Creating Irish Tourism

Anthem Studies in Travel

Anthem Studies in Travel publishes new and pioneering work in the burgeoning field of travel studies. Titles in this series engage with questions of travel, travel writing, literature and history, and encompass some of the most exciting current scholarship in a variety of disciplines, with research representing a broad range of geographical zones and historical contexts.

Editorial Board

Charles Forsdick, University of Liverpool
Mary B. Campbell, Brandeis University
Steve Clark, University of Tokyo
Claire Lindsay, University College London
Loredana Polezzi, University of Warwick
Paul Smethurst, University of Hong Kong

Other Titles in the Series

Travellers to the Middle East from Burckhardt to Thesiger: An Anthology
Edited by Geoffrey Nash

Travel Writing in the Nineteenth Century: Filling the Blank Spaces
Edited by Tim Youngs

Virtual Voyages: Travel Writing and the Antipodes 1605–1837
Paul Longley Arthur

Related Titles from Anthem Press

Russia's Penal Colony in the Far East: A Translation of Vlas Doroshevich's "Sakhalin"
Translated and with an Introduction by Andrew A. Gentes

Govind Narayan's Mumbai: An Urban Biography from 1863
Edited by Murali Ranganathan, with a Foreword by Gyan Prakash

America Magica: When Renaissance Europe Thought it had Conquered Paradise, 2nd edn
Jorge Magasich-Airola and Jean-Marc de Beer,
Translated by Monica Sandor, with a Foreword by David Abulafia

What I Saw in America
G. K. Chesterton, with an Introduction by Simon Newman

Creating Irish Tourism

The First Century, 1750–1850

William H. A. Williams

ANTHEM PRESS
LONDON • NEW YORK • DELHI

Anthem Press
An imprint of Wimbledon Publishing Company
www.anthempress.com

This edition first published in UK and USA 2011
by ANTHEM PRESS
75-76 Blackfriars Road, London SE1 8HA, UK
or PO Box 9779, London SW19 7ZG, UK
and
244 Madison Ave. #116, New York, NY 10016, USA

Copyright © William H. A. Williams 2011

The author asserts the moral right to be identified as the author of this work.
All rights reserved. Without limiting the rights under copyright reserved above,
no part of this publication may be reproduced, stored or introduced into
a retrieval system, or transmitted, in any form or by any means
(electronic, mechanical, photocopying, recording or otherwise),
without the prior written permission of both the copyright
owner and the above publisher of this book.

British Library Cataloguing-in-Publication Data
A catalogue record for this book is available from the British Library.

Library of Congress Cataloging-in-Publication Data
The Library of Congress has catalogued the hardcover edition as follows:
Williams, William H. A.
Creating Irish tourism : the first century, 1750–1850 / William H. A. Williams.
p. cm.
Includes bibliographical references and index.
ISBN-13: 978-1-84331-844-6 (hardcover : alk. paper)
ISBN-10: 1-84331-844-X (hardcover)
ISBN-13: 978-1-84331-899-6 (ebook : alk. paper)
ISBN-10: 1-84331-899-7 (e-book)
1. Tourism–Ireland–History–18th century.
2. Tourism–Ireland–History–19th century. I. Title.
G155.I7W55 2010
338.4'79145–dc22
2010004336

ISBN-13: 978 0 85728 407 5 (Pbk)
ISBN-10: 0 85728 407 X (Pbk)

This title is also available as an eBook.

To Bill and Lavinia

TABLE OF CONTENTS

Preface ix

Introduction xi

Part I 1

Chapter 1: Getting There and Getting About 3

Chapter 2: Tours Grand and Petite 27

Chapter 3: Property, Class and Irish Tourism 49

Part II 67

Chapter 4: The Sublime and the Picturesque in the Irish Landscape 69

Chapter 5: Picturesque Tourist Sites in Ireland 89

Chapter 6: The Tourist Experience 107

Chapter 7: Killarney—A Case Study of the Irish Tourist Experience 129

Part III 151

Chapter 8: Tourist Semeiotics, Stereotypes and the Search for the Exotic 153

Chapter 9: On the Road—In Search of Ireland 165

Chapter 10: The Famine and After 183

Conclusion 193

Notes 199

Bibliography 227

Index 245

PREFACE

Almost twenty years ago I began researching British travel writing relating to the first century of Irish tourism, 1750–1850. Gradually, two paths of enquiry opened up. One concerned how the travelers looked at and sought to account for the Irish landscape and the people they encountered during their tours. This involved investigating the aesthetic, social and ideological biases British tourists brought to the encounter with Ireland and how these preconceptions influenced their ultimate inability to understand pre-Famine Ireland. Based on this research, I published in 2008 *Tourism, Landscape, and the Irish Character: British Travel Writers in Pre-Famine Ireland*.

While tourism provided a context for that book, its focus on the travel writers and their opinions left no room for any real exploration of the phenomenon of tourism itself. The century or so prior to the Great Famine (1845–1852) saw the emergence of modern tourism based primarily on landscape, whether in the carefully designed parklands of the great estates or amid mountains, lakes and sea cliffs. Ireland was in the forefront of the development of the scenic pleasure tour. In fact, the foundations of Irish tourism were laid during the century from 1750–1850. The present book is, therefore, concerned with the evolution of tourism in Ireland and the creation of the Irish tourist experience.

As with my previous work, the primary resources for this book consist of over 100 travel accounts of varying types and lengths, most written between 1750 and 1850. In the almost two decades since I began my research many of these works have recently migrated to the Internet under the auspices of Google Books. While this welcome development has made it convenient to check some footnotes and quotations, most of my research was done years ago the old fashioned way—in libraries. I am, therefore, once again pleased to acknowledge the aid and cooperation of the staffs of the following libraries: the National Library of Ireland; the library of the Royal Irish Academy; the libraries of the National University of Ireland at Trinity College, at Dublin and at Galway; the National Library of Scotland; the Lilly Library, Indiana University, Bloomington; the library of the University of Cincinnati; the Hamilton County Public Library in Cincinnati; and the Gary Library of the Union Institute & University, Montpelier, Vermont.

Lengthy stints at out-of-town libraries would have been impossible without friends who generously gave of their hospitality, the memory of which is undimmed through the passing years. I want to thank once again: Eiléan Ní Chuilleanáin and Macdara Woods, Phyllis Gaffney and Cormac Ó Cuilleanáin of Dublin; Alf and Fionnuala MacLochlain of Galway; Bonnie and Owen Edwards of Edinburgh; and Kenneth Haag, formerly of Bloomington, Indiana.

I want to particularly acknowledge the help of Dr. Christopher J. Woods of the Royal Irish Academy who shared with me his bibliography on Irish travel writing at the very beginning of this project. And, as with the previous book, I want to thank my good friend Kevin McHuge, poet and editor, for his invaluable help in editing the manuscript. His good efforts notwithstanding, any errors and all remaining pot holes in the prose remain my responsibility.

Cincinnati, Ohio 2009

INTRODUCTION

Although modern tourism did not begin there, Ireland was among the first countries to be defined, at least in part, in terms of its scenic attractions. Between 1750 and 1800 the Lakes of Killarney, the Giant's Causeway and the Glens of Wicklow became internationally recognized tourist sites. By 1850, with the beginnings of the country's rail system, Ireland had developed a basic infrastructure required to support tourism. In fact, during the century following 1750, some 570 travel accounts about Ireland had been published, most of them produced by British and Anglo-Irish writers.[1]

While these works take a variety of forms and reflect a multiplicity of interests on the part of their authors, many of them were shaped by the growing enthusiasm for sublime and picturesque scenery. While the already established British "Home Tour" influenced expectations among those who crossed the Irish Sea, the Irish Tour had its own attractions and challenges, providing a unique set of experiences for the British visitors.[2] This study focuses on the emergence of tourism in Ireland and on the nature of the Irish tourist experience.

Irish tourism emerged on the cusp of significant changes in British travel and travel writing. These changes had already manifested themselves by the middle of the eighteenth century, as the Grand Tour was gradually overtaken by the picturesque "pleasure tour." Not that the Grand Tour had lacked potential for pleasures—of almost every possible variety. However, pleasure was not supposed to have been its primary purpose. Starting around 1660, generations of young aristocrats set out from Britain and Ireland to the Continent to be educated in statecraft, manners, military fortification, art and architecture. Half graduate school, half extended "spring break" for the privileged "milords," the Grand Tour was largely an urban-oriented enterprise centered on Rome. While landscape was at best a minor attraction on the Tour, typography, on the other hand, played a major role. As Chloe Chard points out, the Grand Tour entailed "a movement down from the cold North to the warm South…punctuated by the Alps.…"[3] That punctuation was best negotiated by being carried in an "Alpine machine" (a chair) with eyes tightly closed to avoid the terrifying sights of mountains and chasms. Gradually, however, during the first half of the eighteenth century, eyes began to open as a result of a revolution in landscape aesthetics, and the dreaded mountains became tour destinations in their own right. Landscape in the context of the Grand Tour had been something to be traveled *through* not *to*. By the middle of the eighteenth century, however, touring became increasingly oriented toward nature and motivated by what the new Romantic Age called "the sublime" and "the picturesque." These changes in interest and aesthetics were accompanied by a significant shift in the status of "the touring public." While the aristocracy had dominated the Grand Tour, the participation of the upper-middle class characterized the picturesque pleasure tour. The "touring public" of the late eighteenth and early nineteenth centuries was made up primarily of those who, lacking great estates and fortunes, could still afford the time and expense to spend a few weeks (as opposed to the aristocrats' many months) on the road. Not until around the middle of the nineteenth century did steam travel and clever entrepreneurial organization, initiated by such figures as James Cook, inaugurate the age of mass tourism.

The picturesque pleasure tour did not so much supplant the Grand Tour as it took on certain of its touristic habits, its modes of social and cultural inquiry, and combined them with the new fascination with landscapes. Of course, not everyone who traveled was enthralled by nature. Travel remained essential to social, political and economic inquiry about other countries. The literature dealing with pre-Famine Ireland is rich in accounts of British visitors whose primary concerns involved questions of religion, education, agriculture or poverty. Yet, while there are travelogues devoted almost exclusively to either scenery or society, most travel accounts mixed observations on waterfalls and lakes with inquiries about the conditions of the local peasantry. John Bush, author of *Hibernia Curiosa* (1767) largely concerned himself with the sublime and the picturesque. J. C. Curwen, in *Observations on the State of Ireland* (1818), focused primarily on the rural economy. Yet Bush had harsh things to say about Irish landlords, and Curwin dedicated two chapters to the beauties of Killarney. Likewise, Lady Chatterton, a sketcher much devoted to the picturesque, visited a copper mine, while Henry D. Inglis, gathering data on Ireland's social and economic conditions, fell in love with beauties of Connemara.

While some travel works were thematic, with chapters dedicated to different topics, most provided broader impressions of travel in Ireland, based on the visitors' itineraries. Such travelogues may have been influenced by another type of travel literature that had also emerged during the eighteenth century, one based on exploration and scientific research. Such works, as Roy Bridges suggests, began with the known and proceeded to the unknown, with the traveler describing "experiences and observations day to day on the basis of a log or journal."[4] And indeed, many tourists did keep daily records or wrote frequent letters that in some instances became the basis for published travel narratives. Following this approach, the journey itself, the itinerary, organized the tour, with the sights and encounters found along the road strung like beads on the thread of the narrative. As a result, the whole of the host country lay open to visitors, regardless of their primary interests or destination.

The Irish Tour resulted from a convergence of several factors. The changing tastes in landscape and a Romantic fascination for nature was fortuitous for Ireland. With limited mining potential and with the last of its forests rapidly disappearing (along with many small iron works), Ireland had few natural resources other than its spectacular scenery. Even so, had the county still been mired in the turmoil of the sixteenth and seventeenth centuries, no amount of spectacular landscape would have attracted visitors. Too much can be made of the relative stability and prosperity that followed the defeat of King James II and his Catholic forces in 1691. Nevertheless, by the mid-eighteenth century Ireland clearly appeared more inviting to visitors than at any time in its recent past. In fact, with the defeat of Bonny Prince Charlie and his Highlanders at Culloden in 1745, the whole of Britain's Celtic Fringe seemed to invite exploration rather than conquest. In Scotland the military roads the redcoats had built into the Highlands were easily adapted for use by curious tourists. That curiosity was fed by a new fascination with Celtic culture, inspired in part by the publication between 1750 and 1760 of Rev. James MacPherson's forgeries of the legends of Ossian. Wrongly attributed exclusively to Scotland, the original myths, found in their most complete form in Ireland, constituted an essential part of Gaelic culture. Regardless, the cult of Ossian represented a broad cultural shift in Britain away from the dominance of the classical past (and the Grand Tour's focus on Rome) to the ancient peoples of the islands.[5] Again, the timing proved fortuitous. As relations with France grew increasingly difficult toward the end of the century, excursions to parts of the Continent became less attractive to Britons. Their own safe shores offered patriotic opportunities to explore their own history, lands and scenery. Under such circumstances Ireland emerged an inevitable tourist destination.

This does not mean that the Irish Tour was simply an overseas extension of the Home Tour around Great Britain. As most visitors to Ireland were acutely aware, more than the deep channel of the Irish Sea separated the two islands. One theme extended through the travel accounts written between 1750 and the Famine: Britain's lack of knowledge and understanding of Ireland. Most eighteenth-century travel writers acknowledged this ignorance and expressed the hope that their work would help to bridge the gap. Events at the end of the century turned that hope into an imperative. The Rising of 1798 by the United Irishmen briefly plunged Ireland back into rebellious turmoil. Once the rebellion had been crushed and a small French invasion force expelled, the

British government resolved to abolish the Irish Parliament in Dublin and unite some of its members with the Imperial Parliament sitting in Westminster. In 1801 the Act of Union created the United Kingdom of England, Wales, Scotland and Ireland. With that act the Irish and the British became, in theory, fellow citizens. The Imperial Parliament in Westminster, which included Irish representatives, had responsibility for governing Ireland directly. Therefore, understanding the "Sister Island" became essential. In the introduction to his *Journal of a Tour in Ireland, A.D.1806*, Richard Colt Hoare warned that, compared to Wales and Scotland, Ireland yet "remained unvisited and unknown." This was something of an exaggeration. Between 1750 and 1799 some 100 travel accounts relating to Ireland had been published.[6] Nevertheless, with the Continent cut off by wars, Hoare felt that the time was ripe for Britons to recognize that "Our own kingdom still remains unexplored."[7]

Even before the Act of Union, the Irish Tour was very complex. Regardless of the attention bestowed on Ireland's scenery, British visitors, most of whom were Protestants, were exposed to a number of strange sights and experiences. Some of these were amusing, some disturbing, but all reflected the nature of Ireland and its relationship with the rest of the Kingdom. While a British traveler in Naples or Rome might be horrified at the poverty he saw there, he could leave it behind, secure in his knowledge that it had nothing to do with him or his country. Encounters with similar poverty in Dublin left British visitors with no such comfortable retreat. Try as they might, visitors could not completely distance themselves from Irish poverty, which partially explains why travel writing has proved useful in researching previously unexplored aspects of British-Irish social and cultural relations.

Glenn Hooper and I have produced studies about travel writing in the pre-Famine period. Although both of us addressed aspects of tourism, we focused primarily on the travel literature and what the writers could tell us about the attitudes of the British visitors toward Ireland and its people. In *Tourism, Landscape, and the Irish Character* (2008), I argued that British preconceptions about Ireland and the Irish led travel writers not only to misread aspects of the countryside and its people, but also to see the Irish character itself imprinted on the landscape. By focusing on particular authors in *Travel Writing and Ireland, 1760–1860: Culture, History, Politics* (2005), Glenn Hooper traces the evolution of the attitudes of British travelers toward Ireland from optimism to deepening pessimism by the eve of the Famine. Although taking different approaches, both books regard the immediate post-Famine years in the West of Ireland as a triumph of colonialism in which travel writing played a key role.[8]

Unlike these previous works the focus of this book is on tourism. Although I still draw upon traveler accounts, here I am chiefly concerned with the development of Irish tourism and the tourist experience in the first century of

Irish tourism, 1750 to 1850. While the study begins with the evolution of Ireland's tourist infrastructure, it is primarily an inquiry into the very nature of Irish tourism. To what extent did the search for the sublime and the picturesque shape Irish tourism? What defined tourist sites in Ireland, and how were they identified, marked and organized, both physically and perceptually? What did visitors do at certain tourist sites? What guided tourist activities and behavior? How did elements of ritual and even theater contribute to the tourist experience? What was the nature of the guest/host interaction at tourist sites, especially between the upper and middle-class tourists and the peasantry? How did these interactions help define Irish tourism? How did the tourist's search for the stereotypical and the exotic contribute to the Irish tourist experience? In trying to answer these questions, I have drawn upon the work of contemporary researchers in the fields of travel and tourism studies.

However, as noted above, the Irish Tour was complex. Rarely completely dedicated to nature, few tours were devoted entirely to sociological or economic inquiry. Peasants and the picturesque intermingled to some degree in most accounts. In a travel narrative one page might describe a magnificent waterfall; on the next, Paddy's miserable cabin. Or rhapsodic comments on the Irish sublime may be followed by attempts to unravel the Irish character. The same eye that analyzed the beauties of Killarney could also apply aesthetic principles to Irish agriculture. This means that the tourist's experience in pre-Famine Ireland often transcended the sublime and the picturesque to include various non-scenic aspects of Ireland that caught the visitor's attention, already heightened by the desire to know and understand Ireland. As a result, even instances of Irish poverty became part of the tourist experience. Nevertheless, most visitors tried to fit Ireland within the context of the picturesque. And when social and economic realities clashed with beautiful scenery, visitors often perceived a contradiction between Irish society and Irish nature.

This book is divided into three parts. Part One concerns the creation of the basis for tourism in Ireland. Chapter One examines the development of a tourist infrastructure during the first century of Irish tourism. Chapter Two discusses what I call the "petite tour" (as opposed to the Grand Tour) of Ireland, as travelers visited Ireland's towns and cities, investigated institutions, and enquired about the Irish economy and society. Chapter Three returns to the theme of tourist infrastructure but this time focusing on the roles played by the Irish landlords who not only improved roads and towns but also organized their estates for visitors.

Part Two concerns the key role of landscape aesthetics in defining and shaping the Irish Tour. Chapter Four introduces the theme of the sublime and the picturesque, discussing the changes in landscape aesthetics that placed landscape at the center for many tourists. The chapter suggests how Ireland was conceptually reconfigured to accommodate this quest. Chapter Five takes a more detailed look at this process, exploring the various categories of picturesque tourist sites in Ireland and how they were marked for tourism. Chapter Six considers the kinds of activities that engaged visitors and defined the tourist experience at specific sites. It also considers the contribution of the Irish peasantry to both the economy of a tourist site, as well as to the tourist experience. The Lakes of Killarney are used as a kind of case study in Chapter Seven to show how all the various elements of picturesque tourism in pre-Famine Ireland came together in this, the country's most famous tourist site.

Part Three takes the Irish Tour on the road, beyond the picturesque, to look at the non-scenic aspects of the Irish Tour. It examines the extent to which the entire country was open to tourists during the pre-Famine period, and how many of the resulting experiences raised disturbing questions about Ireland. Chapter Eight investigates the tourist's search for "Irishness" in terms of the stereotypical as well as the exotic. Chapter Nine considers how the tourist, by the very nature of travel in pre-Famine Ireland, reacted to non-picturesque aspects of the Irish countryside and its people. It indicates how the physical act of touring added to and greatly complicated the tourist experience in Ireland, creating the sense of a contradiction at the heart of that experience. Chapter Ten briefly suggests how, as a result of the Famine, that contradiction was "resolved."

Part I

Chapter 1
GETTING THERE AND GETTING ABOUT

When they embark on a journey, travelers begin a rite of passage, detaching themselves from their home and homeland, initiating a series of adventures and challenges, which, no matter how minimal, prepare them for their unfamiliar status as strangers in a new and different place. The longer and more difficult the trip, the greater their sense of leaving behind the certain and familiar for the strange and foreign. By the time of arrival the journey has already cost time and money, as well as the inevitable wear and tear on body, mind and spirit. Today's tourists must brave the traffic to the airport, negotiate crowds and endure delayed flights and endless security checks at the airport. Once on board the airplane, they must survive cramped seats and bad food. This is tame stuff, however, compared to travel a few centuries ago. Prior to the age of steam, anything beyond a trip to the next village required careful preparation, a good bit of time and much endurance.

Until the 1820s those British tourists intent on visiting Ireland had to first travel by coach or horseback to a western port and then board a sailing ship for a sea journey of uncertain duration and minimal comfort. For much of the eighteenth century, many Ireland-bound travelers went first to Chester, a six-to-seven day horseback ride from London. There they remained until they could take sail from Parkgate, a harbor twelve miles outside of the city. In the 1740s theatrical manager William Rufus Chetwood was lured out of his comfortable hotel in Chester by a Parkgate innkeeper, who had sent word that the ships would soon embark. It was all a ruse. Once ensconced in an uncomfortable but no less expensive establishment by the harbor, Chetwood found himself cooling his heels, awaiting both a ship and favorable winds. He finally gave up and hired a guide to take him on a three-day trip over the mountains of Wales to Carnarvon and then on to Holyhead. From there, with help of a telescope, he could at least see the Wicklow Mountains across the Irish Sea.[1]

The shortest link between Great Britain and Ireland was from Port Patrick in Galloway, Scotland to Donaghadee in County Down, a route convenient only for those with business in Ulster. By the nineteenth century, however, Liverpool and

Holyhead had become the preferred embarkation points from Britain, although one could also sail from Bristol to Cork. Anne Plumptre considered the Bristol route in 1814, until she realized that, after paying three guineas for the journey, she would still face the cost and time of the overland trip from Cork up to Dublin. She chose instead to pay just one guinea for the direct Liverpool to Dublin route. Sailing to Cork from Bristol sometimes offered worse than inconvenience and added expense. As John Bush noted, that route took ships nearer to the open sea and possible encounters with the French and Spanish privateers prowling Ireland's south coast. Even Samuel Derrick's ship out of Liverpool in the 1760s was attacked by a Frenchman. Fortunately, Derrick's vessel, itself bearing a letter of marque, was armed and easily drove off the intruder.[2]

Usually nature proved more of a threat than pirates. Depending on the time of year, the waters around Britain and Ireland were frequently churned by storms. Around 1810, for instance, John Melish, an American business man, embarked on the usually short passage between Port Patrick to Donaghadee. Unfortunately, he encountered a gale worse than any experienced on his Atlantic crossing. After battling the storm for about for 27 hours within sight of the Irish coast, his ship returned to Port Patrick. When the wind changed, he crossed in just a few hours. In Chetwood's case, by the time he embarked from Holyhead, a storm arose, tossing the ship about so violently that he feared for his life. The vessel missed its Dublin landfall and had to make for Cork instead. In the 1760s John Bush endured a 40-hour storm-plagued trip from Holyhead to Dublin. Under such circumstances those prone to sea sickness could do nothing but accept the opportunity for what Bush called "a good stomach scouring."[3]

Although less harrowing than storms, the complete absence of wind created its own problems. In 1792 Dr. Edward Daniel Clarke's ship out of Holyhead, after initially fighting headwinds, found itself completely becalmed the next day. Clarke's aesthetic sense suffered as much as his timetable: "There is such a degree of insipidity in its [the sea's] appearance: the water, like one vast mirror, smooth and glassy; the canvass all hanging supine…the complexion of a storm contains something awful, grand, and interesting; the attention is awakened, and the mind alarmed, but in a calm I know no single feature of beauty; all is dullness and disappointment." An anonymous writer, becalmed in the Irish Sea in 1804, related how his fellow passages fished for gurnard and mackerel while waiting for a favorable wind. On one day in 1788, strollers along the strand at Bray in Wicklow were surprised to see 30 square-rigged ships becalmed off the Irish coast.[4] Whether by storm or by calm, a delayed sea journey could leave travelers hungry, unless they had furnished themselves with ample provisions. Anne Plumptre had been told that her journey would take no more than 36 hours. Progress was slow, however, and, when her ship was becalmed on the second day, she found herself running short of food. She was still better off than

Dr. Clarke, who discovered too late that the food hamper purchased from his hotel contained rotten meat.[5]

It is little wonder that Anna Maria and Samuel Carter Hall had few good words for the sailing packets, usually small schooners or sloops, that plied the Irish Sea. The cramped accommodations and the lack of on-board food, not to mention the vagaries of the weather, rendered the Irish crossing "a kind of purgatory...." By the 1820s, however, the sea journey from Britain to Ireland had become less uncertain and uncomfortable. As a result of the long wars with France, British ship design had improved, while the introduction of steam in 1819 rendered sea travel less dependent upon fickle winds. Writing in the 1840s, the Halls announced (a bit too optimistically) that steam had essentially transformed England and Ireland into a single island. The sea crossings, they insisted, had become less fatiguing than a land trip from London to York. In addition, the fittings were elegant and the fares moderate. The trip from Bristol to Cork generally took only 24 hours; from Liverpool to Dublin 12 hours and from Holyhead to Dublin only six.[6]

Arrival

The emergence of Liverpool and Holyhead as the standard ports of embarkation for Ireland made Dublin the most frequent port of entry. As such, Ireland's capital city provided traveler's with their initial experience of the country. Depending on weather and time of day, visitors arriving in Dublin Bay were greeted by what Dr. Edward Clarke called in 1791, "one of most enchanting prospects in Europe." With the looming headland of the Hill of Howth dominating the northern end of the bay, the city fans out to the west. Beyond the suburbs on the south side of the bay rise the Dublin and Wicklow mountains, with the conical quartzite peak of Sugar Loaf providing a dramatic southeastern anchor to the view. Whether it was Sugar Loaf or the Hill of Howth that first gave rise to a comparison with the Bay of Naples and its dramatic view of Mount Vesuvius, the idea, once expressed, became a travel-writer's fixation. Typical is Sir John Carr's description in 1805: "On the right was the rugged hill of Howth, with its rocky bays, wanting only a volcano to afford to the surrounding scenery the strongest resemblance, as I was well informed, to the beautiful bay of Naples...." C. T. Bowden seemed pleased enough at the absence of an actual volcano: "Here, you are not terrified with the awful prospect of a Vesuvius, as in the Bay of Naples—but your eye and your heart are at once gratified with the most delightful landscapes...." In fact, the Naples conceit became so ingrained in the tradition of Irish travel writing that it was hard for authors to avoid referring to it, even if only to mock it. In 1843 William Makepeace Thackeray, ever eager to puncture any piece of over-inflated tourist rhetoric, claimed that, having arrived in Dublin Bay on a rainy night, he could form no opinions as to its resemblance to Naples: "It is but to take the similarity for granted, and remain in bed till morning." Sir Francis Bond Head, visiting in the 1850s, congratulated himself on having been delivered into a four-poster bed in Dublin "without having bothered oneself with the old-fashioned controversial comparison between the beauty of its bay and that of Naples." Nevertheless, the comparison echoed on in travel writing for well over a century, rating mention in the second edition of *Walker's Hand-Book of Ireland*, published in 1872.[7]

Whatever the weather or view from the deck, passengers frequently found disembarkation at Dublin anticlimatic, when not actually traumatic. Dublin Bay was heavily silted and lacked a channel deep enough to allow most ocean-going vessels to anchor at the city's quays. No less a personage than Captain William Bligh, formerly of *H. M. S. Bounty*, conducted the first of several engineering surveys of the Bay in 1800, although it was years before the harbor was dredged.[8] Therefore, travelers often found themselves stranded on board ship, waiting hours for the tide to turn so that they could land at the Pigeon House, a hostelry near Ringsend, several miles from the center of the city. Built around 1790 on the South Wall breakwater, the Pigeon House stood upon a spit of land jutting out into the bay near the mouth of the River Liffey. (The hotel allegedly took its name from John Pigeon, its first caretaker.) Alternatively, visitors could disembark to the mainland via a small boat. Confronted by bad weather or darkness, however, many travelers, such as Anne Plumptre, preferred one more uneasy night on board ship.[9] Not until, 1820, two decades after Bligh's survey, did a new harbor at Kingstown (the once and future Dun Laoghaire) welcome travelers to the south side of the bay. Nonetheless, even that improvement left a rather long coach ride into Dublin, an inconvenience not ameliorated unitl 1837 with the opening of the Kingstown-Dublin railroad.

Mary Louise Pratt suggests that the arrival scenes described in travel accounts "serve as particularly potent sites for framing relations of contact and setting the terms of its representation." Such scenes complete the traveler's rite of passage. The familiar has been left behind; land, sea or air space has been crossed; and now the traveler is suddenly exposed to the difference of the "Other." As Michael Cronin suggests, "The arrival scene in the foreign city has a well-rehearsed cast of horrors...," consisting of the weather, aggressive drivers, beggars, bad rooms, and the like.[10] Disembarkation at Dublin had it all. Landing at the Pigeon House, travelers could be excused if they felt they had been thrust suddenly into a very strange and foreign country. In 1805 Sir John Carr compared his initial view of Dublin Bay with what he encountered on shore: "A stranger, in his progress from the Pigeon-house to the capitol, cannot fail of being shocked by a sudden contrast to the beautiful scenes." Leaving the vicinity of the Pigeon House, the visitor entered Ringsend, three miles from the center of Dublin. It was, Carr complained, "one of the most horrible sinks of filth I ever beheld. Every house swarmed with ragged, squalled tenantry, and dung and garbage lay in heaps in the passages, and upon the steps leading to the cellars...." Amid the shouts and demands of car drivers and beggars, arriving passengers had to choose from an odd assortment of conveyances into the city. Many, like Anne Plumptre, took the "Long Coach," which held sixteen passengers inside and sixteen outside (on the roof). Riders on this early version of today's overcrowded airport shuttle bus were at least accompanied by their luggage. Thomas Reid, arriving in 1822, did not like the look of either the Long Coach or the various other cars available to him. He gave a man a shilling to go find a proper coach, which was duly produced an hour and a half later. Before departure, however, the coachman insisted first on going to an inn to treat the messenger, who in turn delayed matters further by insisting upon an additional half crown for his efforts. According to Reid, even onlookers got into the act and demanded money—while he and his luggage sat idle at Ringsend.[11]

Noddies, Jingles and Bians—Inland Transportation

Once settled in Dublin and in need of transportation, visitors had a variety of vehicles to choose from, some of which were as unfamiliar as they were uncomfortable. One was the eighteenth-century Irish form of the chaise, called the "noddy." This light, two-wheeled, one-horse carriage with a collapsible hood was very common around Dublin. As Chetwood described it in the 1740s, the noddy had shafts that hung high on the horse's flanks, "for the Ease of the Horse, not the Rider. The Driver is seated upon a thing like a Stool, with his Back-side near your [the passenger's] Mouth, and a Foot upon each Shaft, and away he drives at a great Rate...." According to John Bush, the vehicle's name derived from the fact that the single passenger could see nothing but the "nod—nod—nodding of your charioteer" taking his motions form the horse. By the late eighteenth century, the noddy had become a outlandish object of wonder and ridicule for tourists, who were assured by Rev. Thomas Campbell that the vehicles were patronized by only the lower order of citizens. Thus, the Dublin expression: "Elegance and ease, like a shoe black in a noddy."[12] For the "quality" there were hackneys and even sedan chairs. The latter in 1771 outnumbered licensed carriages in Dublin, to the benefit of the Dublin Lying-In Hospital, which had been granted a duty on the chairs. The use of sedan chairs persisted in the streets of the largest Irish cities into the 1830s.[13]

By the early nineteenth century the "jingle," a four-wheeled carriage carrying six passengers, had replaced the noddy. According to John Carr, the jingle's appointments were minimal. "This carriage resembles as much of a coach as remains after the doors and the upper sides and roof are removed, and is mounted very high upon four large...wheels. Its motion produces a rattling noise, which furnishes its name: it is drawn by one miserable looking horse...." In Dublin the jingles generally ran between Baggot Street and the Pigeon House on Dublin Bay. In summer they also carried revelers to the seaside at Blackrock for about 6*d*. Similar cars, albeit with roofs and sides, were found in Cork, where Robert Graham appreciated the leather curtains that could be drawn in case of rain. Visitors to Dublin also encountered the "chaise-marine," which John Bush described as an Irish cart with solid wooden wheels and a platform above the axle. Although used primarily for hauling goods, spread with a mat or some straw it could accommodate up to six merry makers, whose legs dangled over the sides a few inches from the ground. Bush found them "the most sociable carriages in use...the drollest, merriest coracles you ever saw." For those travelers with little enthusiasm for hiring cars and dealing with Irish drivers, Richard Colt Hoare had simple advice. He suggested that the visitor could make himself "independent" by traveling with his *own* horse and carriage, whereby "all difficulties will then cease...." Needless to say, Hoare was a member of a wealthy banking family.[14]

Until around the 1820s visitors facing serious journeys outside of Irish cities had a choice of a stage coach or a post-chaise, both of which pursued a few well-established routes, changes of horses not being generally available off the beaten track. The post-chaise was a privately hired car that held two to four people with a servant riding behind them. Light and fast, it was driven by a "post boy" mounted on one of the horses. In 1817, John Gough traveled from Dublin to Kilkenny in a post-chaise with three other passengers. It took twelve hours to cover the fifty-seven Irish miles, including a stop for breakfast and five changes of horses. The post-chaise was not generally popular among visitors to Ireland. In the 1830s, Jonathan Binns hired one in County Down and found it "a dirty, damp, ill-shapened, rattling vehicle...the first and the last we have entered." Around the same time William Belton condemned the vehicles as "the most deficient and most discreditable articles connected with Irish travelling." Woefully neglected and dirty, with their upholstery torn and ripped, they were, he complained, especially to be avoided in bad weather. Worse, the post-chaise was expensive. In 1826 it cost two pounds for a horse and a boy at each stage of a journey. The trip from Kilkenny to Cork by way of Fermoy, for example, cost £8. 10*s*. 6*d*., plus 14*s*. for turnpike fees.[15]

It took a while to expand Ireland's posting infrastructure to include decent inns and reliable changes of horses.[16] To complicate matters further, when hiring a vehicle the traveler could seldom be sure of the quality of the horse or the experience of the driver. Dr. John Forbes, journeying out of Cushendall, Antrim in 1852, complained of only one thing: the exhausted and broken down horses employed to drag cars and carriages, a situation he found general throughout

Ireland. Years earlier, Mrs. Plumptre endured slow progress on her tour of the area around Skibbereen in County Cork. Her horse, as she belatedly learned from her driver, was not used to, perhaps was not fit for, a daily journey of ten to twelve miles. And so her ride to Bantry proceeded at a plodding pace, "What a tedious sixteen miles did I find it!" She offered to pay the author of the *Miseries of Human Life* for including in the next edition of his book a description of the six hours trip from Skibereen to Bantry, since she had found it, "a most superlative MISERY." Not all posting experiences were negative, however. Mr. and Mrs. Frederick West hired a chaise to take them out of Nenagh, Tipperary in 1846. The rider was "a good-looking, cheerful-faced boy in a spick and span blue jacket with bright buttons, velvet cap of hunting cut, top boots and doe skins, bestrowed as shining and well-conditioned a pair of well-groomed little horses as heart could desire. The harnesses glistened like gold....."[17]

Stages and Mail Coaches

In the eighteenth century, only stage coaches (later joined by mail coaches) provided regular passenger service and then only between the cities and principal towns. By the 1780s stages left Dublin two to three times a week for twelve different destinations. In 1784 the Irish Post Office established an English-style mail-coach service, which, once inaugurated in 1789, broadened the links between major towns.[18] Although more numerous by the 1820s, these coaches promised little in terms of comfort. On his trip to Donegal in 1827, Rev. Caesar Otway took the Derry Mail from Dublin. The coach was, he later lamented, "a place of purgatorial suffering;—a public coach, travelling by night and full withal, is my antipathy;—with bent body and contracted limbs, and every sense in a state of suffering, hearing, smelling, feeling, seeing…Oh, it is horrible!"[19] The first mail coaches carried only five passengers, four inside and one outside— on top. As the coaches grew larger, there followed a tendency to overload them. John O'Donovan, travelling on *The Fair Trader* from Derry to Enniskillen in the 1830s, counted twenty-eight fellow passengers; ten inside and eighteen outside.[20] About the same time, John Barrow noted that the roof of a coach pulling into Belfast "was already crowded with passengers, whose numerous legs, like those of so many undertakers on top of a hearse, were dangling down on either side so thickly, as, I should suppose, effectually to exclude the daylight from the unfortunate folks who were cooped up within."[21]

The coaches were also slow and expensive. In the early nineteenth century the Cork Mail to Dublin took 31 hours. Even with later improvements, coach travel between the two cities took 18½ hours. On the eve of the railroad era in the 1830s, a coach from Dublin to Belfast cost 27*s.* 6*d.* for the inside and 15*s.* for the outside. Whatever its shortcomings, however, coaching offered a colorful, if not to say exciting, esperience. Line owners sometimes advertised their political affiliations by the names they gave their coaches, such as "*The Conservative*" and "*The Repealer*." The drivers, a competitive lot, were known to race each other illegally.[22]

The Irish Jaunting Car

The Irish jaunting car provided cheaper transport than either coaching or posting. Moreover, it could travel off of the main routes. According to the Halls, there were three types of jaunting cars. The "covered" car, though weatherproof, afforded limited visibility, unless one tied back the curtains in the rear of the vehicle. These cars were most common in towns where they functioned as hackney coaches. Of the open vehicles (open to the elements as well as to the scenery) the "inside" car was the more comfortable. Here the passengers sat along the sides facing each other. According to the Halls, however, these were generally privately owned and seldom for hire. Visitors typically toured the countryside in "outside" cars, the passengers sitting long-wise, back-to-back, separated by the "well" where their luggage was stacked. Facing the scenery and whatever elements accompanied it, passengers received some protection from a waterproof "apron" that covered their legs and laps. Belton liked the jaunting car because it offered the "pleasantest and most independent mode of traveling possible. You can see the country perfectly; can jump off and on without stopping the vehicle…" At six to eight pence a mile, he found the outside cars relatively cheap.[23]

The jaunting car had certain disadvantages, however. Beggars and souvenir sellers could run along side and negotiate face-to-face with its captive occupants. Moreover, passengers were only able to survey the scenery visible from their side of the vehicle. When Sir Francis Bond Head found that the only vacant seat on his car was at the front, next to the driver, he consoled himself "with the reflection that I was probably the only person travelling through Ireland who was not taking a one-sided view of the country."[24]

Travelers often found their hired cars in poor condition. The anonymous author of *The Sportsman in Ireland* (1840) complained that, because of the accumulated dust and filth, "the harness, horse, and man [driver], are all of a colour, and *that* the natural one—I mean the colour of the earth, in its most impalpable form." Traveling in Ireland clearly required patience, especially since the travel times varied. Thackeray, journeying from Ballynahinch in Galway to Westport in Mayo, a trip of forty-four Irish miles, claimed that the journey could take anywhere from 12 hours to two days, depending on the type of car, horse and luck. The Halls advised travelers to "lay in both a stock of good humour—for petty annoyance will frequently occur—and a plentiful supply of waterproof clothing, for sunny June is no more to be trusted than showery April."[25]

Bians

The most famous and probably best cars in Ireland were those designed and run by an Italian immigrant named Carlo Bianconi. Starting off as an itinerant print seller, Bianconi soon recognized the need for regular connections between towns not well served by the existing transportation networks. He devised several adaptations of the "outside" car, manufactured them and set up his own posting stations, which were well stocked with horses demobbed from Wellington's army after Waterloo. Starting in 1815 with Clonmel as his headquarters, Bianconi quickly organized his network in the South and later in parts of the West of Ireland. Travelling in the 1830s, Henry D. Inglis reported that the Italian's company had between five and six hundred horses and some two hundred vehicles.[26] Bianconi started with short two-wheeled cars known as "Massey Dawsons," named after a popular landlord. As business picked up, he introduced the longer four-wheeled "Finn McCools" that could take up to twenty passengers. His cars were pulled by one to three horses. Dr. James Johnson, who traveled with an air cushion, described a three-horse "Bian": "The luggage was piled up far above the heads of the passengers, and there did not appear room for an additional umbrella, much less a hat-box or trunk, in this caravan of human beings. The high narrow box-seat, with the tall driver, looked like the chimney of a steam engine of a rail-way...."[27]

In addition to the other aspects of his business Bianconi had an canny understanding of advertising. According to the German traveler Johann Georg Kohl, the entrepreneur had small maps of Ireland printed, showing the routes of his cars. Painted yellow with crimson lettering and trim, the cars themselves became so well known that Bianconi commissioned a series of six engravings, depicting "Car Travelling in the South of Ireland, 1836." These prints helped publicize his company's services to the growing tourist trade. By paying strict attention to business details, Bianconi managed to hold down his costs. The basis for his success, however, resulted from his focus on market towns that were off the main coaching (and later rail) lines. While he never tried to compete with the established posting routes, he remorselessly drove out competition at his own level.[28] Bianconi's prices were reasonable, and his schedules well maintained. James Johnson was impressed with the price (a penny or tupence a mile), the speed (eight miles an hour) and the flexibility that allowed passengers to alight at any stop and to resume their journey on a later car. At the end of a 55-mile journey, Jonathan Binns was well satisfied with the cost of 6*s.* 6*d.*, plus the shilling tip to driver. Binns was so impressed with Bianconi's cars that he felt sure that England could benefit from a similar service, a rare instance of Irish superiority and English envy. The only serious criticism of the Bians arose from the passenger's inability to reserve a seat. The wise traveler, therefore, grabbed a place as soon as he arrived at the coach, even if a horse had not yet been harnessed. As Samuel Reynolds Hole observed, however: "People do not look particularly wise when seated, in a public street, upon a vehicle to which no horses are attached; but we were anxious to secure our places on 'the Lake side,'" that is, the side providing the best view of the scenery.[29]

Roads

After the fall of the Roman Empire, bad roads became the norm throughout Europe and bane of the traveler for over a millennium. Even in the eighteenth century, roads were still generally poor, at least in England where domestic tourism was growing rapidly. Arthur Young complained that Yorkshire roads were "detestable, full of ruts whose gaping jaws threaten to swallow up any carriage less than a wagon." In the early part of the century the situation was no better in Ireland. Travelling towards Kinsale in the 1740s, Chetwood noted with some understatement that "the road we passed is very well for Travellers on Horseback, but indifferent for Carriages." Earlier in the century the Irish Parliament had passed legislation encouraging the building of straight roads linking the counties. The resulting routes were often too straight, running directly up hills, rather than twisting and turning to produce manageable gradients. Constructing the required curves represented an unnecessary expense.[30] Beginning in 1729, the Irish Parliament began encouraging turnpikes, believing that toll roads could provide cross-county linkages between major towns without adding to the local rates. By 1758 Ireland had 29 turnpikes, the number eventually reaching around 80. Although of relatively good quality at first, there roadways never attracted sufficient traffic to pay for upkeep and repairs. Moreover, turnpikes eventually faced competition from the county Grand Jury roads (see below) and from canals. Often the bane of weary travelers, most Irish turnpikes had disappeared by 1857.[31]

The Grand Jury or "presentment" system eventually led to considerable improvement in Irish roads. A landlord "presented" a project to his county Grand Jury. If his scheme received approval, he built the road, and the Jury reimbursed him. Although the resulting roads were of generally good quality, the Grand Jury system did have several drawbacks. The landlords, who dominated the Juries, were only interested in building up infrastructure for their own estates. This parochialism often resulted in roads oriented internally within each county with minimal attention given to creating a national network. Nevertheless, as T. W. Freeman has pointed out, by the 1760s Ireland, unlike many other

European countries, was becoming known for the quality of its main roads. A decade later, even Richard Twiss, a travel writer not given to effusive praise of Ireland, had to admit that "the roads are almost universally as good as those about London...." In 1805 Sir John Carr insisted that Irish roads were superior to those of England in beauty and durability, surpassed only by the roads of Sweden.[32]

Opening the West

Although the main Irish roads improved considerably, off the beaten path, especially in West and Southwest, rough roads often discouraged carriage traffic. In the 1760s, the harnesses and springs on Gabriel Beranger's open chaise kept breaking on his trip to Sligo. Forty-five years later, John Carr claimed that few carriages used the road between Abbeyfeal, Limerick and Castleisland, Kerry. In fact, he reported the peasants flocking to their half-doors to see a rare post-chaise rattle by. Travelers crossing the mountains from Cork to Killarney often had to hire locals to help pull their vehicles up the steep inclines.[33]

Even traveling on horseback could prove difficult. In the area around Easky Bridge in Mayo's half barony of Erris, Beranger and his party, having investigated a nearby megalith, decided to take a shortcut through the bog. Suddenly Beranger's horse sank beneath him. While the guides were sent for assistance, Beranger and his companion struggled to find a way out, moving quickly to keep from sinking. They staggered about, lost for two hours. "I confess here," he admitted later, " that I thought it was my last day. The anxiety of mind, the fatigue of the body, the insufferable heat of the day, and the intolerable thirst I felt, made me almost unable to proceed...."[34]

With much of the western population concentrated along or near the coast, people in the West of Ireland often traveled by boat in order to avoid the generally bad roads. Those living inland frequently journeyed on foot. In 1834 Maria Edgeworth reported the condition of the road from Oughterard in Galway to the Martin estate at Ballynahinch as being so poor that the Martins used runners to carry their mail to Galway town.[35] That same year Henry D. Inglis, choosing to spare his carriage the wear and tear of the roads in Connemara, decided to walk through much of the region. Nevertheless, road conditions in the West of Ireland had begun to improve because the post-war economic decline in 1815, followed by several localized food crises, underscored the need for better transportation in the region. Starting in 1822, the government began to hire engineers and to fund roads in the southwestern and western districts. The most immediate progress was made in West Cork, Kerry, Limerick and Tipperary. Scottish-trained engineer Alexander Nimmo did more than anyone to help open up the region. He surveyed bogs and fisheries, built

243 miles of roads and constructed 40 piers. Eventually he became deeply involved in Connemara, where he founded the coastal village of Roundstone and contributed to the development of Leenane. His headquarters in Maum eventually became a hotel.[36]

In 1831 the government created a Board of Public Works, which continued to build roads in the North and West for several decades. This gradual expansion of the West's road network clearly impacted the area. In 1823 only three houses greeted the first wheeled vehicle to pass through Balmullet, County Mayo. In 10 years that hamlet had grown into a town of 185 dwellings.[37] Along with their obvious potential for local economies, the Board's projects opened up tourism in previously remote parts of the West and North. In 1852 Dr. John Forbes delightedly traveled the new road along the Antrim coast, the Board's first project, begun in 1832, that linked Cushindale to the Giant's Causeway. The road not only replaced an almost impassible mountain track, but in Forbes words also "laid open to the traveller scenes of such magnificence and beauty, as would almost of themselves have justified the expense.... I think there is no spot in the island that combines such attractions for the hurried-holiday maker of London as this very road and what it leads to."[38]

Although hopes of economic growth inspired Ireland's road building efforts, the slackening pace of the economy at the end of the Napoleonic Wars ironically helped preserve the quality of Irish highways. Writing in the 1840s, James Johnson remarked: "Few things attract a stranger's notice in Ireland, more than the excellence of the roads, even in the wilds of Kerry and Connaught—and that without any apparent repairs." The reason, Johnson stated, was due to the absence of heavy traffic: "A few Saxon tourists, in the Summer or Autumn, with their jaunting-cars—and a few *barefooted* natives, at other times, are not calculated much to cut up the roads. You may often travel ten, fifteen, or twenty miles in Ireland, without meeting a single cart, carriage, or car! No wonder that highways are excellent!" As Colin Rynne has noted, there was simply not enough economic activity in Ireland to put any real stress on the country's road system. The under-used roadways were but one example of investments in Irish infrastructure that seemed redundant in the post-war years. Visitors marveled at fine, empty warehouses in Clifden, Galway and in Westport, Mayo, seeing in them examples of Irish extravagance and impracticality, not realizing that they represented unrealized expectations based on war-time economic growth.[39]

Even with relatively good roads, finding one's way around Ireland posed a problem, at least in the eighteenth century. If local authorities put up wooden signposts, they were likely to be chopped down by a peasantry sorely in need of fire wood.[40] Fortunately, Irish tourism developed at about the same time that practical road maps became available. In 1778, using a format originated by John Ogilby of England, George Taylor and Andrew Skinner published

Taylor and Skinner's Maps of the Roads of Ireland, Surveyed 1777, based on surveys of 8000 miles of Irish roadways.[41] Taylor and Skinner's two-hundred-page book consisted primarily of strip maps, showing the roads linking the major towns and cities, with most trips originating from Dublin. For example, if someone wanted to travel from Dublin to Killybegs in County Donegal (a serious trip at the time) Taylor and Skinner's maps provided the route from Dublin to Newtown Butler, and from there to Enniskillin, to Ballyshannon, to Donegal town and on to Killybegs. The whole itinerary covered several pages. Tracing the connections *between* the main routes was more complicated, but there was an index of crossroads. Otherwise, one could access the maps by an index of place names. Most pages contain two strip maps, usually showing the mileage in English and Irish measure.

The maps appear to have been intended for the tourist as well as for the business man. They contained symbols for county seats, antiquities, churches, bridges, and the names of principal hills, rivers and lakes. A new edition of the book came out in 1783, and a year later a spin-off, *The Post Chaise Companion*, was published. Without the maps, this volume consisted of typographical descriptions submitted by the original subscribers to the map collection. In 1806 Sir Richard Colt Hoare praised both the *Roads of Ireland* and its *Companion*, which were used well into the new century until made obsolete by the burst of new road building prior to the Famine.[42]

Along the Tow Path

In 1817 John Gough declared that travelling in Ireland had improved since his earlier visits in the 1780s. Back then, a journey between Cork and Dublin by horse took at least four days and frequently five or six. Thirty-seven years later, Gough found the convenience of a post-chaise in almost every town, mail and stage coaches running frequent regular schedules, *and* passenger boats on two cross-country canal lines.[43] The success of England's canal system, an important factor in the country's industrialization, caused some of Ireland's leaders to imagine that canals could be the secret to prosperity as well. In 1731 work started on the Newry Canal, intended to transport coal. Even earlier in 1715, there had been hopes of linking Dublin with the Shannon estuary via a series of river-based navigation systems. Once the river scheme proved of limited value, however, the emphasis shifted to canals. As talk of canals grew, so did interest by the Dublin Corporation, in part because canals would help supply the city with water, as well as providing amenities for strolling. Over the years two lines were surveyed. One, the Grand Canal, runs slightly southwest of the city to link up with the old River Barrow Navigation and then, traversing west through the Bog of Allen and past Tullamore, it meets the great river at Shannon Harbour. It was hoped that, as a by-product of the undertaking, the canal would help to drain the extensive midland bogs.[44] A second line, the Royal Canal, runs northwest from Dublin to Mullingar, eventually connecting with the Shannon system at Richmond Harbour on Lough Ree.

After some public funds had been spent in surveys and in preliminary excavations, the Irish Parliament incorporated the Grand Canal Company in 1772. In 1804 the first trade barge traveled from Dublin to Shannon Harbour. However, the canal companies could not act as carriers for goods shipped on their lines, and, because economic activity slowed after the Act of Union, the shipment of goods produced little in the way of profits. Fortunately, passenger traffic, which the canal companies could control, grew until overtaken by competition from the railroads in the 1840s.[45] The Grand Canal floated its first passenger boat in 1780, providing twice-weekly service from Dublin to Sallins. The boat was 52 feet long, about nine feet wide and could accommodate 45 first-class and 35 second-class passengers. The nine-hour journey cost 1s. 1d. under cover or 6 1/2d. for those traveling in the open. As the line grew and passenger service expanded, the Grand Canal Company built hotels at Dublin, Sallins, Robertstown, Tullamore and finally at Shannon Harbour, Ireland's first hotel chain. Even before the line reached Shannon Harbour in 1804, the company owned 22 passenger boats. Writing around 1820, T. K. Cromwell recommended the canal for those heading west. He noted that the seventy-mile trip from Dublin to Shannon Harbour, which took 18 hours, cost one pound for first-class cabin and 14s.1d. for second class. Competition from the coaching lines quickly forced a reduction in rates to 13s. for a state cabin and 8s. 8d.for second class.[46]

Work on the Royal Canal line did not get underway until 1790. The private company originally behind the venture failed before the line reached Lough Ree, and the Directors General of Ireland took over the project, completing it at public expense in 1817. Although carrying 40,000 passengers a year by 1820, the Royal Canal was less successful than its southern competition. As T. W. Freeman has observed, Ireland did not need two cross-country canal routes.[47]

In 1805 Sir John Carr boarded a canal boat at Athy. He admired the first-class cabin furnished with cushioned benches and a long table. The second class cabin was for servants, and the pantry and kitchen were in the steerage. Carr slept on shore at the canal company's "noble" inn at Robertstown. He was enthusiastic about the food served on his boat, which consisted of a leg of boiled mutton, a turkey and a ham, along with a pint of wine, all for 4s. 10d. Nevertheless, the record suggests that complaints about the food tended to outnumber compliments. Usually, a boat's master was allowed to supplement his meager wages, an average of one-guinea per week, by controlling the on-board food and drink concession, usually operated by his wife. Such arrangements may have discouraged quality. A traveler on the Royal Canal line complained of being served "a leg of mutton, nearly raw—a piece of carrion salt beef—a small bit of good bacon...the port bad—the cider like vinegar...." At least the porter was good.[48]

Because the passenger trade began to face serious competition from expanding coaching lines in the 1830s, there was great pressure on the canal lines to speed up their service. After some failed experiments with steam power, the Irish canals turned to "Scotch boats," or "fly boats," so called because of their speed. Canal operators had known for some time that simply increasing the speed of the average canal boat only added to the water's resistance to the hull. However, John Scott Russell, a Scottish engineer, discovered that at speeds over eight and a half miles per hour a properly designed boat would mount, rather than push, its bow wave, thereby diminishing drag and increasing speed. Two to three horses at a gallop could pull a fly boat at around nine English (seven Irish) miles an hour, a speed comparable to cars and coaches on land. As the fly boats were adopted in Ireland, the older passenger boats, now dubbed "night boats," were kept in service at cheaper rates primarily to serve the peasantry.[49]

Though 65 feet in length, the Irish fly boats spanned only a narrow six-foot width. As a result, the cabins, holding twenty in first class and thirty-two in second, were cramped, and passengers had to remain seated during the journey. Moreover, operators offered only cold food and a more restricted choice of beverages.[50] The Halls complained that the fly boats were, in fact, so narrow that the "passengers are painfully cramped and confined." On the other hand, James Johnson, boarding his flyboat at Portobello, found it small but not too uncomfortable. In good weather, he noted, the passengers could sit outside on the small forecastle. However, when passing through the numerous locks, everyone was crammed into the cabin because of the cascade of water tumbling down close to the bow of the boat.[51]

The fly boats appeared first on the Royal Canal in 1833 and on the Grand Canal a year later. They were not, however, without problems and suffered from corresponding costs. More horses had to be changed more often, necessitating an added investment in animals and stabling. Moreover, the galloping horses damaged the banks, as did the higher wake from the boats. Finally, the Scottish design had to be modified to accommodate Irish locks and canal widths. Still the new boats were faster, reducing the time, for example, between Dublin and Mullingar on the Royal line by four hours.[52] Nevertheless, the canals struggled, and by the 1840s they were losing passengers to the new railroads.

Steam Boats on the Shannon

Well before the development of the major Irish rail lines, steam-powered riverboats had been introduced on the Shannon. The long-term, on-and-off-again engineering efforts associated with the Shannon Navigation were begun in the 1750, when the Irish Parliament, faced with the unpleasant possibility of returning unused funds to London, committed the first of many monetary grants to improve transport on the great river. Eventually, by the 1830s, iron-hulled steamers were plying stretches of the Shannon. An advertisement assured "invalids" travelling from Killaloe to Banagher that, thanks to the new steamers, the journey could be completed "without fatigue and in the most agreeable manner.... Carriages and horses are carefully shipped and carried at a modest charge." Their owners sailed for 4s. 6d.[53]

Mary Knott boarded the steamboat *Garryowen* at Limerick in 1836 to travel with her party to Kilrush, Clare for the overland trip to the seaside resort of Kilkee. She was impressed by the boat's accommodations, by the smooth sailing, and especially by the new steam technology. Soon enough, passenger traffic on the lower Shannon began to attract competition, and in 1839 a rival company launched the *Dover Castle*. Mary Francis Dickson described the scene at the docks at Kilkee as she prepared to depart upriver for Limerick. As the jaunting cars galloped to the pier, touts for each vessel accosted them demanding, "Are you for the *Garryowen*? Are you for the *Dover*?" Passengers for the former had to clamber over the latter to reach their ship. Some confusion inevitably followed, which Dickson described as "men, women and children pushing and jostling each other...goods of every sort piled up...men shouting, halooing, and thundering out orders and counter orders...women screaming and talking, or else vociferously urging their wares, cakes, apples, and oranges upon the passengers; pigs yelling, as only pigs can yell...." Eventually, the *Garryowen*'s owners, the Dublin Steamship Company, bought out their competitor.[54]

The Shannon is a long and complex system, and completing the navigation scheme was difficult. As late as 1842, the German travel writer Johann George Kohl found that there were points along the river where the steamer stopped and passengers and crew had to disembark, mount horses and jaunting cars, and head for a spot where they could once again take to the water. Nevertheless, the Shannon steamboats played a particularly important role in summer tourism. In 1852, Dr. John Forbes found that the majority of passengers on his boat were tourists from Scotland and England.[55]

Railways

Even before it was widely deployed in Ireland, steam technology made a significant impact upon Irish tourism by speeding visitors *to* the island, if not whisking them through it. British trains quickly moved travelers out of London to the ports, and steam packets deposited them in Dublin and Cork in a matter of hours. Travel writers in the early 1840s emphasized the ease with which

Londoners could visit Ireland. In their popular travel book, Mr. and Mrs. Hall assured Londoners that traveling to the picturesque center of County Wicklow involved only a journey of 23 hours, "a journey by no means tedious, troublesome or costly." Following the train journey to Liverpool, steam boats, "the largest, safest and best in the kingdom," sailed twice a day to Dublin. Once in Dublin the glens of Wicklow lay only an hour's drive outside of the capitol. Sir Francis Bond Head, visiting Ireland in 1852, boarded the express from London at 9:15 a.m. and arrived in Holyhead at 5.40 p.m., taking the steamer for Dublin that evening. As Dr. John Forbes noted, thanks to steam travel in Britain, one could leave London, land in Ireland, tour Ulster and return home in eight days. "What clerk," Forbes asked, "what shop keeper, what busy doctor, lawyer, or curate, but could command so short a space of time as this, to pick up a stock of health and delight to last him for months?"[56]

Yet, even in 1852, Forbes' London visitor would have had to do most of his sight-seeing within Ulster via horse-drawn cars. Rail lines were slow to expand in Ireland. As noted earlier, Ireland's first railway line, the Kingstown-Dublin route, opened in 1834. Since Kingstown on the south shore of Dublin Bay had replaced the capitol as the major cross-channel terminus, the train took new arrivals into the city. The line was very successful, carrying over two million passengers in the first twelve years of operation. Interestingly, a survey taken to justify the investment revealed that there were around 70,000 trips a month into Dublin, only a portion of which would have involved tourists. This suggests that the railway may have been the world's first commuter line, linking the southern suburbs to the city. However, Ireland lacked the degree of economic activity and the investment capital that was spurring railway development in Britain at that time. When a second line, the Ulster Railway, running from Belfast to Lisburn and Portadown, opened in 1842, Ireland's accumulated track grew by only thirty-one and a half miles.[57]

During the 1840s, Ireland's national rail system finally began to expand. By 1848 an additional 361 miles of track had been laid. In terms of tourism, the most important developments were the opening of the Great Southern and Western Railway's link between Dublin and Cork in 1849 and its Dublin-Galway route in 1851. In 1859 Samuel Reynolds Hole's trip from Dublin to Galway took only five and a quarter hours. Like the Kingstown and Belfast lines, the Great Southern and Western Railway, along with its several branches, was built by Ireland's leading railway contractor William Dargan. While his work would have a greater impact upon Irish tourism in the second half of the nineteenth century, the company laid much of its track in the shadow of the Great Famine. Workers seeking employment at any wage built the line, and emigrants fleeing hunger for Britain and America were among its first passengers. In fact, the Imperial Government, anxious to revive a country wrecked by economic crisis, encouraged the rapid extension of branches into Wexford, Waterford and parts of Connacht.[58]

The extension of Ireland's railroads promised more than speedier travel. In 1852 Head assured his readers that wherever railways went habits of cleanliness and neatness were sure to follow. Writing a few years earlier, Lydia Jane Fisher was confident that the railroads, simply by increasing the number of tourists, would teach the Irish how to cater more directly to travelers' needs.[59] Indeed, the Great Southern and Western line built its own large hotel at the terminus of its line in Galway. The full impact of rail travel on Irish tourism goes beyond the scope of this study. However, it is important to point out that trains allowed tourists to spend more of their time at major sites and less time in transit. This reversal encouraged the tendency to think of Ireland as a collection of beauty spots, a sort of scenic archipelago.

Accommodations

Touring Ireland in the 1820s, Thomas Reid undertook to explain the "signs" that designated the various accommodations available to the lower ranks of travelers in Ireland: "The neck of a broken bottle, an old tea-cup, and sometimes a *brogue* (an old shoe) fixed on the end of a stick, and placed over the door, apprises the traveler that what at first he, perhaps, mistook for a dunghill, is a house of entertainment!" On the other hand, a wisp of straw tied to a long rod indicated nothing more than a bed for the night. The display of a piece of a turf along with a clay pipe, on the other hand, promised the traveler sugar, tea and tobacco. However, if a besom or twig broom hung before the door, "the traveller may rest assured of refreshment of the very best kind, in which is included whiskey, 'of the right sort, that never saw the face of a gauger.'"[60]

It is unlikely that Reid or many other middle-class tourists had firsthand experience with such establishments. They, of course, stayed in properly designated hotels and inns. Even so, many of them were hard put to find kind words for Irish standards of hostelry. It is not clear to what extent this represented a refocusing of the normal British suspicions of things Irish. British travelers seemed more prepared to read intimations of the national character into the standards of Irish inns than in the quality of the country's superior roads. Even Rathbone's Hotel in Kingstown, one of Ireland's better establishments, failed to come up to Dr. John Forbes exacting standards. Although he found it on the whole an excellent establishment, the hotel nevertheless contained broken bits of furniture, crippled window blinds and other things in general disrepair. It was obvious to Forbes that "we had got into a less nice and more careless country than we had left on the eastern side of the Irish channel."[61]

The quality of Irish accommodations suffered from the fact that the country lacked enough travelers to encourage and support good inns. As Ivor Hering explained, in the eighteenth and early nineteenth centuries many ladies and gentlemen arrived in Ireland armed with letters of introduction, which often resulted in invitations to stay at country estates. The Irish "quality," for their part, tended to visit England or the Continent, rather than tour Ireland and patronize the local hostelry. Nor did the Irish economy generate the volume of internal commercial travel needed to support a number of quality inns. Significantly, the active linen trade in Ulster, where buyers used local inns as their headquarters, supported a better class of accommodations than that generally found in the rest of Ireland. Therefore, finding a clean, comfortable inn could be a problem. In the 1760s John Bush found "extraordinary" the "want of good inns" even in Dublin. He advised new arrivals to the city to get directions from one of several coffee houses in Essex Street near the Customs House for private houses where a neat room might cost half a guinea a week. By around 1800 accommodations in Dublin had improved. An anonymous writer in 1806 found the "better hotels" offered rooms at a "reasonable" two shillings. M'Gregor's *New Picture of Dublin*, published in 1821, deemed four hotels "suitable" for the visitor. As for food, Dublin hotels did not serve dinners, but taverns offered excellent meals for 6*s.* 6*d.*, a price so moderate that, according to one observer, a guest might be thought stingy if he called for less than a bottle of wine.[62]

Travelers putting up in small country inns often had to deal with the exigencies of rural life. In the 1750s, Bishop Richard Pococke luckily found a "tolerable inn" in Carlingford, Louth, "but the Bed chamber being within the kitchen, as soon as I rose, the pigs made my Levee." A decade later, artist Gabriel Beranger managed to find accommodations on the road from Blessington to Baltinglass in Wicklow. He was unable to sleep, however, "as the pigs and dogs of the town were at war the best part of the night, and made a horrid noise." Even the experienced Halls could find themselves frustrated by the quality of Irish hostelry. At the village of Tully between Ballinakill and Killary Harbour in Galway they had to put up at a miserable inn. They were offered neither tea nor bread, and "the horse, the cow, the pigs and the hens were separated from us by a floor, through the dividing boards of which they had ample opportunity for conversing with us—which they did not fail to do." During the night, the hostess continually invaded their room to fetch things needed by other guests. The Halls left an hour before daybreak. Travelling in the 1830s, Jonathan Binns stayed at an inn in Glengariff during the winter and found the room "cold, dark, and dreary." Not only was he unable to get a decent turf fire going, but he found the window broken and had to stuff his clothes into the hole. The inn had neither bellows nor warming pan, "and was devoid of some of the very cheapest and most ordinary luxuries."[63]

Worse things than too much noise or too few warming pans might have disturbed the traveler's rest as well. On his walking tour of Ireland in 1790s, the Breton traveler Jacques-Louis de Latocnaye took shelter in an inn on the road to Limerick. Unhappily, the place turned out to be little better than a pest house. He described his ordeal: "I passed the night defending myself from the monsters who regarded me as their lawful prey, and when the sun rose it was on a bloody scene.... Happily the sea was not far off; to it I fled quickly to drown unwelcome guests...." While Joseph Woods was prepared to admit that his accommodations at McDowell's Hotel in Cork were "good," he still felt entitled to "complain bitterly of the bugs which I almost always escape in England. They are large and numerous in all the inns we had slept at but I think we saw no more of them after leaving Cork." In 1815 Mr. A. Atkinson recommended that travelers pack their own bedding, as Irish innkeepers had the habit of putting their children and servants in unoccupied beds, thus spreading vermin. A few years earlier Sir Richard Colt Hoare, travelling towards Ballyshannon, recalled his accommodations as "a more dirty inn, and worse attendance, I never met with either abroad or at home: the rooms and beds teemed with every kind of vermin, and a dirty barefooted wench acted as our *femme de chambre* and waiter...."[64]

The quality of service was, in fact, another frequent source of complaint. Samuel Derrick, dinning at an inn at Passage, Cork found the food good but the service frightful: "Our attendant was a female...[her] face half covered with dirt, half with snuff, her arms, hands, legs, and feet, (for she had neither shoes nor stockings on)...disgusting to people used to the neatness of English inns." In 1791, Dr. Edward Daniel Clarke complained that at one hotel, "Our waiter had got the itch, his deputy was lousy and the rooms were dark and dirty." Writing in 1840, the anonymous author of *The Sportsman Man in Ireland* complained that, while guests in Ireland could not expect such luxuries as carpets, they could "reckon pretty confidently on finding a red-headed monster, shoeless, stockingless, and capless, acting the part of a waiter—one who will hold back her matted locks...with one hand, while she hands you, between her thumb and finger, whatever edible you may demand, perfectly good-tempered, and wondering what can possible ail the stranger who is surrounded, as she conceives, by every earthly luxury." It is little wonder that Atkinson called for a new attitude towards Irish inns on the part of both travelers and landed proprietors. Conditions would not improve, he warned, "until the press enters into this subject, until travellers pay more attention to their beds and horses, and resist the frauds which are daily practiced upon them in those departments, and finally, as the most sovereign remedy of all, until gentlemen who have towns upon their estates, erect inns for the public accommodation, and place them in the hands of persons who shall be rendered accountable for their conduct."[65]

Some proprietors did build inns in their villages, and conditions did improve, at least for the ladies. Travelling around the same time as Atkinson, Anne Plumptre found that, wherever she went in Ireland, no matter how poor the appearance of an inn, there were always clean, white sheets on the bed. And "indeed, I must say that my accommodations were in every way superior to what could be expected from the first appearance of the house." Perhaps it was a matter of persistence on the part of the traveler, as Atkinson had urged. Thomas Walford, the author of the *Scientific Tourist Through Ireland* (1818), maintained that while one could not expect to find an English level of comfort off the beaten track, if travelers were both careful and demanding, they could usually get clean sheets. Traversing Ireland in 1830s, Henry D. Inglis found Irish inns better than expected, even in more remote parts. At Tarbert near the Shannon he booked into an inn with the sitting room "well and newly carpeted...with good mahogany chairs, three excellent mahogany tables, a handsome glass over the chimney piece, clean chintz window curtains, white blinds, and the walls of the room well papered." Most travel writers were careful to mention the good inns along with the bad, although the latter inevitably made better copy. Even as things improved, however, the allegedly high English standard of hostelry seemed hard for the Irish to attain. In the 1840s, James Johnson stated that unlike hotels in England, the chamber pot under bed, much less the availability of a water closet, remained still a rarity in Irish inns.[66]

Touring in the summer months, tourists were tempted to take advantage of the "stretch" at the end of the long Irish day and not seek lodgings until late in the evening. Unfortunately, with virtually no public lighting in the towns, visitors found it was difficult to judge the quality of an inn by its outward appearance after dark. Theresa Cornwallis West and her husband Frederick, traveling in 1846, pulled into the town of Enfield in Westmeath around ten o'clock. By the light of a full moon the local inn seemed clean enough from outside. "And well it was that night veiled the hideousness of the dirt," which was all too obvious by morning light. "The beds were cold and comfortless; carpets had *never* been shaken or swept in their lives; the wash-hand stand was a disgrace in a civilized country, and I felt afraid of what might happen to it if I laid my hand on the sofa waiting for tea!" This seems to have been the worst Mrs. West encountered, for she was fulsome in her praise of other inns in which she stayed. She was, for example, particularly impressed by the Imperial Hotel in Cork. In the well-appointed sitting room she noticed a portrait of Anna Maria Hall, who, with her husband, had authored the most popular guide book to Ireland. The writers had apparently given the picture to the hotel, which, as the Halls wrote in their book, "for elegance and comfort may vie with any hotel in the kingdom."[67]

Henry D. Inglis' provided a more interesting example of how travel writers sometimes left their imprint on the places they visited. For instance, some of his opinions were picked up by other tourists and then fed back into host community. In 1834, after stopping at Flynn's Half Way House on the road from Oughterard, Galway, to Clifton, Inglis wrote admiringly about the owner's beautiful daughter. She was, he judged, "by far the finest specimen of an Irish girl, I had yet seen in Ireland. She was a magnificent creature...with a fine, expressive and somewhat aristocratic face, and a form of perfect symmetry...." The year after Inglis' book appeared, John Barrow made it a point to stop at Flynn's to see this "magnificent creature." He was pleased to report that she was indeed tall and very beautiful. A year of so later Jonathan Binns, similarly intrigued, also broke his journey at Flynn's but took note of the girl's sister. Arriving at Half-way House in September of 1836, Robert Graham wrote in his journal:

> Mr. Binns, I think, says that the beauty of the younger one, whom he described as a child, was to exceed that of the older. By way of something new I may add that the darker and younger one is now the taller of the two and I believe that she does exceed her sister in personal appearance. They are both very handsome, full-grown women, and give you a good idea of the native productions of Cunnamara [sic]. They are a great cause of all the travellers making a point of stopping here but they heed not the overdone attentions which are paid to them and rather dislike the notoriety the tourists have given them. They like it in so far as it attracts custom to the house but Miss Flynn considers Mr. Inglis to have been very impertinent in writing in the way he did about her.[68]

Like Inglis, Barrow and Binns, Graham's language depersonalizes the young women. The authors could well have been describing heifers.

Security

'Twas on the Gilworth Mountains, he began his wild career,
And many a noble gentlemen before him shook with fear....
("Brennan on the Moor")

Although few of the travel writers in the late eighteenth and nineteenth centuries still used the adjective "wild" before the noun "Irish," that old and familiar English coupling of words (and the images they evoked) was never far from the minds of their readers. Eighteenth-century Ireland (like Britain) had its highwaymen, such as Edward Brennan, famed in song and story as "Brennan on the Moor," who haunted the mountains of Tipperary. By the beginning of the nineteenth century, the mail coaches—considered choice pickings by robbers—usually carried two armed guards. On routes considered particularly dangerous coaches were accompanied by dragoons. One enterprising owner of a Dublin-Cork coaching line tried to reassure his customers by advertising the "bullet proof" copper-lined body of his vehicle. However, by the second decade of the nineteenth century Irish highwaymen like Brennan belonged more to street ballads than to dark roadsides.[69] Of course, by feeding anti-Catholic and anti-Irish stereotypes, the United Irishmen's bloody Rising of 1798 did little to enhance Ireland's reputation for tranquility. An anonymous traveler arriving in Dublin in 1804, the year after Robert Emmett's abortive rebellion in that city, noticed that the market house at end of Thomas Street formed a blockade against further insurrection: "Each window has a sloping cover, from which soldiers can fire without being annoyed by the mob." Suspected of being a French spy, the visitor had his papers searched by the authorities. Sir Richard Colt Hoare, arriving in Dublin two years later, found that the bridges still contained barricades.[70]

With the exception of the Rising and its aftermath, however, agrarian unrest was a more serious problem in Ireland than political rebellion. Starting around the mid-eighteenth century, peasant secret societies, such as the Whiteboys and the Ribbonmen, kept certain parts of the country in turmoil. Nevertheless, in spite of ongoing agrarian violence throughout the pre-Famine years, visitors were seldom in danger. As Henry D. Ingles perceived in the 1830s, "Irish outrages are never committed upon strangers...." Indeed, several travel writers, such as T. K. Cromwell and Anne Plumptre, dismissed the fear of Irish violence as an unjustifiable example of English prejudice. As Plumptre insisted, "my Narrative will show, that it is possible to travel many and many miles over this disturbed country in the most perfect quiet."[71] Leitch Ritchie, warned by his contacts in Ireland to beware of thugs, claimed that the Irish were slandered by their own people, as there was no violence to be encountered. Even when he was hit on the head in a dark street in Athlone, he set the incident down to a case of mistaken identity; his attacker must have taken him for an officer of the law. The Halls were very anxious to reassure their British readers that, if they came to Ireland, they would be safe from violence and even insult. The visitor could always be certain of a hearty welcome. In the second of a series of articles on Irish tourism published in the *Dublin University Magazine* in 1836, Samuel Ferguson, writing anonymously, also sought to bury the security issue. "As to risk of violence, or insult, nay, of rudeness or even incivility, let this suffice, that, to be a stranger, is throughout all Ireland and at all times, a passport to the best offices of a naturally polite and hospitable people."[72] It seems clear that hospitality, one of the prime selling points for modern Irish tourism, had been firmly established well before the Famine, and has remained a key talking point ever since.

Chapter 2

TOURS GRAND AND PETITE

Dublin—In the Shadow of the Grand Tradition

Although Ireland's principal tourist attractions were located in its picturesque countryside, once landed in Dublin, many visitors toured the capital city before setting out for the glens, mountains and lakes. In fact, many travel writers devoted considerable space to describing the Empire's "second city," partly because of genuine interest in Dublin and partly in response to the touring habits established by the urban-centered Grand Tour, to which Georgian Dublin itself owed much of its character. Like their English counterparts, Anglo-Irish grandees returned from their Italian tours with paintings, statues, architectural designs and sketches to be incorporated into their townhouses and country estates. Many of Dublin's buildings, public and private, reflected what one observer, referring to the new Parliament building, called "the true Italian taste."[1] Working with architect Sir William Chambers, Lord Charlemont drew upon his experiences in Italy to design his Palladian mansion on Rutland Square (today's Hugh Lane Gallery of Modern Art) and his exquisite miniature hideaway, the Casino, on his Marino estate overlooking Dublin Bay. C. T. Bowden described it as "one of the most beautiful and elegant seats in the world."[2]

By the middle of the eighteenth century the capital was already on its way to becoming a great Georgian city. Land on both sides of the River Liffey had been reclaimed and the river channeled along the city's quays. As the city developed eastward, Essex Bridge joined the north and south sides of the river, later spanned by Carlisle Bridge in 1794 (eventually replaced by today's O'Connell Street Bridge). To the north, Upper Sackville Street (O'Connell Street) was under development. Just beyond it lay the Dublin Lying-in Hospital (one of the oldest continuing maternity hospitals in the world), begun in 1751 and completed six years later. The subsequent addition of an extensive complex of pleasure gardens and assembly rooms financed this charity institution. These in turn attracted fashionable houses around Rutland Square. South of the river, the rebuilding of much of Trinity College (its charter dating from the reign of

Elizabeth I) occurred between 1755 and 1759. Its new classical facade looked out upon the refurbished Parliament building across College Green. The Earl of Kildare's great Leinster House (present seat of Dáil Éireann) had opened up the southeast side of the city for fashionable development.[3]

The following decades witnessed the erection of other great Georgian structures, such as the Royal Exchange (later the City Hall), the Customs House and the Four Courts, the latter two dramatically situated on the River Liffey. In addition to private and governmental structures, Dublin hosted a remarkable number of charitable institutions, many with imposing Palladian facades. As opposed to the numerous new town houses, most of Georgian Dublin's great public buildings were constructed of stone. Dublin Castle, remodeled in the 1750, remained the last important public structures to be built in brick.[4]

All of this building activity reflected a new sense of confidence and power on the part of Ireland's ruling class, the Protestant Ascendancy. In 1782, under pressures from its wars in America and rising tensions with France, the British government agreed to repeal Poyning's Law, which had forbidden the Irish Parliament from initiating or even considering any legislation not sanctioned in advance by the Crown. Under the leadership of its dynamic Speaker, Henry Grattan, the Parliament at College Green became an important institution with real, if ultimately limited, power. Combined with rising income from rents in the countryside, the new legislative powers to promote the Irish economy provided both the impetus and the funds for rebuilding much of the capital. This involved more than erecting new buildings. The Wide Streets Commission, established in 1757 and controlled by landowners and developers, set about clearing old dark and narrow streets. This opened up major thoroughfares and fashionable neighborhoods, introducing into the urban environment the kind of space and light that the city's grandees enjoyed on their country estates. Luke Gardiner's development of the area around Dorset Street, north of the Liffey, represented an early example of this new type of urbanscape. He dramatically widened the street, installing a pedestrian mall with lamps and obelisks. Dr. Edward Clarke admired the fashionable crowds strolling there every Sunday evening. Renamed Sackville Street, the Mall became a favorite promenade for the wealthy folk who began to build their houses along either side.[5] Writing in the 1760s, John Bush praised the street's width but complained that the developer had failed to carry it further north to the Lying-in Hospital at Rutland Square. Bush also noted that if Sackville Street had been extended southward to the Liffey (accomplished, in fact, by 1798), "it would have been one of the grandest and most beautiful streets perhaps in Europe." By the time T. K. Cromwell provided his detailed descriptions of the city in 1820, the additions of the General Post Office, with its vast classical portico facing Nelson's Pillar, encouraged the writer to declare Sackville Street "one of the novelest in Europe." By then new urban commissions had addressed the lighting and paving of Dublin's main streets. Around 1820 the city boasted some 6000 lamps.[6]

As in London, some of the most fashionable sections of Dublin were built around squares. Rutland Square dominated the main axis North of the Liffey. Describing the south side of the river, Rev. Thomas Campbell in the 1770s called attention to the new Merrion Square, facing Leinster House, with its wide gravel walks for evening and Sunday afternoon promenades. The interior of the square received less formal treatment, however. Visiting in 1814, Anne Plumptre recorded her surprise that, instead of a shaved lawn, the square contained a meadow routinely cut for hay.[7]

Situated at the top of Grafton Street south of College Green, St. Stephen's Green remains the largest residential square in Great Britain and Ireland. The first houses were laid out in 1664 around a commons that became known as "the Green." These early buildings were replaced in the following century by some of the city's finest Georgian houses, many of which have since fallen victim to the wrecker's ball or retain only their facades.[8] Unlike most of the houses around other squares, those on St. Steven's Green are far from uniform in appearance, a fact that offended Richard Twiss, visiting in 1775. He complained that there were "scarcely two of the same height, breadth, materials, or architecture." Perhaps in response to Twiss, the Anglo-Irish clergyman Rev. Thomas Campbell argued that the Green benefitted from this lack of dull regularity in its facades. Sir Richard Colt Hoare, on the other hand, lamented the want of the uniformity, so characteristic of fashionable Bath, and so the debate continued.[9] Like the comparisons between the bays of Dublin and Naples, the surroundings of St. Stephen's Green fueled another travel writers' debate, although this one may have been a family spat between English and Anglo-Irish authors.

In the eighteenth century St. Stephen's Green presented a large open space, its primary ornament a statue of George II (eventually "liberated" to smithereens by IRA gelignite in 1937). Both John Carr and Hoare described the Green as "a fine meadow," its primary feature, a double line of elm trees that arched over a fashionable promenade along its perimeter. Although Hoare noted the "broad gravel walk," he complained that it was "separated from the street by a low wall, and from the green by a dirty and stinking ditch, [that] encircles the whole area...." Carr described the ditch as a "the receptacle of dead cats and dogs." Even the double row of trees, the one feature of the Green generally admired by visitors, received surprisingly casual treatment from the residents living along its perimeter. Anne Plumptre relates the organization of a fireworks display on the Green in August of 1814 to celebrate the century of the Hanoverian succession. So that the square's residents could enjoy unimpeded views of the spectacle, the elms bordering the square were cut to their trunks.

The next year the trees were gone, but so was the offending ditch, replaced by a wrought iron fence.[10]

Most eighteenth and early nineteenth-century travelers, such as Twiss and Carr, dutifully followed the tradition of the Grand Tour by taking in Dublin's public buildings, charities and pleasure gardens and by inspecting art works in public exhibition and private collections. Twiss, for example, claimed to have seen some Rembrandts. Dr. Edward Daniel Clarke visited Trinity College's library but was more interested in its museum with its wax images of females in various stages of pregnancy. He had to cut his inspection short, however, to accommodate some women waiting outside to see the exhibit.[11]

One way in which the city reflected the influence of the Grand Tour could be found in the plaster ceiling and wall decoration in the finer homes, which contrasted dramatically with the rather austere brick Georgian exteriors. Ornate stucco work on the ceilings and in the stairwells reflected Italian influences, especially in the work of the immigrant Franchini brothers. Tastes in such decoration alternated between elaborate baroque extravagance and more restrained classical influences. The lavishly decorated ceiling of the chapel in the Dublin Lying-in Hospital boasts what is probably the best example of rococo plaster work in Britain and Ireland. Even tourists not sufficiently well placed to gain admittance to the houses of Dublin's grandees could still glimpse some of this plaster work. In many houses the high windows of the most richly decorated room, the *piano noble*, situated on the first story in the front, allowed those in the street below to catch a view of the decorated ceilings.[12]

In the tradition of the Grand Tour, a tried and true method for starting one's visit to a strange city consisted in finding a high point that provided a panoramic view. Unfortunately, Dublin is relatively flat. Recommending the view from the Phoenix Park west of the city, Rev. Thomas Campbell promised that the sight of the blue slating of the city's roofs offered "a finer effect than you can imagine." Otherwise, eighteenth-century Dublin offered few of the towers, steeples and domes available to tourists in most Continental cities. This anomaly struck Sir John Carr, who wondered if Dubliners were possibly averse to heights, perhaps out of an inordinate fear of lightning.[13] In 1816 a pillar commemorating Admiral Horatio Nelson, erected on Sackville Street opposite the General Post Office, redeemed the situation. The pillar had a viewing platform below the statue of the famous commander (James Joyce's "one-handled Nelson"). It survived as Dublin's most famous landmark until 1966, when, on the fiftieth anniversary of the 1916 Easter Rising, the IRA blew it up—an unofficial contribution to the urban renewal that has continued to clear away so much of Dublin's Georgian heritage.[14]

Eighteenth-century Dublin had been fortunate in attracting talented architects skilled in the Palladian style, most notably Richard Castle (originally

Cassel). Visitors admired his Parliament building on College Green (now the Bank of Ireland), Leinster House and his design for the Dublin Lying-in Hospital, better known as the Rotunda. (Castle also designed several fine houses in Stephen's Green, as well as Carton House in Kildare and Westport House in Mayo.) Built through the unflagging efforts of its founder Bartholomew Mosse in 1759, the maternity hospital depended for support on lotteries and on income from the adjacent Pleasure Garden, much admired by tourists. Rev. Thomas Campbell opined that, while the entertainment within the Garden might not be defensible on religious principles, the enterprise did support a worthy cause. Anne Plumptre described the grounds as "open every night during the summer as a promenade, with a band of music and lights, each person paying six pence at the entrance, and they are much frequented even by very good company. About seventy thousand have been admitted since opening of the hospital...." Reflecting the emerging taste for the picturesque and the parallel interest in estate landscaping, John Gough admired the Garden's gravel walks, shrubs and bowling green, and especially its lofty upper terrace and rows of grown elms trees. It all presented, he thought, as much rural beauty as one could expect in nine urban acres.[15]

Modeled on London's Vauxhall and Ranelagh pleasure grounds, the garden at Rutland Square inspired competition south of the river, which soon boasted its own "Renelagh Gardens" along with Marlborough Green. All of Dublin's pleasure establishments offered music, theater, fireworks, bowling greens and tea rooms.[16] The Lying-in Hospital sought to meet the competition by erecting the Rotunda, a large circular room similar to one in London's Ranelagh Gardens but unobstructed by any central supports. The new building extended the entertainment season by providing an indoor promenade space in which the fashionable and would-be fashionable could see and be seen. The Breton Chevalier Jacques-Louis de Latocnaye, touring Ireland in the 1790s, observed that, while a certain freedom of movement prevailed, "people only mix with and speak to members of their own circle." Nevertheless, once settled at the tea tables, "everywhere there reigned a kind of quiet enjoyment.... The good mothers were not very numerous, and those who were present appeared to be absent-minded. The young folk on the other hand, were very numerous and making good use of their time...." A later addition, the Assembly Rooms soon added to the Rotunda complex, providing meeting and dining space.[17]

Most visitors found Irish society, especially in Dublin, freer and less formal than that of London. T. K. Cromwell described Dublin society as "excellent," combining the polish of Paris with the "wit, raciness, frankness, and hilarity of Hibernia...." He felt that the inclusion of members of the gentry, the professions, and even academia, gave Dublin society a distinct urbanity. Nevertheless, however hearty the welcome, the visitor to eighteenth-century

Ireland sometimes found the hospitality of Irish high society more curse than blessing. Not only did the tables groan with food, but the copious amounts of drink challenged, when it did not stagger, visitors. Shocked at the display of such lavishness in a country rife with poverty, John Bush claimed that if the Englishman "will but *drink* like an *Irishman*, he is welcome to *eat* like an Englishman." He found Irish intemperance an "inconvenience," that left him with feelings of disgust. The philosopher Bishop Berkeley wondered "whether any kingdom in Europe be so good a customer of Bordeaux as Ireland?" As Viceroy of Ireland, Lord Chesterfield lamented the 5,000 tons of wine imported into Ireland annually, to the determent of the "constitutions, the faculties, and too often the fortunes of those of superior rank."[18]

The situation began to change during the later part of the eighteenth century. The hypercritical Richard Twiss observed in 1775 that, "since the excesses of the table have been so judiciously abolished, hospitality is not so violently practiced as heretofore, when it might have been imputed to them [the Irish] as a fault." As with almost everything else he wrote, this apparent compliment was so left-handed in its expression that Twiss' Irish readers took his comments as a slur on their much-regarded sense of hospitality. For his troubles Dublin immortalized him by putting his likeness on the inside of a chamber pot, inscribed with the invitation to salute the distinguished visitor in the fashion appropriate to the utensil.[19]

Visitors sometimes found other characteristics of Irish society more disturbing than the excessive drinking. The admixture in society of "half-mounted gentleman," squireens, buckeens and general fortune hunters provided the occasional spice of scandal and even of danger for the natives, if not for the visitors. Dueling appears to have been a popular avocation among the Irish upper classes, well supported by dueling clubs. Writing in 1790, C. T. Bowden claimed that dueling seemed more prevalent in Dublin than in any other city he had visited. Upon arriving in the capital, he called upon a man he had met in Bath only to find him dead, the victim of an exchange of honor that very morning. Indeed, the number of duels fought in Marlborough Green contributed to the decline in its popularity.[20]

Squalor Amid Splendor

Always anxious to establish their *bone fides* as experienced travelers quite conscious of the alleged superiority of their own country, British travel writers could never completely agree as to whether Dublin was, in fact, one of the finest cities of the Empire or a provincial upstart striving but failing to impress. While John Bush found Dublin "a well built city" without much "ornament," Richard Twiss, anxious to display his own superior tastes, sniffed that "to write of this city with the solemnity of a geographical description, would have the appearance of a very frivolous ostentation." While few visitors could be totally indifferent to the splendors of Georgian Dublin, the city's chief characteristic remained for many the unavoidable contrast between its very conspicuous wealth and its appalling poverty, something which greeted tourists the instant they arrived at the city's outskirts. In 1822 Thomas Reid recorded his initial impression of Ringsend: "The place where we landed was crowded with creatures of whom it would be difficult to give a correct description. Their dress, or, more properly speaking, their undress, together with their emaciated, haggard looks, was well calculated to awaken feelings of commiseration." The new harbor at Kingstown, several miles southeast of Dublin, did little to improve first impressions. Landing there, Leitch Ritchie complained that "the stranger is welcomed to Ireland by the beggars." In other countries, he maintained, porters would push the beggars out of the way. "Here they [the beggars] take a distinct and prominent part in the scene. They are sacred from interference; and their voice has something of authority in it as they cry—'God bless your honour! Welcome to the country sir; and joy be on the day our eyes look upon you!'" One of the few writers to go beyond typography in comparing Naples and Dublin, Ritchie noted the deep poverty in both places. However, he added, "The lazzarone of Naples enjoys life; he of Ireland endures it...."[21]

The visitors' initial dockside impressions did not wear off once ensconced in Dublin. The city's alleys of squalor and poverty were only steps from its most fashionable streets and squares. Though St. Patrick's Cathedral stands only a few blocks from Dublin Castle, the Rev. Thomas Campbell had to hold his nose against the stench as he walked to the Cathedral, pitying, as he went, Dr. Jonathan Swift, the Cathedral's late Dean. Seventy years later James Johnson almost waxed poetic as he described the poverty of the adjacent "Liberties," a district of weavers since medieval times: "Thus the wind and the rains have *liberty* to enter freely through the windows of half the houses in this locality...the pigs have *liberty* to ramble about without rings in their nose...[the silk weaver] has the *liberty* to starve, to go into the workhouse.... Lastly he has *liberty* to beg...." T. K. Cromwell found the Liberties memorable for the "accumulation of filth, stench, and every variety of wretchedness," noting that there, as in many other parts of Dublin, the backyards were the only available receptacle for human waste.[22]

Dublin poverty could not be viewed from a comfortable distance; it pressed itself up against the visitor. Dr. Edward Clarke warned any reader seeking to enter a Dublin shop that the city's beggars "infest the door, through which you must press your way, and deem yourself fortunate if you escape the detached parties of vermin which, wandering from the republic of their hair, hang on all parts of their bodies." De Latocnaye complained that the beggars "may be seen hanging on for hours to the railings of basement stories, forcing charity by depriving those who live in these places of light and air." Writing of Dublin in the 1830s, Ritchie described the poor lounging on the steps of the great houses and almost blocking the doors of the shops. To his dismay he also found two nearly naked children lying shivering and moaning on the sidewalk near the fashionable Gresham Hotel in upper Sackville Street. In all cities, he observed, visitors could find this "commingling of wealth and poverty; but here the extremes of both meet in a manner that would be ludicrous were it not dismal...everywhere we see Want staring Luxury in the face, and pointing with her lean finger to the contrast."[23]

Surveying the piles of manure, the barely-clothed children and the numerous prostitutes in the vicinity of Thomas Street, one visitor, writing anonymously in 1804, claimed, "It would be difficult to convey an idea of the vice, filth, and wretchedness, in which the lower orders dwell, and seem to delight, everywhere in this district; compared with which, [London's] St.Giles is a palace in comfort, and a paradise in morality." He summed up Dublin by charging that "everything...is pomp or poverty, splendor or squalid wretchedness. No decent comforts of the middle ranks unite, as in London, the magnificence and misery."[24] One must wonder if Dublin was, in fact, really poorer than London or if its slums were worse than those of Britain's industrial cities such as Birmingham and Manchester. At one quarter the size of London, it may be that Dublin differed not in the depth of its poverty as much as in the close proximity of its privation to its splendor. Perhaps, as will be argued later, tourist amnesia precluded realistic comparisons between home and abroad, since one of the essentials of touring culture is the traveler's conviction that "home" is superior and therefore sacred.

Whatever the accuracy of their complaints, these writers summed up the impressions of many visitors to Ireland during the country's first century of tourism. Travelers extended this contrast between splendor and destitution, beyond Dublin and the other cities and towns, deep into the countryside. There the juxtaposition of spectacular scenery and abject peasant poverty was noted in almost all travel accounts of pre-Famine Ireland. As will be discussed in the last chapter, observing Irish poverty became part of the Irish tourist experience.

The Petite Tour and the Built Environment—Cities

Given its position as a capital city, its size, wealth and the quality of its new buildings and streetscapes, eighteenth and early nineteenth-century Dublin fitted easily into the habits of the Grand Tour. Most of Ireland's other cities and towns were not on the scale typical of stops on the Grand Tour. Nevertheless, tourists visited them and travel writers described them. Along with the country's natural scenery, Ireland's built environment remained an essential part of the Irish tour for several reasons. As noted in the "Introduction," the well-established habits of the Grand Tour would have made it difficult for most visitors to ignore urban Ireland. Public buildings, churches and cathedrals, bridges, charitable institutions, prisons, schools, military barracks and the like were among the sights tourists were supposed to notice. Moreover, many British visitors regarded the Irish tour as a search for knowledge about the Sister Isle, which, after 1801 became the newest member of the United Kingdom. Many British visitors took Ireland's social and economic life seriously. In contrast to the Grand Tour, however, this aspect of Irish tourism might be referred to as the "petite tour." The visitor to pre-Famine Ireland inspected cities, buildings and institutions similar in type to what they might have encountered in Europe, except that in Ireland the scale was usually much more modest. In 1800 Cork, the island's second city, had 80,000 people; Limerick, 60,000: and Belfast, 20,000, although the latter grew very rapidly because of its industrial development. The old medieval administrative center of Kilkenny reported a population of 15,000, and the city of Derry, only 11,000.[25] Yet, all had their points of interest and all received attention from visitors.

Many travelers were impressed by Cork's setting on the River Lee, backed by the surrounding hills, although the visitors generally had less enthusiasm for the city itself. Built upon marshes, throughout much of the eighteenth century Cork had been divided by numerous canals, its streets connected, as Richard Twiss observed, by numerous small draw bridges. Although he noted a few fine buildings, Twiss decided that "the *forte* of the citizens" did not lie in the sciences or fine arts but rather "in the more essential arts relative to eating and drinking"; that is, in the processing and shipping of Ireland's agricultural produce, especially its livestock. Twiss was accurate enough regarding the city's important role in Ireland's agricultural export trade, a point repeated by Rev. Thomas Campbell, who, before his visit, had been led to believe Cork a "magazine of nastiness." Campbell ended up impressed by "the busy bustle of prosperous trade and its concomitant blessings." The export trade in livestock and meat had its drawbacks, however. Visiting in the 1790s, C. T. Bowden decided that the large number of slaughter houses worked against "any idea of the salubrity of its air." Around the same time the French counsel Charles de Montbret declared the city's remaining open canals dirty and odorous.[26]

As to Cork's appearance, most visitors commented on its seven churches, its barracks, the customs house and other public buildings. Several eighteenth-century writers noted that many houses were "weather slated," unusual for Ireland, giving the city a dull and heavy look. An anonymous contributor to *Walker's Hibernian Magazine* suggested that "if rebuilt of brick," Cork "would be one of the best in the kingdom." Anne Plumptre thought that visitors who looked too hard for impressive buildings might miss the mark. Cork, she claimed, "is upon the whole recommendable to the eye only as having a general appearance of comfort and prosperity, not as offering any particular subjects to dwell upon." Leitch Ritchie declared that Cork had no distinguished buildings, only houses. However, because the city had been founded on islands and canals, he noted: "The ground is so irregular that at almost every turning you are presented with a new picture; and the houses themselves, in height, form, and color, are as unlike each other as human caprice could well make them." Nevertheless everything came together on "one grand meeting-point—the desire of forming, out of these irregular materials, a wide, massive, and regular street."[27]

Indeed, visitors did seem most impressed by Cork's major thoroughfares, such as Patrick Street and the Grand Parade, which the correspondent for *Walker's* called "a noble street lately formed by arching over one of the small canals."[28] Most visitors were also impressed by the mile-long Mardyke promenade shaded by elm trees. Carr admired its "handsome" houses and "elegant" society. Visiting Cork forty years earlier, Samuel Derrick had complained about the Mardyke's uneven paving but admitted, "I have seen it filled with very genteel company, and a greater number of pretty women than I ever saw together in any other town." In spite of such comfort and elegance, Cork also had more than its share of poverty. Dr. John Forbes found the city's poor clustered in its center in what he described as "extensive masses of hidden streets of the most squalid description."[29]

Even more than Cork and Dublin, Limerick seemed to strike many tourists as a city of contrasts. Made up, as William Makepeace Thackeray pointed out, of three historic sections—Irish Town, English Town and Newtown-Pery— only the latter with its warehouses, fine shops and clubs, suggested prosperity. Yet, as Thackeray insisted, initial appearances could be deceiving. Once out of that area, the visitor "entered a labyrinth of busy swarming poverty and squalid commerce as was never before seen—no, not in Saint Giles." Thus, while Ireland's poor could be found in all of the country's cities and towns, poverty seems to have been the principle impression that tourists took away from their visits to Limerick. Situated on the banks of the Shannon, Limerick, the largest city in the west of Ireland, reflected some of the region's characteristics. Carr, for example, was surprised to encounter beggars conversing and seeking alms in the Irish language. Poverty represented another factor all too common in the West. Travelers who had already encountered extreme poverty elsewhere in Ireland were, nevertheless, shocked by what they saw in Limerick. Spencer T. Hall admitted that the city had some fine buildings, but he added, "I can never expect to see human beings more miserable, denuded, or in all respects more deplorable than may be found abiding among its poor." Leitch Ritchie claimed that, if he had stuck to the main thoroughfares, he would have come away with a good impression of the city. But "I cannot, and dare not if I could, describe the horrors of Limerick destitution. Their existence is alone sufficient to blast the character of Great Britain in civilized Europe, and to all succeeding ages."[30]

Belfast, which overtook Limerick during the nineteenth century as Ireland's third city, generally received a better press. Belfast was the only city in Ireland to actually experience the Industrial Revolution. Even before the Famine it was becoming a center for textile manufacture. And because of its explosive growth, Belfast actually looked new. According to Henry D. Ingles, who visited it in 1834, at least one third of Belfast had been built over the previous fifteen years, and its population stood at around 65,000, up from 20,000 in 1800.[31] Since poverty seemed so characteristic of Ireland's older cities, such as Dublin, Cork and Limerick, Belfast's very modern industrial-based prosperity struck visitors as a pleasing anomaly. Inglis spoke for many British visitors when he claimed that the city seemed to have almost nothing in common with the rest of Ireland: "No mud cabins,—these I had left behind me long ago...." Nor did he see any beggars. "There is, in fact, *no trace of an Irish population among any class*: the lower orders are not ragged, and starving; and idle,—because unemployed: the middle and upper classes are not loungers and men of pleasure. Pleasure, in Belfast, is a very secondary consideration.... Everyone has something to do; and every one appears to find pleasure in doing something...."[32]

Inglis' extraordinary contention that Belfast was not truly Irish was echoed by other British visitors, who seemed to see Belfast positioned on the hinge of Irish history. If any place in Ireland had less to do with the country's Gaelic, Roman Catholic, agrarian heritage it was Belfast. In fact, Belfast appeared more in tune with industrial Britain's present and future than any other Irish city. Ritchie maintained that, if transplanted with it population to England, Belfast would be recognized as a credit to that country. Probably referring to the supposed moral basis of political economy, Ritchie claimed that Belfast, having become the third city in Ireland in terms of size, represented the country's first city from the "moral point of view." For his part, Inglis found the key to the city's success in its population, dominated like much of eastern Ulster by descendants of Lowland Scottish Protestants and Dissenters: "It is impossible that Cork, Limerick, or Waterford, should ever become altogether like Belfast; because the character of the Scotch and the Irish is essentially different...." Inglis was, of course, himself a Scot. Nevertheless, most visitors were inclined to see Belfast, along with much of Ulster, standing apart from the rest of Ireland. It remained for Lord John Manners, touring in 1846, to wonder what might happen if Belfast's combination of the spinning-jenny and Calvinism could be extended over the whole of Ireland. The country would no doubt lose its poetry but perhaps, he speculated, Roman Catholicism would "soften" the features of industrialism.[33]

Few visitors, in fact, spent much time extolling the beauties of Belfast. Neither Inglis nor Ritchie, for example, mistook industrial progress as a recipe for the city beautiful. "A chaste architectural design," Inglis suggested, "is not at all inconsistent with moderate expense; but anything is better than the...*hungry* look of the modern streets of Belfast. If a beautiful architectural design is too high a flight for the architect, let him, at last, take refuge in the picturesque." And for all of his admiration of city's "moral" achievement, Ritchie had to admit that "upon the whole Belfast is not a place which can delay long the steps of him who travels in search of the picturesque, whether in nature, or human character; and, after a very brief sojourn, I pursued my route northward."[34]

Leaving Belfast and traveling north and then west, visitors eventually found their way to the city of Derry (or Londonderry) on Lough Foyle. Although lacking the industrial swagger of Belfast, Derry had an even greater purchase on the history of Protestant domination of Ulster. It stood in many respects as Ireland's "first" *Protestant* city. Having closed its gates to the Catholic forces supporting James II in 1690, the city survived a 105-day siege safe behind its walls, which stand to this day. So, like Belfast, Derry conveyed a Protestant aura much appreciated by most British visitors. In his book, John Barrow hailed the city as the Edinburgh of Ireland and included a brief history of the siege. Dr. James Johnson claimed Derry as the "Jungfrau" of Ireland, the maiden city. "There she sits majestic on her lofty throne, crowned with a cathedral and guarded by a church-militant," a reference to the Bible-bearing statue of George Walker, a Protestant clergyman who helped defend the city and who later died a martyr to the Protestant cause at the Battle of the Boyne.[35]

Towns

In historical terms, much of urban Ireland was relatively new when compared to England. The old Gaelic polity had never fully embraced towns. Ireland's monastic centers and its few Viking-founded seaports were what Anngret Simms has called "incipient" or "proto-towns," having some of the social and economic functions of towns but lacking the sort of organization and town law brought to Ireland by the Anglo-Normans in the twelfth century. Ireland's subsequent medieval towns and manorial villages were generally of Norman origin and most were clustered around or were within the Pale. Even these settlements were not numerous. Kevin Whelan observes that of 270 town charters granted during the Anglo-Norman period, only 56 became significant walled towns.

The situation changed dramatically with the plantations of the seventeenth century. The new masters of the land often established new towns and villages, some of them replacing the older medieval settlements. Plantation towns, usually centered on a castle or fortified house and a new Protestant church, often included a triangular market green, called "the diamond" in Ulster. A spate of urban expansion had occurred during the Restoration period. However, the first half of the eighteenth century witnessed a significant wave of construction of estate towns, encouraged by the political stability and the economic growth that followed solidification of the Protestant Ascendancy's power after the Battle of the Boyne. Many proprietors, busy building or remodeling their own manor houses, went on to develop the towns in their demesnes. Rebuilt older villages or the new estate towns of the eighteenth century usually assembled themselves around a market house erected by the town's owner. Such towns often included an imposing entrance to the proprietor's walled-in estate, as well as a military barracks and a Protestant church. The shift of road building to the county Grand Juries after 1760, mentioned in the last chapter, gave further impetus to town construction, as the landlords who owned the villages sought to improve access. In addition, landlords often established local industries and trades as part of the development of their estate towns. For example, Arthur Young noted the efforts of Mr. Jeffrey, proprietor of Blarney Castle in Cork, in establishing textile manufactures—linens, woolens and stocking—in his town.[36]

In some of the smaller estate towns, where the landlords usually had considerable control, tourists sometimes found results more impressive than what they had seen in the cities. In 1817 John Gough compared the relatively new town of Caher, Tipperary on the banks of the Suir to the city of Limerick. He found the little town "very beautiful, and its exterior view is splendid, beyond most country towns in Ireland, from a tall spire steeple to a new church just built, another equally elegant on the Romish chapel; its venerable old castle and the handsome new cupola on the market house...." Caher could boast "four elevated edifices while the great city of Limerick has but one."[37]

Whatever their size and appearance, most Irish towns shared one feature few visitors failed to notice. In 1769 John Bush decried the "long strings of despicable huts, or cabbins [sic]" that spoiled the entrances of most Irish towns. Similarly, T. K. Cromwell complained of the "long avenue of mud cottages, by which we usually approach and quit" Irish towns. This clustering of the poor cabins at the entrances and exits of Irish towns resulted from two significant changes that occurred in the eighteenth century. Around the same time that the country's road system improved and expanded, Ireland's farmers, tired of the poor cabins huddling around them, began pushing their workers off of the land. The displaced peasants followed the new roads to the growing towns, where the proprietors seldom bothered to provide space for them. And so they filled in vacant land within the towns and congregated on the outskirts.[38]

The inevitable military barracks constituted another feature of Irish towns that most visitors noticed, but seldom questioned. British travelers would less frequently encounter such structures back home, where they would have found the visible presence of a large standing army unwelcome. In Ireland, on the other hand, invasion threats from France, not to mention potential unrest among the lower orders, made the military a welcome presence, at least to the Ascendancy class. In the 1760s Ireland contained over 15,000 regular troops housed in every city and in most towns of any size. Landlords frequently built barracks within their new estate towns. Whether foot or horse, military units helped underwrite a town's economy, going some way in reducing Ireland's burden for maintaining much of the Empire's "home" forces. John Gough, revisiting Clonmel in 1817, found the town much improved, mainly because of the presence of the military. Alexis de Tocqueville attributed the relative prosperity of the landlord town of Fremoy to the presence of two regiments of foot. However, he considered the military "a nasty source for a country's prosperity."[39]

In fact, those in search of the picturesque were not always pleased by the ubiquitous presence of the military. Touring Ross Island at Killarney, Richard Colt Hoare complained that the barracks in the old castle "sadly disfigured the place." Anne Plumptre also condemned the "vile barracks" in so picturesque a setting. John Carr found the white stucco barracks at Glendalough out of place with the "dusky scenery" of the site. On a more practical level, some tourists felt that the military spoiled tourism. The anonymous author of *The Sportsman in Ireland* complained that easy money from the soldiers encouraged the "boys" around Athlone and the Shannon to be too demanding in their tips for services rendered.[40]

Naturally, Irish towns differed greatly from one another, in part because of the great differences in the quality of the agricultural land that formed their economic bases. Some were new elegant estate towns like Caher, while others were old and decayed, like Callen ("of the Ructions") in County Kilkenny. Most towns were somewhere in between. Spencer T. Hall had to confess that although Irish towns were not all alike, some were so much so that the visitor soon forgot which was which. Many were disorganized and "odd-looking, desolate, dirty streeted, pi-bald sort of places, in which every object of consequence appeared in remarkable contrast with its neighbor." Hall claimed that one might see a venerable abbey in ruins right next to a new, white-washed Roman Catholic chapel.[41]

Industrial Sites and Irish Tourism

According to Chris Rojek, "a tourist sight may be defined as a spatial location which is distinguished from everyday life by virtue of its natural, historical or cultural extraordinariness."[42] All this is relative, however. What might appear mundane or even off-putting to the tourists of one age or country could be considered extraordinary, or at least curious to those of another. Even an object or an institution that at home might seem humdrum could excite interest when encountered abroad. As noted earlier, in the tradition of the Grand Tour travelers often concerned themselves with foreign customs and institutions. This habit carried over into the "petit tour" of Ireland, where, because of Ireland's relationship with Great Britain, many visitors took at least passing interest in some of the basic structures of Ireland's society and its economy. Based on the Irish travelogues, it seems that most visitors combined the search for picturesque scenery with at least some curiosity about business and institutions, and vice versa. This section will briefly consider some of Ireland's economic activities that attracted the attention of British tourists.

During the eighteenth and early nineteenth centuries, some visitors were interested in the country's industrial or proto-industrial activity. In addition to those already mentioned, there were several reasons why tourists visited Irish iron works, mines and mills. Industrial sites provided examples of "progress" through the application of science and technology, and, strange as it may seem to twenty-first century readers, certain kinds of industrial works were not at odds with the appeal of the picturesque. Just as eighteenth-century English tourists detoured to take in salt mines and cotton mills on their way to the Lake District, some visitors to Ireland took in mines and iron works along with the picturesque scenery.

Since science and industry were beginning to probe the secrets of nature, seeking to harness its power, some painters and travelers in this period were fascinated by furnaces and steam-driven engines. Such "unnatural" control of nature hinted at the sublime. Depending on the amount of flame, smoke, steam, noise and (in mines) darkness, industrial sites might provide occasional triggers for the emotions of fear and wonder, not unlike those elicited by the sublime in nature.[43] In the 1790s George Holmes and John Harden passed through some abandoned mining works at Silvermines in Tipperary. Holmes' description shows how an imagination attuned to the sublime and the picturesque managed to conjure up an aesthetic reaction to mine tailings. He never saw, he wrote, "finer studies for the painter, the various stains, the effects of mineral water dripping from them, and oozing through their jagged sides, the shattered fragments split from the mountain's side, where the dark gashes, torn and blackened by the explosion of the powder in mining, a few blasted stumps and burnt herbage, give it all the character of Salvator's savagely picturesque pencil...."[44]

While not all visitors shared Holmes' aesthetic appreciation for the detritus of mining, some found other industrial activities compatible with the picturesque. The painting of *A View Near Avoca* by George Barret, the Elder, features dramatic cliffs on either side of the River Wicklow. Yet, in foreground stands a water wheel and some low structures, probably part of the glen's copper works. Between 1818 and 1820 Irish artist James Arthur O'Connor painted two pictures of Duffy's Cotton Mills at Ballsbridge, then on the outskirts of Dublin. Placing the factory in the background within a sylvan setting provided by the River Dodder in the foreground, the barely noticeable smoke from the mills is easily incorporated into the picturesque setting.[45]

Iron smelting represented one type of proto-industrial site that attracted the attention of eighteenth-century visitors. Landlords and entrepreneurs once ran as many as 160 small charcoal-fired blast furnaces all over Ireland. Much of the ore consisted of bog iron of such low quality that it would not have been smelted had it not been for the once-plentiful supply of wood. This fuel supply was so cheap and abundant that better quality iron ore was shipped in from Britain to be processed in Ireland.[46] Usually the smelting operations were established within woods nearest to the source of the ore. Samuel Molyneux in his tour in 1709 visited Mount Melick and its "great" iron works, fired by wood from Lord Digby's forest in Killaigh in Kings County (Offaly). Molyneux also visited iron works at Black Combs on banks of Lough Cair, in the barony of Dunkeron. The *Traveller's New Guide through Ireland* (1815) promised that visitors to the Veasy estate along the Liffey would find extensive iron works, as well as various types of mills. Around the same time Anne Plumptre included some iron works in her Wicklow itinerary.[47]

These later blast furnaces would have been coal fired, as the last of Ireland's small charcoal operations had ceased by 1778 or 1779.[48] In a great act of environmental destruction, most of Ireland's great aboriginal forests had been decimated by the end of the eighteenth century, much of the wood having gone to feed the country's relatively insignificant small estate-based smelters. Even as early as the 1750s both Charles Smith and Richard Barton commented on the closing of the iron works at the Herbert estate at Muckross, Killarney, due to the near exhaustion of the estate's supply of arbutus wood. George Holmes, traveling in 1797, blamed iron operations for the loss of trees around Cappoquin, Waterford. Rev. Caesar Otway, visiting Glengariff in Kerry in 1827 complained of the lack of oak and birch in the area, sacrificed to a "villainous furnace" with an "open and cupidious throat."[49] Unlike England, where careful forest management had kept some degree of forest exploitation sustainable, most of Ireland's losses remained unreplaced until the twentieth century.

Some tourists, such as Charles de Montbret, descended into coal mines. Mr. A. Atkinson enthused over them at Coalbrook, Tipperary. Although he did not find the scenery particularly inviting, he was interested to learn that the proprietor, Charles Llangley, ran three mines that employed 150 hands and took out 45 tons per day. However, unlike the well-preserved coal fields of Great Britain, many of Ireland's deposits had been geologically shifted and exposed, either eroding them or making them otherwise difficult to mine.[50]

Tourists were particularly intrigued by the coal mined and used in County Kilkenny, its "smokeless" fires something of a traveler's tale. De Montbret and C. T. Bowden both commented on the phenomenon. Although unable to visit a local mine, the sight of the "noble fire" she saw in Kilkenny's kitchens impressed Anne Plumptre: "The coal is of a remarkable quality, burning entirely without smoke; having much more the appearance of a fire of charcoal than of mineral coal." T. K. Cromwell believed that the clear air above the city of Kilkenny could be credited to this relatively clean-burning fuel. Barrow claimed that such "blind coal" also could be found in the mines around Ballycastle, County Antrim. The coal mined around Kilkenny was anthracite, which, with its high carbon content, burns slowly and with minimum smoke.[51] The British visitors' fascination with it suggests little experience with this type of fuel. However, several tourists did warn of the dangers of what would later be recognized as carbon monoxide poisoning resulting from the burning of the coal in a closed room. In the 1740s William Rufus Chetwood woke up in a Kilkenny inn with a headache. Over half a century later Sir John Carr claimed that he was almost asphyxiated in the town.[52]

Ireland also had some of the oldest copper mines in Europe. The Napoleonic Wars led to a brief expansion of some operations, although most were short lived. Yet, in the 1830s, Mrs. Chatterton, the epitome of the picturesque tourist, reported on her visit to some copper workings at Allihies in Cork, one of the few such mines then in operation. Her party went into the mine itself just to see the steam engine at work. She also took in mines near Ennistymon in County Clare.[53] Unfortunately, the run-off from mines caused pollution, even in tourist areas, including some of the most popular glens of Wicklow. As early as the 1750s, Bishop Pococke noted that the mines north of the town of Arklow had killed the fish in the areas rivers. In 1801 Sir John Carr toured the area around the famous Vale of Avoca in County Wicklow. Although he maintained that the Vale itself remained little affected by the mining of copper and iron pyrites in the vicinity, he complained: "The savage sterility of these mountains, varied by the green, red, and yellow stains of their vitriolic streams, which scantily dripped down their sides, presented a striking contrast to the soft verdure and luxuriant foliage which marked the termination of their desolate features." He, too, noted that leaching from the mine had killed fish all the way to the sea. Carr nevertheless made it a point to visit the mine. Almost half a century later, Dr. John Forbes objected to the pollution in the Vale itself, "which not only troubles but poisons the 'waters,' and mingles its squalid ruins and its gigantic mechanism with the pure charms of nature."[54]

Severely undercapitalized, most of Ireland's industrial activity operated at low levels of production. In fact, after the Act of Union, Ireland could no longer protect its industries from English or Scottish competition. Various enterprises that had seemed promising in the eighteenth and early nineteenth centuries closed down. Meanwhile, as industrialization continued to expand in Britain, its once fascinating accompaniments of smoke and noise seemed less extraordinary, and so middle-class tourists gradually lost interest in seeking the picturesque in billows of smoke, steam and thumping engines.

Interestingly, this did not deter some tourists from visiting Ulster's textile mills, the one aspect of Irish industry that did grow after 1815. Some of Ulster's mills were powered primarily by water. Indeed, the very lack of steam power attracted the Halls to Sion Mills in Country Tyrone in the early 1840s. Turned by the river Mourne, the mills' water wheels powered eight thousand spindles, providing employment to hundreds of peasants without fouling the air. But Ulster's main industrial activity occurred in Belfast, where steam power predominated. Its multistory factories, illuminated at night by gas light, fascinated some visitors. Around 1840 Thackeray wrote that "a fine night-exhibition in the town is that of the huge spinning-mills which surround it, and of which the thousand windows are lighted up at nightfall, and may be seen from almost all quarters of the city." Thackeray went on to explain the workings of a typical steam-powered mill in fanciful, almost romantic terms. He visited one that employed nearly 500 girls and described the scene: "They work in huge long chambers, lighted by numbers of windows, hot with steam, buzzing, and humming with hundreds of thousands of whirling wheels, that all take their motion from a steam-engine which lives apart in a hot cast-iron temple of its own." The engine, to Thackeray's mind, did all the work. "The five hundred girls stand by to feed him, or take his material from him, when he has had his will of it." Under Thackeray's gaze the girls themselves seemed to thrive: "I have seldom, I think, seen more good looks than amongst the young women employed in this place. They work for twelve hours daily, in rooms of which the heat is intolerable to a stranger; but in spite of it they looked gay, stout, and healthy; nor were their forms much concealed by the very simple clothes they wear while at the mill." Thackeray even provided a sketch of one mill lassie in his book.[55] Clearly the author gave no thought to the effect that standing long hours might have had upon the bodies of girls and young women, some of whom would later have difficulty bearing children as a result.

Ulster's textile industry had one other feature that appealed to the tourist with an eye for the picturesque: the bleaching of raw linen. As John Barrow described the process in 1838, "The linen is laid out in long narrow strips, the width of the web, and, with the blades of grass standing up between them, has the effect from a little distance, which is produced just when the snow is in the act of dissolving with the warmth of the sun."[56] Other aspects of linen industry were not as benign, however. In order to separate the flax from its woody stem, the cut plants had to be retted or rotted in ponds, which gave off a powerful odor. Surgeon

Thomas Reid wondered if the stench emanating from the retting dams could be detrimental to people's health. Henry D. Inglis warned visitors to the flax-growing regions to carry a bottle of smelling salts. And pedestrian tourist William Whittaker Barry, disadvantaged by having to walk rather than ride past the odoriferous retting dams, noted that the run off polluted the steams around them.[57]

Institutions

The "petite tour" of Ireland potentially involved virtually any institution or social and economic condition that might interest a visiting Briton. Thomas Reid signaled the socio-economic orientation of his travelogue in his title: *Travels in Ireland in the Year 1822, exhibiting brief sketches of the moral, physical, and political state of the country*. As part of his inquiry into the condition of the poor, he inspected almost every asylum and prison on his itinerary, including a prison ship anchored in Cork harbor. The Halls inspected the jail at Clonmel, complaining about the "grievous want of classification," resulting in the mixing of hardened criminals with petty offenders.[58]

After the enactment of the Poor Law for Ireland in 1838, workhouses became part of the itinerary for some civic-minded travelers. Although attracted by picturesque scenery, Dr John Forbes still dutifully inspected the workhouse in almost every large town he visited. Touring during the Famine, Thomas Carlyle assiduously visited Poor Law Union workhouses until he reached Galway, at which point he appears to have had enough. He jotted in his notebook, "Workhouse, well enough for *it*—'human swinery;' can't be bothered looking much at any more of them."[59]

Given the growing importance of education in Britain, many visitors were naturally interested in Ireland's schools. In fact, since Irish education was bound up with politics and religion, such interest proved inevitable. Touring the country, travelers took note of roadside "hedge schools," organized by Roman Catholic farmers for their children and taught by itinerant schoolmasters. On a more formal level, depending on where and when they made their tours, visitors found a variety of schools to inspect, Protestant and Catholic. Protestant travelers found it difficult to subdue their discomfort regarding Catholic schools, however. Inglis admired the motives behind a Christian Brother school in Waterford but doubted its value, assuming that learning would be sacrificed to theology. Lord John Manners, who frequently visited Irish schools, viewed the Christian Brothers' efforts more positively.[60] Theresa Cornwallis West visited Irish schools with almost the same enthusiasm that took her to the Lakes of Killarney. Travelers like John Barrow and Sir John Forbes included schools as a basic part of their tours.

Not surprisingly, some of the most compelling dynamics of the Irish tour involved religion. A predominately Roman Catholic country, Ireland received British tourists who were predominately Protestant. Given religion's role in Ireland's history and its relations with Britain since the Anglican Reformation, it is hardly surprising that sectarian concerns figured in so many travelogues. Some tourists visited Protestant churches, Roman Catholic "chapels" or "mass houses," as well as religious schools and institutions. St.Patrick's College at Maynooth was a frequent destination for Protestant visitors keen to demonstrate their tolerance—or to possibly sniff out the enemy in its lair.

Some travel accounts concentrated almost exclusively on religion. The anonymous author of *A Journal of A Tour in Ireland during the Months of October and November, 1835* was a sort of religious Inglis, devoting most of his rain-soaked trip to churches, schools, priests and ministers. Although he advertised his 1836 tour thorough the Irish Midlands as an inquiry into the conditions of the peasantry, Baptist Wriothesley Noel's tour constituted a progress among Protestant congregations and their schools. Even when he ventured into the more scenic parts of Ireland, such as around Rostrevor, County Down, Noel quickly scurried on with his mission, complaining, "But, alas, in Ireland nature can never be fully enjoyed. There priestcraft is ubiquitous." It seems that a local priest had recently ejected a Protestant woman from the house of one of his parishioners.[61]

Anti-Catholic attitudes lay intertwined within many travel narratives. Few visitors railed as vociferously against "priest craft" as did Noel. Yet, many visitors voiced their own suspicions of Roman Catholic priests. For example, Dr. Forbes had to admit that Fr. Matthew Theobald, the leader of the Irish Temperance movement, had done some good. However, Forbes worried that these efforts had also strengthened the power of the Catholic clergy. William Bennett, a Quaker famine relief worker, placed some of the blame for the catastrophe on the Irish priests, arguing that they had encouraged early marriages among the peasantry only to increase their incomes. Theresa Cornwallis West was one of the few travel writers to praise priests for their work among the poor.[62]

Attentive Protestant eyes spotted evidence of Catholicism almost everywhere in Ireland. Even so common and innocuous a custom as the everyday greeting, "God bless you" or "God bless all here," set Rev. Spencer T. Hall's Protestant teeth on edge. Many visitors disapproved of what they considered Catholic Ireland's lax observance of the Sabbath. Mary Knott, a Quaker lady from Cork, became upset when the locals peddled produce to the tourist lodges in Kilkee on a Sunday. Much to the locals' surprise, Mrs.Knott refused to buy anything! In 1810 Thomas Walford indignantly observed that, if one began his tour with "moral investigations…he will at once observe, that in the Protestant district six days in each week are dedicated to labour, and the sabbath dedicated to the office of religion; whilst in other [Roman Catholic] districts half the week is passed in the idleness or dissipation of holidays, and the sabbath neglected."[63]

More common expressions of disapproval of Catholic practices focused on "patterns" and pilgrimages. These outdoor events (to be discussed later in more detail) occurred all over Ireland, and while most visitors acknowledged the genuine display of piety, some found such practices disturbing. The author of the *Traveller's New Guide through Ireland* (1815) described the arduous pilgrimage to Great Skellig off the Kerry coast and lamented that the people do not "adopt a more rational mode of worshipping the Deity, conformable to that spiritual purity enjoined in the gospel dispensation." The famous pilgrimage sites of Croagh Patrick on the shores of Clew Bay and of Lough Derg in Donegal attracted the hostile and despairing attention of writers such as Inglis, Rev. Caesar Otway and William Makepeace Thackeray. The latter, who had managed to get through mass at the Catholic "chapel" in Tralee in tolerant good humor, exploded when confronted with the barefoot pilgrims toiling their way up Croagh Patrick to make the Stations on their bare knees: "But it's too hard to think that in our days any priests of any religion should be found superintending such a hideous series of self-sacrifices as are, it appears, performed on this hill.... Better have over a company of Fakeers at once, and set the Suttee going."[64]

Several writers saw the pilgrimage sites encapsulated within a confessional landscape in which nature itself conspired to create a "Romish" scene. Thus, the anonymous author of *The Irish Tourist* (1837) described the ancient pilgrimage site of Lough Derg in Donegal: "It seemed as if nature had put on her darkest, as best suited the gloomy haunt we were to visit for black clouds rolled sternly up in our faces, and threatening winds began to howl around us." Most of the writers who criticized these practices tried to separate their hostility to the Church and its priests from the obvious devotion of the peasantry. The author of *The Irish Tourist* expressed surprise at the "seriousness and earnestness" of the pilgrims at Lough Derg.[65] Even the Rev. Caesar Otway set aside his Evangelical wrath at Popish practices long enough to admit that the Irish peasants, in the midst of their "well-worshiping and sundry absurd superstitions," nevertheless evidenced the "germ of fervent devotional religion, and bursts of genuine piety...which bespeak hearts capable of a high attainment in Christian holiness...."[66]

The Irish landscape could take on confessional aspects in numerous if less dramatic ways. During the pre-Famine decades, Catholic churches grew in number and visibility, a trend that provided an unpleasant shock to British Protestants not used to seeing them in Great Britain. An anonymous writer in the 1830s visited a "dirty town" and saw the Catholic "chapel" overtopping the Anglican church in height—"an ominous sign."[67] Rev. Otway complained of the "unseemly" practice of peasants scooping out and taking home soil from the graves of revered priests. The Halls, among other travelers, noted the many little roadside cairns around Cong, Mayo, erected in memory of the dead. Some contained a hollow in the center which, when filled with pebbles, would allegedly free the soul from Purgatory.[68]

While many travel writers took notice of religion, it was not unusual for some, such as Dr. John Forbes and Sir Digby Neave, to devote whole chapters to the subject. The 1820s and 1830s saw the emergence of a particular, narrowly focused kind of travel literature written by British and some Anglo-Irish Evangelicals, intent on furthering charity, "progress" and what some called "The Second Reformation" in Ireland. As Edward Lengel has noted, they looked upon the West of Ireland as a sort of "Protestant frontier."[69] To facilitate their efforts, Evangelicals established settlements or "colonies" of missionaries and converts in West Cork, in Dingle, Kerry, on Achill Island, Mayo and in Connemara, mostly under the auspices of such organizations as the Protestant Colonization Society and the Society for Irish Church Missions. The latter, being well funded, was especially active in Connemara during the Famine. Even before that, however, the colonies received their support from a network of proselytizing clergy and sympathetic landlords and their wives.[70]

Two of the most prominent Evangelical settlements were Rev. Alexander Dallas' colony on Lough Corrib in Galway and Rev. Edward Nangle's settlement founded at Dugort on Achill Island on Clew Bay.[71] In addition to Bible readings in Irish, the colony on Achill offered free elementary education and training in modern agricultural methods. Nangle's mission at Dugort on the eastern flanks of Slievemore became a compelling site for sympathetic or at least curious tourists. In fact, the mission opened its own hotel to cater to visitors interested in its work. Among these were John Barrow, James Johnson, the Halls and Harriet Martineau. Rev. Caesar Otway, who appears to have been a director for the Missionary Society supporting Nangle's efforts, devoted some space in his book on Connaught to describing the feuding between the Evangelical colony and the Roman Catholic inhabitants of the island. Some visitors, such as the Halls and the American relief worker Anesath Nicholson, worried that Nangle might be too sectarian.[72]

This brief survey of the "petite tour" serves as a reminder of the variety of interests visitors brought with them to Ireland. It presents something of the complex social, political and cultural background against which the Irish picturesque tour took place. Whatever pleasant memories of Ireland's splendid scenery visitors took back with them to Britain, it was the sort of information gleaned on the "petite tour" that turned up in newspaper articles and parliamentary debates. Picturesque Ireland was to be savored; prosaic, everyday Ireland had to be governed.

Chapter 3

PROPERTY, CLASS AND IRISH TOURISM

Estate Tourism

According to Dean MacCannell, "sightseeing is a ritual performed to the differentiation of society."[1] Certainly, tourism in Great Britain and Ireland originated within the differentiation between the very top of society and all that lay beneath. On both islands pleasurable travel began with visits to the great estates. As early as the sixteenth century, improved roads and maps had encouraged the English to explore their own country. Not until the eighteenth century, however, did travelling for pleasure within Britain, the "Home Tour," begin to emerge in its modern form. By then, a general curiosity regarding the next shire had given way to visiting the estates of the landed aristocracy.

Many of those estates dated to 1537 when Henry VIII dissolved the monasteries and vast amounts of property suddenly fell into the hands of the aristocracy in England and Ireland. In England the enthusiasm for building great country houses, begun during the Tudor and Stewart eras, continued through the eighteenth century, spurred on, in the case of the great Whig families at least, by their secure positions in the wake of the Glorious Revolution.[2] The grandeur lavished on British estates went beyond private satisfaction. Power and status were on public display. Writing about the great English houses, Ian Ousby has affirmed that "attracting tourists has always been part of their function...." Even as picturesque scenery, antiquities and, for a time, mines and mills, became incorporated into the Home Tour, the country house remained an enduring tourist attraction in Britain for several centuries.[3]

Until the eighteenth century, what Esther Moir has called "the Tour of Britain" remained the exclusive prerogative of "the governing classes." Only they had the money, leisure time and "taste" to visit and to be accepted into the great houses. However, by the middle of the eighteenth century wealthier members of the middle class were becoming part of the "touring public." Although letters of introduction were sometimes required of those who were not part of the peerage, visiting a "seat" became a rather informal affair, "a matter of etiquette," as Ousby suggests, "rather than regulation; a social custom rather than an organized system." According to Peter Mandler, however, such informality did not prevent the housekeeper (who admitted guests and collected tips) from carefully scrutinizing the "dress, servants, vehicles, and calling cards" of supplicants. Nevertheless, throughout the eighteenth century, the touring public continued to grow to the point where Horace Walpole, owner of the Strawberry Hill estate, complained in 1783 that tourists had become a veritable "plague." He responded by posting a set of rules to regulate their admittance and behavior.[4]

By the eighteenth century, both proprietors and visitors alike accepted estate tourism as a way to extend "taste" and all that implied to the middle classes. Carol Fabricant argues that, as the middle class became part of the traveling public, tourism helped "seduce" it and the lower orders into "identification with the tastes and interests of the landed rich through the manipulation of voyeuristic delights and vicarious pleasures—through the illusion of shared participation in a world not in any meaningful way their own." A new tourist literature emerged, consisting of guidebooks for particular houses, catalogues of their art works, and published engravings of mansions and park lands, all publicizing the great estates.[5]

Estate tourism emerged later in Ireland. For one thing continued political instability limited the initial impact of the dissolution of the monasteries. Most of the great houses built in the sixteenth and seventeenth centuries were fortified structures, often tower houses, reflecting the importance of defense over displays of grandeur. Not until the rout of James II at the Battle of the Boyne in 1690 and the subsequent Treaty of Limerick the following year did Ireland's Protestant Ascendancy finally begin to feel secure. Even then the unrest and upheaval of the seventeenth century had reduced rents and for a time slowed rebuilding.[6] By the 1730s, however, a new generation of proprietors began taking over the estates. Thirty years of peace and the protection of the Penal Laws enabled the Ascendancy to present to the world a more confident front represented by Palladian-style mansions and carefully landscaped grounds. In Kevin Whelan's words, "portcullis yielded to portico, battlement to pediment, loophole to sash windows...." By mid-century rents had recovered and continued to grow, and Ireland experienced a boom in the construction of country houses.[7]

On the surface, English and Irish estates would have looked much alike. Socially and politically, they were nonetheless quite different. While the English aristocracy was not always popular at home, it was at least English and played a significant role in defining the national identity. In Ireland the display of the aristocratic self proved more complicated. While the English estate with its park lands and gardens proclaimed itself separate from the local community, in Ireland the estate stood apart from the nation. Peter Mandler suggests that the

English estate represented change amid a sense of national continuity. Conversely, the Irish estate stood as a denial of continuity. Unlike the English aristocracy, Anglo-Irish proprietors represented an ethnic and religious, as well as an economic minority. As a consequence, according to Toby Barnard, the "big house" and its surrounding park lands reflected a particularly Irish mix of aesthetics and ideology. For example, the ruling Protestant Ascendancy presented a public face of power intended to differentiate itself from all that was Roman Catholic as well as Irish. In the process it was supposed to shun the sort of ostentation that might attract ridicule, a danger not easily avoided in Ireland.[8]

The Estate in the Irish Landscape

As Toby Barnard suggests, "To build in the correct style was turned into a sign of cultivation, even gentility...." But what constituted the correct style of construction and landscaping for Ireland's Protestant Ascendancy? Emerging from the turmoil of the seventeenth century, the building and rebuilding of Irish estates progressed slowly and with tentative steps. Until the 1740s, many of Ireland's country houses had what Barnard calls a "Spartan" look about them when compared to the growing splendor of Georgian Dublin. A psychology of uncertainty seems to have lingered on, even in the newer houses. Desmond Guinness remarks that many country houses presented "a massive, durable quality and a certain heaviness" intended, perhaps, to impart "a feeling of security and permanence...."[9]

Even the Irish landscape reflected this apparent concern for Ascendancy security. While an English aristocrat enclosed his deer park, an Irish landlord often walled in his entire demesne, a nineteenth-century example being Robert Gregory's 600-acre Coole Park. As Louis Cullen points out, these walled estates, along with the gate houses and newly constructed or expanded villages, dominated the Irish countryside. According to Cullen, enclosing a whole estate made "the impact of the Irish house...more dramatic than that of the contemporary English house with its open park land close to an old rather than new village." The walled Irish estate represented, therefore, a bald statement of power and possession combined with separation that announced its presence to every passerby.[10] William Rufus Chetwood, touring in the vicinity of Kilkenny in 1740, observed that "the Paddocks, Meadows, and even the common Fields are enclosed with high white Stone Walls, some more than two Miles in the Square...." A short time later he visited another estate park of some 200 acres encompassed within a stone wall nine feet high. In 1777 Rev. Thomas Campbell noted that the country around Carlow seemed "entirely occupied by gentlemen's parks, walled in and recently planted...."[11]

Visitors to Ireland, who wanted to see fine houses and landscaped gardens, were not pleased when confronted by the endless miles of walls that often obstructed their views. An anonymous author, writing for *Walker's Hibernian Magazine* in September, 1807, declared his surprise that he could actually *see* the house of Mr. Edgeworth of Edgeworthstown from the road, since it was not barricaded from sight. Too many Irish gentlemen, the writer complained, resided in "a kind of secluded grandeur," appearing "more on the defensive from the dreaded eruptions of some barbarians, than living secure in the middle of [their] country." That same writer later grumble: "I am no admirer of these heavy walls. They almost preclude any view of the improvements from the observations of the traveller; and surely their proprietors might be as secret with nice hedges and railings...." Mr. A. Atkinson expressed his pleasure with a small estate near Parsonstown that "laid out as to expose its little group of beauties in full view—no black walls or heavy gates...."[12]

Nevertheless, within the walls some of the wealthier proprietors attempted to create what Finola O'Kane has called "ideal landscapes," Ascendancy visions "of an Irish Utopia." The shape of this Utopia varied throughout the eighteenth and early nineteenth centuries, as tastes in Irish landscape designs and their underlying ideological and aesthetic concerns changed. Central to these various Protestant "visions" loomed the proprietors' overwhelming desire to differentiate themselves and their lands from the "mere" Irish and the "wild" landscapes they supposedly inhabited. Their attempts to project a physical representation of Protestantism onto both house and grounds attracted many Irish proprietors to the calm and "rational" symmetries of various types of classical designs. On great estates, such as Stradbally in Cork, and Castletown and Carton in Kildare, this preference initially resulted in the adaption of the seventeenth-century Anglo-Dutch style of landscape design in which geometrical patterns, parallel lines and sharp angles determined the shapes of floral beds, tree plantings and waterways. An anonymous traveler in 1740 described the seat of Sir John Rawdon, Bart, near Moyrah: "The Avenue leading to the House, and the Gardens...are formed in good Taste; the Walks, Vista's and Espaliers [are] regular, and thrive well. Here is a pretty Labyrinth, and several Ponds and Canals."[13]

Finola O'Kane points out that, given their position as a colonial elite, the Ascendancy proprietors could not easily look to an Irish tradition for architectural and landscape inspiration; thus their attraction to the Palladian style in house design. She also interprets the inclination of some proprietors to cling well into the eighteenth century to the very rigid Anglo-Dutch landscape style as an ideological gesture of admiration for William I, the "Protestant Prince" from Holland. Whatever the reason, as Terence Reeves-Smyth argues, the strict formality of the Anglo-Dutch style encouraged proprietors to design their estates on a large scale and to extend them (and their owner's claim to power) out into the countryside.[14]

By the middle of the eighteenth century the deployment of tree-lined avenues had become an effective landscaping technique that established the centrality of the big house within the estate. These sylvan corridors converged upon the house. Large estates often featured a complex series of aisles radiating through the park. Describing the Dromore estate two miles from Mallow, Charles Smith admired its three avenues, each ending in a pleasing vista: respectively, a mountain, a "roman temple" and a waterfall.[15] William Rufus Chetwood, writing in the 1740s, claimed that he recognized the sources from which the owner of Burton Hall (near Carlow) had borrowed to create his vistas and to set off his woodland: "The fine Vista here is determined by a Statue of a Gladiator, a good copy of that finished Original now in *Hampton-Court* Gardens. The Wood in this spacious Park, upon any memorable Day, is illuminated with a large Number of Lamps, placed in regular Order, after the Manner of *Ranelagh* Gardens at *Chelsey*. The beautiful Cascade is adorned with elegant Statues, some of which are Originals, brought from Italy."[16]

Elaborate artificial lakes and canals, often extensions of an estate's agricultural hydrological works, added grandeur and at times fed the fantasies of their owners. On the road from Kildare to Dublin, Chetwood stopped at the Chetwood Eustace's estate, situated on a rise above the River Liffey. There the visitor discovered, lying at anchor in an artificial lake, "a Ship completely furnished, as if ready to make a long Voyage by Sea; her Sails spread, her Colours flying, Anchors weighed, Guns firing, and the Sailors neatly dressed, every one at their proper Function, with the usual Sea-Terms." With the ship's guns echoing in adjacent mountains and woods, the whole scene "seemed to us like a Piece of Inchantment [sic].[17]

As the eighteenth century progressed, tastes in landscape design began to move away from the rigid Anglo-Dutch formula, which travelers increasingly condemned as out of fashion. Visiting a large estate near Mitchelstown in County Cork in 1778, Rev. Thomas Campbell complained: "Behind the house is a square parterre of flowers, with terraces thickly studded with busts and statues; before it, a long and blind avenue, planted with treble rows of well-grown trees, extends its awkward length…. The whole park is thrown into squares and parallelograms, with numerous avenues fenced and planted; where if a hillock dared to interpose its little head, it was cut off as an excrescence, or at least cut through; that the roads might be as level, as they are straight. Thus was this delightful spot, treated by some *Procrustes* of the last age." Campbell argued in favor of less formal approaches to landscaping, suggesting that "instead of torturing the place to the plan, they had accommodated the plan to the place. Indeed, all predisposed plans for laying out grounds are dangerous;

for every place has within itself a plan, from which true taste can never deviate. Nature may be improved, but never changed to advantage."[18]

By the time Campbell had unburdened himself on the subject, Irish proprietors had already begun abandoning the geometric artifice of the seventeenth century for a more "natural," Romantic approach in landscaping, replacing angles with curves, formal canals with rounded lakes, rectangular flower beds with great expanses of lawn, rigid straight-line plantings by informal groupings of trees.[19] Dean Patrick Delany's miniature Delville estate at Glasnevin outside of Dublin contained one of the first Irish parks to break away from the rigidity of the seventeenth-century style. Laid out around the mid-eighteenth century by Dr. Delany (a friend of Swift's and the second husband of the artistically inclined Mary Delany, née Grenville), the gardens reflected a style in which, according to one visitor, "the obdurate and straight line of the Dutch was softened into a curve, the terrace melted into the swelling bank, and the walks opened to catch the vicinal country."[20]

In spite of the conceits of Romantic poets, when landscapers spoke of "imitating nature" they generally meant "improving" upon it, without obliterating it under a blanket of geometric design. However, the simulation of artless nature sometimes involved a high degree of artifice. John Harden admired Blarney Castle's carefully landscaped Rock Glen (the famous "Sweet Rock Close") as "a wonderful specimen of what taste & money can accomplish, whole mountains moved & piled together in happy combination...." Sometimes, more than mountains were moved. In 1752 Bishop Richard Pococke, visiting Westport, Mayo, reported that the proprietor intended to remove the village on his property in order to enlarge his park.[21]

The new approach to landscaping generally sought to make "the big house," the mansion, appear even more dominating by clearing away encroaching trees. Instead of approaching it down a long straight sylvan corridor, the house might suddenly appear around a curving screen of trees, standing in the open on an elevated site surrounded by vast "sheets" of green lawn. This is how Leixlip Castle appears in a painting produced around 1750 by an anonymous artist. James Arthur O'Connor's paintings of Ballinrobe House and Westport House depict the mansions and their immediate grounds standing free from the mass of trees behind them, suggesting a sense of spaciousness, calm and nobility. By necessity, the vast lawns around the big house represented a happy intersection of aesthetics and economics. Only by opening them to sheep or cattle could the acres of grass be kept neatly trimmed. Traveling in the 1770s, Arthur Young noted approvingly the vast expanse of lawn at Carton House, Lord Harcourt's seat in Kildare, maintained in the "highest order" by 1100 sheep. The beasts were kept away from the house by a "ha-ha," a ditch invisible at ground level.[22] Just as the old-fashioned canals and waterways had supported carp and tench, the new landscaping offered some recompense in the value of the sheep grazing on the lawn before the big house.

Nevertheless, taking vast acreage out of production and devoting it to romantically landscaped parks represented a very conspicuous form of consumption. Based on a study of the mid-nineteenth-century Irish Ordinance Survey maps, an estimated 7000 landscaped estate parks accounted for between 0.8 and 0.9 million acres—four percent of Ireland's total land mass. Cormac Ó Gráda points out that, if cultivated, much of this acreage could have been prime farm land that might have provided work for 100,000 small holders. Nevertheless, the removal of park land from production constituted some sort of investment, "from the outside looking in," according to Raymond Williams, "a visible stamping of power, of displayed wealth and command.... Much of the real profit of a more modern agriculture went not into productive investment but into that explicit social declaration...of an established and commanding class power."[23]

In Ireland, proprietors often co-opted nature in the cause of power. Many of Ireland's famous scenic beauty spots were situated on estate land or were at least incorporated into landscaping vistas. John Hutchinson points out that most of the picturesque sites in County Wicklow could be seen on or from the grounds of the great estates, making the proprietor's seats aesthetic, as well political and economic, centers. Hutchinson calls attention to the inclusion of Sugar Loaf Mountain in George Barret, the Elder's painting of Powerscourt House (designed by Richard Castle). According to Hutchinson, the use of such a well-known feature of the Wicklow landscape "reflects the attempt by the wealthy classes to disguise the hierarchies of society by 'naturalizing' the signs of their authority."[24]

The Big House as Tourist Attraction

Irish estates contributed to the establishment and development of Irish tourism in several ways. First of all, as in England, the big house and its surrounding gardens and parklands were among the first tourist attractions in Ireland. As Irish tourism grew, the country drew Britain visitors for whom the habit of exploring country houses had become part of their touring culture. Chetwood's 1740s tour was little more than a circuit of estates. The great houses themselves held a variety of attractions, not the least their art collections. Since there were no museums and only occasional public exhibitions, paintings were usually found in private collections. And though Ireland was not as rich in art as England, visitors did their best to seek out important paintings. As noted earlier, Richard Twiss listed the paintings in the great mansions in Dublin. John Barrow saw paintings by Rubens in Florence Court, seat of Earl of Enniskillen, and in the house of

Lord Sligo at Westport. Reverend Daniel A. Beaufort saw one of Henri Fuseli's Shakespeare paintings—"Macbeth"—hanging in Lord Glendores otherwise "ill-conceived and ugly" house. Jacques-Louis de Latocnaye and C. T. Bowden admired the collections of Lord Bristol and the Marquis of Downshire respectively.[25]

Still, most tourists would see only the exterior of the house and its parklands. In fact, for much of the eighteenth and early nineteenth centuries, visitors evaluated a day's journey in terms of the quality of the "seats" seen from the road. Fortunately, travelers could usually easily see the newer houses, since they were situated on slopes where they commanded a view. This often placed them on the edges of their demesnes rather than hiding them away in the interior. Chetwood's journey toward Kilkenny initially disappointed him: "The first Part of our Way here was but indifferent, I mean for eminent Seats, though the country was pleasant and rich...." Along the banks of the River Suir the scene changed, however: "...you see delightful Meadows, with beautiful Houses and Plantations, mixed with more eminent Structures, both ancient and modern." When the author visited the seat of George Mathews near Thomastown (where Jonathan Swift had once passed three pleasant months), Chetwood could barely contain himself: "What do I call a Seat! It is a Paradise.... I cannot find Words to describe this Place."[26]

James Howley points out that Ireland's common hill-and-lake topography, as well as its mild climate, made landscape gardening easier than in England.[27] Accordingly, many proprietors tried to incorporate elements of the new Romantic aesthetics into their landscape designs. Although he found Lord Limerick's house "very bad," Bishop Pococke admired his grounds, which included an "artificial serpentine river, a Chinese bridge, a thatch'd open house supported by the bodies of fir trees...." At Curraghmore, seat of the Earl of Tyrone, the Bishop saw another serpentine river, the setting for Lady Tyrone's "grotto," itself adorned with a "grand profusion of curious shells and Corals," as well as a statue of her ladyship.[28] While their husbands oversaw the shifting of vast amounts of earth to "naturalize" their estates, the ladies often concentrated on grottos, moss houses and shell houses. Mary Deleny decorated her shell house at Delville and designed a grotto for the Bishop of Killala, Mayo. The Marquise of Downshire at Blessington created a moss house and grotto to set off the Poulaphouca waterfall.[29] To further adorn their parks, proprietors often built "follies," ranging from imitation classical temples and monuments to pseudo medieval ruins and faux hermitages (sometimes complete with hired "hermits"). Such structures sometimes enabled proprietors to display ideas picked up on the Grand Tour or inspired by the Italian landscape paintings.[30]

Some estates boasted a "wilderness" area, groves of specially planted trees and shrubs or rocky dells like Blarney Castle's Rock Close. Visiting Lord

Moira's castle, Gabriel Beranger enjoyed the way the Earl had landscaped an abandoned quarry on his estates: "[I]t forms at present delightful shrubbery with ups and downs, either by steps or slops, and has so many turns and windings, that it appears a labyrinth, and contains shady walks, and close recesses, in which...buildings and seats are judiciously placed, with a little wooden bridge to pass a small rill of water. Jasmine, woodbine, many flowering shrubs are in this charming place."[31]

Many of the features of romantic landscaping came together at the 500–600 acre estate of John Foster, Baron Oriel. In addition to its famous "temple," an almost overwhelmed Atkinson listed some of the estate's many features: "The botanic garden—the flower-garden—the cottage—the grotto—the lake in a low moor enveloped in a thick wood, and the planted hill which rises on the south above it, are but a few of the features which mark this scene...." Atkinson could perceive no contradiction in dedicating artifice to the imitation of nature: "and though the wood and water, the temple and the cottage, the grotto and gardens are all art, yet all assume the appearance of nature, or at least produce the effect of nature upon the feelings." Of course, such efforts also underscored what Raymond Williams has called the "the real invention of the landlords...that kind of confidence, to make Nature move to an arranged design."[32]

As the new fashion in landscaping took hold, tourists came to expect an unencumbered view of the big house, and they became annoyed when their expectations were denied them. In fact, some Irish manor houses remained hidden behind walls or among trees well into the nineteenth century, perhaps reflecting the older defensive attitude on the part of a Protestant aristocracy still uncertain of its place and its security in Ireland. As late as 1852, Dr. John Forbes complained about beautiful residences that were "too much shut in with dense and extensive woods...being often more like a forest than a park...."[33]

Estate Forestry

It is not as though British visitors to Ireland had anything against trees. As will be explained later, they usually could not get enough of them in Ireland. Tourists, in fact, often evaluated a demesne in part by the deployment of its trees and woodland. On the larger estates, however, trees could represent a significant part of an estate's economy. Unfortunately, estate woodlands in Ireland had been poorly managed, and by the time tourism developed, the country's forests had been destroyed. The deforestation of Ireland began in Neolithic times after the first farmsteads appeared. The conversion of woodland into farms eventually contributed to the formation of bogs, as climate changes suppressed the regrowth of trees in many areas, especially in the West. Nevertheless, by the end of the Middle Ages, Ireland still had vast tracks of dense forests. In a period of about two hundred years, however, from 1600 to 1800, English adventurers and Anglo-Irish proprietors logged most of the remaining aboriginal forests. Although some clearings had been undertaken for security reasons, intended to deny shelter to native Irish raiders, economic factors dictated most lumbering. In the seventeenth century leases often required tenants to clear a certain number of trees from the land. Moreover, by simply selling the lumber from their estates, landlords reaped quick profits in unstable times from land forfeited to them as the result of various rebellions. The Civil Survey of Ireland, compiled between 1654 and 1656, suggests that even at that time between only two and three percent of the island remained under wood.[34] Vast numbers of trees were converted into building materials for houses and ships or into utensils, furniture, pipe staves, bark for tanning and fuel for the production of glass and iron. As noted earlier, iron furnaces on estate lands consumed copious quantities of wood. As a result, by 1800 very little remained of Ireland's aboriginal oak forests.

In England, which had also seen large-scale deforestation, tree planting represented a characteristic activity of progressive landlords. Such investments in the future, however, assumed stability, the lack of which, prior to the eighteenth century, had encouraged ruthless exploitation of Ireland's forests in the first place. Reforestation did finally begin in Ireland around the middle of the eighteenth century. New plantations not only graced the landlord's parks, but, with careful management, they provided sustainable sources of income. The resulting policy of cutting and replanting, what Eoin Neeson has called "estate forestry," received support and encouragement, first from the Dublin Society and later from the Irish Parliament. The Society, founded in 1731, helped propagate knowledge of forest management and offered prizes to landlords who led the way in establishing plantations. Traveling in 1806, Rev. Joseph Robertson recorded the destruction of many of the ancient woods of County Tyrone. He reassured his readers, however, that the Dublin Society and the proprietors were cooperating to develop new plantations. Between 1766 and 1806, the Society claimed that it had helped encourage the planting of some 25,000,000 trees, although that number is suspect. Unfortunately, fraud contributed to the discontinuance of its forestry prizes.[35]

Proprietors' interest in trees went beyond their economic potential. Recalling Roland Barthes' observations concerning the ideological power of trees to symbolize the union of the "political" and the "natural," John Hutchinson notes the ubiquitous presence of "plantations" in period illustrations and paintings of Irish demesnes: "The planting of trees accentuated an impression of naturalized power, with devices such as avenues, clearings, rides, belts, clumps, and screens creating particular visual and ideological effects." Trees were deployed to set off the big house itself, while simultaneously demonstrating the proprietor's tasteful subjugation of nature. As Kevin Whelan points out, most demesnes were frequently designed "as set pieces. The cocooning effect of the boundary planting, the focus on the big house and its manicured lawns all reflected precise planning, creating an island effect within the more organically evolved surrounding countryside." Writing about landscaping in England, Nigel Everett associates the new Romantic style of park design with "Capability" Brown, who served his clients by excluding from the view of the proprietor's mansion any sight of fields, outbuildings and the village. Using trees as screens, "the house and its improved grounds [appeared] as the entire world. Everything appears to be owned and controlled, clearly under the eye and authority of the proprietor."[36] Thomas Sautelle Roberts' watercolor of Curraghmore House, Portlaw, Waterford provides a good depiction of a well-planted estate, a quarter of which was under wood. Probably painted toward the end of the eighteenth century, the picture shows the big house positioned in the open middle ground. Around it, especially in the foreground, rise clumps of trees planted in imitation of a "natural" landscape. Nearby are larger groups that provide mass to set off the house. Beyond them, screened by a line of ornamental trees, stands a large, regular plantation, presumably awaiting harvesting.[37]

Many visitors to Ireland recognized and appreciated the ways in which trees could set off an estate. Arthur Young, agronomist and a pioneer of the picturesque, admired Lord Harcout's deployment of trees at Carton, Kildare: "The park...is a vast lawn, which waves over gentle hills, surrounded by plantations of great extent, and which break and divide in places so as to give much variety." Visiting Woodlawn, seat of Frederick Trench, in Galway, Young recorded how the estate grounds were "prettily scattered with clumps and single trees, and surrounded by a margin of wood." In his enthusiastic description of Oriel, the demesne of John Foster, Atkinson noted the "numerous beautiful walks—the various borders of trees and plants—the healthful and judicious openings in the plantations, for the admission of air and the command of prospect...." Where the aesthetic principles of landscaping were violated, however, some travel writers did not shrink from offering advice. On relatively flat land, Rev. Thomas Campbell argued that the owners could give "boldness and variety" to the estate by planting tall trees on gentle rises. On the other hand, hilly land required planting at foot rather than the top of the hills in order to "raise" the valley. "By planting on great eminences, instead of correcting," Campbell maintained, "you exaggerate the deformity of your grounds." Clearly, one had to have the right trees in the right places.[38]

Besides enhancing their estate grounds, many proprietors were seriously involved in estate forestry. As will be seen in later chapters, the plant and harvest cycle of estate forestry gave a dynamic character to the Irish countryside, sometimes to the dismay of tourists in search of the picturesque.

They could never be sure that wooded tracts described in guidebooks were still standing. Around 1815, Atkinson commended the picturesque effect of the Stokestown woods in County Wexford, adding parenthetically "if not since cut down." His warning was very apt. When John Gough first visited the village of Ballitore, Kildare, in 1780, "it appeared as if built in a wood." He returned in 1817 to find it totally stripped of its old timber. William Makepeace Thackeray set off in 1843 from Limerick in search of what his guidebook described as "the aboriginal" forests of the region. All he found were some ruined tower houses with a few old trees about them: "For the fact is, that though the forest has always been there, the trees have not, the proprietors cutting them regularly when grown to no great height; and the monarchs of the woods which I saw round about would scarcely have afforded timber for a bedpost."[39]

Interactive Tourism: Critiquing the Estates

Obviously, when it came to inspecting Irish estates, tourists were not passive visitors. Critiquing estates constituted, in fact, an essential part of estate tourism. It was what tourists did when they visited a demesne. If the design of the house, gardens and parklands stood for an expression of the proprietor's taste, then evaluating the results represented the tourist's role in the game. Travel writers found this especially important, since it enabled them go beyond the role of passive reporters to exhibit their own command of "taste." Of course, inviting critiques from commoners was not what the great proprietors had in mind when they opened their demesnes to the public. Yet, enabling the middle class to evaluate the big house and its parkland involved tourists in the ideology of power and taste upon which the estates had been founded. Having no demesnes of their own, members of the touring public could play at being proprietors and mentally inhabit their world. When a visitor complained that an Irish big house lacked a commanding prospect, he or she said, in effect, that the owner had failed in the presentation of his position in the world. As Carol Fabricant suggests: "The relationship between spectator and prospect view, no less than that between owner and estate, reflected the desire to assert mastery over one's surroundings, to lay claims to pieces of an environment otherwise beyond one's control."[40]

Atkinson's appraisal of the rather "modest" seat of a Mr. Reynolds typifies this "interactive" process. In his description Atkinson illustrates how landscape design controlled the visitor's appreciation of the big house. The tree-lined road into the estate screened everything until he passed through the gate, at which point "the beauties of the house and demesne begin to open upon the view." Searching for a commanding prospect from which to make a final judgment, Atkinson climbed an elevation overlooking the big house. From there he admired "its snowy front, inclosed [sic] by plantations on the right and left, with openings between them to more distant prospects; while two or three clumps [of trees], placed with great judgment on little hills remote from the interior improvements, give an appearance of amplitude to the demesne, and by their distant and conspicuous position form a kind of grand outline to the scenery...."[41]

The Reynolds' estate passed muster, but sometimes the grounds of other gentlemen did not. Atkinson peppered his book with complaints about missing lakes, absent Chinese bridges and misplaced plantations, which would have beautified any number of poorly designed estates, or so he argued. Some estates simply failed to impress, as did the house and grounds at Brittas in Kings (now County Offaly), which Atkinson encountered buried in its own woods: "When the superfluous timber on the demesne of Brittas is felled and disposed of," he scolded: "When light and ornamental plantations are substituted in their stead—When the prospect from all parts of the neighborhood is opened to the house and surrounding improvements; then Brittas will be an object of high interest in that bleak and mountainous country...." And all of this from a man who had to do most of his touring on foot because he could not afford a carriage or jaunting car.[42]

Organizing the Ground for Tourism

At a certain level tourism is a self-organizing system; once visitors turn up, people and facilities catering to them somehow appear. Nevertheless, at the dawn of the age of modern tourism, even the most basic infrastructure required for travel and sight-seeing had to be created. Visitors not only needed to know what to see; they also required access to the sights as well. In this regard, Ireland's proprietors played major roles in opening up scenic spots and creating accommodations for visitors, as well as building roads and towns. The Kenmare and Herbert families developed virtually the whole of the Lakes of Killarney (see Chapter Seven). The famous waterfalls and glens of County Wicklow (to be discussed in Chapter Five) were enhanced by the proprietors, who outfitted them with paths, resting places and viewing stations. Proprietors also erected ornate "cottages" or "temples" in which tourists could picnic and prepare food. Bishop Pococke, visiting the estate of Lord Limerick in the 1750s, found that the proprietor had built on a ledge overlooking a stream, "a thatch'd open place to dine in, which is very Romantick [sic], with a stove near to prepare the Entertainment...." An anonymous writer, walking through Wicklow's Glen of the Downs in 1826, expressed astonishment at the octagon banqueting room that Mr. La Touche had built on an overlook. In 1770s Lady Caroline Dawson observed that "it is quite the fashion in Ireland to have a cottage, neatly fitted up with Tunbridge ware, and to drink tea in it in the summer."[43]

The proprietors' contribution to tourism could be seen around Leixlip, a village in County Kildare near Dublin, long famous for its salmon leap on the River Liffey. The land along the river was, of course, in private hands. Yet, John Gough, visiting in 1813, noted that several of the demesnes had only just been opened to the general public, providing legal access to the river and the cascade. Some of the landlords had even erected pavilions to accommodate picnickers. In fact, Gough observed that tourists could walk upriver on estate land to Newbridge and then on to the demesnes of Castletown, Carton and eventually on to Maynooth.[44]

Engravings of great estates, picturesque scenery and antiquities, sometimes collected into books, fed directly into tourism, especially in Wicklow and adjacent Kildare. Finola O'Kane discusses how the publication of Jonathan Fisher's collection, *Scenery of Ireland* (1795), influenced the way proprietors along the Liffey organized their grounds for visitors. "Although the demesnes had not necessarily been designed with Fisher's selected viewpoints in mind, once published, those selected affected the valley's future interpretations and designs." With tourists keen on seeing the views depicted in Fisher's illustrations, proprietors tended to both preserve and provide access to them.[45] Although such efforts originally may have been intended for the benefit of their peers and neighbors, Gough's remarks further suggest how the proprietors ultimately contributed to the shaping of Irish tourism.

One aspect of estate tourism that did not extend too far down the social ladder was a sort of high-class bed and breakfast available at many big houses. Rev. Thomas Campbell reported that William Conolly of Castletown had set up a coffee room for those guests who, rising too early or arriving too late, could not dine with the family. Thomastown, with its forty bedrooms, boasted a "coffee room," or common dining room, and a tavern. Many manor houses had "barrack rooms," dormitories that accommodated large numbers of guests, most of whom would have been part of the country-house social scene. Arthur Young, a frequent visitor to various houses, described receiving in one a " 'shakedown'… some clean straw spread upon the floor, with blankets and sheets, in what was called the barrackroom, one containing several beds for single men."[46]

The Decline of Estate Tourism

As noted earlier, manor house construction peaked in Ireland between 1760s and 1790s, when there was a rash of building, landscaping and in many cases over-spending on estates. Some level of extravagance could be managed for a while, as long as rents continued to rise. In the long run, however, this most conspicuous of consumptions left a serious burden of debt on many Irish estates.[47] When the Act of Union abolished the Irish Parliament in 1801, about a third of its members crossed the Irish Sea to sit in Westminster. Some of them simply abandoned their houses in Ireland. Nevertheless, some new country houses continued to be built into the early decades of the nineteenth century, as those proprietors who remained in Ireland closed their Dublin town houses and moved onto their estates.

For the first few decades of the nineteenth century, in fact, landed estates remained an important part of Ireland's tourist landscape. Taking in the panorama from Killiney Hill south of Dublin Bay, surgeon Thomas Reid, touring in the 1820s, admired the "luxuriantly cultivated" lands "thickly set with numerable country seats, rivaling each other in taste and decoration...." The engravings of manor houses in Rev. George Wright's illustrated *Guide to Wicklow* (1822) demonstrated a continuation of what John Hutchinson has called the fascination with the big house and its estate. For those with the right connections and interests, estate tourism continued unabated. In his journal Robert Graham, himself the proprietor of the Scottish estate of Redgorton, recorded his progress in the 1830s from one Irish estate to another. Likewise, John Barrow and Jonathan Binns, also touring in 1830s, kept to the older tourist habit of admiring "seats." Along his route from Passage to Cork in 1834, Henry D. Inglis noted along the way, "not boxes with their acre, or half-acre of lawn, shrubbery, and garden; but handsome houses, with room enough about them, to give them an air of independence and respectability."[48]

Nevertheless, the tastes of many middle-class tourists in Ireland were changing. Instead of confining themselves largely to the rounds of demesnes, most tourists after 1815 wanted to see natural landscapes and even the peasants who lived in them. Anne Plumptre articulated the newer attitude when she announced in 1814 that she had little interest in estates: "There must inevitably be a kind of sameness in these seats, and when one has seen a few, little is to be attained by seeing many more: but in the works of Nature there is an unceasing variety which can never pall; they are always presenting something new, something to charm, to fill the mind." Certainly, the big house could not long compete with the growing attraction of the spectacular scenery of Ireland's northern and western coasts. Desmond Guinness points out that, with the exception of places such as Powerscourt in Wicklow and Westport House on Clew Bay in Mayo, many of the richest Irish houses lacked spectacular scenic settings. The best rents came from the richest agricultural lands, which were often in the relatively flat interior of the country far from the picturesque sea coast and mountains. In many instances nineteenth-century visitors would have had to detour from the most popular tourist paths just to see some of the greatest estates.[49]

Even where estates could boast picturesque scenery, nature was beginning to win out over the big house and its parkland. Referring to the string of estates along the River Liffey, Finula O'Kane confirms that, "interest in bounded estate landscapes was replaced by the composite landscapes of the [Liffey] river valley and eventually moved toward landscapes with no visible connection to a great house and demesne." Elizabeth Smith, herself the mistress of an estate in Baltinglass, Wicklow, might have spoken for many of her contemporaries when she visited Powerscourt in 1849. She had to admit that the great Palladian house, which she dubbed "the Custom House on the Quay at Dublin transplanted to the country," was impressive. But its gravel walks and balustrades, interposing between the house and the formal gardens, were emblematic of a style far too grand and formal for her tastes. As for the surrounding Wicklow countryside, "the beauty of the scenery is spoiled by the many villas which the near neighborhood of Dublin has crowded the ground with." Such sentiments completely reversed the attitudes of Chetwood's day, a century earlier. It is noteworthy that the Halls' popular guidebook to Ireland, published in the 1840s, devoted relatively little space to the country's great estates.[50]

Estate tourism in Ireland never matched the heights of popularity it enjoyed in England. It started later and drew upon a smaller base of potential visitors. By contrast, the English railways in the 1840s made it possible for weekend and day trippers to head out from the great industrial cities for a day or two in the country. Among the sights to be seen were the nearest country houses. When the young Queen Victoria opened parts of the Royal Palace at Hampton Court to the public without charge, country house visiting entered the dawning age of mass tourism. During the nineteenth century, in response to England's rapid industrialization, the public indulged itself in a vogue for popular history that looked back to the Tudor and Stewart eras, celebrated as the "Olden Time" or "Merrie Olde England." Because many of the great houses of the sixteenth and seventeenth centuries had survived, they attracted great attention from the newly expanded traveling public. Proprietors and tourists alike regarded these architectural remnants of an earlier age as essential symbols of national heritage and identity.[51]

Compared to nineteenth-century England, Ireland could boast relatively few surviving great sixteenth and seventeenth homes that didn't look more like fortifications. More to the point, however, not much in Irish history could benefit from such romantically comfortable labels as "Merrie" and "Olden Times." And, of course, concepts such as "national heritage" and "national identity" were problematic at best in the Irish context. Whose nation? Whose heritage? As noted earlier, Ireland's great estates represented a dominant class of Protestant arrivistes, along with some older Catholic and Gaelic families who had seen fit to embrace the new order. Even in the eyes of Protestants, English and Anglo-Irish alike, the great estates could never represent in Ireland, as they did in England, symbols of national unity.

Instead, as Brian Graham notes, since the Anglo-Irish big house was intended to legitimate a contested power, nationalist Ireland would eventually see it as a symbol of British exploitation to be excluded from the iconography of Ireland.[52] Many of the manor houses that attracted tourist attention two hundred years ago today lie in ruins; many have disappeared completely. Some estates were abandoned by their owners, while others were burned in the last century during the Anglo-Irish War. In subsequent decades, some houses were demolished by their owners who could not manage the taxes, while many others fell victim to developers. Vestiges of estate tourism do survive in contemporary Ireland, with some very fine houses open to the public. Yet, few of them feature the extensive landscaping of the eighteenth century. Where even the gardens survive, they often have been redesigned in later styles. And even though the Powerscourt Garden may still suggest the original eighteenth-century design beneath a nineteenth-century overlay, the estate's romantic Glen of the Dargle, originally created by the Powerscourts and the Grattans and once laid out with pathways, lookouts and resting places, is now only a muddy track.[53] At Killarney some of the park lands and gardens that once belonged to the Kenmare and the Herbert estates are now part of a national park. Yet, while the ruined abbey on the island of Innishfallen is still accessible by boat, Lord Kenmare's original landscaping has disappeared beneath a tangle of trees and bushes. The cheap surplus labor that kept the great estates in splendor has long since departed from Ireland.

However, even though the big house did lose some of its preeminence as a tourist attraction, estate tourism did play a vital role in opening up Ireland for tourism. As already noted, the landlords' efforts in building roads, villages and inns helped to create the infrastructure upon which Irish tourism came to depend. And by incorporating scenic attractions into landscape designs and by opening their estates to visitors, the proprietors also organized Irish tourism on the ground.

Part II

Chapter 4

THE SUBLIME AND THE PICTURESQUE IN THE IRISH LANDSCAPE

Landscape Perception and the Visual Imagination

Today's tourists are part of a global culture increasingly dominated by television and computer screens. They often carry electronic devices in their pockets with which they can take pictures when not making phone calls. It may come as something of a surprise, therefore, to realize that by the late eighteenth century British tourists may have possessed an even more acute visual awareness than their modern-day counterparts. Without the benefit (or hindrance) of a camera, these travelers knew how to recognize, frame and even analyze the scenery they encountered. Many could sketch, paint or write detailed descriptions of what they had seen.

Within the context of tourism this visual acuity represented a relatively new phenomenon. The idea of travelling to "see" scenery had only begun to emerge late in the seventeenth century. Up to that time the early modern traveler sought education rather than pleasure. As discussed in the "Introduction," the Grand Tour originally enabled young aristocratic males to prepare themselves to serve the state. In search of knowledge and social polish, young travelers went abroad, writes Judith Adler, "for *discourse* rather than for picturesque views or scenes." Young men toured with a tutor, a.k.a. "bear leader," with whom they inspected great buildings and fortifications, met learned men, practiced their social skills, and admired works of art. (They also did other things as well whenever they managed to lose the bear leader.) As Adler suggests, "The word, not the image, the ear and the tongue, not the eye, stand at the center of such treatment."[1] Except within the context of architecture and fortifications, early modern travel literature contained few references to landscape until near the end of the seventeenth century. But the growing interest in Natural Philosophy and a new sense of individualism helped shift emphasis toward the more visual aspects of travel. Individuals were to *see* the world for themselves, and the world included natural scenery. Even then, the traveler's appreciation for landscape did not fully emerge until the second half of the eighteenth century. By that time Ireland had become one of the primary European sites for the appreciation of romantic scenery.[2]

The English word "landscape" is derived from the German *Landschaft*, the Dutch *landschap* and the Old English *landskip* or *landscipe*. Anne Whiston Spirn suggests that these words combine two roots: "'*Land*' means both a place and the people living there. *Skabe* and *schaffen* meant 'to shape'...." A "landscape" was, therefore, a place shaped or altered by some sort of human intervention. In the case of the Netherlands, the word originally referred to land reclaimed from the sea. As "landscape" evolved, it continued to refer to nature as modified by man, initially through engineering, agriculture, or estate design, later as represented in painting or in literature. Spirn's maintains: "*Landscape* connotes a sense of the purposefully shaped, the sensual and aesthetic, the embeddedness in culture." Thus, the concept was and remains a social and cultural artifact. Malcolm Andrews defines a landscape as "what the viewer has selected from the land, edited and modified in accordance with certain conventional ideas about what constitutes a 'good view.' It is land organized and reduced to the point where the human eye can comprehend its breadth and depth within one frame or short scan."[3]

This more focused view involved another aspect of landscape. The German word *Landschaft* originally referred to the countryside surrounding a town. This corresponds to the Old English *landscape*, suggesting a region. In this sense a landscape is a sort of container; there is something within it. Originally this denoted a town, its extra-mural fields and farms, or an estate. Gradually, the contents of a landscape became a "view" or a "scene." As W. J. T. Mitchell explains, a landscape not only calls our attention to itself, but also invites us to contemplate its contents. To Mitchell, landscape is both signifier and signified. It not only represents nature made over into a human artifact, but it can also become "operational"; that is, it can so absorb the viewer as to mask its "artificiality," its human-bestowed qualities. As a consequence, that which is cultural in a landscape often appears to be "natural" and therefore inevitable. "To call some landscapes natural and others artificial or cultural," Spirn argues, "misses the truth that all landscapes are never wholly one or the other." Therefore, landscape is not only a matter of aesthetics. Denis Cosgrove argues: "Landscape is an ideological concept. It represents a way in which certain classes of people have signified themselves and their world through their imagined relationship with nature, and through which they have underlined and communicated their own social role and that of others with respect to external nature."[4] To understand British tourists in Ireland one must try to understand the sources of their perceptions of landscape.

At the moment when Irish tourism began to emerge, the very idea of landscape as a "view" or a "scene" was also evolving. The roots of this change in modern landscape appreciation lay in seventeenth-century painting rather than in travel descriptions. Returning from the Grand Tour, many wealthy aristocratic travelers brought back to Britain and Ireland examples of Italian art, including landscapes. Although intended for the private enjoyment of their owners, paintings by artists such as Claude Lorrain, Nicholas and Gaspard Poussin, and Salvator Rosa became well known in Britain. While there were no museums until the nineteenth century, the public could inspect paintings at auction houses, at commercial galleries and at exhibition venues, such as the Royal Academy of Art, founded in 1768, and the British Institution, established in 1805. Moreover, as mentioned earlier, by the eighteenth century many of the aristocratic manor houses were open to visitors who often came armed with catalogues and guidebooks that detailed the works to art on display.[5]

The middle class itself entered the art market, collecting prints, however, rather than the paintings on which they were based. Having lagged behind the Continent in print making since the fifteenth century, England emerged as the center of the European print trade by around 1700.[6] The spectacular growth of the market for prints and books of engravings provided a key stimulus for the British middle class's burgeoning interest in art, as well as in travel. As a result, interest grew dramatically in engravings of the works of the Old Masters—portraits, historical paintings and eventually landscapes. In fact, after 1740 the emerging enthusiasm for landscapes helped to expand the British print market, which became so important that artists began exhibiting their paintings with the intention of selling engraved reproductions. Many manor houses had a "print room," the walls of which were decorated by the women of the family with cutouts of pictorial and decorative illustrations. A rare surviving specimen of an Irish print room can be found in Castletown House in Kildare. Since the great expansion in print sales occurred in the moderate price range, many middle-class families could build modest collections of engravings.[7]

Visual education for the British middle classes extended beyond the perusal of prints and illustrated books. The same increased leisure that made tourism possible tempted many men and women to take up sketching and watercoloring. Kay Dian Kriz notes the growth around 1800 of interest in watercolor painting and sketching, which paralleled the considerable expansion of domestic tourism in Britain. As books on sketching, as well as reasonably priced paints and brushes, became available in the late eighteenth century, amateur involvement grew. In 1800 James Roberts brought out the first manual on watercoloring. Periodicals catering to the interest in landscapes were readily available by the 1820s. A decade later the popularity of sketching and watercoloring among the British traveling public reached its peak. (By the time photography emerged, tourists had already established the habit of bringing home visual representations of the places they had visited.) The anonymous author of *The Sportsman in Ireland* (1840) noticed ladies sketching on deck as his steam packet left for Ireland.[8] Lady Chatterton, who wrote *Rambles in the South of Ireland* (1838), was an ardent sketcher. Men also learned the art. Anne Plumptre engaged two "gentlemen" to illustrate her Irish travelogue, while both William Makepeace Thackeray and Jonathan Binns illustrated their books with their own drawings.

The Claudean Landscape

Whether as sketchers, as watercolorists or simply as admirers of landscapes, British tourists based their appreciation on aesthetic principles and artistic techniques established by prominent seventeenth-century Italian artists. Although a British school of landscape painting established itself in the early decades of the nineteenth century, the Italian "Old Masters" remained reference points for the traveling public. Chief among these painters was Claude Gellée (1600–82), usually referred to as Claude Lorrain or simply as Claude.

The Claudean landscape was, according to W. F. Axton, "invented in the studio from a recipe of conventional features, rules of composition, and prescribed methods of handling it." Claude's subject matter and motifs usually suggested idyllic scenes in classical settings. His paintings often included columned temples peopled by toga-clad figures or pastoral rustics, all set in imagined Italianate landscapes infused with glowing Mediterranean light. Axton describes the structure of a typical Claudean painting as

> composed of three or more *coulisses* (receding planes rather like theatrical "flats"): a foreground frame of dark broadly handled, generalized trees, a middle distance in local color, and a distant mountainous backdrop and sky, in pale blue. Spatial depth and recession were established between *coulisses* by transitional objects—cattle wading a stream, bridges, temples—and by atmospheric perspective, that is, by lightening the color and value (the degree of black in a color) of increasingly distant objects. Glazing promoted an overall harmony of color and richness of shadow to Claude's landscapes, lending them the mellow golden glow and unity of tone for which they were famed.[9]

In Claude's landscapes the viewer may sense a harmonious relationship between objects and among the various plains within the picture. The eye is easily drawn in a smooth transition from the carefully framed and elevated prospect in the foreground, through a series of light and dark bands of color in the middle ground, toward the blue mountains on the horizon.

The fact that Claude's scenes were imaginary did not prevent British viewers from absorbing his vision and methods and then finding or creating Claudean landscapes in Britain and Ireland. As John Barrell has remarked, for a time eighteenth-century Britain had no other way of imagining landscape except as realized by Claude.[10] Poets described their favorite haunts as they might have appeared in his paintings. Aristocrats designed their parks and gardens to reflect Claudean vistas and perspective. And so as travelers fanned out across England, Wales, Scotland and Ireland, they were predisposed to find in nature what they had already seen in paintings and prints.

By the late eighteenth century the ability to render a landscape in Claudean terms had passed from painters and poets to travel writers.[11] Typical is George Holmes, who, in describing the view from the Rock of Cashel in Tipperary in 1797, moves the reader's imaginative eye along the Claudean path from foreground to the painterly blue of the distance hills: "...the town stretches along to the left; its new cathedral, the archiepiscopal house and gardens, with the suburbs, form an excellent middle distance, beyond which the eye wanders over a tract of country, fraught with innumerable beauties: the little village, and lordly demesne; the humble cottage and ruined tower; the grove, lawn, and rivulet, all in their turn court the eye, till at length it reposes on the distant Galtee mountains, whose clear ethereal blue gives a delightful finish to the picture." Mary Frances Dickson, in describing her trip to Clare in 1841, also displayed a trained eye for color and Claudean organization. One of the few writers to find beauty in Ireland's bogs, she extolled "that fine, rich, dark, Vandyke brown, that forms so beautiful a back-ground, and throws out so well the figures seen against it....men with their straw hats, and white shirt sleeves—women in their picturesque variety of costume.... Imagine all these figures in vivid and distinct relief, against the fine brown of the turf, and a line of blue mountain beyond, the tender azure of whose changeful hues, melting away into the clouds, contrasts well with the bold, rich, pronounced colour of the middle tints; and you will have a picture of no mean attraction."[12]

Seventeenth-century Italian landscape painters so influenced eighteenth and nineteenth-century British visual perception that travel writers often invoked their names in describing particular scenes. Riding from Passage to Cork in the 1760s, Samuel Derrick enjoyed "the variety of beautiful landscapes, which the genius, fancy, and spirit, of Pousin [sic] or Claude Lorrain could never exceed.[13] In 1804 Robert Bell, describing the passing of a storm around Kells, declared that it produced "...the grandest sunset I ever beheld.... Claude Lorrain himself might have been inspired by the prospect," A few years latter Edward Wakefield thought of Claude's paintings while in Wicklow. Malcolm Andrews suggests that such name dropping provided a sort of shorthand that writers assumed their readers shared.[14] At the same time such references helped writers established their own aesthetic credentials.

The compelling influence of landscape painting and engravings upon British visual culture can be seen in the ways in which some tourists thought of Nature herself as an artist. Comparing Kilkenny Castle and its environs to the Royal seat at Windsor in England, Rev. Thomas Campbell, while granting the grandeur of the latter, insisted that the views from its windows offered nothing to "lavish variety to the landskip-painter [sic], as these Hibernian scenes." At Windsor "Nature has painted with her more correct pencil, here [in Kilkenny] she has dashed with a more careless hand. This is the fanciful and fiery sketch of a great master, that [in Windsor] the touched and finished work of a studious composer." In 1851 John Ashworth found himself caught in a sleet storm on a mountainside. When it lifted, he described how "the deep glens below, with their glittering streams, their verdant spots and craggy sides, browsed by the sheep, opened upon us with all the loveliness of a *finished picture*." Lady Chatterton, an ardent sketcher, claimed that "when the sun shines after one of the frequent showers, the whole landscape resembles a *highly finished and freshly varnished picture* not by a known artist—different—though quite fine as a Claude."[15]

The Irish Sublime

Not all of the landscapes travelers encountered in Ireland could be appreciated in terms of Claudean calm and beauty. In the 1820s Reverend Caesar Otway climbed the flanks of a mountain in northwest Donegal. Looking up toward the peak, he marveled at the sight of the "compact siliceous sandstone, so bare, so white, so serrated, so tempest-worn, so vexed with all the storms on the Atlantic, that if mere matter could suffer, we must suppose that this lofty and precipitous peak presented the portrait of material endurance…."[16] Far from striking him as grim and off-putting, however, Otway found the sight exhilarating.

Had Caesar Otway been writing a few generations earlier, his attitude might have been much different. Mountains had long been problematic for most Europeans. In the vocabulary of seventeenth-century English poets, mountains were considered the "Wens, Warts, Pimples, Blisters, and Imposthumes" of nature. Behind this prejudice lay two old and well-established ideas. Classical aesthetics long had sought beauty in the smooth and the regular, categories into which most mountains did not fit. Christian theology, on the other hand, did have a category for them—the awful debris of a postdiluvian landscape, the miserable sweepings of a sinful world. Mountainous regions—barren and windswept, the haunts of beasts—could be found in most European countries. Even so, one must have some sympathy for those travelers from the North whose path on the Grand Tour to sunny Italy lay through the vast and terrifying Alps. Many travelers found it a horrific experience, as did poor Horace Walpole in 1739, who watched his beloved lap dog snatched away by a wolf on the rugged path up Mount Cenis. In response, Walpole's companion, the poet-to-be Thomas Gray, speculated that perhaps Cenis had carried "the permission mountains have of being frightful too far."[17]

Nevertheless, British attitudes toward mountains were changing. Far from approaching them with traditional foreboding, Walpole and Gray actually had looked forward to the thrill of crossing the Alps. At Grenoble "not a precipice, not a torrent, not a cliff but is pregnant with religion and poetry." Indeed, half a century earlier in 1688. John Dennis had described his Alpine experience as walking "upon the very brink in a literal sense, of Destruction," which nonetheless produced "a *delightful Horrour*, a terrible joy and at the same time that I was infinitely pleased, I trembled." This gradual shift in landscape aesthetics, from what Marjorie Nicolson has termed "mountain gloom" to "mountain glory," was more or less complete by the middle of the eighteenth century. Theological attempts to embrace the multiplicity of God's creation combined with Newtonian science to produce what Nicolson defines as "the Aesthetics of the Infinite." At the same time, as Simon Schama points out, Romanticism found within disorder and chaos a sort of "agreeable horror."[18] Western culture had discovered the power of the *Sublime*.

Although he did not invent the concept, an Irishman, Edmund Burke (1729–97), helped to solidify and articulate the sublime in his famous essay, *A Philosophical Enquiry into the Origin of our Ideas of the Sublime and Beautiful*, published in 1757. Burke rooted the sublime deep within the human psyche: "Whatever is fitted in any sort to excite the ideas of pain and danger, that is to say, whatever is in any sort terrible, or is conversant about terrible objects, or operates in a manner analogous to terror, is a source of the *sublime*, that is, it is productive of the strongest emotions which the mind is capable of feeling." There is, of course, no pleasure to be found in actually facing real dangers or pain, "but at a certain distance, and with certain modifications, they may be, and they are delightful...."[19] In the presence of the sublime it is the mind, the imagination, rather than the body, that teeters on the brink of self-preservation. Thus, John Dennis' "delightful Horrour" as he crossed the Alps. In that inhospitable alien region the travelers found themselves surrounded by intimations of danger—towering mountains, fearful chasms. But, having set their feet firmly on the path so many had safely trod before them, they could savor their sense of dread.

A decade before his essay, Burke himself had experienced his own brush with such delicious fear. Around 1746 he found himself trapped in his Dublin house when the River Liffey burst its banks. As the water began to enter the ground floor, he recorded his impressions of the gathering gloom, the howling wind and the rumble of the water. "It gives me pleasure," he confided in a letter to a friend, "to see nature in those great though terrible scenes. It fills the mind with grand ideas, and turns the Soul in upon itself."[20] Because the sublime works upon the imagination, the sense of pain and danger it triggers might threaten to overwhelm the individual. This ominous possibility provoked what Burke identified as an "astonishment...that state of the soul, in which all motions are suspended, with some degree of horror [and] the mind is so entirely filled with its object, that it cannot entertain any other...." Among the qualities that might trigger the sublime are objects that are "vast," "infinite," "dark," "obscure," "rugged," all of which contrast with the small in scale, the bright and the smooth—in other words, the beautiful.[21]

The Burkean sublime appealed to the radical individualism born of Romanticism. While certain objects possessed innate qualities that could arouse strong emotions, the arousal itself occurred within the individual's own senses. This empowered people to react to and report on what they encountered, with obvious implications for travel writing. While Burke's essay went far beyond the aesthetics of nature, his philosophy, nonetheless invited travelers to open themselves to those aspects of nature that, like mountains, had been shunned or ignored. In Ireland, beyond the Ascendancy's carefully landscaped parks with their Palladian mansions and Claudean order, there loomed a wild, Burkean world of dark glens, looming cliffs, thundering waterfalls and stark, inhospitable mountains—all waiting to be seen.[22] However, after Burke, landscape was no longer something just to be "seen"; it had to be *experienced* at first hand. In 1805 Sir John Carr, entering the Gap of Dunloe at Killarney, marveled at what seemed a frightful scene of desolation. "It is a hideous pass through two prodigious mountains of barren rock and masses of stone, which looked as if all the rubbish of the creation, after the great Creator had completed his work, had been collected together."[23] Although the term "rubbish of the creation" harkened back to pre-Burkean repugnance for mountains, it was precisely this kind of landscape that Carr wanted to experience—and enjoy.

Few travel writers quoted Burke, and it is impossible to know what direct influence he may have had upon them. However, his *Enquiry* was published just on the cusp of the appearance of the Irish travelogues. John Bush's *Hibernia Curiosa*, one of the first Irish travelogues to focus on the country's scenery, appeared in 1767, a decade after the publication of Burke's essay. Bush articulated a popular version of the sublime, as the he struggled to describe his emotional reaction to Ireland's wilder scenery. For example, he claimed that the narrow valley of Wicklow's Glen of the Downs, confronted the traveler with "a prospect of the most horrible impending precipices, that from their terrifying height, and broken ruins at the bottom, appear to threaten him with destruction.... I never rode through a valley where there was such a mixture of beauty, or grandeur, of *sublimity*, if you will allow me the use of the expression here, and of something really awful, as is exhibited in this monstrous Glyn [sic]...." [24] This passage, typical of many in his book, clearly shows Bush deploying the vocabulary of the Burkean sublime and even invoking imaginary threats of danger.

By the time George Holmes published his 1797 tour the sublime had become a familiar item in Irish travelogues. Holmes and his partner John Harden rode through the Knockmealdown Mountains in Waterford on a gloomy, misty day, accompanied, appropriately enough, by some iconic ravens. The somber birds "now and then heavily passed us close by...flapping their moist wings, and hoarsely croaking...keeping up their discordant shrieks, by no means unpleasing, *as it assisted in adding to the general and horrific sublimity of the whole.*" The scene represented a sensation that Holmes admitted he longed to repeat. In 1806 Rev. Joseph Robertson climbed Slieve Gullion in Armagh. Almost overwhelmed by the mountain "towering in awful majesty" with its "barren rocks, rugged cliffs and deep glyns [sic]," he found the scene "at once awful and pleasing."[25] Some travelers learned how to manipulate their emotional responses to a scene, encouraging their imaginations to yield to pleasurable terror. In 1837 Leitch Ritchie, coming down from Lugduff above Glendalough in Wicklow, suddenly found himself enveloped within a mist. "While descending the steep of the waterfall and the precipitous ravine into which it plunged, clinging by the trees and lichens, and, owing to the darkness formed at once by the mist and over-arching foliage, with little else to guide me but the cry of the little mountain-torrent by my side, *I could have imagined myself in the wildest region of the Alps.*"[26]

Ian Ousby calls attention to the "stock, highly stylized vocabulary" employed by the cult of the sublime: "fells and high moorland are described as 'barren,' 'gloomy,' and 'desolate'; crags and valleys are 'wild,' 'chaotic,' 'confused' and 'primeval.'" "Horrible," "dreadful," and "awful" usually combined with "terrific," "tremendous" and "stupendous," suggested experiences of both fear and grandeur.[27] Today, the vocabulary of the sublime that stalks its way through these Irish travel accounts may seem more than a bit self conscious and theatrical. Nevertheless, in the eighteenth and very early nineteenth centuries, such attempts to articulate the Burkean sublime were relatively new, and sensitive souls were not shy in revealing their emotional susceptibility to it. Moreover, it could be argued that Burke himself had encouraged the use of emotional language. In his essay he insisted on the superiority of words over the power of images to convey sublime emotions. However, mere "naked description," he argued, conveyed "a poor and insufficient an idea" of objects. An author had to "call in to his aid those modes of speech that mark a strong and lively feeling in himself."[28] The emotional power of carefully chosen words most effectively conveyed the sense of the sublime.

Finally, it is important to remember that, apart from their clothing, very little of civilization and its technologies interposed themselves between travelers and the environments through which they moved. The modern tourist zips through a landscape partially glimpsed from the windows of a car or bus. The slow-moving tourist of the earlier periods, traveling on foot, on horseback or in a roofless "car" or carriage, directly experienced the unimpeded presence of the close, rough walls of narrow valleys or of looming over-hanging rocky outcroppings. In such circumstances, these earlier tourists felt themselves at the mercy of the impressions wrought by their immediate surroundings—the beautiful, the sublime or the ugly. Atkinson struggled to give the impressions of the solitary individual on foot, wending his way down the rocky Glen of the Downs. "The pedestrian pilgrimage necessarily imposed upon the visitor...the relative horror of the place...." The glen's romantic castle, waterfall, and mountains of "lofty and terrific aspect" all conspired "to seal upon the mind and imagination of the beholder an awful impression of the grandeur of this place...."[29]

Just as Claude's paintings stood as exemplars of idyllic classical landscapes, so the work of fellow Italian Salvator Rosa (1615–1673) was often evoked by those fascinated with the sublime. Instead of the open landscapes favored by Claude Lorrain, Rosa produced more romantic, closed-in scenes—lonely mountain passes, or bare cross-roads hemmed in by dark trees.[30] As Gina Crandell points out, instead of Claudean smoothness, Rosa could produce jagged and broken landscapes and harsh textures, peopled, not by shepherds and philosophers, but by what English viewers took to be untamed figures—gypsies, beggars and *banditti*, marginal yet romantic characters freed from the fetters of society. The words "wild," "savage," even "outlaw" were frequently associated with Rosa's paintings. John Sunderland suggests that after the publication of Burke's essay, "Rosa's name and the word, 'sublime,' as [applied to] landscape, became almost synonymous and interchangeable." According to Samuel H. Monk, the term "savage Rosa" became "a sort of shorthand" for British society's enthusiasm for his paintings.[31]

British travelers in Ireland found as many opportunities to invoke Salvator Rosa as they did Claude Lorrain. In a visit to the Wicklow's Devil's Glen, a remote valley once frequented by rebels in the wake of the Rising of 1798, Sir John Carr mused: "Groups of such figures must have augmented the gloomy grandeur of the scene, and made it rendered a subject worthy of the pencil of a Salvator." Dunn, contemplating the Eagle's Nest, rising 700 feet above the Long Range River at Killarney, proclaimed: "It has that bold freedom in its general outline which sets at naught description, and demands the pencil of Salvator himself to express justly." On first seeing Connemara's Killary Harbour in 1851, George Preston White claimed that "a more wild or romantic scene cannot be conceived,—it would have been worthy of the pencil of Salvator Rosa." To such writers Rosa's approach to nature demonstrated that even the wildest landscapes could be easily aestheticized, placing them within the viewer's perceptual control.[32]

The Sounds of the Sublime

"The eye is not the only organ of sensation by which a sublime passion may be produced," wrote Burke. "Sounds have a great power...." Surrounded by constant man-made sound, much of it in the high decibel range, many people today may have difficulty appreciating the role that the unamplified sounds of nature played in the lives of our ancestors. Sound was an important part of the emotional and spiritual side of tourism. In Burke's words" "The noise of vast cataracts, raging storms, thunder...awakens a great and awful sensation in the mind...."[33] The tourist in search of the sublime appreciated not only landscape but soundscape as well.

John Bush, for example, was thrilled by the thunder of a cascade in full flood: "the noise and impetuous fall of the water is astonishing, and *possesses the mind* of the curious spectator, unused to scenes of this kind, with a degree of terror mixed with admiration." Stopping in Mayo by the shores of Clew Bay after a day of heavy rains, artist Gabriel Beranger and his party were startled by the sound of the runoff pouring down Croagh Patrick, pushing rocks and boulders in its path. The travellers ventured outside to look and to listen. "It would require the pen of a poet to describe the awful scene that presented itself to us. *The thundering noise and roarings of torrents* at various distances, heightened by the stillness of the night: the moon covered with clouds, which, gliding over it now and then, afforded us a sight of the immense region of Croagh Patrick, filled us with a kind of horror, which made us quake, though we were sure that there was no danger. We stayed for some time looking and listening, and lost in contemplation, and returned home, the mind filled with the grand objects we had seen, which made us grave the whole evening." The evening Sir John Carr arrived at Killarney the storm that had greeted him cleared and the moon came out. As he stood by Ross Castle, he recalled how the reflection of the moon on the waters combined with *"the sound of distant cascades,"* which "formed a sublime and solemn scene too powerful and impressive for the pen to convey."[34]

Echoes proved particularly fascinating. Common enough so that travelers could expect to encounter them, they remained peculiar to a particular place, giving it character and fixing it in the memory of the visitor. Creating their own echoes also provided tourists with something to do. Addison, for example, shot his pistol in Pallazo Simonetta in Millan and counted 56 reports. Visiting some time later, Boswell, firing off his own weapon, enjoyed 58 echoes.[35] As tourism developed in eighteenth-century England, singers in the caverns at the Peak District took advantage of the echoes to provide a unique experience for visitors. Likewise, the Lake District, too, was particularly well known for its echoes.[36]

Travel accounts of pre-Famine Ireland also provide many examples of tourists seeking out and experimenting with echoes. On his walking tour of Ireland in the 1790s, Jacques Louis de Latocnaye found a single-arched bridge over the Blackwater at Lismore. He spent at least fifteen minutes underneath it, testing the echoes. In 1792 when C. T. Bowden visited the waterfall at Poulaphouca, his guide brought along a gun to demonstrate the echoes, producing, the writer noted, "an effect awful and sublime." Thomas Crofton Croker and his companions used a blunderbuss to experiment with the echoes around Gougane Barra, Cork. While hunting in the Muskerry Mountains, the "Sportsman in Ireland" fired off his duck gun just to enjoy the echoes, while the toot of his companion's bugle mingled with the screams of the rock birds.[37] As will be discussed in Chapter Seven, much of the tourist experience at Killarney was fashioned around echoes.

Echoes comprised a liminal experience. In a culture in which nature was increasingly probed by scientific explanations and dominated by industrial exploitation, echoes allowed the Romantic imagination to continue to play with the mystery and wonder of nature. They offered travelers an opportunity to interact with nature in ways that called forth, in their minds, some transcendental quality that otherwise might have remained potential, unrealized within a landscape. When Lydia Jane Fisher and her party boated into a sea cave off Valentia Island, she found that "the echo here is one which is wonderful…and its replies seem to come from voices deeply buried in the bowels of the earth. It is fearful to awaken these solemn sleepers! One of our young ladies was asked to sing. 'I cannot—I feel more ready to cry,' was her touching answer…."[38]

The Aesthetics of the Irrational

Lurking at the heart of sublime Romantic terror lay what Burke called the "idea of vast power" and the irrational fear it could produce. As Malcolm Andrews has noted, "The essence of the Burkean sublime was its irrationality: it seized hold of the mind before the mind could begin consciously to organize any response." Or, as Burke himself put it, the sublime takes over the mind. It "anticipates our reasonings, and hurries us on by an irresistible force…."[39] In Ireland nothing produced this sensation of irrational force more than the sight and sound of the great Atlantic crashing against the island's western sea cliffs. In the 1820s

Rev. Caesar Otway, visiting the coast around Horn Head at the northern tip of Donegal, found the mists "hanging over the Atlantic...like the way into the eternal world....there was no wind, it was a perfect calm, and yet the roll of the waves and the roar of the tides as they rushed and rolled amidst the caverned cliffs communicated an awful grandeur to the whole scene." In such a situation writers like Otway could easily imagine that they were surveying the remains of some enormous, inexplicable catastrophe. Otway believed that the Atlantic coast, from Donegal to Achill Island to the Cliffs of Moher, had experienced some disruption, some great cataclysm that had occurred long before human habitation. Perhaps, he mused, Ireland stood at the eastern end of the continent of Atlantis or Hy Brazil.[40] Likewise, James Johnson, surveying similar scenery between Bantry Bay and Cork, believed that "some terrible convulsion of Nature" had split Ireland's west coast. Later, contemplating Donegal seascapes, (the "wildest of all wilds in Ireland!") Johnson insisted that "its perpendicular cliffs hanging over the roaring surge—its jutting headlands...all bespeaks some awful catastrophe—some stupendous convulsion, by water, fire, or both, that buried a Continent...leaving a shattered angle, a mere fragment of it, above the deep—not indeed to tell the tale, but to shadow forth to the people of other and more remote ages, the indications of some horrible tragedy!"[41]

Even inland at Killarney the apprehension of the irrational power of nature could seize the mind. In 1786, Mrs. Dorothy Herbert described the mountains looming up behind the Eagle's Nest as "piled in such grand Confusion that they set the Head quite giddy to look at them—It seemed as if there had been a Battle of Giants there and Mountains torn up by the Roots and hurled in dread disorder...." A few years earlier Dunn described the mountains of Kerry, as seen from the top of Mangerton at Killarney, as "thrown together in a tumultuous, and wild an assemblage, as if *Chaos* had been here arrested in his billowy career, and chained to stability by the supreme *fiat*." However, he went on to judge the scene "inferior even to the maritime Alps in grandeur," because Kerry's mountains exhibited "the turns of nature so uncommon, as must furnish the best informed fancy with new, and *picturesque* images."[42] In Ireland sublime terror frequently blended into the realm of the picturesque.

Romancing the Picturesque

As Luke Gibbons points out, "One of the paradoxes of the sublime...was that even though it appeared to extol the savage wilderness, in the end it was a case of 'evil, be thou my good.'" According to Gibbons, the coupling of beauty with the sublime softened the terror of the latter. This mitigation enabled many tourists to aestheticize and enjoy the wilder aspects of Ireland without looking too deeply into the dark challenge of the Burkean sublime. For example, traveling in 1847 near Glenbeigh in what would eventually be called the Ring of Kerry, Lidia Jane Fisher managed to balance the high emotions summoned by the sublime with a calming effect of beauty. "Oh! for a pen of fire to describe out route!... I despair of conveying any idea of this enchanting country...closed in by the gigantic M'Gillicudy's Reeks on one side and the mighty Atlantic on the other.... I cannot attempt to describe the effect it produces to find yourself driving on a smooth road, with a high mountain, fragrant with heath and rich in bloom, close at one side, and the sea sleeping in the summer's evening calm, two hundred feet immediately beneath, lapping the base of your track! I felt my soul filled with *beauty and sublimity*—fully satisfied. Nature had completely performed her part, and it was perfect bliss to enjoy and admire her work."[43] In the theater of the sublime, nature may shake her mighty thunder sheet, whirl her howling wind machine, and then bathe the scene in a soothing, beautiful golden light.

In spite of the agitated enthusiasm for the sublime that travelers invested in the glens of Wicklow or in the Gap of Dunloe, some found it difficult to hang on to all that anticipated horror and terror. As Dunn reminded his readers, the McGillicudy's Reeks were not the Alps. Although he claimed that only a Salvator Rosa could do justice to the Eagle's Nest, he had to admit that "from the ruggedness of its impending cliffs, which almost overshadow the river, it would be truly awful, if the trees and shrubs which cover them, *did not counteract the effect, by defusing an air of festivity over the whole, which strips it of its terrors.* The parts of it, considered singly, are beautiful...."[44] Yet the word "beautiful" was too broad, too unfocused, too imprecise for a culture discovering new ways to look at and describe natural scenery. Travelers needed another word, one that allowed beauty to mingle with the rough and the rugged. And, as noted at the end of the previous section, Dunn, writing in 1776, had the word: *picturesque.*

The word can be traced back to the early eighteenth century, when "picturesque" referred to something that had the qualities of a picture. By the 1730s writers had begun occasionally to apply the term to landscape. Not until the 1790's, however, did Uvedall Price proclaimed it an aesthetic category, theoretically distinct from the "beautiful" and the "sublime."[45] By that time the word had been used for several decades to refer to certain types of scenery. In fact it appears in most of the major Irish travelogues published in the 1770s, as authors tried to describe landscapes that were neither Burkean nor Claudean. Here is Dunn's description of O'Sullivan's Cascade at Killarney, in which he stresses the liveliness and agitation of the falls, which, nonetheless, did not suggest the sublime. "The water is so agitated in its course down the mountain, that from the instant it breaks upon the eye, it is one entire sheet of foam; and dashing from stage to stage, enlivens everything around it, by the reflection of the scattered rays which fall upon it; serving at once to illuminate, and contrast, the shady green trees and shrubs which overhang it.... The whole scene abounds with the most *picturesque* beauties, but the minuteness of the objects, and the air of regularity which is diffused over the whole, strikes it out of the class of grandeur and sublimity." Also writing in the 1770s, Rev. Thomas Campbell expressed his sense of the picturesque in a slightly different way. The most attractive countries, he argued, were "those which are gently varied with hill and dale; equally removed from the roughness of the mountain, or the deadness of the flat.... And in this *picturesque* mixture of hill and dale, few countries are, I suppose, more happy than Ireland...."[46]

The idea of the picturesque gradually came to include not only landscapes but also specific elements within them. As tourists fanned out across the countryside, their eyes guided by paintings and prints, they looked for qualities that had once been excluded from aesthetic appreciation—the rough, the ruined, the exotic. While these did not necessarily evoke the emotions associated with the sublime, objects that possessed these qualities attracted interest through their departure from conventional ideas of beauty. As the travelling public learned to visually organize landscapes, it found that satisfying "views" could be formed around a jagged rocky outcropping, a ruined abbey, a rustic bridge, a shepherd's hovel, a crumbling tower house, or a group of colorful peasants.

Kay Dian Kriz suggests two additional characteristics of the picturesque: contrast and variety. Nothing offended picturesque sensibilities more than uniformity. The restless eye of the traveler required a variety of subjects to fix upon. As early as the 1756, Charles Smith extolled the scenery around Sneem in County Kerry: "Every half mile shifts the scenery, affording a pleasing novelty, that strikes the traveller with astonishment...." Like Campbell, Smith was impatient with uniformity, preferring landscapes "diversified with mountains and hills" to the flat plains of the Low Countries, where, "there is a sameness of objects everywhere, that leaves the field of description very barren."[47]

Ireland's maritime climate with its frequent changes in atmosphere and light also contributes contrast and variety to its landscapes. Describing Connemara in West Galway, a member of the Blake family observed, "There are not indeed two landscapes in the year that perfectly resemble each other." Visiting Killarney around 1776, Dunn was entranced by the "hourly revolutions in the face of the heavens"; "The vast volumes of clouds, which are rolled together from the Atlantic, and rest on the summits of the mountains, clothe them with majesty: the different masses of light and shade, traversing the lakes in succession.... [T]he wandering vapours flitting from cliff to cliff...amuse the eye with their varieties and irregular motions." Even the legendary Irish rain played its role in the tourist's search for picturesque variety. In the 1830s William Belton described a passing shower at Lough Mask in County Mayo: "the rocks, *here* wreathed in a veil of mist, or *there* projecting their pointed summits through the mass of vapour into the blue sky above; the rain-drops falling to earth like molten silver; and the whole overarched and beautified by the broken segments of a most vivid rainbow...." While Irish rain does not always fall in manageable picturesque doses, for the traveler who can wait it out, the effect of seeing the same landscape first in rain and then in sunshine can be rewarding. Dr. John Forbes experienced this contrast near Skibbereen in County Cork: "Yesterday was wet and gloomy, and the country all around seemed to present nothing but a sense of barren wilderness, and scarcely a trace of beauty. When viewed now, however, under a cloudless sky, and lighted up by the morning sun, it was manifest that the natural beauties of the landscape were far from inconsiderable...."[48]

Along with the sunlight, however, travelers encountered shadows, ruin and decay, and they would have been disappointed had it been otherwise. Such qualities often lacked quantity; that is, they did not loom large on the sublime scale. Yet, these darker aspects of the landscape attracted travelers, who, by borrowing from a sentimentalized sublime, were able to incorporate a ruined abbey or a broken bridge into a picturesque scene. In the process, Burkean terror gave way to more manageable but even more pleasing *melancholy*. Lowenthal and Prince have suggested that, like the sublime, the picturesque was supposed to "stimulate moral reflection, to appeal to the emotions." As they point out, British travelers looked for scenes that "induced reflection about puny man confronted by the force of the Creation. The feeling of 'melancholy' was aroused by the silent pool, the deep dark grotto, the gloom of overhanging branches, the falling ruin."[49] As we will see in the next chapter, ruins or "antiquities" were favorite sources for picturesque melancholy.

The Picturesque as Technique

Serious theoretical and philosophical debates about the terms "sublime" and "picturesque" had little resonance in the travel literature. According to Standring, as the picturesque entered middle-class popular culture, the term "became so overused as to become virtually meaningless by the turn of the century." As Ousby points out, some travel writers even used "sublime" and "picturesque" interchangeably. In fact, by the early decades of the nineteenth century, all attempts to fix the concept of the "picturesque" to any particular theory had ended since, as Malcolm Andrews has noted, "even among the theorists, let alone the touring amateurs and connoisseurs, the term changes meaning as it is handed one from one to another."[50] Whatever the sources— Claude's calm or Rosa's dramatic landscapes, even flashes of Burkean sublime—all were taken up by tourists to be celebrated as "the picturesque," an idea that had degenerated into a series of techniques.

As Jacque Ellul contends in *The Technological Society*, the primary characteristic of modern urban societies is an emphasis upon *technique*, which "has become a reality in itself. It is no longer merely a means and an intermediary. It is an object in itself, an independent reality with which we must reckon."[51] In fact, a fascination with the how-to of things often suffices when trying to grasp the inner essence of a subject seems too difficult or complicated. Thus, the picturesque equipped the urban middle class with a set of rules for interpreting, dissecting, deconstructing and reconstructing, or just talking about, landscape without having to actually wrestle with the intricacies of aesthetics and philosophy.

The chief popularizer of these techniques of the picturesque was the Rev. William Gilpin (1724–1804). Unlike upper-class aesthetic theorists and philosophers, such as Uvedale Price and Payne Knight, Gilpin wrote for middle-class tourists. He was, according to Charles L. Batten, Jr., one of the first writers to provide non-fictional descriptions of landscapes for the readers' entertainment, with the implication that they, too, could experience an aesthetic and emotional response, if they were to visit the same sites. Gilpin produced several "tours" of England, Wales and Scotland, as well as essays on landscape. His books were illustrated by the new aquatint process that reproduced his ink wash sketches made during his travels. These sketches themselves considerably influenced how tourists looked at landscapes.[52]

Gilpin's book on the Wye River valley, published in 1782, is often regarded as instrumental in popularizing the fashion for picturesque tourism. Gilpin offered his readers precise methods for looking at, analyzing, and, when possible, sketching or describing landscapes. His techniques or "rules" seem based on a simplified understanding of the Claudean landscape. He stated that there were "four grand parts" to any scene: the "area" or foreground, the "two side screens," which framed the scene and provided perspective, and the "front screen," the framed vista. Under Gilpin's tutelage the viewer could recognize the various elements within a scene and understand how the parts might be related to the whole in order to produce a proper view or picture. For tourists this meant finding the right spot or "station" from which to enjoy the best view—to see the "picture." For example, in the Lake District crosses were actually cut into the sod to mark "*the* spot" from which to view a particular scene. Among other things, such "stations" confirmed the "authenticity" of the view. Only by standing at the "right" spot could tourists be sure of seeing the "real" view.[53]

Gilpin's methods encouraged tourists to discover and to mentally frame their views, as if their trip itself constituted a progression through a collection of landscape engravings. The publication in the 1780s of detailed guides to the Britain's Lake District reinforced this approach for many tourists. As Ian Ousby has observed, "By interpreting the Lake District as a series of static, approved pictures and by providing a language in which these pictures could be admired,..[these writers] set a pattern which tourism still follows...."[54] Yet, the authors of the Lake District guides were merely reflecting the already powerful influence of paintings, illustrations and even theater design upon the British tourist's visual orientation. The theater's influence on tourism can be found in various travel accounts. William Ockenden (1767) tells how he and his companion, boating on one of Killarney's lakes, "rested on our oars within the bowery bosom of this sublime theatre, (for so I call it, though the curve is small)...." An anonymous traveler in 1783 described a view suddenly glimpsed through a gap in the Knockmealdown Mountains: "it resembled part of a beautiful scene in a theatre, exposed by drawing up a corner of the curtain."[55]

The tourist's tendency to seek out static "scenes" in nature, as though they were stage sets or engravings, surfaces in John Bush's description of the Lakes of Killarney published in 1767, before most of the popular accounts of the Lake District had appeared.[56] In Bush's work the search for "views" already had become a part of the tourist's gaze. Describing Killarney, Bush wrote: "For sail which way you will, there is continually some opening prospect of islands unseen, or different views of the mountains, or of the rocks and horrid precipices, a new cascade or water-fall, before undiscovered, from which mixture and diversity the spectator is perpetually getting a variety of entertainment, either from new objects, or from different views of those before seen." Bush reasoned that Nature accommodated humanity's "imperfection" when "confounded in its choice, in one point of view, by too great a multiplicity of inviting objects." Thus, at Killarney she kindly reveals herself, scene by scene, as attractions previously concealed, come successively into view.[57]

Finding and mentally composing Nature's "pictures" had become a basic part of the tourist experience by the late eighteenth century, defining what tourists did at a site and determining how they moved within it. This practice was reinforced in the 1820s by an increasing number of books, illustrations and magazines catering to middle-class picturesque tastes. Timothy J. Standring suggests that these publications "conditioned a large audience about what to look for and how to look at it. The point of view adopted for the landscape image, as well as its composition, helped create a common visual language for landscape painting." This common language of the picturesque helped travel writers to organize and describe the scenes before them, enabling them to give their readers some sort of visual impression of particular places.

Many tourists therefore commanded a vocabulary of color and form derived from art and illustration. With their eyes trained to take apart a scene and relate its various parts to each other, the writers among them attempted "word paintings," scenic descriptions that verbally mimicked the ways in which painters constructed their landscapes. Describing the "Salmon Leap" on the River Liffey at Leixlip, Anne Plumptre thus depicted a "charming wild romantic dell, where high slopes covered with wood rise on each side directly above the water. In the midst of this dell the water falls over some rocks, forming a very beautiful though not very high cascade.... A broken fragment of a bridge on one side of the fall adds much to the picturesque effect of the whole." It is that bit of a bridge, which readers might have imagined "framing" the scene, that particularizes this description. The passage could have reminded Plumptre's reader of illustrations of other river scenes framed by old bridges. Of course, any sketcher under the influence of Gilpin might have inserted a bridge, if reality had neglected to provide one. In this case, however, Plumptre description was accurate.[58] Another writer, Lydia Jane Fisher, attempted a verbal sketch of the town of Listowel in Kerry. From her vantage point atop a hill, she described "the winding river with its handsome bridge, the solitary pillar, the church steeple, the ivy-covered chapel with its stone cross, and the old castle, combined to make Listowel a place to rest on the memory."[59] The author had filled in her picture with the items common to picturesque illustrations, thereby inviting her readers to imagine that they too had "seen" Listowel. In other words, the picturesque became self-referential, particular landscapes mirroring whole classes of scenes that viewers and readers had already encountered in illustrations and descriptions.

As Gina Crandell notes, "The techniques of framing, distancing, and irregularly balancing compositions, learned from painting, had been internalized in the spectator." Some tourists even tired to take away with them mental "pictures" of the places they had visited. Indeed, once the proper images had been formed in the mind, it was best not to disturb it. Dr. John Forbes decided against climbing Mangerton, which overlooks Killarney's Lakes, because, "my mind was so full of the charms of the Upper Lake, the successive scenes presented by it were so lively delineated in my fancy, in all their individual and peculiar beauty, that I feared to alter in any way the now-familiar picture."[60]

Comparing the scene before them to others they had visited (or about which they had read) represented another characteristic of tourists in search of the picturesque. In 1815 an anonymous writer finished his flowery description of Rostrevor in County Down by insisting that the scene provided "an assemblage of objects which Greece or Italy might not distain."[61] John Barrell points out that this tendency to compare landscapes marked a privilege that the tourists' native hosts, rooted as they usually were in one place, normally could not enjoy. Yet, according to Barrell, such comparisons threatened to obscure the reality of a *specific* place in the eyes of the travelers. The picturesque tourist's main concern, "to be always moving through a place, to see it never primarily as a place-in-itself, but always as mediated by its connection to one place to the east, and another to the west, produces a sense of space which is defined always by this linear movement, so that to stop at a place is still be in a state of potential motion...." Barrell also finds significance in the common phrase to "look over" a collection of landscape prints. It suggests that viewers dealt with aesthetic generalizations, instead of the actual typography of specific places. Such habits produced "an impression of the order of [the eye's] own progress over the objects in the landscape, rather than of those objects themselves."[62]

One certainly can find examples of such generalizing in the attempts at word painting in the Irish travelogues. Still, some writers did focus their attention on very particular objects in an Irish landscape—a beggar, an ill-thatched cabin, a nearly starving half-naked peasant. Perhaps the very nature of the Irish Tour itself meant that few visitors were so besotted with the picturesque that they could completely ignore the less attractive realities of Irish life. Passing through the one village, Henry D. Inglis complained: "Over almost every half-door, somebody was leaning with crossed arms and many others were sitting at their doors, doing nothing." Thomas Reid expressed disgust at the sight of peasants sitting in front of cabins, the men shaving each other, the women examining and dressing each other's hair, prior to putting on their Sunday clothes. Had Inglis and Reid been writing about peasants in Italy or France, they might have presented these as picturesque scenes. Within the Irish context, however, they were anything but. Even when a writer managed to turn the peasantry into picturesque objects, "figures in a landscape" so to speak, the pleasant effects were often fleeting and ragged reality intruded all too quickly. Jonathan Binns spied a colorful group of peasants going to mass. He admired "the white and scarlet dresses of the women, shining brightly in the sun, and backed by the scenery." However, his picturesque tableaux faded as they drew nearer and the plain and dingy condition of their clothing became obvious.[63]

Nevertheless, travel writers sometimes tried to take refuge in the picturesque. After having described the dirtiness of the town of Dingle in County Kerry, Lydia Jane Fisher confidently anticipated the time when "this romantic little town, seated on her sloping hills, and by her rushing streams, is pictured in my 'minds-eye,' and refreshes my imagination with the recollections of nature's sublime handy work! Poverty and filth will not then mar the luster of the picture, for, thanks to the wise ordering of our gracious Creator, we forget the evil and remember the good."[64] In this passage Fisher clearly made an effort to stave off the contradiction that she intuited—the clash of poverty amid the picturesque—a point to be discussed further in Chapter Nine.

Having discussed the importance of the sublime and the picturesque in landscape aesthetics, it is important to understand how these concepts effectively reconfigured Ireland and redefined it in terms of tourism. Therefore, the next chapter will exam the identification of picturesque tourist sites in Ireland and the evolution of tourist practices at those sites.

Chapter 5

PICTURESQUE TOURIST SITES IN IRELAND

Marking Tourist Sites

As tourism develops, it reconfigures the host country into a succession of specific sites that shape the visitors' itinerary. In Britain, as Esther Moir points out, newly awakened curiosity sent early tourists off to explore as much of their country as was accessible. However once the great estates became organized for visitors, as ruins, mountains and lakes were "discovered" and noted in guidebooks, tourism came to define itself as a progress from one designated site to another.[1] The same was true of Ireland.

What constitutes a tourist attraction? Dean MacCannell maintains that "no *naturalistic* definition of a tourist sight is possible." Instead, it is the result of "an empirical relationship between a *tourist*, a *sight*, and a *marker*...."[2] A marker "points" to a place. It can be any piece of information about a site, including travel accounts, guidebooks, the guides themselves, souvenirs and pictures. John Hutchinson suggests that engravings of scenes in Wicklow, which began to appear as early as 1730s, contributed to the popularity of certain tourist sites in that county.[3] Literary associations also can act as markers. For instance, the ruins of Kilcolman Castle in County Cork, no more picturesque than those of many other abandoned Irish tower houses, could boast as its marker its connection to Edmund Spenser, author of *The Faerie Queene*.

Marking also facilitates the organization of a site or sight for visitors, not only physically in terms of accessibility, but conceptually as well. In Ireland writers produced accounts and guide books. Publishers issued collections of prints of manor houses and scenic spots. Poets memorialized castles and glens. As John Urry observes, the tourist gaze "cannot be left to chance. People have to learn how, when and where to 'gaze.' Clear markers have to be provided, and in some cases the object of the gaze is merely the marker that indicates some event or experience which previously happened at that spot." For example, the obelisk at Celbridge in County Meath, commemorating the Battle of the Boyne and the victory of Protestant King Billy over Catholic James II, once attracted a good deal of tourist attention, in spite of the fact that, apart from the monument, there was nothing to see but some pleasant rural scenery.[4]

Once it becomes famous, the very name of a place can act as its own marker. "Killarney," for example, still summons up for many tourists the promise of ideal natural beauty. The tourist's Killarney, however, is actually a collection of specific sights—lakes, waterfalls, mountains, islands and ruins. As MacCannell suggests, tourists do not "see" a place in an empirical sense.[5] Thus, visitors do not "see" Killarney. They see, instead, a series of internal "markers" that point to individual sights that define the larger whole. Sometimes a marker itself earns a name and becomes what one might call a "meta-site," a well-known place that points to the "real" site. At the southwestern end of Killarney, for example, an elevated spot provides a panoramic view of the Lakes. This location was familiar to tourists (or at least their guides) years before Queen Victoria and her entourage stopped there in 1861. Ever since then it has been known as the "Ladies' View," a tourist spot in its own right that "points" to the principal attraction, the lakes themselves.

Often tourism itself may generate a series of markers representing or symbolizing the generic attractions available in a host country. As early as 1775, the fold-out map in the front of Richard Twiss' *Tour of Ireland* included miniature engravings of a round tower, the basalt columns of the Giant's Causeway, a Celtic cross and a view of Glendalough. These icons had already become stereotypical symbols of the tourist's Ireland, itself little more than a quarter century old. Such is the power of markers that they can sometimes act as substitutes for the actual attraction. In 1814 Anne Plumptre contemplated visiting Gougane Barra at the headwaters of the River Lee in County Cork. At the time no good road ran into the lough, and she could find no one who had actually been there to reassure her of either its accessibility or value. Balancing a two mile walk over boggy mountains with the professional writer's concern for time, not to mention comfort, she settled on inspecting a "marker," in this case a painting of the place.[6]

Neil Leiper emphasizes the systemic nature of the relationship between tourist, site/sight and maker, by which each element influences the other.[7] During Ireland's first century of tourism, landscape aesthetics held this triad together, as visitors traveled through Ireland seeking the sublime and the picturesque. This in turn determined which places to visit and which sights to see. The picturesque and the sublime were most often associated with certain categories of natural scenery: mountains, lakes, glens, waterfalls, caves, seascapes, as well as antiquities.

The Glens and Vales of County Wicklow

Largely because of its proximity to Dublin, County Wicklow provided the first opportunity for most visitors to Ireland to seek out the sublime and the picturesque. The county's mountains, glens, waterfalls and seacoasts were popular tourist attractions, their access facilitated by the efforts of the proprietors on whose estates these sights were often located. Wicklow's glens were particularly fashionable. Narrow, dark, wooded, usually with a rushing river at the bottom, places such as the Devil's Glen, the Glen of the Downs, the Glen of the Dargle and Glendalough ("The Glen of Two Lakes") excited the imagination. In the 1750s Richard Pococke found the county's glens "most exceeding Romantick [sic] & beautiful...." Arthur Young described the Glen of the Dargle as "a specimen of what is to be expected by a romantic glen of wood, where the high lands almost lock into each other, and leave scarce a passage for the river at bottom, which rages, as if with difficulty forcing its way.... The extent of wood that hangs to the eye in every direction is great, the depth of the precipice on which you stand immense, which with the roar of the water at bottom forms a scene truly interesting."[8]

The Glen of the Dargle, also known as the "Dark Glen," provides a good example of how proprietors organized portions of their estates to accommodate visitors. According to Philip Luckcombe, the Powerscourt family constructed three miles of paths along their side of the Glen, providing the public "an opportunity of viewing, in different prospects, the most delightful romantic, and surprising landscapes in the world, which would have been imperceptible to all human sight...had it not been for these improvements." Along the carefully maintained path the visitor encountered alcoves, chairs and a pavilion for picnicking. Sets of stone stairs led down to the bottom of the glen.[9] John Carr reported that Mr. Grattan (who divided the Glen with the Powerscourt family) also built walkways on his side of the river. He cleared lookouts and even constructed a "rustic temple" where the backs of seats were formed by "intertwisted branches, softened by moss, and whose arches opened upon one of the most favorite spots of the Dargle: it seemed to be suspended, like an aeronautic car, from some vast impending oaks, which spread far over it an umbrella of leaves." (In the upper right-hand corner of George Barret's oil painting, *View of the River Dargle*, one can see a small, ornate open structure on a bluff above the river.)[10]

No matter how awe-inspiring a scene, it can always be personalized for tourists by a legend, a story or a poem. Such narrative markers bring a place more easily within the realm of human emotions. Although the story connected to it seems vague at best, the Glen of the Dargle boasted a "lover's leap," which Dr. Edward Daniel Clarke described in the 1790s as "an enormous rock, which projects forward on the side of the river in the form of a castle. It is bold, lofty, and terrible, from its great height overhanging the woods and the river." Mr. A. Atkinson, who seems to have been afflicted by vertigo and shortness of breath, found the Lover's Leap a particular challenge. It presented "a most horrid prospect of the precipice beneath; so that even to contemplate for a moment the possibility of a human being casting himself from this Alpine pinnacle...is sufficient to throw a weak mind into disorder...."[11]

Literature, as noted earlier, can provide markers that help to popularize tourist sites. Sir Walter Scott almost single-handedly created the tourist map of Scotland with his *Waverly* novels. Ireland lacked a novelist of Scott's stature and productivity, although Lady Morgan (Sidney Owenson) did feature Irish landscapes and antiquities in her novels. However, the country could boast one of the nineteenth century's most famous poets and song writers: Thomas Moore. Two of the most popular attractions in Wicklow, the Vale of Avoca and Glendalough, were both memorialized by Moore, whose *Irish Melodies* began appearing in 1808. In the first collection Moore's "The Meeting of the Waters" celebrated the beauty of the spot where the rivers Avonmor and the Avonbeg meet in Wicklow's Vale of Avoca, a place easily accessible to tourists coming from either Bray or Dublin. Moore did not "discover" the Vale. Sir John Carr wrote up the site in 1805. Once published in 1808, however, Moore's song became so wedded to the place that few visitors could resist quoting at least its opening lines.

> There is not in the wide world a valley so sweet,
> As that vale in whose bosom the white waters meet;
> Oh! the last rays of feeling and life must depart,
> Ere the bloom of that valley, will fade from my heart.[12]

Like the Vale of Avoca, Glendalough had attracted tourists before Moore wrote about it. James Dodd's *The Traveller's Director Through Ireland* (1801) suggests that the new carriage road from Dublin had opened up the site for visitors. In 1805 Carr used Burkean terms to describe this old monastic site, with its round tower and ruined churches. He called it, "this awful spot" with its "stupendous mountains" surrounding "the gloomy dark lake." Moore's song, the title of which is contained in the first line, constituted a powerful marker that helped to fix the word "gloomy" to Glendalough: "By that Lake, whose gloomy Shores / Sky-lark never warbles o'er." In its subsequent lines the lyrics also recall a famous legend about St. Kevin, the founder of the monastery. An extreme ascetic, the Saint slept in a cave above the upper lough. One night, when the temptress Kathleen dared track him to his cliffside retreat, he hurled her into the lough's dark waters. The legend became a marker for the site, becoming part of the standard patter of the glen's guides.[13]

"Gloom," whatever its source, did not constitute a drawback for those in search of the sublime and the picturesque. The ruined churches, the legends of St. Kevin and Kathleen, and a treeless setting all combined to lend the place a certain "gothik" atmosphere steeped in picturesque melancholy. Leitch Ritchie described his impressions of the place in the 1830s: "On reaching the shores of the upper lake, it is not easy for the pen to describe the solemnity of the scene which met my view. The blackness of water, and its depth—for the cliffs plunging sheer down give the idea of an almost bottomless gulf; the dreary and savage aspect of the hills, with the mist tumbling and swirling on the summits; together with the profound silence which reigned around—all gave a most strange and unworldlike character to the spot. Turning back to look out of this recess into the broader Valley, there were only tombs and ruins before me...."[14]

Tourists, however, if they arrive in sufficient numbers, can change the tone of almost any place. Writing about Glendalough in 1870s, Sir William Wilde noted a new bridge over the glen's river, as well as "an admirable hotel" with shrubbery and gravel walks around the ruins. In addition, the good doctor observed that "loud-clothed young men from Dublin establishments play accordions; or brass bands proceed in procession with their respective crowds of admiring gossoons and colleens to make the circuit of the place." Unfortunately, industrial pollution from the lead mines above the Glen had also altered the scene. As Wilde sadly noted, "streams of grey material from the mines pour down mountain sides, poisoning the lakes."[15]

The Vanishing Trees: Estate Forestry and Irish Tourism

Industrial pollution presented less a problem for tourists in Ireland than the disappearance of trees from popular picturesque sites. No one came to Ireland just to see trees, but the prevailing landscape aesthetics made them an expected part to any but the starkest, most barren monuments to the sublime. Arriving at a well-known beauty spot, however, visitors to Ireland might have been shocked to discover that the proprietor had recently logged its trees. The woods of Glendalough had been lumbered in the early part of the nineteenth century, no doubt contributing to, if not producing, its "gloomy" reputation. It is not clear just when and how often the area had been cut. The glen's original oak forests had disappeared by the time Carr visited it in 1805. He noted that only place names, such as Derrybawn, Kemyderry and Kyle, recalled the Gaelic designation of former woodlands.[16] The illustration accompanying Carr's description of the glen shows the surrounding mountains, as well as the valley floor, devoid of trees. Joseph Peacock's 1813 oil painting of the pattern at Glendalough shows a similarly denuded view of the area. In 1815 Atkinson complained that he could not conceive of how nature could have formed a more admirable spot if only the mountain sides had still been covered with oak. When the Halls visited some decades later they found that "except along the borders of the lower lake and on the heights that divide the mountains of Lugduff and

Derrybawn not a tree is to be seen, and there is scarcely a shrub large enough to shelter a lamb—nothing, indeed, to humanize its utter loneliness."[17] In all likelihood aggressive estate forestry contributed to Glendalough's famous gloom.

As will be seen in Chapter Nine, Killarney also became a frequent victim of landlord logging, as did Gougane Barra, Cork, a site associated with St. Finbar and noted for the wild splendor of its setting. However, J. Stirling Coyne writing in the 1840s, feared that the "natural beauty of this scene has been considerably impaired by the destruction of the woods which clothed the islands, that skirted the shores of the lough." Apparently the new road, which had made the site only recently accessible to tourists, had facilitated logging as well. George Petrie's 1831 romantic watercolor of Gougane Barra's lake and its hermitage suggests the deforestation of the surrounding hills.[18]

Nevertheless, at some tourist sites trees, once cut, had a habit of seeming to reappear within a matter of a few years. Estate forestry, properly managed, sometimes involved replanting logged-over areas. Indeed, the foliage at sites such as Glendalough and Killarney seem to have disappeared and reappeared with startling regularity. In spite of frequent logging at Glendalough, when T. K. Cromwell visited just before 1820, he reported that he found the surrounding mountains were clothed in trees.[19] The fact that he mentions that the area remained green all year round, however, suggests that some sections had been reforested with relatively quick-growing, non-native pine. As noted above, when the Halls wrote about the Glen some twenty years later, most of the trees had once again disappeared.

In addition to replanting, estate forestry employed other techniques that kept the hillsides green. Writing in 1823 Wakefield quotes the first-person account of a Mr. Hayes, author of *Treatise on Planting*: "I have been eye-witness to the fall of well-growing oak in a romantic valley, on the see land of Glendalough...*three times* within the space of *twenty-four years*." Hayes reported that the owners eventually sold off the copse wood, leaving no reserves. Although apparently sacrificed at Glendalough, copse wood, mentioned by Hayes, represented another forest management technique belatedly employed on some Irish estates. Coppicing involves cutting hardwoods so that the roots and a few inches of the trunks remain in the ground. These quickly sprout "saps," new growth, that within a decade or so may be thick enough to cut for poles or fuel. The root systems supporting this sort of regrowth can go on producing for centuries. Trees may also be pollarded: the trunk and its main branches are left intact while the lesser branches are cut. Again saps quickly grow, eventually yielding wood for future harvests. These techniques may explain the cycle of disappearance and reappearance of trees at some Irish tourist sites. When viewed from a distance, new growth on coppiced and especially on pollarded woods could appear green enough to satisfy a visitor. When Mrs. Plumptre arrived at Killarney in 1814, only seven years after a popular guide book had announced the area's deforestation, she found that the slopes of Glena were once again green.[20]

Lakes and Waterfalls

Water, too, constituted an essential element in picturesque scenery. According to Thomas Whatley, an eighteenth-century expert on gardening, water "captivates the eye at a distance, invites approach, and is delightful when near...it animates a shade; cheers the dreariness of a waste, and enriches the most crowded view...[and may] add splendor to a gay, and extravagance to a romantic, situation."[21] Travelers enjoyed following the river valleys of the Boyne, the Barrow and the Suir, and almost anywhere they turned in Ireland they found lakes, from the numberless small loughs to large bodies of water such as Lough Erne and Lough Neagh. The most famous of all, the Lakes of Killarney, will be discussed in Chapter Nine.

Waterfalls particularly won favor with the picturesque traveler. Combining the play of movement and light with sound, they represented an important element in the Burkean sublime. In addition waterfalls suggested great natural forces that could erode seemingly impenetrable rock. This "energized nature," as Barbara Stafford calls it, fascinated the eighteenth and early nineteenth-century travelers. Neither Ireland nor Great Britain contain falls on the massive scale of Niagara or Victoria, spectacles so magnificent that they act as primary destinations around which tourists plan their trips. Nevertheless, as John Bush observed in his *Hibernia Curiosa*, hardly a river in Ireland was not "ornamented" with cascades, falls or salmon leaps.[22] In Wicklow the Powerscourt and Poulaphouca cataracts were among the most popular waterfall sites on the Irish tourist itinerary, promising peak moments in the tourist's search for the picturesque.

In the Powerscourt demesne, before entering the glen that bears its name, the Dargle pours over an almost four hundred foot-drop to create what is still one of Wicklow's most popular tourist attractions. Already well known in the 1760s, the falls had been painted sometime during that decade by the Dublin-born artist George Barret, the Elder. Featured in the theatrical set of an Irish play, *A Trip to the Dargle* (1762), Powerscourt Falls provides an interesting example of the connections between estate development, theater and tourism.[23] John Bush provided one of the earliest full descriptions of the falls in his 1767 travelogue. Reflecting the influence of landscape design upon tourist perception, Bush began by describing the setting of the falls: "It is found at the very bottom of a lofty semi-circular hill, into which, after a most agreeable ride through a park well planted with wood, you enter, by a sudden turn round the extremity of one of the curvatures, and at once, unexpectedly get into the midst of a most entertaining scenery of lofty slopes on either hand, verdant from top to bottom, with trees or every kind. The distant view of this water-fall, at first entering within the scope of the surrounding verdant hills, is inexpressibly fine." In his description of the falls itself, Bush revealed an almost painterly eye trained in noticing natural details. He described how the water's initial drop of 200 feet is broken by rocks. The resulting spray "in beautiful curves...produces an infinite number of frothy streaks behind the larger sheets of water...." More rocks at the bottom caused the water to "fly off in a thousand different directions, exhibiting...in the morning, with the sun in the east shining full on it, most curious and beautiful representations of the rainbow...." In a Berkean manner Bush assured his readers that the falls would "possess" the mind of the spectator and fill it with astonishment. However, when he went on to praise its "terrific grandeur" after a good rain, he may have dragged nature too far into the theater of sublime emotions. Dr. Edward Daniel Clarke, visiting Powerscourt during a rare dry spell, found little grandeur. He claimed, moreover, that he was not impressed by "temporary" rain-swollen waterfalls: "they are rather the offspring of caprice than a regular feature in the visage of nature; it is necessary to be wet to the skin in order to see them to perfection...." In his opinion Powerscourt could not compare to Monarch falls in Wales.[24]

While nature had created the waterfall on the Powerscourt estate, the family greatly enhanced its setting, as well as providing access. On his visit to the estate, Atkinson passed over a wooden bridge onto a finely ornamented lawn: "Here you see the waterfall to more advantage than from the lands on the other side of the river, and here, the banqueting house provided for the reception of select companies, will protect you from the storm, or afford you a genteel resting place after the fatigue of travel." Anne Plumptre, however, did not appreciate the proprietor's carefully designed approach to the falls. She felt that the estate's deer park, off limits to the public, promised the best view. Undaunted, she and her companions had no hesitation in wetting their shoes and crossing a stream: "like true descendants of Eve, enjoying our walk more for its being taken in opposition to the imposed *taboo*."[25]

The waterfall at Powerscourt apparently provided a favorite picnicking spot for parties from Dublin. In the 1830s Jonathan Binns picked whortleberries at the site, while noticing that others had brought along more substantial repasts: "Some seated on rustic benches and others on the ground—their gay summer dresses enlivening the sequestered and beautiful glen, and the rich notes of the bugle mingling with the scarcely less rich melody of the waterfall." At around the same time, Robert Graham noticed the cottage for "tea drinkings" near the foot of the waterfall. However, by the 1840s changes had taken place in the character of Wicklow's tourism, as the numbers of visitors grew and their social status broadened. Leitch Ritchie reported that because of "depredations," the Powerscourt family had closed the walk through the Glen of the Dargle on Sundays, opening it only on certain weekdays, when presumably, the "lower" classes were otherwise occupied in the Dublin.[26]

Poulaphouca, another popular although less spectacular waterfall, lay on the other side of the Wicklow Mountains near Blessington. At the point where the River Liffey passed through a narrow gorge, it formed a falls some forty feet wide, dropping one hundred and fifty feet in three stages. Having already visited Powerscourt, Anne Plumptre, warned that she would be disappointed by Poulaphouca, nevertheless found the falls charming. Not as high as Powerscourt, it was broader, "consequently making a much finer rush and foam." In the 1820s, Alexander Nimmo built a bridge over the Pollaphuca gorge, which Ritchie described as spanning "the gulf from rock to rock, in a manner at once beautiful and daring." From that vantage point "the traveller looks down from the parapet into the middle of the whirlpool."[27] The Halls, who never missed an opportunity to introduce the drama of local legends into their accounts, described "the solemn and dreary solitude out of which rushes the waterfall of Phoul-a-phooka, which terminates in a whirlpool of unfathomed depth and where it is said, the famous spirit horse holds its nightly revels, luring unhappy wayfarers into the frightful vortex formed by the waters of the cataract."[28]

As noted earlier, estate-based sites sometimes benefited from the efforts of proprietors' wives, who staved off boredom by designing and decorating fanciful small structures that appealed to the visitor's imagination. On his visit to Poulaphouca Mr. A. Atkinson found a moss house, which contained a black oak desk and a book in which visitors could inscribe their names and impressions. Situated at the top of the falls, a ballroom catered to those fond of dancing to the sound of the cascading water. Near the foot of the falls the windows of a tea room provided what Elizabeth Smith considered the best views. In addition to Poulaphouca, C. T. Bowden also visited Coolaphouca Falls near Bunclody in Wexford. There he found a moss house in which a living tree had been shaped to form a table.[29]

Caves

Caves, inland or carved into sea cliffs, attracted the attention of tourists ever in search of new sensations, especially when they promised a touch of the sublime. Barbara Stafford suggests that, to explorers and casual tourists alike, "These hollows in mountainsides were now seen to expose the universal matrix of matter, while themselves embodying yet another individualized expression of the potency of the earth's core...the protean dynamism of nature...." She suggests that tourists' fascination with mines and caves allowed them to combine scientific curiosity with sublime emotions.[30]

Although described in a recent guidebook as "decidedly unexciting and not worth a big detour," Dunmore Cave near Ballyfoyle, County Kilkenny, represented an early and frequently visited spot on Ireland's tourist map. Dr. Thomas Molyneux and his party descended into the caves in 1701, where they entertained themselves by firing off their pistols to "awaken" the echoes. William Rufus Chetwood, who visited the cave in the 1740s, had his romantic sensibilities aroused by a "monstrous Flight of different Species of birds," which issued from the mouth of the cave and darkened the sky. Once inside the cave, Chetwood, a Dublin theatrical manager, allowed his imagination full play: "Our Faces, through this Gloom, looked as if we were a Collection of Ghosts, and the Lights in our Hands seemed as if we were making a Visit to the infernal Shades.... the Shining of the petrified Water...forms so many different Objects that it is not unpleasing; and by the help of a little Imagination, we might make out Organ Pipes, Pillars, Cylinders, Pyramids inverted, and ten thousand various Things in Art, all formed form the dropping of the Water." The flight of birds and mineral formations described by Chetwood became a part of the tourist literature and, thus, a part of tourist expectations. Mrs. Plumptre, having read about Dunmore's attractions in the *Post Chaise Companion*, also visited the cave but saw neither birds, organ pipes nor inverted pyramids. T. K. Cromwell also failed to distinguish the fanciful formations from the cave's "dark gray limestone rock," in spite of the best efforts of his guides. Although the Halls mentioned Dunmore Cave, they were more enthusiastic about the caves at Mitchelstown in Country Tipperary. Discovered in 1833, these caves quickly became a popular tourist attraction.[31]

Visitors to the Giant's Causeway had the opportunity to visit nearby sea caves, which Inglis declared as "bordering on the sublime." Combining darkness and sound, such caves promised intimations of the Burkean sublime. Inglis described their "gloominess and solitariness" and "the rush and deep thunder of the resistless waves that bound into it." He retained, however, enough of his Scottish presence of mind to remember that the guide and boat came to 17s. Leitch Ritchie's description of his visit to Portcoon, a sea cave near the Causeway, provides an example of how sound helped augment the sensation of the sublime. The cave "is entered dryshod, or nearly so, by a lateral passage; but the sea comes in by the front opening in huge billows, and presents an appearance not less grand that the stranger is seized, in spite of himself, with the idea that the cavern will be filled to the roof.... The effect is supposed to be increased by the report of a pistol which is usually fired on the occasion; but on a tempestuous day, like that of my visit, nothing can be finer than the rush and roar of the sea exaggerated by the thousand echoes of the cave."[32]

Mary Francis Dickson experienced a bit of Burkean awe as she and her party floated into a cave near Kilkee, County Clare: "The passing from the gay sunshine and bright skies outside, into the solemn and gradually deepening gloom within; ...the sudden check that seemed to come over the spirits as the silence and darkness increased—the peculiar smell of the place, and feeling the air compressed as it were and rendered heavier on the chest by the low roof— the unearthly sounds, 'old ocean's husky voice,' rumbling in hoarse and muffled tones—the white sea birds perched here and there on the sides of the cavern...all these, together with the sense of danger that must unavoidably enter the mind...all these produced a thrilling sensation of awe, a sort of deep, silent, breathless delight, that is quite indescribable." Alas, such moods are easily shattered. Someone in another boat had brought along a keyed bugle. "[A]nd there, in the midst of nature's mighty music, when even a whisper would have seemed an impertinent intrusion, we had to endure the intolerable annoyance of 'Jenny Jones,' and 'Jim Crow,' and such tunes, redolent of London streets, and barrel organs, and hurdy-gurdies, and dancing monkeys." Escaping the cave, she could still hear the annoying bugle punctuated by rifle shots, intended to augment the echoes.[33]

Seascapes

In addition to a number of spas, Ireland offered many locations for sea bathing. A few, such as Kilkee in Clare and Bray in Wicklow, attracted the attention of British tourists. Sea coasts offered more than the bracing promise of a good, cold swim. As Alain Corbin points out, by the middle of the eighteenth century, the seashore had become a "focal point for the world's enigmas." Strange rock formations, occasional fossils and the dramatic power of the sea itself invited speculation and meditation. The sublime vastness of the sea shattered itself as waves crashed against cliffs and surged into rocky inlets. Jagged coastlines provided an endless number of picturesque planes over which the tourist's eye could play.[34] Such dramatic combination of rock and sea is one of the characteristics of Irish topography. With most of its mountains ranged on its periphery, Ireland offers striking examples of surging seas dashing themselves dramatically against high cliffs. This is particularly true for the southwestern, western and northern coasts. Visiting the Bay of Schull in County Cork, Caesar Otway felt that he stood on the edge of the last "redoubts of the continent of Europe against the force of the great ocean."[35]

The North Antrim coast also offers very dramatic and unusual scenery, including romantic ruins, such as Dunluce Castle, perched on the edge of a sea cliff. There are also many dramatic promontories in the region, including Fair Head, from which one can see the islands of Rathlin and Mull. Intrepid traveler though she was, Anne Plumptre felt almost overpowered as she approached the edge of Fair Head: "It is indeed awful to look down this precipice: I could not have done it standing, I was obliged to go on my hands and knees to get near the edge." From that vantage point, however, she managed to provide detailed descriptions of the rocks below.[36]

Carrick-a-rede near Ballintoy offered another sight that gave travelers pause. Since at least 1786, when William Hamilton described it in his study of the North Antrim coast, to the present day, travelers have been fascinated by the dramatic sight of a rope bridge linking the mainland to a small island. The bridge spans a chasm some sixty feet wide with a drop of eighty feet into the sea, clearly evident in the old days between the boards lashed to the supporting ropes. Fishermen threw up the bridge each year to give them access to the salmon runs that occur around the island. William Hamilton described it as, "a beautiful bridge in the scenery of a landscape, but a frightful one in real life." Carrick-a-rede in fact afforded an experience of the sublime that yielded some genuine terror. Even the no-nonsense Anne Plumptre took one look at the rope and board construction swinging away in the wind with the sea boiling beneath it and felt no compulsion to set foot on it. And this, in spite of the example of a twelve-year old boy who happily scampered back and forth across the bridge to encourage her. Barrow, writing in the 1820s, felt impressed by the danger of looking down and losing his balance. The Halls visited the bridge on a stormy day, and they too were disinclined to cross. For many tourists the mere sight of Carrick-a-rede offered sufficient thrill, requiring no further action. Philip Dixon Hardy had the best advice for tourists—see it from below from the deck of a steamboat.[37]

The Giant's Causeway

A unique type of seascape, the Giant's Causeway on the North Antrim coast particularly interested those fascinated by the mysterious forces of Nature. The Causeway combines cliffs and sea caves with unique rock formations. Some sixty million years ago, molten rock, forced through fissures in a chalk base, created the largest lava plateau in Europe. The flows, continuing on and off over several million years, created some 35,000 polygonal basaltic columns currently visible, some almost one hundred feet high. The basalt structures form the sides of sea cliffs, as well as free standing columns of varying size, and disappear under the sea, reappearing around nearby Rathlin Island. They emerge again around Scotland's Staffa island some eighty miles across the North Channel where giant columns frame the entrance to Fingal's Cave.[38]

The Causeway came to the public's attention in 1692 when Sir Richard Bulkeley visited it and described it in a paper sent to the Royal Society in London the following year. Other reports followed, and in 1697 Dr. Thomas Molyneux commissioned the first drawings. The Giant's Causeway attracted considerable interest because its basalt columns were supposed to reveal, as Barbara Stafford suggests, the very processes of their creation. "No formation was deemed more worthy of apprehension as a natural monument or considered more controversial...than those formed from basalt.... Unlike primary strata, which underwent slow transformation and hence were symbolic of lastingness, basalt (depending on one's scientific prejudices) was thought to be the result of volcanic activity." Intense speculation continued throughout most of the eighteenth century regarding the origins of Antirm's strange columns. Two schools of thought shaped the debated. According to Charlotte Klonk, "volcanism" suggested dramatic, cataclysmic origins of the columns, while "neptunism" implied the gradual building up resulting from repeated precipitation from water or mud.[39] Eventually, the tide of scientific opinion began to swing in favor of the vulcanists. In 1771 a French scientist reasoned that the basalt stacks were of volcanic origin. It was not until 1786, however, when the Anglo-Irish cleric and scientist Rev. William Hamilton published his *Letter Concerning the Northern Coast of Antrim*, that a relatively comprehensive and accurate account of the Causeway became available. Even so, J. C. Curwen, in his discussion of the columns in 1818, took a careful middle ground between fire and water.[40]

Some visitors hailed the Causeway as a profoundly sublime experience. In 1801 James Solas Dodd, viewing the approach to the Causeway from the Portrush side, claimed that it exhibited "an awful wreck of the terraqueous globe." Many of the eighteenth-century visitors, such as Rev. Hamilton himself, were inspired by a vaguely scientific theology that sought for signs of God's design within the forces of nature. Hamilton believed that art and nature were one, and, although he described the complex formations he found in the Causeway as forming "a scene of horror," he also saw evidence of divine design, an orderly universe, "a world self-balanced."[41]

Even by the time Hamilton published his work, the Giant's Causeway had already become a tourist attraction. As noted earlier, the fold-out map in the front of Richard Twiss' 1775 *Tour of Ireland* featured engravings of the Causeway, a marker for Irish tourism as well as for the site itself. However, its renown, coupled with the images of grandeur that its name implied, involved the site in the classic tourist dispute: did it live up to expectations or did it disappoint? For some expecting an instant rush of awe, the Causeway appeared more odd than sublime. One problem lay in the drawings and engravings of the Causeway reproduced in travel books. Although the cliffs rising behind the Causeway and running eastward along the coast can be impressive, the Causeway proper is wide rather than high. As a consequence, illustrators, struggling for effect, tended to exaggerated the height and the "sublime" character of the columns.

Anne Plumptre, in fact, placed part of the blame on those would-be artists who strained to make the site appear dramatic and sublime, instead of adhering to "the truth." Indeed, the endless number of columns tended to bring out the draftsman in some of those who sketched them, making their drawings look more like improbable architectural renditions. Interestingly, one of the best attempts to capture the site was also one of the earliest. Susannah Drury's remarkable gouache painted around 1740 effectively focuses on the width of the site rather than trying to exaggerate its height.[42]

The travel writer's debate about the Giant's Causeway began in the 1770s when the hypercritical Mr. Twiss refused to be impressed. Around the same time, Jacques-Louis de Latocnaye also found the jumble of columns disappointing. In describing the site in 1818, J. C. Curwen recalled the words of Dr. Samuel Johnson: "the Giant's Causeway might be worth seeing, but was not with going to see." Part of the problem lay in the very name of the site, a sort of metamarker recalling the legends of the Irish giant Finn Mac Coul. In some minds it raised expectations that simply could not be met. In 1834, Henry D. Inglis found the Causeway the disappointment of a lifetime. "I had heard of the Giant's Causeway from my earliest childhood; I had read in the guide-books, of the sublimity of this wonderful spectacle; and although I had long ago learned to appreciate the bombast of a guide-book, the very name—the Giant's Causeway seemed inseparably connected with scenes of the sublimest character. Imagination had pictured a far-spread congregation of rocks, broad enough for giants to plant their footsteps on; and wide enough asunder, for the stride of a giant. My picture was dissolved in a moment." Visiting the Causeway in 1849, Lord John Manners grumpily concluded that "...more lies are told of it than of any other wonder of nature...."[43]

Nevertheless, for those willing to spend some time and effort investigating the Giant's Causeway, the site could prove fascinating. Anne Plumptre brought an informed interest in geology to her travel writing. A generation after Bishop Pococke lavished his attention on the columns (and hauled a few away as souvenirs), Plumptre devoted a chapter to the formations, arguing that, in order to appreciate the Causeway, one had to contemplate the basalt columns through minute examination. If visitors were prepared to momentarily surrender the search for overpowering sublime scenery and to speculate instead about the origins of the geological features of the Causeway, they would, as Dr. John Forbes insisted in 1852, experience a "great elemental feeling [of] WONDER...." The sublime, in other words, could be sought within the details of nature. James Johnson enthused over "the romance of geology...wherever the eye wanders, we behold, as it were, a huge laboratory, a supernatural repository of the materials from some incomprehensible undertaking by gods or demons, rather than man!" Even J. C. Curwen, who had confessed to an initial disappointment, admitted, "I had erroneously considered its magnitude to be equal to the wonders in its formation....but I cannot describe the feelings of admiration excited by the examination of is structure or the sentiment with which I was inspired, while I exclaimed— 'Wonderful are the works of God.'"[44]

Antiquarian Landscapes

Ancient and medieval ruins, "antiquities" as they were called, constituted another important feature of the picturesque tour. In Ireland ruins were so ubiquitous and were incorporated into so many picturesque paintings and engravings that Patrick J. Duffy writes about "antiquarian landscapes." Over the centuries, and in some cases millennia, nature had done its best to absorb Ireland's ancient tombs and ruined abbeys and castles. In many cases they were almost buried in ivy, with trees growing from arches and turrets. Today's tourists, visiting a historic site, such as Jerpoint Abbey near Kilkenny, walk through a medieval ruin that has been cleaned and partially repaired. The visitor walks on gravel aisles and enjoys a clear view the stonework, traceries and surviving carvings. Such settings were different two hundred years ago. Inspecting the remains of Holy Cross Abbey in Tipperary in the 1790s, George Holmes found "the east end...so thickly mantled over with ivy that the great window is nearly choked up, admitting but a few partial rays of the sun...." Nature nonetheless produced a pleasing theatrical effect. The few sunbeams that penetrated the foliage "rested upon the tomb of Donald, king of Limerick, the founder, and produced a most happy effect." Arthur Young, found Muckross Abbey at Killarney "half obscured in the shade of some venerable ash trees; ivy has given the picturesque circumstance, which that plant alone can confer...."[45]

The melding of nature's green with the medieval builder's gray stone primarily pleased those whose interest in antiquities did not extend beyond an appreciation of picturesque effects. Those who took the past seriously and actually wanted to see what lay beneath all of that ivy often found conditions frustrating. Blaymire, a dedicated antiquarian touring Connacht in the 1790, struggled with the encumbering trees and ivy at Boyle Abbey in Sligo, trying to take measurements. Exploring a tomb at nearby Rath Muleak, he fell into a hole obscured by sallys, hurt his leg and lost is candle. A few decades later, Richard Colt Hoare, who also had a keen interest in antiquities, complained about the overgrown state of the ruined abbey at Adare in County Kerry. He recommended some "judicious pruning" of the ivy to reveal the building's details. Any such tidying at a site depended upon the proprietor or ecclesiastical authorities, however. The Halls were pleased to report that, where once the ruined cathedral at the Rock of Cashel had to be examined through banks of nettles and weeds, the late Archdeacon Cotton had devoted much of his time to improving the site.[46]

John Dixon Hunt has suggested that the aesthetic appreciation of ruins initially arose from the picturesque fascination with the broken, the rough and the unfinished, which the imagination was called upon to complete. The average tourist, however, found "impressionistic suggestions of decay and loss" much easier to deal with than history or architectural details. In fact, under the spell of the sublime and picturesque, most tourists approached ruins in a spirit more attuned to their emotions than to antiquarian research. Richard Twiss, inspecting some cromlechs in the vicinity of Dublin, felt moved to proclaim: "In contemplating these venerable remains of remote antiquity, the attentive spectator feels almost instantaneously a pleasing train of sensations, more easily to be imagined than described." Travelers frequently reached for one word to describe those emotions: "melancholy." Thus, George Holmes felt overwhelmed by the ruins of Lismore Castle, "lifting its high embattled towers in a kind of *melancholy grandeur*, bordering on sadness...." Although thoughts of past grandeur and power could easily induce this emotion, Lady Chatterton pointed to the principal source of romantic melancholy: "Of all the many venerable objects of antiquity, there is not one that calls forth deeper respect in my mind, than the moldering walls of an old church...." John Harden, seeing the abbey at Adare with Holmes wrote, "there is no walking thru' this venerable pile without feeling a religious melancholy prey on y[ou]r spirit."[47] Travelers contemplating ecclesiastical ruins commonly used the words "melancholy," "gloom," "sadness," "decay" and even "horror."

Not all such emotions were related to the picturesque, however. These mostly Protestant visitors to Ireland were not above scaring themselves with anti-Catholic "gothic" thoughts of monkish "gloom" and "superstition." As Luke Gibbons points out, among the "familiar stage-prompts of the gothic *mise-en-scene*," were ruined castles, graveyards and, of course "moldering abbeys and monasteries." In his book on Killarney Rev. Isaac Weld described the "melancholy and religious awe" he felt at Muckross Abbey. "At the same time," he cautioned, "we cannot behold these ancient fabrics, their dismal aisles, their dark and narrow cells, without drawing a comparison favorable to ourselves between the gloomy and bigoted notions of monkery and the more enlightened opinions of modern day."[48]

Even when observers intended no overt criticism of Catholicism, few failed to comment on their horror and disgust at what must have been the most gothic feature of Irish antiquities, the human remains found in Irish graveyards that were often attached to ruined medieval abbeys and monastic sites. Whether scattered randomly about or heaped in carefully designed arrangements, as at Muckross Abbey, bones were a common accompaniment to the Irish antiquarian landscape. As will be discussed in Chapter Eight, Irish antiquities embodied still other, somewhat gothic associations not normally encountered in Britain. On the roads leading to old graveyards and their ruined churches, visitors frequently heard keening, the traditional sound of Irish lamentation that usually accompanied funeral processions. Also the annual "patterns" held on the feast days of a local saints often took place around ecclesiastical sites. These patterns attracted large numbers of peasants who, after making their devotions, often enjoyed fair-like celebrations involving drinking, dancing and sometimes faction fighting. Obviously, whatever their aesthetic and philosophical implications for the picturesque, Ireland's ecclesiastical antiquities acted as centers for aspects of Irish peasant life that visitors found exotic, bizarre and foreign.

Considerable debate raged regarding the origins of certain types of Irish antiquities. Eighteenth and early nineteenth-century scholars puzzled over the country's pre-Christian past. Ireland is particularly rich in pre-Christian sites— exposed cromlechs or dolmens and passage graves. Welsh antiquary Edward Lhywd visited the famous passage graves around the Bend of the Boyne in 1699 and found the entrance to the great Newgrange tumulus. The intrepid Halls, never to let a bit of dirt and mud deter them, crawled and squirmed along the sixty-foot passage at Newgrange to marvel at inner dome. In 1775 Gabriel Beranger drew the tomb at nearby Dowth, discovered only a few years earlier in 1769. On their sketching tour through Connacht in 1779 Beranger and his artist companion Angelo Maria Bigari produced illustrations of cairns and dolmens, which formed part of the rich prehistoric remains found around the Sligo area.[49] Some eighteenth-century antiquarians believed the passage graves to have been of Christian origin. Later scholars argued for pagan sources, although they split on whether they were of "Gothic" (later "Celtic") northern European origins or "Phoenician," or "Oriental" origins. As Clare O'Halloran has pointed out, questions of national origins lay at the center of these debates. At stake were issues of sectarianism, colonialism and nationalism.[50]

Only a few visitors to Ireland brought with them any real knowledge of these controversies. This did not prevent them from speculating, especially about the one feature of the Irish antiquarian landscape that appealed most to picturesque tourism: the famous round towers. In spite of the fact that these uniquely Irish structures are only found on or in close proximity to medieval monastic sites, the "Phonecianists" maintained that they were pagan fire temples given over to God-knew-what sorts of practices. In spite of the efforts of some Irish antiquarians led by George Petrie to establish their medieval, Christian origins, the more romantic, "Oriental" and pagan notions enlivened popular travel books. The Halls were enamored with the "fire temple" concept, as they were with the idea that Newgrange had been the site of "Druidical" human sacrifices. Until Petrie and his colleagues finally prevailed after 1847, anyone who wished could express an opinion on the round towers. Although familiar with Petrie's ideas, Theresa Cornwallis West, traveling in 1846, remained sufficiently convinced by the structures' Oriental origins to reproduce several sketches of ancient Middle Eastern towers.[51]

With the exception of round towers, most of Ireland's medieval antiquities looked like those travelers had seen in Great Britain. However, their underlying cultural meanings differed profoundly. In Britain Medieval ruins represented visible markers of national identity and told the story of historical progress from feudalism and Roman Catholicism to nationhood and "true religion."[52] Such comforting assumptions could not easily accompany the British tourist across the Irish Sea. In Ireland, if the ruins stood for conquest, the "nation" they represented had been defeated, its religion bereft of its churches and abbeys. Yet neither the sense of an Irish nation nor the country's Roman Catholics had disappeared. One of Daniel O'Connell's "monster meetings," held as part of his Repeal campaign, took place on the Hill of Tara, a site deeply associated with the ancient roots of the Irish nation.

In Ireland the picturesque was where the tourists found it. It was not limited to lakes, falls, mountains or crumbling monasteries. With their eyes trained to spot and organize scenes, tourists were adept at finding a picturesque sight in a chance encounters along the road. This was, and remains, one of the great joys of touring. However, the tourist experience is based on more than simply seeing something. Tourism involves much more than moving from one site to another. The next chapter will examine how tourist experiences were created at some of Ireland's most popular sites.

Chapter 6

THE TOURIST EXPERIENCE

The tourist experience begins and ends in the mind of the visitor, bounded by anticipation and recollection. The experience consists of those on-site activities, encounters, sights, and other sensations, along with any accumulation of souvenirs, that promise to make the tourist's visit memorable. Of course, the experiences of visitors to Ireland varied from one individual to another, depending on interests and itinerary. Many centered their primary experiences on picturesque scenery, trying perhaps to capture it in watercolors or sketches. For others the tourist experience may have included collecting information about schools, roads, ruins, farming practices or poverty. Some busied themselves investigating the conditions of the peasantry, while others were happy enough merely to be entertained by them. At the end of each day tourists made notes, finished sketches, updated their journals, wrote letters and planned the next day's activities.

The process by which a site becomes incorporated into tourism involves a series of steps. Although they often occur in combination with each other, initially there may be a particular sequence. For example, before a site can be toured it first must be "discovered." This means that it is perceptually abstracted from the "ordinary" and placed in the "extraordinary" context of tourism. It becomes a sight that must be seen. Then it must be "marked"—placed on the tourist's mental as well as paper map. Although a tourist sight can be marked in many ways, naming is most important. More than anything else, naming objectifies a sight and places it within the context of tourism. "A waterfall on the Powerscourt Estate" is not the same as "the Powerscourt Waterfall." The first is a part of a proprietor's park; the second, a tourist attraction.

Once marked and named, a site must be made accessible, although actual ease of access may come later. Killarney, for example, had earned its reputation as a tourist spot before it became easy to reach. Access, however, may be perceptual as well as physical. If the site is large and involves more than a single feature, the landscape must be broken up into discrete and recognizable parts that can be viewed in sequence, comprehended easily and remembered. The visitor to Killarney did not just see "the Lakes," but instead engaged in a series of tours around the Lower, Middle and Upper

Lakes, taking in waterfalls, mountains and ruins. In addition, providing perceptual access to a site often involves naming specific features within it. This may entail incorporating a site into a narrative—a history, a story or a legend—thus creating a context within which the place may be appreciated. Eventually, of course, the site itself must be toured, often with the help of guides or guidebooks. There may also be activities and entertainments to engage the visitor, involving them in bits of ritual or even elements of theater. Finally, the visitor may purchase souvenirs, mementos that act as proof of having "been there." Ultimately, these ingredients all combine, not just to create a memorable tourist experience unique to a particular site, but to contribute to the trip as a whole.

Anticipation

Anticipation is a vital aspect of tourism. Long before tourists *see* their destinations, they anticipate them. As James Buzard points out, the anticipation of seeing what one has read about or imagined underlies the tourist's search for the new and different. As travel narratives (the products of previous travelers' experiences) and guidebooks became available, visitors to Ireland knew (or thought they knew) what they were going to see, and, as at the Giant's Causeway for example, they were prepared to compare imagination with reality. Since traveling by horse power took time, the tourist's anticipation for each succeeding site had to sustain itself for a relatively long time. This enforced delayed gratification explains George Holmes' poetical suggestion that anticipation represented "one of the greatest pleasures which the traveler himself experiences.... [It] is his staff, and he naturally leans on it for support: it bears him over many a solitary hill, and by its all consoling help, keeps curiosity alive, and softens his fatigue."[1]

Basing their anticipation upon reading and illustrations, tourists were often satisfied with the results. As a professional travel writer, Anne Plumptre had carefully prepared herself for her visit to Killarney by reading several guidebooks. When she finally visited the Lakes, she had the sense of "renewing an acquaintance of long standing;—everything seemed perfectly familiar to me; I found everything conformable to the ideas arranged in my mind—a strong proof at once of the accuracy of the descriptions given and of the transcendent beauty of the scene, which thus answered the high expectation raised." On the other hand, William Belton, felt disappointment in his initial impression of the Lakes: "I think each tourist has created in his mind an ideal Killarney, which perhaps can scarcely be realized in this world, and of which the actual Killarney falls short." Eventually, he judged Killarney the most beautiful place he had ever seen. However, this was only after he had invoked the picturesque technique of mentally comparing the Lakes to his recollection of similar sites in Scotland and England. For his part Isaac Weld preferred dispensing with the anticipation of seeing frequently described views from prescribed "stations" in favor of spontaneous discovery: "In this as in other instances where the object is of higher import, the pleasure arising from attainment of our desires is often lessened by anticipation during moments of pursuit." It was important, therefore, not to let the travel writer's hyperbole raise unreasonable expectations. Leitch Ritchie warned his readers that the Wicklow Mountains were not really "mountains" but "romantic hills" that occasionally took on some majesty. Like the mountains along the Rhine, he argued, the hills of Wicklow, if they were to be appreciated, had first to be stripped of guidebook exaggeration.[2]

Naming Things

Assigning names to specific features within a site, even to the place itself, is an essential component in the evolution of a tourist destination. Dean MacCannell lists naming as the first step in the "sacralization" of a tourist sight. At the very least, names function as markers, semiotic pointers that help the tourist to "see" and to remember what is seen. The larger the site, the more features within it, the more important naming becomes. Since the visitor requires a landscape that can be recognized, understood, appreciated and remembered, a complex site may, therefore, be broken up and offered to the tourist as discrete elements to be focused upon one at a time. Naming individual features within a landscape greatly facilitates this process. For example, the scores of little islands in the Lakes of Killarney are in reality just so many rocks and bits of land. But once *named* they stand out individually, taking on at least momentary significance. As early as 1751, Richard Barton noted that the rock formations in the Lakes been christened with whimsical names, such as "Man of War."[3]

Indeed, at certain types of tourist sites, such as those containing numerous rock formations, for example, it becomes necessary to individualize such objects with names. In this way, naming functions much like a spotlight that can reconfigure even empty space on a stage. Names also have the effect of making tourists think they "see" more than they actually do. For example, a good cavern guide can kindle and extend a tourist's sense of awe by pointing out specific named rock formations. In 1835 when Robert Graham visited Ireland's best known cave at Michelstown a few years after it had opened, he recalled seeing the "Turkish Tent" and the "Four Courts of Dublin" (complete with stalactites resembling judges' wigs), "St. George's Steeple," the "King's Candelabra," the "Queens Bed" and "Lot's Wife," in addition to several sets of "organ pipes." The formations in a newly opened part of the cave, Graham noted, had not yet acquired their stock of names, although he did see a set of "bells," from which the guides produced some musical tones.[4]

As suggested earlier, the Giant's Causeway on the North Antrim coast presented a particular problem for tourists who might have tired of viewing its endless stacks of basaltic columns. While each basalt polygon is in some way unique, to the average visitor the array of columns may appear as pretty much a jumble of sameness. What has the visitor seen after the tenth or hundredth column? And, of course, how could the poor travel writer describe this remarkable but somewhat repetitive attraction? It helped that, by the beginning of the nineteenth century, guidebooks had divided the site into three sections: the Little, the Middle and the Great Causeway. As at Killarney, such demarcation provided visitors with an instant mini-geography that helped them find their way around. Moreover, by this time, many columns had received names. As early as 1775, Richard Twiss reported that the guides at the Causeway referred to some of the larger basalt formations as "looms" or "organs." In 1814 Anne Plumptre observed the "Giant's Organ," the "Chimney Top" and the "Giant's Well." Several decades later Mr. and Mrs. Hall reeled off a plethora of named formations, including the "Honey Comb," the "Giant's Gateway," the "Giant's Loom," not to mention the "Giant's Ball-Alley," his "Pulpit," his "Bagpipes" and, not to forget, his "Granny"—all suggesting a triumph of tourist nomenclature.[5] It is not clear to what extent, if any, these names had roots in local lore. Naming at tourist sites is often inspired by the inner dynamics of tourism itself and so may draw little or nothing from local traditions or language. Interestingly, the names of the bays and rocks that William Makepeace Thackeray mentions in his mad boat ride along the Causeway's coast appear to be of Gaelic origin, hinting at the very different and older naming habits by which the locals had labeled topographical features important to them.

Myths, Legends, Folklore and Fakelore

However artificial or touristy the "Giant's" this and the "Giant's" that may have sounded, such nomenclature at least derived from the name of the site itself, based in turn on a series of ancient legends and folk tales. According to one version of the story, the giant Finn Mac Coul, to facilitate his planned pummeling of his Scottish counterpart, Bennadonner, built the Causeway so that his neighbor and intended victim would not get his feet wet travelling from Staffa in Scotland to the Antrim coast. In a romantic age, such legends helped to both create and mark the tourist landscape.

So numerous were the legends tied to the topography of Killarney that T. Crofton Croker gathered them into a two-volume collection. From the standpoint of tourism, the most famous and most useful legends concerned "the O'Donoghue," a clan chief whose castle stands on Ross Island by the shore of Lough Leane. O'Donoghues had controlled the lands around Killarney until the death of the O'Donoghue Mór in the Second Desmond war in 1583, after which the territory eventually fell into the hands of the Browne family. In an interesting case where politics merged with local lore, the O'Donoghue became confused or associated with what originally may have been an ancient lake deity. At any rate, on May Day morning, one of the moments in the Celtic calendar when the fairy realms penetrate the world of man, the O'Donoghue could be seen riding his battle steed upon the misty waters of the lake, preceded by a retinue of youths and accompanied by unearthly music[6] One of the early accounts of the story derives from William Ockenden's *Letters Describing the Lakes of Killarney, and Muckross Gardens*, published in the 1760s, one of the first extensive traveler's pieces devoted to the area. Almost every subsequent writer who visited the Lakes repeated the O'Donoghue tale, retaining the essential elements of Ockenden's account. Thomas Moore reinforced (and elaborated upon) the legend in his song "O'Donoghue's Mistress," thereby providing yet another Killarney marker.[7] The O'Donoghue tale, like the stories of Finn Mac Coul at the Giant's Causeway, inevitably generated names for the islands and rock formations around the lakes. In their *Ireland, Its Scenery and Character* (better known as *Halls's Ireland*), the Halls noted that the guides associated almost every unusual rock in the Lake with O'Donoghue—"his horse, his prison, his stable, library, pigeon-house, table, cellar, honeycombs, pulpit, his broom...." The summit of Mangerton also had a similar cache of O'Donoghue memorabilia and tales.[8]

The Halls were content to just report the O'Donoghue myths in their first book. However, in *A Week in Killarney*, originally published in 1843, they tried to explain the phenomenon. They concluded that the O'Donoghue's aquatic rides on May Day morn could be set down to a type of optical illusion encountered in many parts of the world. Luke Gibbons interprets the Halls' explanation as part of a bourgeois "disenchantment of the landscape," the triumph of a "Whiggish" desire for mental, economic and political improvement over the superstitious and ineffective world of the Irish peasant. Still, the Halls gave their readers what they wanted—a good story *and* a rational explanation, which, incidentally, left open the possibility that even the most hard-headed Manchester merchant might see the O'Donoghue "illusion" if the weather were right. The Halls offered their readers neither enchantment nor disenchantment but rather the kind of "theater" that a good tourist site could provide (see below). Thus, smoke and mirrors, even if derived from nature, could make up part of the show. Such stories were gifts to tour guides and travel writers, as long as authenticity was not required. Inevitably, the demands to feed the tourist experience lead to a certain amount of what Richard Dorson has called "fakelore," stories manufactured often for commercial purposes.[9] And, there can be little doubt that guides embellished and perhaps occasionally invented a good story.

The Tourist Experience as Ritual

Sometimes the naming or the association of legends with a site became the basis for tourist rituals. On her tour of one of Killarney's lakes Anne Plumptre's boatmen told her that many of islands and rocks had been named for visitors, and they promptly offered to name a rock to commemorate her visit. The proposed recipient of this honor showed a certain sophistication regarding how names and stories evolved within the context of tourism. Although ready to play along, Plumptre insisted that "I would not...permit my name to be given: as the habit of the world has been ever to pronounce it as if it were a *Plum-tree*, I was sure that the island would never be called anything but *Plum-Tree Island*; and a tradition would soon be affixed to it that it was once covered with *Plum-trees*." So she decided to name the spot "Kean's Island" after a friend. The whole party landed on the designated piece of rock and gathered in a circle, "in midst of which the bugle-horn player came forward, and repeated the proper formulary in a jargon of English, Irish, and Latin, perfectly unintelligible to me, then applying to me as the god mother, I gave the name, which he repeated with the addition of a little more jargon, and the ceremony concluded with throwing down upon the rock a bottle of whiskey," without which, the boatmen explained, the island "would not have been regularly christened...." The baptismal sacrifice of a perfectly good bottle of whiskey surprised the island's "god-mother" until the men suggested that she buy them a bowl of punch "to drink the god-mother's health...." At that point Plumptre admitted: "I then perfectly understood the general eagerness for the christening."[10]

Although she knew that the whole exercise was nonsense, Plumptre played her role in the game, as should any good tourist. Dean MacCannell defines a tourist ritual as "a perfunctory, conventionalized act through which an individual portrays his respect and regard for some object of ultimate value or to its stand-in."[11] Such activities on the part of the tourist and the guides often became embedded in the travel literature and consequently anticipated by subsequent visitors. The most famous Irish example of a tourist ritual still takes place at Blarney Castle, the tower house built in 1446 by Cormac McCarthy of Muskerry in County Cork. Its proximity to Cork city helped to establish the castle's presence on the tourist's beaten track. Although the structure and its grounds are still of great interest, Blarney has long been associated with one of the most peculiar of all tourist rituals—the kissing of a certain stone set in the walls of one of its battlements. According to legend, such an act would bestow upon the celebrant the gift of oratory (or the ability to lie with impunity, as one guidebook put it)—in other words, the gift of "blarney."[12] Kissing the Blarney Stone had not always been the defining moment of the tourist experience at Blarney Castle, however. Chetwood does not mention it in connection with his visit there in 1746. In fact, during the eighteenth-century, the site was generally renowned instead for its landscaping and the panoramic views from its walls. Visitors in the 1770s, such as Arthur Young, were often as impressed by the growing industry in the adjoining village as by the Castle itself. Although *The Itinerant*, a book of engravings of major tourist sites in Britain and Ireland published in 1799, mentions kissing the stone, neither George Holmes nor John Harden, who travelled there in the same decade, refer to it. Nor did Richard Millikin include the stone among the castle's attractions in his extravagantly comic poem, "The Groves of Blarney" (1799), leaving it to "Father Prout" (Francis Mahony) to add a verse in praise of the stone decades later.[13] Certainly, the Blarney Stone appears to have become a more prominent feature of the castle after 1800. Visiting in 1821, T. Crofton Croker mentioned the loquacious powers of "a stone in the highest part of the castle wall," and Anne Plumptre, who visited in 1814, suggests that kissing the stone had become a well-established ritual.[14]

Once established, the ritual seems to have involved different stones at different locations on the castle walls. There were two stones inscribed with dates: the nearly inaccessible "1446" stone and a more easily reached "1703" stone. Accessibility, or the lack there of, seems to have been the criteria for designating "the stone." One in the northeast angle of the wall could be reached only by rope and tackle. During the mid-nineteenth century, a water-worn stone with a depression in the center sat comfortably on the northeast parapet, easily reached by ladies. In order to salute it Anne Plumptre had only to climb a set of winding stairs. A decade later Mrs. Chatterton described a stone that used to project over the machicolations of the old tower, making it difficult to kiss. However, in 1838, she reported: "now [it] lies maimed and helpless, and looking very foolish on the battlements." According to the Halls, a madman had thrown it over the walls where it broke into three pieces. Perhaps this is why J. Sterling Coyne reported in the 1840s that the guides at Blarney could not agree on which stone was "the stone." It was up to the tourist to choose.[15] Nevertheless, some stone—if not *the* stone—has now survived into the new millennium, a token of the enduring power of the tourist ritual at Blarney Castle.

Some tourist rituals appear to have been little more than tourist traps designed by the locals to cage a few coins. Driving about the countryside,

Mary Knott and other visitors to West Clare found their carriages frequently stopped by groups of women spinning by the roadside. The women held a length of yarn across the road and politely demanded a modest "toll." The drivers claimed reluctance to continue, as it would have been "bad luck" to break the string. As a Quaker, Mrs. Knott engaged in charity on her visits to Clare, but she lost patience with the constant repetition of the ritual of the "toll": "If these demands were only occasionally made, they might be complied with; but the inmates of every cottage think they have a right to do so every day. It has now become a complete annoyance, and it is high time that it should be put an end to."[16]

From Ritual to Performance: The Theater of Tourism

Tourism itself is, of course, a type of performance. It begins, as Tim Edensor suggests, with travel accounts and guidebooks that tell the tourist what to visit, perhaps even where to stand, and what to do at each the site. Once described, such performances become imperative: the visitor *must* see that view, sketch that scene, hear the echo. As visitors arrive at a site, the guides take over the stage management and choreograph the tourist's movements.[17]

In the class-based societies of the eighteenth and nineteenth centuries the relative informality of this tourist/guide relationship was somewhat unnatural. In fact, that very abnormality added to the theatricality of such encounters, with each side playing inevitable assigned roles. Thus Philip Crang sees tourism as "a cultural reconstruction of the work place as stage" with performance as the "product." Theron Nuñez, looking for a way to characterize the host-guest interaction, also suggests a "dramaturgical" metaphor: "Tourists and more often their hosts are almost always *on stage* when they meet in face-to-face encounters. They have prepared for their performances backstage; the tourist has read his travel brochures, consulted previous visitors, planned his wardrobe...before going on stage; his host may count the house, assess the mood of the audience, arrange the lighting and props, consult with fellow performers, and rehearse a friendly smile."[18]

This staged aspect of Irish tourism began to manifest itself by the beginning of the nineteenth century. Bits of landscape became incorporated as props in this theater of tourism. Guides might pick out a certain distinctive spot or topographical feature tied to a local legend or, if necessary, invent a story on the spot. With the stage set and a "plot" in hand, the tourist experience then consisted of the interaction among the visitor, the guide and an object or view. In the process both guide and tourist became actors. For example, Wright, in his 1823 guidebook to Killarney observed a particular crab apple tree on the north end of island of Innisfallen. The tree's divided trunk formed a large oblong aperture, called the "eye of the needle." The guides urged ladies to pass through it, assuring them of the benefits of "a certain charm." Wright also described a projecting rock overshadowed by an old yew tree. This so-called "bed of honour" supposedly commemorated the visit of the Duke of Rutland, a former Viceroy for Ireland. Some years later the Halls were introduced to both the "needle" and "the bed." Mrs. Hall squeezed through the former, an act that would, she was assured, "have a powerful influence on the after-destiny of any of the gentler sex who ventured through it." Then she and her husband had to sit on "the bed." However, the Halls found their guide's attempts to explain the traditions behind these objects "confusing and contradictory." In Irish folklore such natural formations as the "eye of the needle" and "the bed" were often associated with fertility or luck in childbirth. While the Halls hinted obscurely at the supposed powers of the "needle," apparently neither they nor their guide were prepared to delve too deeply into the possible significance of the "bed." Perhaps the guide may have been uncertain about the Halls and feared that too clear an explanation of the "bed's" function might have embarrassed his clients. For their part, the Halls—sharing perhaps a similar concern for their readers— feigned ignorance and puzzlement.[19]

As suggested earlier, caves, theatrical by nature, are filled with rock formations that, once illuminated, named and picked out by guides, become props in potentially dramatic displays. Even in the early candle-lit days of tourism, caves offered opportunities for creating dramatic lighting effects. When the Halls visited Mitchelstown Cave their guides pushed forward with their candles to "arrange themselves so that a sudden turn exhibits in an instant one of the most splendid of the caves in all its beauty and grandeur." William Bennett described how, in his visit to Mitchelstown Cave, his guides led him down into a side chamber. When he turned around he found that one of them had remained behind and had placed her candle behind a translucent stalactite screen, producing a ruddy glow. Bennett declared it "a fine effect."[20]

Most tourist theater simply requires a passive audience. At the subterranean river at the Pigeon Hole near Cong, Mayo, the Halls, like many visitors before them, encountered a "crone," who first showed them the "holy trout" that had lived there "since St. Patrick blessed the abbey of Cong." Then she lit some straw and cast it upon the underground stream, which carried it along, briefly lighting the further reaches of the cavern. The Halls were impressed. "Although the entire of this singular natural excavation was exhibited but for a moment, the sight was very startling, and it is worth a far longer pilgrimage to see it." By the time Dr. William Wilde visited the spot in the 1860s, however, the presentation of the Pigeon Hole had evolved into a melodramatic performance. "Lo! Presently on the top of one of these immense blocks stands for a moment a weird female figure, bearing a lighted flambeau, the *genius loci*—the Meg

Merrilies [sic] of the scene. Away she flits—darkness again...then, emerging from an unobserved passage, she stands on another and more distant crag, with her white locks, and pale aged face, personifying the banshee of the ancient Firbolgs. She hurls stones into the deep pools beneath, and utters a loud wail, that reverberates through the cavern, till the repeated echoes fade into the distance, and we watch the lurid light of the expiring *glossogs* she has thrown on the waters...."[21] Wilde did not spoil this somewhat gothic presentation with any thoughts about an old woman having to pursue this method of earning a pittance. Tourists seldom think beyond the show.

The more features that can be discovered or invented and crammed into a site, the more opportunities the locals have for delineating the theater of tourism, while multiplying the opportunities for tips. The Giant's Causeway offers some modest examples. Ritchie recorded the presence of "a smoke-dried carline [who] gives you to drink of the Giant's Well, a spring of pure water which oozes up between two of the pillars, and which, on tasting, you find to have been miraculously converted *in transitu* by the old witch into whisky [sic]." Visiting the spring a few years later, Thackeray described "an old grey hag beside, who has been there for hundreds and hundreds of years, and there sits and sells whisky [sic] at the extremity of creation! How do you dare to sell whisky there, old woman? Did you serve Old Saturn with a glass when he lay along the Causeway here? In reply, she says, she has no change for a shilling: she never has; but her whisky is good." Twenty years later this particular tourist experience had become more elaborate, if somewhat abstemious. In 1865 when William Barry visited the spot, the drink seller was an old man and his potation mere water. However, he had custody over the adjacent "Wishing Chair." Ian Ousby maintains that the cult of the sublime encouraged the tendency for tourists to treat natives serving at tourist sites as "stage extras." Thus, the ease by which an old woman may become a "carline," a "witch," "hag," or in Dr. Wilde's account of the Pigeon Hole, a Meg Merrilees. Such conceits represent the tourist's imagination embroidering the details of his experience. Unfortunately, the process tended to demean those who worked the sites.[22]

As suggested earlier, a literary marker, such as a novel, a poem, a song or a legend, might endow a site with qualities that the tourist then expects to encounter. Thomas Moore's song about Glendalough not only helped to fix the "gloomy" image of the place, it also helped popularize the legend of St. Kevin and Kathleen. Eventually, as tourism grew, it became customary for a peasant woman to show visitors St. Kevin's bed on its rock ledge above the lake by demonstrating how the unfortunate Kathleen had climbed up to it. These women were, of course, always called "Kathleen." Thomas Carlyle, visiting Glendalough during the Famine, was more alert than most tourists to the grim reality beneath any show offered him. He recalled seeing a "woman squirrel clambering on the rocks to show St. Kevin's Bed, which needed no 'showing' at all; husband had deserted her, children all dead or in workhouse…a shed under a cliff; food as the ravens." While there is no suggestion that the "Kathleens" actually dived into the chilly waters of the lough, Theresa Cornwallis West described the woman descending "from her perilous post on the rocks, for a shilling; then, remounting, she woke the echoes with shriek, and dived into the Saint's Bed,—a hole in the side of the cliff, turning in it three times for our sakes, by which our souls are in some way benefitted."[23] It is impossible to know whether this particular Kathleen's "blessing" represented the incorporation of folklore or fakelore into her routine. Either way, it added to the tourist theater at Glendalough.

Exploitation never lay far beneath the surface of these peasant "performances." In the West of Ireland, tourists were sometimes entertained by watching the daring endeavors by which the locals made their living. Martin Haverty, in his account of the trip of the Ethnological Section of the British Association to the Aran Islands in 1857, saw a piece of peasant life turned into tourist theater. The august assemblage was "treated to a view of [an] appalling feat performed in the most perfect manner." Fifteen or twenty islanders used homemade ropes to lower themselves down a cliff face to gather gulls' eggs. Haverty described one man of around sixty, who, having tied the rope about his waist, descended, "striking the rock with his foot, holding the rope with one hand, and preserving his balance with the other, [he] flew, as it were, outwards and downwards, his feet constantly moving like paddles in the air…[when] in imminent danger of being dashed to pieces, he struck out again with a bold and graceful movement, until at last, becoming smaller to our eyes as he descended, he reached the bottom." The grandees of the society applauded at the end of this feat, which Haverty assured his readers, did not really seem to be particularly dangerous because of the men's experience.[24]

In the 1830s Mary Knott described a similar exhibition—bird catching—on Clare's Atlantic coast. A dozen or so men approached a cliff above the ledges where sea birds nested. They then sat one behind the other, holding a rope, the free end of which one man tied around his waist. That man then rappelled down the cliff face to a lower ledge. Another man then joined the first. Both deployed long sticks with nooses at one end, with which they caught sea birds, wringing their necks before putting them in a basket. In this way, according to Mrs. Knott, each man earned 2s. 6d. to 3s. per day for the birds' down. Even the retrieval of sheep from the cliff ledges became an exciting spectator sport for Mary Knott and her friends: "It is customary for persons to go from Kilkee to see the hardy coast climbers ascend to bring the sheep down." She describes the relief of the "anxious spectators, whose nerves are strongly excited during the perilous descent." Nevertheless, she assured her readers that "practice from childhood enables the men to scale and overlook these giddy heights without danger."[25]

Similar feats take place today in what John Urry calls "tourist space," the contrived and artificial performance areas that supposedly represent for visitors the "real life" of the locals. Setting up a fake village, for example, allows the natives to earn money by pretending to be "real," while keeping the tourists away from what *is* real—the natives' own private space.[26] The Irish peasant enjoyed no such protection from the tourist gaze. It is not clear to what extent these exhibitions in rappelling were organized for the benefit of the tourists and to what extent the tourist audience formed spontaneously to watch them. Either way, such activities were very much a part of everyday peasant life in the West of Ireland. Witnessed or not, the peasant's reward for going over a cliff, some gulls' egg or a bag of down, remained the same. At the very least, the tourists were spying on a particularly risky slice of peasant life. If not quite exploitative, it was certainly voyeuristic. By turning peasant life into theater, the tourists, without admitting it, could take vicarious pleasure in watching the natives risk their lives, while reassuring themselves from the safety of their vantage point that no real risk was involved.

Reading through travel narratives, it is difficult to distinguish the "authentic" from the "staged," assuming that in the context of tourism there *is* any real difference between the two. For example, visitors to pre-Famine Ireland often came upon outdoor peasant dances, organized by the locals themselves for their own enjoyment. However, as tourism increased, it appears that dances were sometimes staged at popular tourist sites for the visitors' entertainment. An anonymous author writing in 1853 described such a performance during a picnic at Lady Kenmare's cottage at Killarney. After the meal, a fiddle came out and one of daughters of the woman who ran the concession danced with a boatman while the visitor's sketched the scene. The Halls reported a similar scene in their guidebook to the Lakes.[27]

Still, tourists occasionally create their own experiences without the help of the locals. Through their graffiti, for instance, they physically memorialize their presence, as if to make themselves a permanent part of the landscape. At Glendalough, the Halls noted that the area around St. Kevin's Bed above the upper lough contained the initials of visitors, those of Sir Walter Scott among them, carved there by his son. At the Giant's Causeway the Halls found numerous initials carved on the columns around a formation known as "Lord Antrim's Parlour," the earliest dated 1717.[28]

In the vicinity of Ventry on the Dingle Peninsula, M. F. Dickson and her party bestowed names such as "Merlin Cliff" and "Elfin Cove" on intriguing parts of the a strand. Visitors to Kilkee invented their own theater of nature.

Lady Chatterton particularly admired a rocky inlet the visitors had dubbed "the amphitheatre—or better the Theater, having the sea as its stage." According to Dickson, the "amphitheatre," while affording a particularly good view of the bay, also provided a gathering point for the seasonal residents. She recalled that when the waves crashed dramatically and the wind blew from the right direction, "the amphitheatre is then 'in beauty,' and the whole *village of visitors* flock to admire the scene." There were even occasional concerts given there for the assemblage. Those who ventured too far out along the rocks, however, risked being knocked down by a rogue wave, as happened to the Dickson herself.[29]

Sometimes tourists malevolently turned peasants into unintended performers. M. F. Dickson's party came across some children dancing on the strand. Unfortunately, one of her group spoiled the charming scene: "How vexed I was with my companion for throwing pence amongst them, thereby awakening sordid passions, and disturbing the harmony of their innocent amusement!" The author of *A Sportsman In Ireland* expressed his annoyance at the English "gentlemen" who amused themselves by tossing ha'pence from their car at the crowds of poor on road into Killarney. One offered a "miserable" youth a crown if he could keep up with the coach over the broken flint, and laughed when the child collapsed in exhaustion.[30]

The Tourist Site as Social Space

At some point during the first half of the eighteenth century, a visitor to the Giant's Causeway would have had the place pretty much to himself, except for a few peasants gathering kelp. Admittedly, his or her experience there would have been a somewhat lonely one, accompanied primarily by wind, waves and rocks. Toward the end of the century, however, such a solitary, nature-filled moment would have been difficult to achieve. In the process of becoming a popular site, the Causeway had become overrun with guides, boatmen, vendors and beggars, not to mention tourists. It was society rather than nature that really defined the tourist experience at the Giant's Causeway.

Tourists at most such sites find themselves confronted by what some tourism specialists today identify as "heterogeneous spaces," the result of what Tim Edensor calls "an unplanned and contingent process" produced by tourism itself. "As part of a mixed purpose space," Edensor continues, "facilities co-exist with local small businesses, shops, street vendors, public and private institutions, and domestic housing...." The heterogeneous spaces in pre-Famine Ireland were peopled, as noted above, by guides, jarvies, beggars and vendors, all vying for the tourists' attention. For example, visiting a sea cave near the Giant's Causeway, Ritchie encountered a group of functionaries, in addition to boatmen and guides, all of whom sought employment or at least a tip: "One man fires the pistol which produces the echo prescribed by the books; another professes to keep the path to the cave clear for your honour's feet."[31]

Although proprietors and businessmen organized the basic infrastructure of Irish tourism—roads, inns, on-site access—the locals, sometimes under the direction of landlords or entrepreneurs but often on their own, filled in the details of the tourist experience. They were quick to understand the many ways by which they could provide services or entertainment for visitors and, in the process, earn some money, thereby creating for themselves a place within the tourist economy. This now familiar feature of modern tourism developed early in the process. Tourists arriving in 1750 at the entrance to England's Peak Cavern in Darbyshire found the entrance surrounded by a growing cluster of poor cottages belonging to those who supported themselves as guides, cavern singers and beggars. Many visitors expressed their disgust at what their own presence had conjured up.[32] Travelers in Ireland had similar reactions. Tourists there complained of the swarms of guides and beggars. Yet, the visitors were never at a loss for a body to carry a bag, to fetch something, to answer a question or to show the way, all for a coin.

There were, in fact, few places in Ireland so remote that someone would fail to pop up to offer a tourist assistance when needed. Journeying from Derrynane to Caherciveen on a particularly slow-witted Kerry pony, Jonathan Binns became lost on a desolate mountain. Suddenly "a tall, wild-looking man, with long hair floating in the wind, without shoes and stockings, and nearly without clothes, made his appearance...." Although the man spoke only Irish, he figured out Binns' destination, and he acted as a guide the rest of the way. During the Famine, William Bennett took time out from his relief efforts to do some sightseeing. He and his party, having rounded a part of the Mayo coast by boat, were dropped off to make their way back to Rossport on foot. When they came to a stream, the gentlemen crossed it "in a manner not uncommon in this country by hailing a stout fellow at a distance, who voluntarily offers his back, and is more than satisfied by a few pence from the stranger." Sometimes the traveler required no initiative at all in summoning help. While standing by a stream, wondering if he should wet his boots to cross it, Ritchie suddenly found himself "caught up by some one behind, carried with great rapidity through the stream, and set down dryshod on the other side. My bearer was a very young girl, who had taken this mode, not uncommon here, of earning a penny." Stubborn determination, goaded by necessity, often forced both children and adults into physically exhausting and humiliating attempts to earn a coin. Carlyle tells how one "beggar" ran for two or perhaps three miles, following his party's car. When the travelers reached their destination, they permitted the man to carry their coats for a shilling. In post-Famine Connemara the open tourist cars were often accompanied for miles by swarms of barefoot girls, running alongside, trying to sell the passengers hand-knit stockings or wildflowers.[33]

Peasant Sales and Services

When considered at this immediate and very personal level, tourism can be seen as a self-organizing system. In Ireland the mere presence of tourists created innumerable small but vital opportunities for the locals to earn a bit of cash—the only limitations being the locals' imagination and of the good humor and patience of the tourists. So desperate for whatever money they might garner, and no doubt curious about the visitors with their fine clothes and carriages, Irish peasants inundated travelers with proffers of aid, food, drink, souvenirs and calls for alms. Sometimes their presence was relative unobtrusive. Climbing around the Hag's Jaw near the Cliffs of Moher, Mary Knott described how "the little girls from the cabins nearest to the top, followed the travellers with dishes of potatoes smoking from the pot, and butter or milk. They do not press the provisions, the best the house affords; neither ask for payment, but thankfully receive a trifle; for, as may be supposed, in this wild region money is an object of much rarity."[34]

Often, however, the competition for the tourists' attention and pennies overwhelmed the quiet contemplation of nature. Rev. Wright complained that when visitors to Killarney sat down to rest within a grotto near O'Sullivan's Cascade, hoping to reflect on the wonders of nature, they were inevitably startled by the sudden appearance of inhabitants of the glens and mountains prepared to sell them "the wild fruit of their happy vales."[35] At Killarney these delights tended to be wild strawberries or the fruit of the arbutus or "strawberry tree," neither of which are particularly tasty. Or the visitors might have been offered that bane of Irish tourism—goat's milk laced with *potín*.

Managing to get and to hold a prominent position as a guide or vendor at a popular site probably called forth a high degree of self-assertion. In 1865 William Whittaker Barry felt that any description of the Giant's Causeway would be incomplete without some notice of "a pretty young woman with flaxen hair and a red petticoat, who takes up her position there to sell fossils and photographs." Barry suggested that the gentleman visitors were better disposed to her than were the ladies, one of whom recorded in her guide book that the Giant's Causeway would do well enough "were it not for that young fiend in a red petticoat" "Ah! My lady," Barry commented, "that child of Nature possess those artless ways of pleasing which you, born to wealth and dignity, and continually moving in the drawing-rooms of the rich, have endeavored in vain to acquire." The girl had apparently been at her station at the Causeway since childhood.[36]

Irish peasants offered one service, essential to any tourist site—the sale of souvenirs. Part of the tourist experience is the accumulation of artifacts that can be taken back home, where they become reminders, as well as markers, of particular attractions. In some ways souvenirs help to justify a journey, making tourists feel that they have indeed been somewhere different and seen extraordinary things. In fact, Nelson H. H. Graburn, in defining tourism as a "sacred journey," identifies souvenirs as the tourist's "holy grail." The nature of the journey and the destination determine what the traveler should bring home as a totemic reminder of the trip and proof of its success.[37] Of course, in pre-Famine Ireland tourists could and did produce some of their own souvenirs— notes, letters, sketches, watercolors—but they also purchased items to take home. The Halls were particularly good in reporting on the availability of quality goods, such as "tabbinet," fine hand-loomed cloth made in the Liberties of Dublin, or Limerick gloves so delicate that they fit into a walnut nutshell. At Killarney tourists could buy toys and boxes made from the wood of the arbutus, a Mediterranean shrub that grows to tree size at the Lakes. The Halls had hardly settled into their Killarney hotel "before a fair messenger from one of the 'arbutus factories' makes her appearance, and with winning looks and wiling words endeavors to effect sales from the full basked she carries with her."[38]

Everyone who visited the Giant's Causeway complained of being constantly pestered by boys selling rock samples or "specimens." On her visit there Anne Plumptre admired a particular crystal but not its asking price. The persistent seller followed her about all day. By the time the price had fallen from a guinea to five shillings, the testy tourist was too angry to buy it. Ritchie complained that at the Causeway "more than a dozen men and boys follow you through the whole adventure, in spite of your expostulations, to offer boxes of mineralogical specimens." He found it impossible to refuse them and so bought the lot, asking that only the best pieces be sent to his hotel. Ritchie did not expect to be further troubled by any specimens, but to his surprise found his entire purchase intact and waiting for him. He admitted his surprise: "After all, there are so many good points in the character of this unhappy people, that I am sometimes tempted to blame myself for speaking the truth about the bad ones."[39]

At certain sites, such as Killarney and the Giant's Causeway, taking to water offered visitors a special, indeed, a rather dramatic experience. In the theater of tourism, however, tourists do not always play the dominant role; sometimes the role dominates them. At the Causeway Robert Graham found himself hurried into a boat to see the basaltic columns from the sea, in spite of rather rough weather. "For this achievement," he later grumbled, "I paid five shillings more, and I should have been happy to have compromised for ten shillings, if they [the boatmen] had saved themselves the trouble and me the glory of having gone the last two miles on the water." Upon emerging from his hotel near the Causeway, Thackeray, too, found himself besieged by boatmen: "I had no friends, I was perfectly helpless. I wanted to walk down to the shore by myself, but they would not let me, and I had nothing for it but to yield myself into the hands of the guide who had seized me...four men seized a boat, pushed it shouting into the water, and ravished me into it.... we were up one swelling wave that came in a huge advancing body ten feet above us, and were plunging madly down another...before I had leisure to ask myself why the duce I was in that boat, with four rowers hurrooing and bounding madly from one high liquid mountain to another—four rowers whom I was bound to pay." Not for the first time, and certainly not the last, had the tourist experience become a mold into which guides expected the tourist to fit. Thackeray advised future visitors to elude the boatmen if they could and take a good look at the state of the ocean to see if they wished to venture out on it. "For after all," he reminded his readers, "it must be remembered that it *is* pleasure we come for—that we are not *obliged* to take those boats."[40]

Guides and Jarvies

Even as guidebooks became more available, tourists in Ireland still needed real guides, who often doubled as car drivers or jarvies. They not only pointed out the sights and acted as translators, but they were also expected to supply "information," the quality of which, however, could not be taken for granted. Jonathan Binns warned his readers that Irish drivers "do not scruple to make the most confident assertions on matters with which they are perfectly unacquainted." Rejoicing in the gullibility of some of his fellow travel writers, Thackeray relished reporting on "the glee with which a gentleman in Muster told me how he had sent off MM. Tocqueville and Beaumont 'with *such* a set of stories.' Inglis was seized, as I am told, and mystified in the same way. In the midst of all these truths, attested with 'I give ye my sacred honour and word,' which is the stranger to select? And how are we to trust philosophers who make theories upon such data?"[41]

According to Dennison Nash, in the unique type of social space that tourism creates, "tourists are separated from their hosts by the facts of strangerhood, the work-leisure distinction, and whatever cultural differences obtain in a particular situation." Nevertheless, tourism forces strangers, hosts and guests, to interact with each other across linguistic, class and ethnic boundaries. On the host's part this calls for a variety of communication skills and careful organization, not to mention an acute sense of opportunity and ingenuity, especially in the face of language barriers. Not surprisingly, in Ireland would-be guides competed with one another, inundating tourists with offers of their services. James Johnson declared the Killarney guides "an amusing race. They swarm about the hotels like the Hindoos and Mahomedans [sic] on the beach at Madras, when there is a fresh arrival from Europe." (Johnson's comment suggests that he was well travelled, while his "Oriental" reference fixes the Irish guides in their place on the social and even ethnic scales.) In the Halls' classic account of the Giant's Causeway, the visitor, having arrived at the hotel on the edge of the Causeway, strolls to the back door to check the weather before inspecting the site: "The instant he shows himself, he is surrounded by THE GUIDES!" Indeed, upon exiting the back door of Mrs. Henry's Hotel, Thackeray found himself surrounded by a mob that proceeded to "yell and bawl incessantly.... 'I'm the guide Miss Henry recommends,' shouts one. 'I'm Mr. Macdonald's guide,' pushes another. 'This way,' roars a third, and drags his prey down to a precipice; the rest of them clambering and quarrelling after."[42]

There may have been a bit more order to this apparent chaos than the average tourist could discern. The Halls reported that most of the guides at the Causeway seemed to have been members of the extended MacMullen family. The Earl of Antrim appointed one of them, Neil MacMullen, as his "chief guide." Peasants outside this inner circle may have made it a point to meet the tourists' cars *before* they arrived at the Causeway, as did the one who intercepted Ritchie: "He kept up with the vehicle by running; and in the meanwhile, took care to describe the country as we passed, in order to show us that he had already entered upon his office."[43]

For all of the helter-skelterism with which some travel writers liked to invest their Irish guides, these men played an essential role in creating the Irish tourist experience. In addition to their more obvious functions, they worked the direct interface between the upper- and middle-class British visitors and the Irish peasantry. In Gaelic-speaking areas, the guides acted as translators, but, as Michael Cronin suggests, they were really interpreters of culture. In most tourist situations the guides are "generally part of the host community and as such are conduits for privileged 'inside' information on the society and culture. They confer authenticity and verisimilitude on that account. For this reason, the interpreter may become as much an object as an instrument of inquiry in travel writing."[44]

Although travel writers tended to scorn the peasants who crowded about them, as often as not, they found the guide they hired at least satisfactory, and sometimes extraordinary enough to be gratefully named in print. Like most visitors to the Giant's Causeway, Mrs. Plumptre complained bitterly about being pestered by guides. She nevertheless commended her chose, a man named Currie, The Halls sang the praises of the Spillane's, father and sons, who became famous bugling guides at Killarney, performers in every sense of the word. At Glendalough Ritchie enjoyed the services of Joe Irwin, a well-known guide whose "invention" of tales and "his carelessness of dress" constituted his "genius." The Halls described George Wynder, Irwin's successor, as "a wild and picturesque-looking fellow, with loose drapery and a long beard."[45] When he visited Glendalough, this "ragged bearded genius of a guide" regaled Thackeray with stories of the other famous writers he had served: "This is the spot which Mr. Henry Inglis particularly admired, and said it was exactly like Norway. Many's the song I've heard Mr. Sam Lover sing here—a pleasant gentleman entirely. Have you seen my picture that's taken off in Mrs. Hall's book? all the strangers know me by it, though it makes me much cleverer than I am."[46] The Halls were enthusiastic although patronizing champions of Irish guides, whom, they insisted, "are the most amusing fellows in the world; always ready to do anything, explain any matter, go anywhere; for if the Tourist proposed a trip to the moon, the guide will undertake to lead the way—'Bedad he will, wid all de pleasure in life.' They are inevitably heart-anxious to please; sparing no personal exertion...." Rev. Caesar Otway had his own system for choosing a guide. He advised the traveler to find a young lad of twelve or thirteen or an old woman: "...the boy's fresh memory and youthful unsuspectingness would have helped me to all the traditional lore he had heard during the winter's night; or the old woman, from her garrulity, *when properly managed*, would have poured forth all her store."[47]

Such patronizing attitudes placed Irish guides in a sort of double bind when interacting with visitors. If Paddy did not talk, he seemed surly. If he did, his loquaciousness rendered him suspect of having, in the words of Michael Cronin, "a characteristically female attitude to language and truth, spendthrift with the former and economical with the latter."[48] But then, part of Paddy's function in filling out the tourist experience lay in his speech and its entertainment value. In the hands of the travel writers the brogue and its accompanying locutions provided readers with humor of the Stage-Irish variety. Yet, in light of Philip Crang's idea that tourism forces both locals and tourists to assume and perform assigned roles, it seems likely that the writers, while they no doubt embellished it, did not totally invent the kind of blarney they quoted in their accounts. A bit of stage Irishry was often part of the guide's performance, expected and therefore delivered *and* rewarded (tips completing the feedback loop between a guide's performance and a tourist's appreciation). At Killarney Theresa Cornwallis West not only enjoyed the music of one of the Spillanes but also the banter between the bugler and her boatmen: "Listening to their *bon mots* and witticisms, rather distracted my attention from the scenes before me; it was the first opportunity ever afforded me of hearing the genuine Irish humor in full play, and I entered into it heartily." She went on to provide some examples of what amounted to a bit of performance the Kerrymen put on for their client. As Crang suggests, "talk" is one of the "consuming practices" that characterizes tourism, resulting in the "commoditization of many...forms of talk...." Given the social inequalities that characterized Irish tourism, the roles that each party assumed shaped and structured such talk. The guide's patter and persona constituted part of the service he offered, and most travel writers seem to have been impressed and often pleased by the Irish guides' ability to cut through the class barriers and to establish themselves as personalities.[49]

Beggars

This sort of interaction between host and gust, guide and tourist, extended even to the beggars who populated virtually every stop on the tourists' itinerary. Whether at tourist sites or outside hotels and shops in the towns or cities, from the moment they arrived until they left, tourists were regaled with pleas for alms. Outside of the Kenmare Arms in Killarney town John Barrow's coach encountered a mob of would-be guides and souvenir sellers, with the outer circle filled in by beggars. The latter "chime in with their pious ejaculations, blessing and praying, and preserving his honour's long life, and his your honour's father and mother, and his wife and children...." Interchanges between beggars and visitors sometimes reached the level of impromptu tourist theater. Inglis reported on an exchange between some beggars and a passenger in a coach. When the tourist claimed that he had nothing less than half-crowns, the beggars responded with, "May your honour never have less...." When the passenger claimed, "'You would take my coat off my back," they answered, "And if your honour gave it with good will, maybe we would."[50]

The Halls, who peopled their travel books with happy-go-lucky Irish peasants, nevertheless urged their readers to look beyond the beggars' entertainment value: "Their wit and wisdom are as proverbial as their rags and wretchedness, and both too frequently excite a laugh at the cost of serious reflection upon their misery and the means by which it might be lessened. Age, decrepitude, imbecility and disease surround the car the moment it stops." This represented the darker side of the beggar's contribution to the tourist experience. Reaching the town of Kildare in 1822, Thomas Reid tried to count the beggars as he had in Ulster. However, "they were so excessively frequent" as to render the task was impossible. By the time he arrived in Macroom, Cork, he had to report that "the number of beggars that surrounded the coach, during this short time, exceeded anything I had before seen." Their "wretchedness" left him deeply disturbed.[51] Chapter Nine will discuss how the extent and depth of Irish poverty usually managed to cut through the visitors' most romantic, or, for that matter, cynical attitudes.

British travel writers often presented their exchanges with beggars as though they were performances. However, the beggar-tourist relationship occurred within a context more complex than many seemed to realize. Rev. Spencer T. Hall understood something of the social context of Irish begging. Although he complained about the beggars following him into the shops, he had to admit that "it was impossible not to respect the humanity of the shopkeepers in allowing it." He believed that the habit of begging in Ireland arose originally "out of a virtue": "...[I]t is my serious belief that, when they [the Irish poor] have the means, there is scarcely to be found on earth another such a race of unselfish GIVERS!" It seemed natural, he wrote, that, since they gave when they had food, they would ask for it when did not. Hall, among other observes, noted that Irish beggars who received something would then beg for those who had not.[52]

There could be a kind of reciprocity involved in the beggars' request and the donor's gift. As Mary Louise Pratt suggests, reciprocity is "the basis for social interaction" in non-capitalist societies.[53] The Irish beggars, part of an almost pre-capitalist peasant society, pulled the British tourists into a kind of relationship involving two possible forms of reciprocity. First, the beggars were an integral part of a Roman Catholic society that regarded the giving of charity as part of a religious duty. In this context begging constituted part of a social/spiritual "contract," in which, having acted as a vehicle for good works, the beggar bestowed a blessing in response to a gift. Unfortunately, some Protestant tourists may have felt that they had received little in return for their coins. There was another kind reciprocity involved with begging, however—if only on a psychological level. The tourist's superior social status and sense of self-importance were reinforced by the beggars, who usually addressed even middle-class travelers as "your Honour." If they gave, the tourists experienced a philanthropic sense of well-being; if they did not give, they reasserted their moralistic insistence that unearned gifts could damage the character of the recipient. Either way, their egos received a boost, and that, too, was part of the complete tourist experience.

Of course, not all tourists insist on the "complete" experience. The author's late father-in-law is alleged to have driven his family from Pennsylvania to Arizona to see the Grand Canyon. When they got there, everyone jumped out of the car and went up to the Canyon's rim. "Still there," he said and then piled the family back in the car and drove home. This is tourism reduced to its barest, minimalist act. Go to it; see it; leave it. For the most part, however, tourism is usually more complicated than that. A visit to a tourist site is like taking up a blank slate or an empty glass; it needs to be filled in or filled up. And so things must happen to engage the tourist with the site. An experience or set of experiences must be created. As this chapter has suggested, visitors and locals, from the landlords to the beggars, willy-nilly managed to create a wide variety of opportunities for engagement with Ireland's tourist sites. The next chapter, using Killarney as a kind of case study, will demonstrate how all of the elements of picturesque tourism came together at a complex site to create the ultimate in the Irish tourist experience.

Chapter 7

KILLARNEY—A CASE STUDY OF THE IRISH TOURIST EXPERIENCE

By Killarney's Lakes and fells,
  Emerald Isles and winding bays;
Mountain paths, and woodland dells,
  Mem'ry ever fondly strays,
Bounteous nature loves all lands,
  Beauty wanders ev'rywhere;
Footprints leaves on many strands
  But her home is surely there!
Angels fold their wings and rest
  In that Eden of the west,
Beauty's Home, Killarney,
  Ever fair Killarney.

By the time Edmund Falconer and William Balfe published their song "Killarney" in 1861, the Lakes had been Ireland's preeminent scenic attraction for well over a century.[1] With mountains rising steeply from its shores, Killarney held out promises of the sublime. In 1764 John Bush described these "horrible and frightful precipices," using the stock vocabulary of the sublime that would soon be applied to the British Lake District. As Luke Gibbons suggests, the opening up of Killarney to tourists after the 1740s represented "one of the founding moments of European Romanticism."[2]

As far back as 1735, Lord Orrery had described the area in a letter to his friend John Kemp: "This Llaugh [sic] is one of the Beauties of Nature, exclusive of Art... It is a vast Lake of Water in which forty & fifty little islands, all cover'd with wild Evergreens, stand erect. The high mountains, that are its Boundaries, are likewise cover'd, in the same Manner with Arbutus, Oak, Holly & Yew.... Eccho [sic] lives in the Woods; & the Musick of a Pack of Hounds, chasing the Stag up & down the almost perpendicular Hills, made a Harmony much more agreeable to the Ears than one of Handle's best Chorus's." While one might question his lordship's taste in music, his account did pick out most of the essential features of Killarney, described hundreds of times in subsequent letters, journals and books. By as early as 1777, in his *Philosophical Survey of the South of Ireland*, Thomas Campbell ignored the Lakes because he felt they already had been described so often. Killarney, therefore, provides a kind of case study that illustrates how all of the elements of tourism in pre-Famine Ireland came together to create a total tourist experience in the age of the picturesque tour.[3]

As Lord Orrery observed, Killarney combines the lush beauty of lakes and tree covered islands with the dramatic mountain scenery. In his 1756 description Charles Smith added waterfalls: "the lofty mountains hanging over the lake wooded almost to their summits; cascades pouring down from several of them...." Running from south to north, the three distinct but connected lakes begin with the Upper Lake, joined by the two-and-a-half-mile Long Range River to the Middle or Muckross Lake, which in turn connects to the largest of the three, Lough Leane. While the land to the north and east of the middle and lower loughs is generally flat, mountains rise abruptly from the southern and western shores. Behind the western mountains rear the Macgillycuddy Reeks, which include some of the highest mountains in Ireland, five or six peaks rising over 3000 feet. The Gap of Dunloe, carved like Lough Leane by glaciers, parallels the Lakes and climbs between the Macgillycuddy Reeks and the Tomies and Purple Mountain. The Gap was a particularly popular attraction for the seeker of the sublime. Writing around 1840, the anonymous author of *The Sportsman in Ireland* reveled in its dark power: "The entrance to the Gap is very narrow, and the mountains on either side are perpendicular. The pass is directed by the side of a small black lake—black from the reflection of the high and perpendicular mountains which overshadow it—and narrows so fearfully, yet so wildly, that many have failed in achieving the ascent from the horror which is calculated to overwhelm timid and nervous persons."[4]

The climate of this corner of Kerry contributed to Killarney's uniqueness. Winter comes early and stays long in Killarney's mountains. In the valleys and along the lake shore, however, the climate, although very wet, is generally mild. Combined with the contributions from migratory birds, this has made the Lakes home to a variety of Mediterranean and even American plants not generally found elsewhere in Ireland or Great Britain. With no killing frosts, many of Killarney's plants and trees tend to keep on growing throughout the year, producing a lush flora. In fact, one Mediterranean shrub, the *arbutus unedo* grows to the size of a tree in Killarney, where it is often called the "strawberry tree" from the bright red fruit that it produces in fall.[5]

According to T. J. Barrington, "Kerry has little climate but much weather." If a "rain day" is defined as producing 0.2mm of precipitation, then Killarney is blessed with between 200 and 250 such days a year. A rain day is not necessarily a full day of rain, however. On the average the rain might last three-and-a-half hours. In Ireland, where the weather and therefore the light is so variable, the character of a place like Killarney can quickly change from calm beauty to wild mists and storms, and back again over a short space of time. George Holmes, visiting in the 1790s, described being caught on the lakes in a sudden storm: "Before we reached the island of Innisfallen, the face of the lake became totally changed; the sky began to lower, and darkened the surface of the water, assuming an alarming aspect.... Thick mists hung down the hills and hid them entirely. By degrees the general gloom involved the whole, while the wind swept down the sides of Glenaá [sic] and Tomish; lifting the waves to an alarming height, giving it all the appearance of the angry Atlantic." Holmes and his party gained shelter on the island, where a fire and dinner had been already laid on for them. By the time they had eaten, serenity had returned with only the roaring of the rain-swollen O'Sullivan cascade to remind the travelers of the recent storm.[6]

Killarney's Landlords and Estate Tourism

As mentioned in Chapter Three, part of the reason for Killarney's early renown as a tourist spot stemmed from the efforts of its leading proprietors, especially the Brownes of Kenmare. The Brownes, a planter dynasty, acquired the lands around Killarney at the end of the Second Desmond Rebellion in 1683. The family became Catholic, but later, finding themselves on the wrong side in the Williamite war, temporarily lost their lands after 1691. Valentine Browne, the Third Viscount of Kenmare, managed to regain the estate and, although a Catholic, kept it intact and within the family.[7]

Having regained control of the estate, the Brownes around 1750 began to develop their lands. Luke Gibbons suggests that, as the most prominent Catholic proprietor in Ireland and the head of the Catholic Association, Thomas Browne, the fourth Viscount, was anxious to demonstrate that Catholic landlords could modernize and improve their estates as well as any Protestant. Gibbons, therefore, places Kenmare's efforts at enclosing his lands and opening up of Killarney for tourism within a political context. Kenmare sought the approval and trust of liberal-minded Protestants who might have looked favorably at some point on Catholic relief. He refurbished the old ecclesiastical ruin on Innisfallen, turning it into a dining place for visitors, an example of modernization celebrated by the Protestant poet John Leslie in 1772:

> How proud the ruin! once the ruthless home
> Of pale Austerity, and monkish gloom,
> The seat of Woe, now by its princely Lord,
> To Mirth devoted, and the social board.[8]

While intent on spreading the fame of their mountains and lakes, Killarney's proprietors were also interested in exploiting their estates in other ways. The area seemed rich in possibilities. Thanks to the once plentiful supply of oak bark, tanneries developed in the area during the eighteenth century. According to Charles Smith, writing in the 1750s, the water flowing from the Devil's Punch Bowel near the summit of Mangerton went to the nearby Muckross iron works. And Lakes themselves formed part of a transportation system that once carried copper and iron from the Herbert family's works at Muckross to the River Laune and then to Killorglin and the sea.[9]

Beginning in 1765, the Brownes, as well as the Herberts and other local landlords in the area, began using the Grand Jury system, which they, of course, dominated, to improve the roads, a necessity for the development of both trade and tourism. Even so, it took some time before traveling to Killarney became relatively easy. In 1827, Caesar Otway described the difficulty in getting his chaise over the steep hills on the road out of Glengarriff. Seven years later in 1834 Henry D. Inglis, like Otway, had to a hire a gang of peasants to pull his carriage up the hill and then to lower it down the other side. Such inconveniences ended by the 1840s, when a new thoroughfare and tunnel replaced the old mountain road. The Halls hailed the results as one of the best roads in the Kingdom.[10]

The Brownes also put considerable effort into developing the town of Killarney. Writing in the 1750s, Charles Smith described it as a "small thriving place, being considerably improved" after Lord Kenmare had encouraged several gentlemen (along with some linen manufactures) to settle there. Although Kenmare wanted to develop businesses in the town, Smith already saw the potential of tourism, noting that "the curiosities of the neighbouring lake, have of late, drawn great numbers of curious travellers to visit it...." By 1815 the *Traveller's New Guide through Ireland* claimed that not only did Killarney experience an "immense influx of visitors," but, thanks to efforts of the Kenmares, it also attracted "new settlers who build new houses," promising a "little colony" for the future. Unfortunately, the general economic slow-down in the wake of Waterloo caused the collapse of some of the small industries Kenmare had encouraged. By then, however, tourism had become the town's major source of income. The town served as a convenient base for exploring much of Kerry and West Cork, as well as the Lakes themselves.[11]

Having recognized the potential for tourism at Killarney as early as the 1750s, Charles Smith assumed that the number of visitors would increase "when they can be assured of being commodiously and cheaply entertained." Oddly, the Kenmares seem to have been slow to provide the town with adequate inns and hotels. In the 1770s Arthur Young maintained that the want of proper accommodations at a reasonable cost to visitors robbed Killarney of what today would be called "tourist nights." The "inns are miserable," he complained, "and the lodgings little better." With proper accommodations, "The resort of strangers to Killarney would then be much increased, and their stay would be greatly prolonged; they would not view it post haste, and fly away the first moment to avoid dirt and imposition." In 1822 Rev. G. N. Wright, author of a guide to the Lakes, noted that the British Lake District had better accommodations, although he did find at least three "tolerable" hotels in Killarney.[12]

Most visitors complained that the walls of the Kenmare estate cut the town off from a proper view of the Lakes. This may not have been considered a great problem in the eighteenth century when visitors to the Lakes were likely to be people of quality who might stay with one of the area's proprietors. But as more middle-class tourists began arriving, the complaints grew. Anne Plumptre lamented in 1814 that there was no hotel on the lakeshore. "It is mortifying, when one would not wish to have the eye a moment detached from the exhaustless store of beauty presented to it, to be obliged to take up one's quarters in the town, from no part of which any of the lake scenery is visible." Wright complained of the mile walk from the town to the lake, particularly at the end of a rainy ten to twelve hours of exertion. The anonymous "Sportsman in Ireland" objected bitterly to" the proud obstructions of high walls, around that part of the lake which belongs to…[the Earl of Kenmare], shutting even from the view of an ordinary walker the objects he has come to Killarney to see…." As in other parts of Ireland, estate tourism had its critics.[13]

Organizing the Ground for Tourists

In spite of such complaints, the Kenmares, the Herberts and other proprietors did organize the area for visitors, and their endeavors were sometimes appreciated. For example, most tourists were often charmed by the proprietors efforts in landscaping some of the Lakes' larger islands and outfitting them for visitors. In 1758 Bishop Pococke praised the way Lord Kenmare had laid out the island of Innisfallen (*Inis Faithleann*) with walkways and a dining place. Rev. G. N. Wright admired the large bay-window built into one side of the island's reconstructed Abbey, "from which a delightful view may be had of Ross Island, Muckross shore, Mangerton, Tork and Glena," the principal mountains rising from the southern and western shores. Tenants of a nearby cottage saw to the needs of the visitors.[14]

Much of the eastern shore of the Middle Lake was bounded by the Herbert estate at Muckross. After having leased it for some years, the family reoccupied the grounds in 1770 and immediately began to follow the lead of the Brownes, improving their lands and developing the estate with an eye to impressing visitors. Thanks to her family's landscaping of Dinish Island, Mrs. Dorothea

Herbert enjoyed "the Luxuriance of the various Heaths along the half natural, half cultivated Walks and Vistas which intersect its delightful Groves and velvet Lawns...." Decades later, Dr. John Forbes admired the Herberts' ornamental cottage on Dinish, which had become a customary resting place for those taking a boat down the Long Range River from the Upper Lake.[15]

In keeping with the interactive nature of the picturesque tour, the proprietors' innovations inevitably prompted suggestions and critiques from visitors. For example, in spite of Rev. Wright's earlier admiration for it, Robert Graham complained that the bay window added to Innishfallen's Abbey looked as if it belonged on a London shop. Indeed, the poor island came in for more than its share of criticism. The "Sportsman" complained of the hefty tips the family in charge of the banqueting room expected for their services, although the visitors themselves had to provide the food. He felt that the Kenmares should have placed a proper inn or tavern on the island. Rev. Wright expressed dissatisfaction with the upkeep of the grounds. The island's scenery he noted, "is of the soft, gentle, and civilized character, in which a degree of neatness is necessary to beauty...." He acknowledged that a certain element of ruggedness and neglect would bring out the "noblest features of the view." However, "the walk through the grass should be clean and strewn with gravel from the shore; the briars and brambles, that are daily chocking up the natural evergreens, should be removed..." Out of a presumed concern for visitors' footwear, Wright urged that "*sheep alone*," rather than horned cattle, be "permitted to pasture on the lawns." As previously noted, landlords risked their aesthetic reputations when they developed their lands for tourists. Wright, for example, concluded that, had the proprietor of Innisfallen but seen the improvements Mr. Curwen had made on his island on Windemere in the Lake District, "he would perceive what can be accomplished by a man of taste," with a "degree of attention to neatness."[16]

Estate Forestry at Killarney

As noted in Chapter Five, visitors to major tourist sites were sometimes horrified by the all too active practice of estate forestry. Even while promoting tourism, the proprietors at Killarney logged the splendid forests that covered the islands and the mountain sides. Dunn, visiting the Lakes in 1776, described the "bleak sides" of Mangerton, which apparently had been recently cut. By 1797, when John Harden visited the Lakes, Mangerton had recovered somewhat, but by then the sides of Turk (Torc) mountain looked "rude bare & Rocky being entirely with[ou]t trees."[17] After the Act of Union the newly ennobled Earl of Kenmare, an absentee, sold off the remaining trees on his mountainsides and islands to raise much needed cash. (He even briefly entertained the idea of draining the lower lake to recover more land.)

In 1807 Isaac Weld mourned, "It is painful to reflect how much the beauty of the lake has been impaired by the destruction of the forests; and still more so to think that the few remaining venerable trees have been devoted to the axe. By their removal, the scenery is likely to sustain an injury irreparable during the present generation...." Ross Island had once been, in Weld's words, "one of the most enchanting spots within the whole surrounding region...covered to the water's edge with majestic oaks...." Its "stately trees" were felled in the summer of 1804. Weld went on to complain: "Painful is the task which now devolves upon me, of relating that the woods of Glena, its glory and ornament for ages have been consigned for a trifling compensation, to the timber-merchant. Cold must be the heart of that man, and insensible to the beauties of nature, who, conscious of their impending fate, could behold their romantic and venerable shade without heaving a sigh." Weld's carefully phrased ending narrowly dodged a direct criticism of the Earl of Kenmare.[18]

Coppicing contributed to some recovery of tree cover. Edward Wakefield, visiting the Lakes a few years after Weld's lament, acknowledged that the stumps on Glena had regrown. The young coppice growth, however, had not yet attained sufficient height to cover mountain with foliage: "It is indeed a general complaint, that the views of Killarney have been destroyed by the sweeping fall of timber...." Nevertheless, he reassured would-be visitors that Killarney's splendors were such that the hand of man could not diminish them. Richard Colt Hoare acknowledged evidence of some reforestation but complained that native oaks had been replaced by "Scotch" firs on the Herbert estate: "The *Fir* tree, from its uniform and never varied shape, but ill accords with scenery so wild and natural as that which environs these lakes on all sides...."[19]

Touring Killarney

Killarney is a large, complex site. Such areas, as noted in Chapter Five, must be broken down into convenient individual features, each offering tourists discrete sights and activities. In fact, one did not visit Killarney so much as tour its various elements, and each travel writer seemed to have his or her own preferred system. As early as 1801, James Solas Dodd's *The Traveller's Director Through Ireland* provided a very detailed and exact itinerary for seeing the area, demonstrating the extent to which tourism at Killarney had already been organized. Writing in 1806, Richard Colt Hoare recommended spending at least one week at Killarney, although even that would consign the visitor to only the well-beaten paths. Hoare believed that an extended stay would reward the more independent-minded visitor. Near the end of his 1822 guidebook to Killarney, Rev. Wright provided a series of routes for one, two, or three-day tours. However, Barrow, strapped for time, decided to do the lakes in just one day on land, rather than three in a boat, which would have required ideally three days of good weather, "a monstrous supposition in Ireland."[20] In their guidebook to the Lakes, the Halls urged visitors to plan to spend a week, and they laid out an itinerary for each day, careful to specify the locations from which the best views could be enjoyed.

Even back then time was money, and so behind the confident assertions that the visitor spend at least a week at Killarney lay the assumption that those addressed could afford such a luxury. Nevertheless, some travel writers seemed anxious to combat the already well-established idea that a tourist could *see* something by merely casting eyes upon it. William Belton feared that most tourists were simply out to "'kill a lion,' in the shortest possible time; and…go through the appointed routine with admirable perseverance, be the weather favorable or not…such tourists lose all the beautiful effects that result from the ever-changing play of tints and lights, so especially various and lovely in this fickle element." The hotel keepers, however, did their best to prevent their guests from hurrying through their stay. Forbes complained that although there was plenty of time to do both the Upper and at least the Middle Lakes in one day, his boatmen had been reluctant to accommodate him. He later discovered that the hoteliers, who booked the guides for tourists, had ordained that one day be devoted to the Gap of Dunloe and the Upper Lake, and a second for the lower Lakes and their islands, thereby squeezing at least another night out of their guests.[21]

The Red Deer Hunt

Killarney offered visitors a variety of activities. Many tourists considered a trip through the Gap of Dunloe almost as important as boating on the Lakes. In addition, tourists could climb Mangerton and visit romantic ruins, such as Muckross Friary, Aghadoe Abbey and Ross Castle. Moreover, the fishing was good. And, on occasion, the Kenmare estate staged one of Ireland's most famous sporting events: the hunt for a red deer stag. The chase was unique in that, having begun on the steep mountains slopes, it often ended in the waters of the Lakes themselves, as George Holmes dramatically described in the 1797:

> The echoes caused by this sport reverberate the sounds in a manner not to be believed by any but those who have heard them…. The deer are roused from the deep woods which skirt the lake by hunters…on foot, as horses are useless, not being able to make their way through the bottoms nor rise the steep declivities. The hills are lined with hardy peasants, who encounter the most imminent danger and extreme fatigue to assist and enjoy the chase; while on the lake are scattered numerous boats, full of anxious spectators. The animal darting from his covert, makes towards the soft lawns, which sometimes verge

upon the lake; and bounding along the shore, he is hotly pursued by his loud-tongued enemies, whose various notes and the cheering shouts of men along the hills, joined with the sounding horns through the woods and on the lake, cause one continued roll of harmonic thunder among the hills and hanging forests. He now looks upward and panting seeks the rock eminence, but in vain; his lofty antlers, once his pride, are now, alas, his ruin!

The brush and trees were too thick and the dogs pressed on, forcing the stag to turn again to the shore: "[H]ere he is assailed by the loud shouts and horns, of the enjoying spectators in their crowded boats.... Suddenly, in desperation, he plunges from the bank, and gives his ample breast unto the wave. But, alas! his fate is fixed—he gains but a few minutes respite—the shouting boatmen surround the victim—he is dragged with ropes into the boat—and with peals of exultation that thunder through the woods, he is brought to land."[22]

In 1840 the anonymous "Sportsman" provided a less romantic description of the hunt. Just as the bugles signaled that the stag had been sighted, a gale hit the Lake: "Ludicrous were the scenes of apprehension, screaming, and splashing, as the lake, now wild with storm, dashed its angry spray over the dignified spectators.... [T]he shores were crowded with spectators—the mountains reverberated the sounds in continued echoes—the clamping of a thousand oars—the resounding bugles from the boats—the cries of cargoes upset in the melee—the alarm of the drowning, and the shouts of the foremost, raised altogether a din that must fail in description." The writer found the hunt artificial "and therefore, to the true sportsman, uninteresting." Indeed, the deer hunt at Killarney may be the first example in Ireland of a characteristic of modern tourism that John Urry, borrowing from Daniel Boorstin, calls a "pseudo-event," in this case a staged hunt in which the spectacle seems to have ended with the deer, once caught by the boatmen, being landed and released. Unlike the organized grouse hunts in Scotland, where guests at least had a chance to bring down (and possibly eat) the quarry, Killarney's famous hunt was primarily tourist theater.[23]

Antiquities

Ruins, sacred and secular, constitute another type of attraction in the Killarney area. As noted in Chapter Five, Ross Castle holds an important place in the region's history and legends. And the monastic ruins on Innisfallen represent a historic ecclesiastical site where the eleventh-century "Annals" that bear the island's name had been once kept. The island is also commemorated in a song by Thomas Moore ("Sweet Innisfallen, fare thee well / May calm and sunshine long be thine!"). At the north end of Lough Leane are the ruins of Aghadoe Abbey. Most popular with the tourists, however, is the old Friary built in 1448 on the grounds of the Herbert estate at Muckross. The yew tree that still stands in the center of the cloister was already old and large when Arthur Young described it in the 1770s as "the most prodigious yew tree I ever beheld, in one great stem two feet in diameter...from whence a vast head of branches spreads on every side, so as to form a perfect canopy to the whole space." Twenty years later John Harden estimated that the tree stood at fifty to sixty feet high and measured nine feet in circumference. According to Rev. Wright, who associated ecclesiastical ruins with the sublime, the tree with its enormous shading canopy so effectively contributed to the general "gloominess" of the cloister that "some persons have not nerves sufficiently strong to endure a lengthened visit within its precincts."[24] Inside and along the walls of the Friary, however, tourists found a bit more of the sublime than they may have wanted. Disinterred bones were arranged in fantastic patterns. In fact, the amount of human remains underfoot elicited numerous complaints from travel writers, and the Herberts eventually cleaned up the site, removing cartloads of bones.[25]

Echoes—Killarney's Soundscape

Music there for Echo dwells,
    Makes each sound a harmony,
Many voie'c the chorus swells,
    Till it faints in ecstasy ("Killarney")

John Urry discusses the process of "sacralization" that "renders a particular natural or cultural artifact a sacred object of the tourist ritual." Among the stages involved in this process—naming, framing, enshrinement—Urry also mentions the "mechanical reproduction of the sacred object."[26] While Urry is referring to images, the chief "artifact" in the case of Killarney was aural rather than physical. Sound in the form of echoes made Killarney an unusual tourist attraction. As discussed in Chapter Four, the aesthetics of the sublime extended beyond the visual to the aural. Sometimes, as with waterfalls and surf, nature provided sound to accompany the spectacle. However, in mountainous areas, in caves and even under the arches of bridges people literally used nature as a sounding board to produce echoes. Some tourist sites became renowned for the quality of their echoes, and Killarney ranked among the most famous, its sound as important as its scenery.

Alfred Lord Tennyson's visit to Ross Castle in 1848 inspired him to write a poem, which he later appended to *The Princess: A Medley*:

The splendor falls on castle walls
    And snowy summits old in story;

The long light shakes across the lakes
  And the wild cataract leaps in glory.
Blow, bugle, blow, set the wild echoes flying,
Blow, bugle; answer, echoes, dying, dying, dying.[27]

Just as the visual thrill for the visitor to Killarney lay in finding the right juxtaposition of sublime mountains and picturesque lakes and islands, so the Lakes' auditory pleasures were stimulated by a carefully manipulated combination of black gun power and music. Writing around 1760, William Ockenden, whose early detailed description of Killarney influenced later writers, tells how his party rowed to a position opposite the Eagle's Nest, a high promontory rising abruptly 700 feet from the Long Range River. From there they were admiring "the marble chasm in the perpendicular side in the mountain...when suddenly, to our inexpressible amazement, we were surprised with music, sweeter than any I had ever heard before, which seemed to arise from the rock, at which we gazed; and breaking upon us in short melodious strains, filled the very soul with transport." After fifteen minutes of serenade a sudden explosion "rent the mountain with its roar and filled us with the apprehension of being instantly buried in a chaos of hill, wood, and water: but the horror was as suddenly dissipated by the return of the same soothing strains which had before enchanted us." A cannoneer and musicians, secretly positioned on the shore behind a hillock where they could be heard but not seen, continued to bounce sound and fury off of the Eagle's Nest to the astonishment and admiration of Ockenden and his friends.[28]

Holmes, who published his account of Killarney in 1801, gloried in the interchange between cannon and horns. He describes the echoes of the cannon as "the most dreadful thunder rolling from side to side...[mingling] into one continued sound, seeming as if the mountains groaned in dreadful labour, such as precedes the most horrible commotion of nature. The sad and awful impressions made upon the mind by this terrible sublime effect, are delightfully displaced by the echoes from the horn, which are exquisite, and the very soul of harmony." Isaac Weld claimed that, given the right atmospheric conditions, at least twelve reverberations of the cannon, sometimes more, could be counted, "and what appears extraordinary, after the sound has been totally lost, it occasionally revives, becoming louder and louder for a few seconds, and then again dies away."[29] While the cannons provided auditory enhancement to the visual sense of the sublime, musical echoes translated the gentler sense of the picturesque into sound. After noting the thunderous echoes of the cannon, John Bush described the music that followed: "But the most delightful effect of these echoes is the *musical*, particularly of the horn and trumpet...attacking the ears form all sides in succession, as if twenty instruments were blowing in concert at different distances and elevations." According to Bush, Killarney's scenery "affects the mind of the spectator in a manner unspeakable, and possesses the imagination with the highest conceptions of natural sublimity." Yet, "to add to the effect of such a supereminent landscape, which will carry [the traveler's] imaginations to the highest pitch of frantic enthusiasm is the melodious echoing of the horn.... If any scene in the world can elevate [the traveler's] conceptions to the sublime of nature, it must be a situation like this."[30] For romantic travelers like Bush and Holmes, the sought-after echoes of Killarney served not as a mere accompaniment to the emotions aroused by the scenery but, instead, extended and expanded those emotions and the spiritual intimations that they were imagined to suggest.

This total tourist experience could not be enjoyed spontaneously, however. It involved carefully planned effort, both on the part of those who organized and controlled the sites and of the tourists themselves, who served as willing participants rather than passive spectators. Right from the start it seems as if Lord Kenmare had intended to exploit Killarney's echoes: he positioned cannons at choice spots on the shore, mounted small guns in his boats, and found locals to supply the horns and bugles. Of course, some visitors merited special treatment. The Rev. Daniel A. Beaufort, one of Ireland's principal cartographers, enjoyed his 1788 trip on the Lakes in an eight-oared barge, complete with cannon. The music was provided by the band of the 55th Regiment, then billeted in the town.[31]

While echoes of some sort might be enjoyed almost anywhere on the Lakes and in the Gap of Dunloe, to experience the full impact the visitor had to be at a designated spot at the right time and with the necessary equipment. At the Eagle's Nest, for example, musicians had to be placed correctly to produce the desired sound. James Johnson, a visitor to Killarney in the 1840s, suggested situating a bugler on the shore behind a small rise, out of sight of the listeners. Johnson suggested that musicians direct their notes, not at their auditors but at the "grand reverberator," the hill itself. In this way, the audience would hear only the echoes and not the original notes, which, rough and shrill, would spoil the intended effect. Through such careful stage management, the visitors could "listen, with astonishment and delight, to a *continuous* stream of music from the mountain, so mellowed as to be hardly thought earthly, but rather the emanation of some celestial organ." Writing earlier, Isaac Weld even supplied directions for the type of music to be played at the Eagle's Nest, suggesting simple melodies with simple harmonies, "played slowly," so that the notes would not become jumbled or confused.[32]

Inevitably, not all visitors to the Lakes found the echoes up to their expectations. Taking her place before the Eagle's Nest, Anne Plumptre felt disappointed. Having read Weld's guidebook, she had expected twelve reverberations. She lamented, however: "I could never distinguish more than four…, [but] this I am informed depends very much upon the state of the atmosphere; and, as the people said, it happened to be an unfavorable day for the reverberation." Lord Manners, at first charmed by the echoes, condemned their constant pursuit as "Cockneyish," appealing primarily to the "lower" sort of tourist. Nevertheless, he had to admire the excellent bugle playing of one of the Spillane family: "I listened in a sort of dreamy ecstasy to the wild and mournful notes as they lingered in the air that would not part with them." Isaac Weld recalled one evening when musicians were placed in a separate boat at a distance from the visitors so that the notes were softened by passage over the waters: "He who has never sailed along the shores of Glena by the light of the moon, or ever listened to the dying cadence of the echoes during the stillness of the night, may be justly pronounced a stranger to the most fascinating charms of Killarney."[33]

Unfortunately, many tourists inevitably departed "strangers" to the ultimate Killarney experience, since for a time the quality of the local musicians could not be guaranteed. Only those with good connections to the proprietors or with deep pockets could enjoy, as did Beaufort, the music of the resident military band. For the average visitor, Weld himself repeated Ockenden's warning that most visitors to Killarney would not really have an opportunity to judge the effect of musical sounds, "as the only musicians who reside on the spot are two wretched performers on the French horn and bugle." For example, Joseph Woods discovered that the horn players he had engaged knew only one tune, "God Save the King." Anne Plumptre grumbled that "there was something to me of a *petitesse* in the strains of our one solitary bugle-horn player, which seemed ill to accord with the grandeur and sublimity of the objects around."[34] By the 1840s, however, members of the Spillane family had made themselves famous as skillful buglers.

The Costs of Sublimity

Good, bad or indifferent, the musicians had to be paid, boats had to be hired and black powder for the canon had to be purchased. Sadly, Killarney's echoes were not free, and the quality of the total tourist experience there depended upon more than the vagaries of the Irish weather or even the quality of the resident musicians. It depended on how much one was willing to pay. In 1859 Samuel Reynolds Hole quoted the *Times* to the effect that "You cannot have guides, and horses, and boats, and bugles (especially where the demand is temporary and irregular), without paying highly for them…."[35] While most visitors to Killarney found the echoes exemplary, there were frequent complaints about the costs required to awaken them.

The greatest source of complaints from tourists had to do with the boats, however. To really experience Killarney and its echoes one had to be on the Lakes themselves. And there, Lord Kenmare, who controlled the surface of the waters, made his most important and controversial contribution to organizing tourism at Killarney. He created a fleet of boats and barges and made them available to visitors. The craft were oared because sudden squalls gusting down the mountainsides made sails unsafe. Kenmare, in fact, forbad them. Of course, Lord Kenmare's boats were not free, except to *his* guests. Visitors had to hire them and their crews through the hotels at a fixed price. And here was the rub. Since the boatmen's fees were set by Lord Kenmare, holding out for more and better victuals and whiskey represented the only way the boatmen had of capitalizing on their monopoly. If the boatmen were dissatisfied by the amount of refreshment supplied for the trip, they simply refused to move until the deficit had been remedied, as botanist Joseph Woods discovered in 1809. Nevertheless, Woods blamed the proprietor: "...no traveller can visit Killarney without wishing Lord Kenmare at the Devil for his pains. If everyone were at liberty to let out his boat and the pay both for the boat & for the men published, the traveller would be less open to imposition." Also, as Hoare pointed out, the limited number of boats prevented tourists from exploring the Lakes at their leisure.[36]

One anonymous author in 1804 found the boats too costly and the crews too inclined "to impose," and so confined his sightseeing to the shore instead. Anne Plumptre explained that the cost of a boat varied according to its size—whether it required six or four oars—and whether it went on the upper or lower lakes (the lower lake cost half a crown less). The boatmen expected to see a freight of provisions and whiskey carried on board—or else the tourist paid out two shillings per man. She doubted that this was part of Lord Kenmare's plan, but "in such places," observed this most experienced professional tourist, "impositions are regarded as positive privileges."[37]

The costs of boating and echoing could be pretty steep. When Richard Twiss visited the Lakes in 1775, he complained that the oarsmen had to be paid eighteen pence a day, while the boatswain received five shillings. Nothing less than a brace of French horns to wake the echoes would do, but "the *corni primi* must be paid a guinea a day and the *corni secondi* are at half price." In addition, the tourist had to purchase eight to ten pounds of black powder for the cannons and supply provisions and liquors "of every kind" for the crew for a total cost of eight guineas over two days. Rev. Wright claimed that, with demands for food, drink and tips, the hiring of a boat for the Lakes would be "the most disgraceful circumstance" connected with the tourist's visit to Killarney. And, he added: "How different from the modest charges of Derwent and Windemere" in the English Lake District. By the early 1840s the

Halls figured that, "the moderate tourist will calculate his necessary expenses at Killarney at something less than seven shillings per day. The only charge at which he will complain is the hire of a boat—sixteen shillings—but that includes the dinners of five men." A pony at Mangerton or the Gap of Dunloe cost an extra five shillings.[38]

Plucking the Pigeon's Wing

While the proprietors and hoteliers organized the Killarney experience on the macro level, the peasantry managed it on the micro level. Guides, boatmen, buglers, porters, vendors and general hangers-on, filled in the details, just as they filled up the landscape, and in so doing found opportunities to help themselves in ways that even the most experienced and jaded tourist might not have imagined. Sometimes the guides managed to create their own "traditions" for entertaining and for extracting extra money, food or whiskey from the travelers. Anne Plumbtre's experience in naming an island was noted in Chapter Six. William Belton, author of *The Angler in Ireland*, 1834, recorded the clever way by which the boatmen had worked Killarney's famous echoes into another bit of tourist theater. Stopping below the walls of the ruined Ross Castle (whose echoes so inspired Tennyson), the boatmen used them to form a dialogue called "Paddy Blake's Echo."

> "Paddy Blake, are you at home?"
> Answer [Echo]. "At home."
> "Are you sober or drunk?"
> Answer. "Drunk."
> "We've got a good gentleman on board."
> Answer. "Good gentleman on board.
> "He's the gentleman to give whiskey to the men."
> "Give whiskey to the men."
> "Your Honor hears what Paddy Blake says"—slyly remark the impudent crew.[39]

Harden was amused by "Paddy Blake" back in 1797 and Crofton Croker reprinted a version of the "dialogue" in his book on Killarney.[40]

Most guides and buglers learned how to cater to the tourists and to build entertainment into their patter and their demonstrations of the famous echoes. Theresa Cornwallis West enjoyed Spillane's version of "The Groves of Blarney" bounced off of the Eagle's Nest. In their 1865 guidebook to Killarney, the Halls explained how one of the Spillanes (whom they had helped make famous) would pick a spot in a cave on Torc Mountain, where he would say, "Now's a fine time for the laugh—O'Donoghue's laugh," referring to the legendary warrior who supposedly haunted the region. He would then blow a series of discordant notes in imitation of satanic laughter. "Crash, crash it went, and roused the angry echoes, which repeated, now loudly, now faintly, then in the distance—far off—the phantom like sounds." Suitably impressed, the Halls describe it as unearthly music, thus establishing another tourist event that those who came after were sure to expect and to pay for.[41]

Whereas in other parts of Ireland tourists might chance upon the sound of pipes or fiddle and come upon some peasants dancing in a meadow, at Killarney by the middle of the nineteenth century such events seem to have been staged for the benefit of the tourists. When Mrs. West's hotelier asked if she and her party wanted a concert from Gandsay, a famous local piper, she was thrilled: "Thanks to Croker's Legends of the Lakes—[Mr. Gandsay] was an old familiar of mine...." Unfortunately, Gandsay never appeared to fulfill the booking. In their guidebook to the Lakes, the Halls describe a sort of "folk" entertainment that one might find today at Bunratty Castle. After dinner at the tourist's cottage at the foot of Glenna, O'Leary set things off with his pipes: "The chances are that a merry Irish girl—a maid-of-all-work to visitors—will be there also; and, if so, be sure you can see an Irish jig, for there is little doubt that one of the boatman will call for 'Green Grow the Rushes, O!' and the effect will be irresistible. The dance is as certain to follow it as a bugle sound when you round the corner at parting from beautiful Glenna."[42] No modern tourist brochure could have laid it on any better. Killarney had become a stage set for the tourist experience.

However, no matter how sublime the location in sight and in sound, the Killarney tourist experience quickly became a series of commodities; the tourists became essentially purchasers of sights, sounds, services, entertainment and goods. Anne Plumptre described the scene as her party set out alone to climb Mangerton, towering above the Lakes: "[B]y the time we arrived at the top of the mountain we were not less than a cavalcade of fifteen or sixteen. A man followed with a bugle-horn, which he blew in different parts about the Punch-bowl and the other lake, the reverberations of which by the echoes was really fine. Some girls from a cottage at the foot of the mountain followed with goats-milk, several boys pursued us with offers to relieve the guide from the trouble of the basket of provisions, and carry it, none making their offers in pure love, all hoped some token in return." For those not fortunate enough to earn a "token," there remained the possibility of scavenging the leavings of the tourists' picnic. Plumptre reported: "When the regularly employed party had finished their meal by the side of the Devil's Punch-bowl...all the rest sat down to a scramble for what remained." As a veteran of many a romantic but expensive tourist site, she added wearily: "It is curious to observe, in all places which are much the resort of travellers, the ingenious devices the people about have, each to pluck a feather out of the pigeon's wing."[43]

In pre-Famine Ireland the economic circumstances of the peasantry shaped much of the tourist experience. The teeming population took advantage of any opportunity it could to earn a bit of cash. Wright complained bitterly that at Killarney "the tourist is subject to great annoyance, arising from the number of men and boys, who run on every side of him, without uttering a syllable, but merely keeping up with his horse. Entreaties to desist on this undertaking, as *one* would be sufficient to point the way and tell the names of distant objects, are of no avail...." And so the visitor might end up with six or eight "guides." Killarney's army of guides and vendors extended up into the Gap of Dunloe, as acknowledged by the Halls: "As you approach the Gap, you will be arrested by some of the thousand and one women, boys, and girls, who will gather like a rolling snow-ball as you proceed. They will try to tempt you with goats-milk and 'mountain dew;' but some of them will offer you stockings of their own knitting; and always they will try to wile the visitor out of half pence—with a good supply of which you should therefore be provided." Something of this atmosphere is captured in the August 4, 1849 issue of the *Illustrated London News*, which carried a woodcut of pony-mounted tourists trying to negotiate their way up the Gap through a throng of beggars and vendors.[44]

Kate Kearney's Cottage, still a fixture at the entrance to the Gap, is an interesting example how a literary marker could be combined with some clever entrepreneurship (and fakelore) to create one of the longest-running tourist traps in history. Around 1807 Lady Morgan wrote a poem, "Kate Kearney," which begins, "Oh, did you not hear of Kate Kearney?/She lives on the banks of Killarney...." Set to music, it became a popular parlor song that in all probability inspired a local landlord named O'Mahony to build "Kate Kearney's Cottage" at the mouth of the Gap of Dunloe (several miles from the "banks of Killarney") where tourists could buy refreshment. While the cottage, or at least its descendent, still survives, the old house specialty, goat's milk and *potín* (cottage-made whiskey), are no longer on tap. The Kate Kearney phenomenon seems to have taken off around 1850. And, just as a "Kathleen" climbed up to St. Kevin's Bed at Glendalough, so—according to the Halls, a "Kate Kearney" presided over the cottage in the Gap. With or without her, however, the Gap of Dunloe never wanted for peasant girls peddling their goat's milk concoction. Theresa West having tried it, declared it "horrible," and passed it on to her guides.[45]

The travel accounts suggest the extent to which tourism reshaped the lives of the peasantry in Killarney. The Halls exaggerated only a little when they claimed: "Every boy or girl child, from the time they are able to crawl over the door-step, seems to have a strong natural instinct to become a guide, and to climb—or rather trot—up Mangerton...and what is worse for the traveller, disturb the solemnity of the Eagle's Nest with their importunities that you will drink goat's milk fresh from the cow [sic], taste poteen [sic] or eat wild strawberries." Nevertheless, recognizing the various ways by which the guides contributed to the tourist experience at Killarney, the Halls defended the best of them, whom they characterized as "sparing no personal exertion...[to] willingly endure the extreme fatigue, carrying as much luggage as a packhorse, familiar but never intrusive, never out of temper, never wearied either of walking or talking and generally full of good humour...." As for the tip, "the guides of all countries extort, the Irish guide does so only by 'laving it to yer honour.'" For their part, the locals were aware of the extent to which travel writers helped to promote Killarney. "I was the man that was with Sir Walter Scott and Mister Moore himself, yer honour," one guide assured the Halls. "I'm the boy that's mentioned in Mr. Crofton Croker's book," claimed another. On his second visit to Killarney, Tennyson's bugler, after learning his patron's identity, is supposed to have remarked, "Oh! then you're the gentleman that's brought so much money to the place!"[46]

Tourist Heaven or Tourist Hell? The Paradox of Tourism

By the 1840s Killarney, like the Giant's Causeway, seems to have taken on all of the trappings of the modern tourist site, the very popularity of which turns it into its own worst enemy. Henry D. Inglis complained in 1834 that the town itself was large, noisy and rather unattractive. According to the Halls, it had grown from about a hundred mostly thatched houses in 1747 to around a thousand structures with a population of 8000 almost a century later. The town's only thriving manufacturing activity, the production of arbutus-wood souvenirs, depended upon tourism.[47]

In one respect Killarney inevitably failed. Professionals in the tourist industry stress the importance of keeping the surroundings or at least the approaches to a tourist site free from elements that might distract the tourist and produce an unsatisfactory experience.[48] On this score Killarney fell victim to an early case of what John Urry characterizes as "social contamination," the presence of people whom tourists deem as inappropriate, even if they are native to the place. Thus, descending from his coach at the Kenmare Arms, John Barrow found himself beset by locals offering everything from boats to trinkets. Beggars were everywhere. When Thomas Carlyle's party arrived at the Weir Bridge, where the boats were to be shifted from one lake to another, they were greeted by a cheery group of beggar girls. "We been waiting for ye all day!" they chirped. Usually an admirer of perseverance, Carlyle was not pleased. Even many of the attempts to sell goods and services amounted to little more than begging. In the 1790s, Harden was pestered by barely clad children selling nuts and wild strawberries, neither of which he nor his party wanted. Nevertheless, "we could never get away with([ou]t) leaving 6*d*. or 1*s*. behind with them—that received away they ran—[to] prepare for the next stranger...."[49]

According to the anonymous author of *A Run Around Ireland* (1850), solitude and freedom of movement were the last thing a tourist could expect at Killarney: "Guides, buglemen, boatmen, performers on the pipes, vendors of bog oak and arbutus trinkets, firers of cannon and carriers of *yells* to awake the echoes, and nameless hangers on, offering all kinds of miscellaneous services, make a net-work around [the tourist] from which it is impossible to escape." Ironically, in a place famed for its sound as much as for its sight, the writer lamented that "...the external noise everywhere—the multitude of people...would spoil any landscape that nature could spread before the eye." In desperation the writer dismissed his guide at the entrance of Gap of Dunloe, only to find the rest of his path lined with nuisances and his ears filled with the constant noise of cannon and bugles. Even before the Famine, Killarney—town, lakes, mountains, gaps—suffered from what John Urry has called "visual contamination," although, given the nature of the tourist experience there, the pollution was aural as well. Thus, the hopelessness of the modern tourists' situation. As Urry points out, their desire to visit pristine sites is rendered nearly impossible by the nature of tourism itself. The popularity of such places erodes the very qualities that attract visitors to them in the first place. This is, in effect, the "catch 22," the real "tourist trap."[50]

With its lakes, fells and echoes, Killarney is a perfect example of this paradox of modern tourism, especially in its scenic mode. There the search for the ultimate experience of nature was anything but natural. When Anne Plumptre complained about the mob around her picnic at the Devil's Punch Bowl, she revealed a bit of the machinery of tourism as it clanked and groaned behind the visitors' search for the picturesque and the sublime. Generally, that search was no more spontaneous than any other activity in which the elite classes engaged, whether hosting a party or going to an opera. At Killarney, as at the theater, one had to get to the right place and sit in the exact spot in order to enjoy the performance. Because they had already read the "libretto," guidebooks and travel accounts, the tourists knew exactly what to expect and how they were supposed to interpret their experience. Unfortunately, that experience could be spoiled by bad weather and importuning peasants, not to mention other tourists. In fact, by the middle of the century, the tourists themselves constituted perhaps the greatest obstacle to enjoying the Killarney experience. On his visit, the "Sportsman" found that by mid-afternoon the Lakes were crowded: "Numerous boats floated on its surface; parties, accompanied by flags and bands of music (if so execrable an association of performers can be so called), were everywhere seen and heard...." When William Makepeace Thackeray visited Sweet Innisfallen he had plenty of company: "one large barge especially had landed some sixty people, being the Temperance band, with its drums, trumpets, and wives."[51]

Of course, without the presence of others in large numbers, the kind of services the individual tourist wanted might not have been available. Moreover, the crowds at tourist sites such as Killarney did at least confirm the importance of the place and, in a way, justified the visit. The problem, as Urry points out, rests in the role that consumption plays in scenic tourism. True, the objects of the gaze—the mountains, lakes, waterfalls—are not actually "consumed." But as more tourists flock to a site, its carrying capacity is threatened, if not physically then perceptually. Natural objects are, in Urry's words, "positional goods," shrines to nature that individuals wish to enjoy in solitude. Unfortunately, solitude is "consumed" by the tourists themselves.[52]

The Romantic tourist's frantic search for visual and aural sublimity, exploitative of both nature and people, may seem absurd today. However, the enthusiasm of one age can too easily become the absurdity of enlightened skeptics in another (as most people learn, if they live long enough). What drove these tourists to search out picturesque and sublime landscapes and soundscapes in an age before speed and good hotels could guarantee comfortable travel? Seeking to establish some relationship with nature, the romantic tourists sought a third path between those of the scientist, who desired to analyze and understand nature, and the industrialist, who wanted to exploit it. The Romantics sought to transcend through nature the materialism engulfing their culture. Denis Cosgrove sees this impulse to search out the sublime as "a cultural response to the advent of an industrial market society." This meant more than just journeying out into the countryside. Since the appreciation of nature represented an "organic intrinsic value located in the soul of the individual," the sublime provided an alternative to the scientific and technological approach to nature. The sublime held the promise of "the continued existence of the divine in nature, reasoning by analogy rather than by cause."[53]

Yet, what did the tourists actually hear but their own voices, when the great echoes had been teased (at some cost) from the mountains around Killarney? Whether shouts, shots or bugle calls, men made sounds, and nature echoed them. It was as if the tourists were ventriloquists, and nature their dummy; or as if the echoes were commodities, the quality of which varied according to price expended. Kim Ian Michasiw warns, however, against the "cultural materialist" assumption that aesthetics are simply economically or ideologically determined. Since the picturesque dealt with nature, it is particularly tempting for today's cultural critics to assume, according to Michasiw, that "the footprints of the ideological are most visible where nature is announced." In general, current critiques of the sublime and the picturesque do not take aesthetics seriously, treating it "as a *faux pas* on the way to something else or as a by-way entirely." Today's reader must be willing, Michasiw suggests, to meet the picturesque tourists on their own ground, no matter how strange it may seem.[54]

Clearly, tourists found more than novelty or consumer satisfaction in the echoes of Killarney. Those reverberations carried intimations of nature's soul, profound and liminal, partially hidden within the landscape, which the visitors sought to call forth, indeed, command. Inglis took time out from his investigation of the rural economy to visit the Lakes in 1834. He was, of course, careful to hire the best bugler and to equip himself with a larger cannon than the public boats usually provided. Contemplating the results, which he considered "sublime", Inglis expressed doubts about Edmund Burke's contention that the force of sublimity lay in the emotion of terror. Inglis traced it instead to its "truer origin – power." Although Burke actually had a lot to say about power, Inglis, nevertheless, went on to maintain that, "when we hear the call [of the bugle] repeated and answered from mountain to mountain—sometimes loud, and without interval, and then fainter and fainter—and after a solemn pause, again rising, as if from some far distant glen—our imagination endows the mountains with life; and to their attributes of magnitude, and silence, and solitude, we, for a moment, add the power of listening, and a voice."[55]

For the Romantic traveler, Killarney's echoes were supposed to produce the total tourist experience. Visually overwhelmed by water and mountains and momentarily surrounded by sound, the visitor to Killarney was (or was expected to be) emotionally engulfed by nature. Yet the tourists were not and did not intend to be passive collectors of sublime experiences. Nor, for obvious reasons, did most of them wish to recognize the artificial and exploitative aspects of the social and economic arrangements that supported their quest. Yet, they were certainly aware that the sublime moment, when it occurred, was the product of *human* intention and intervention, of imagination working with and upon nature.

Samuel Monk, in explaining the impact of William Wordsworth's poetry upon the Romantic approach to nature, has theorized: "The result was a new ability to see and love the natural world for its own sake, a care for the expression of what they saw and the imagination decreed to be significant." Wordsworth's *Preludes* stood as "a vindication of the imagination as an interpreter of experience." To seek after the sublime was, in Monk's words, to "see and reveal the light that never was on sea or land."[56] As Wordsworth (who had authored a guidebook to the Lake District) wrote:

... I would walk alone,
Under the quiet stars, and at the time

> Have felt whate'er there is of power in sound
> To breathe an elevated mood, by form
> Or image unprofaned; and I would stand
> If the night blackened with a coming storm
> Beneath some rock, listening to notes that are
> The ghostly language of the ancient earth,
> Or make their dim abode in some distant winds,
> Thence did I drink the visionary power.[57]

The tourists sought such "visionary power" in Killarney's scenery and longed to hear the ancient earth's "ghostly language" in its echoes. Unfortunately, they did not seek sublimity "alone under quite stars." As visitors to a very popular site, they turned a spiritual quest into social ritual and economic enterprise.

And so it is with all modern tourism. One must, therefore, have a certain sympathy for Thackeray who, having "done" Killarney, declared, "The writer wishes ingenuously to announce that he will not see any more lakes, ascend any mountains or towers, visit any gaps of Dunloe, or any prospects whatever, except such as nature shall fling in his way in the course of a quiet reasonable walk." Writing in his persona as a "Cockney," Thackeray claimed to feel like the ostrich: "Press us too much, and we become flurried and run off, and bury our heads in the quite bosom of dear mother earth, and so get rid of the din, and the dazzle, and the shouting."[58]

Indeed, Killarney teetered on the edge of what James Buzard identifies as the inevitable result of the tourist's search for something that promises to encompass the "wholeness" of a place. Too often it becomes "the wholeness of the wholly touristic place, inauthentic, trumped-up, corrupted, commodified," where, in the words of W. H. Auden's "First Things First,"

> …a world where every sacred location
> Is a sand-buried site all cultured Texans do,
> Misinformed and thoroughly fleeced by their guides.[59]

Part III

Chapter 8

TOURIST SEMEIOTICS, STEREOTYPES AND THE SEARCH FOR THE EXOTIC

Brogues and Blarney—The Semeiotics of Language

From its earliest days, tourism has primarily involved the search for difference. Tourists leave home to experience something different, even when they insist on enjoying all the comforts of home. Ironically, however, they may find unpleasant—sometimes even frightening or disgusting—the very the differences they've set out to explore. Nevertheless, they travel to encounter sights and sensations considered unique to the host country. In this respect tourists are, as Dean MacConnell and Jonathan Culler have argued, semioticians, looking for signs of Frenchness, Englishness or Irishness.[1] Inevitably, many such signs derive from and point back to stereotypes visitors hold regarding the host nation and its people. Moreover, this search for signs of foreign difference based on stereotypes manufactured back home may not reflect native realities. As Johathan Culler suggests, a "chanteuse" in Paris singing in English with a French accent may seem more "authentic" to an American tourist than if the woman sang in French.[2] Similarly, tourists scanned the behavior, dress and speech of their Irish hosts for "authentic" signs of Paddy—based on stereotypes of British invention

Speech was one potential source for Irishness. Since many Irish stereotypes had been propagated in the theater, British tourists expected their hosts to sound like the Stage Irishman. However, in crossing the Irish Sea British visitors crossed several linguistic frontiers, taking them beyond Paddy's Stage-Irish drolleries. As elsewhere along the Celtic Fringe, tourists in pre-Famine Ireland often encountered a Celtic language—Gaelic, still spoken in all four provinces at the end of the eighteenth century. The French counsel Charles de Montbret reported in the 1790s that, although peasants in County Kildare spoke English, many of those he had encountered in adjacent Wicklow still used Irish. Across the border in Kilkenny Montbret claimed that the local guides "pretended" not to speak English, and he found Irish freely used in Clonmel, Tipperary.[3]

Like Montbret, some British visitors, obviously frustrated with the linguistic difficulties they encountered, complained that although the locals in some places understood English they simply refused to speak it. Touring Killarney in 1767 Samuel Derrick managed to find a peasant family who engaged him in English, unlike many of their neighbors whom, he claimed, were too stubborn to oblige him. Travelling in 1843 in Connemara, where Irish was widely spoken, William Makepeace Thackeray complained that he could get little out of the locals in their cabins: "The people are suspicious of the stranger...and are shy, sly and silent." It never seems to have occurred to such visitors that Irish speakers, even if they knew some English, might have been uncomfortable in trying to negotiate the language of their upper-class foreign visitors. As J. G. Woods noted in 1809, while women and children in more remote parts of Ireland often seemed to have no English, most men understood it but spoke it with hesitation, as with a foreign tongue, which, of course, it was.[4]

When encountered without the immediate benefit of a translator, the language barrier could prove annoying. Mary Knott, summering in Kilkee in the 1830s, complained that local girls bearing baskets of fish would simply walk in on her family as they sat in the parlor, unaware that their intrusion had breached etiquette. Compounding Mrs. Knott's frustration, the girls had no English and she, therefore, had no means to correct them. In some towns in the West market women had found a way to negotiate the language problem. Thomas Reid, entering a town between Galway and Castlebar, discovered that the English speakers among the women wore colored ribbons in their caps.[5]

Occasionally, the visitors' ignorance of Gaelic produced frustrations of a different kind. Gabriel Beranger, on a sketching tour around Sligo in the 1790s, generally traveled with an interpreter. Visiting the local peasantry with a Col. Irwin, who spoke Irish, Beranger noticed that his host frequently embraced and kissed the young women. Pleased with this "custom," Beranger tried to practice it in Mayo, where, upon entering a cabin, he would call out, "Torum pogue Calinogue"—"give me a kiss, young girl." He claimed that he had great success. Having pretty well exhausted his meager store of Irish, however, he complained, "how unfortunate it was I could ask no more!"[6]

In pre-Famine Ireland the Gaelic language was the voice of a still vibrant vernacular culture, the energy and vociferousness of which occasionally startled visitors. Lady Chatterton visited Michelstown Cave, where the farmer in charge of the site shouted orders to his men in Irish: "...I have always found, that the wild eagerness of the Irish gestures and tones, inspires with a feeling of fear those who are not accustomed to them; it is almost impossible to imagine that they are not quarreling." Lady Chatterton went on to reassure her readers that all of this was quite normal, and the visitor had no need to worry.[7]

The language barrier was impenetrable in both directions. In 1852 Sir Francis Head stood in the market at Clifden in Connemara amid a group of girls seated with their baskets of fish and fruit. He records that they chatted among themselves in Irish, taking no notice of him as he made his notes. He could, of course, have been the sole object or butt of their conversation. However, in the reverse position of Mrs. Knott's peasant girls in her Kilkee parlor, Head had no Gaelic and, therefore, no way of knowing what the girls were saying. The unwritten history of Irish tourism lies in what the Irish speakers said to each other as they reversed the tourist gaze and regarded the strangers who walked uncomprehendingly amongst them. A hint may be found in Fr. Patrick Dinneen's discussion of the word *rúcach*, which means "a rook, a crow; a close-fisted person; a clown." He states that the "summer visitors to Kilkee are called *rúcach*, while those who frequent Lisdoonvarna and Liscannor are called *fámairí*...a kind of dogfish."[8]

Rarely a serious obstacle to the tourist, the gulf between English and Gaelic was at least obvious and to be expected. Not generally anticipated, however, were the problems resulting from the collision of two types of English: the speech of the British tourists and the Hiberno-English of their hosts. Atkinson, traveling between Waterford and Kilkenny in 1815, warned visitors that they would have trouble understanding whatever English they heard in those areas. A half century earlier in 1740, William Rufus Chetwood, walking through the town of Youghal, passed a group of locals, who bestowed a seemingly friendly greeting. However, as he passed by, one of the Irishmen said to his friends: "*I believe they are all Bugs.*" Chetwood hoped that "Bug" might be some kind of Irish compliment, "but when I asked the Meaning of it from the Gentlemen that accompanied us, I was informed, I might take the Word *Bug* in the *English* literal Sense; for by that the Vulgar of this Kingdom intitle [sic] all of our [English] Nation." In his book *Slanguage* Bernard Share affirms that "bug" could refer to Englishmen, based on the belief that they brought bugs to Ireland.[9]

As in Scotland and Wales (or areas of England where the local dialect might lay thick on the tongue), the vernacular English the tourists encountered in Ireland was not always standard. This problem resulted in a situation that Michael Cronin calls "intralingual" travel, the collision of two dialects of the same language, between which easy translatability is assumed but not always achieved. Tourists found that Hiberno-English could differ from British modes of speech in syntax, meaning and accent. The results could be annoying to tourists because, as Cronin points out, a language barrier is not supposed to exist *within* English. Yet, since Gaelic was impenetrable to most British, Hiberno-English took on the exotic qualities—and some of the difficulties—of an actual foreign language.[10] Consider Leitch Ritchie's problem when he asked a waiter in a hotel for a pin to repair a draw string: "A pin, Sir," came the reply;

"is it a *wroiting pin*, Sir?" Interestingly, Ritchie put the problem down to a flaw in the Irish character: an over-eager assumption of comprehension before all the facts were in.[11]

Even before tourism came to Ireland, British writers had labeled Hiberno-English as the "brogue," the comic sounds and locutions of the Stage Irishman. While not anticipating incomprehensibility, the tourists were at least expecting to be entertained by the speech of their drivers, guides, waiters, servants and whatever peasants came their way. Although few travel writers attempted to reproduce the dialect sounds they heard, some delighted in giving their readers alleged samples of Hiberno-English vocabulary and syntax. This added "authenticity" and entertaining color to their accounts, which certainly reflected the Irish stereotype. It is impossible to know the extent to which such exchanges were invented by the authors and what actually came from the mouths of their subjects. As noted in Chapter Six, within the context of tourism it is certainly possible that some Irish men and women, whose livelihoods depended upon pleasing visitors, took up the role and played the anticipated stereotype. In such cases, "intralingual" travel became a part of the theater of tourism. Whether he wished it not, when the Irishman addressed a tourist, he often assumed a character and played a role.[12]

Searching for the Exotic—Market Days and Celtic Chaos

It is a short but vaguely mapped journey from the stereotypical to the exotic. Within the context of tourism both represent a visitor's discovery of foreignness within the host country. The stereotypical represents expected "everyday" foreignness, such as a Frenchman's beret or Paddy's short clay pipe—his "dudeen." Even if it is largely the product of tourism itself, such as the sight of a Dutchman in wooden shoes in contemporary Amsterdam, the stereotypical is the sort of thing many tourists expect to encounter. The exotic is less typical but, nevertheless, essential; it represents a more profound and exciting sign of the Other. The exotic, of course, can easily slip into the realm of the bizarre. For example, many women in the West of Ireland wore hooded cloaks. Rev. Spencer T. Hall, touring the West, observed that some peasant women wore their cloaks over any burdens they carried on their backs as they headed to market. So garbed, a woman appeared to have "a large hunch on her back," as can be seen in some period illustrations.[13]

Certainly, the crowds at Irish markets and fairs provided endless opportunities for tourists practicing their semeiotics in search of the wilder shores of Irishness. Since Irish towns might have anywhere from two to three market days a week, anyone traveling even a short distance in Ireland inevitably encountered at least one of them. Markets, in fact, pumped the life blood of the

Irish economy, especially in the rural areas. In many landlord-owned towns, the proprietors built market houses, complete with scales, a weigh bridge, clock and bell, as well as an enclosed area for buying and selling. Some towns were built around large greens that accommodated these activities, which often attracted crowds. After having traversed roads and countryside that seemed quiet and even empty, tourists were often surprised at the masses of people attending markets. Robert Bell was amazed when he entered Cootehill, Cavan on a market day: "One is apt to wonder where such a multitude can be collected form." Just outside of Baltinglass on a fair day, T. K. Cromwell noticed girls, who, having walked the roads barefooted, were washing their feet at the brook before putting on shoes and stockings. Entering the town, Cromwell was astounded: "The over-grown population of the country shewed itself in the single living mass which filled the town, and through which it was scarcely possible for our vehicle to force a passage."[14]

The confusion of fair day was not only visual. British visitors were surprised and fascinated by the loud raucous sound of the Irish *en masse*. Visiting Ballinrobe on a market day, John Harvey Ashworth noted that the throngs in attendance "seemed busy...that is to say, so far as shouting and talking, the violent gesticulation, can convey that idea." Several decades earlier, Inglis, visiting the market in Galway town, felt that the noise and gestures of the swarm suggested immediate violence, although none ensued. Thackeray may have put his finger on what bothered his fellow Britons. Wandering among the throngs in the streets of Limerick, he noted that "the buzz, and hum, and chattering of this crowd is quite inconceivable to us in England, where a crowd is generally silent...." At any rate, given the sudden transition from quiet rural roads to market throngs, the apparent chaos of the scene could be disturbing to the visitor. Lady Chatterton reminded her readers not to be concerned when entering a crowded market town with is masses of people, pigs and dogs: "The whole scene looks in the most dreadful confusion. The horses rear, the post boys look as if they could not keep their seats.... The populace haloo, the pigs squeak, the jingle-men vociferate in Irish—jabbering it quicker and more vehemently than ever. But again I say it—do not be in the least afraid, for no accident ever happens."[15] Sensible advice, except that her Ladyship also managed to reinforce the British stereotype of the Irish as a wild, blundering, chaotic people.

A tourist able to view the scene from a secure perch, such as a hotel window overlooking a market square, might have discovered a certain picturesque quality to the scene. Several writers visiting the West of Ireland commented on the colorful effect of the blue or red cloaks and red petticoats worn by the large numbers of women in attendance. On the other hand Inglis observed that in Galway the women wore no shoes and that the numerous boys were clad at best only in ragged shirts. For his part Thomas Carlyle found nothing picturesque in the sight he beheld from his hotel window in Gort, Galway: "Old blue cloaks on women, greasy-looking rags on most of the men—defacing the summer sun this fine morning!" Happily, he spied a troop of cavalry coming down a street, exercising their horses; "very trim and regular they."[16] Carlyle seemed oblivious to the irrelevance of this contrast between Celtic chaos and Imperial regularity.

Interesting as they were for tourists in search of signs of Irishness, markets and fairs could also be a nuisance for those in transit. Just getting through a town on market day could be a problem, as Ritchie found at Youghal: "The empty carts, waiting probably for their four-footed freight, were huddled together without order, and advanced so far into the street as to render the channel intricate." The ever-practical Anne Plumptre recommended that tourists consult the *Traveller's New Guide in Ireland*, published in 1815, which listed all the fairs held in different parts of country. This enabled the traveler to avoid a town on such days when finding lodgings could be difficult.[17]

Patterns and Fairs

While markets took place several times a week, larger fairs occurred at specific times during the year, most lasting several days. Some focused on specific commodities—there were horse or cattle fairs, even goose fairs. Others were associated with "patterns" held in honor of local patron saints.[18] The crowds at patterns mixed religious practices with commerce and a carnival atmosphere. Needless to say, fairs and patterns proved ideal for the tourist searching for the more exotic signs of Irishness.

The fair held at Donnybrook just over the Dodder River in south Dublin was perhaps the most famous fair in Ireland. It seems to have been a largely secular affair, with elements of the circus. Cromwell described the scene around 1820: "The green is completely covered with tents, or with pipers, fiddlers, and dancers; and of late years mountebanks have also been introduced, together with shews of wild beasts.... The din and tumult is inconceivable; and from the union of the vociferation, laughter, quarrelling, and fighting...a noise ascends that is heard for several miles in all directions." The fair occurred in August and may have originally been part of the old Celtic harvest festival. To end it, Dublin's Lord Mayor frequently had to come out to the grounds to help strike the tents and to clear out the people.[19]

Although sometimes accompanied by a fair, patterns were religious in nature and, therefore, provided British tourists with glimpses into some of the older layers of Irish culture. Many patterns took place around the picturesque ecclesiastic ruins frequented by tourists. Like other types of pilgrimages, patterns moved the folk aspects of Irish Catholicism out of doors and made them visible to visitors. The religious observances that characterized these events—making the stations of the cross, bathing in or praying at holy wells—struck the mostly Protestant tourists who witnessed them as strange if not exotic. Moreover, tourists found outlandish the mingling of devout, if seemingly "Popish," practices with the carnival aspect of a fair. Dr. William Wilde described the great crowds who came to Glendalough every twenty-third of June for a pattern and fair. Once devotees had made their rounds of the Seven Churches, they retired to the vendors' tents for food and drink. Then began the "dancing, drinking, thimble-rigging—prick o'-the-loop, and other amusements, even while bare-headed venerable pilgrims, and bare-kneed voteens who are going their prescribed rounds, continued. Toward the evening the fun became fast and furious." Such activities are depicted in Joseph Peacock's 1813 painting of the pattern at Glendalough. However, along with the seller's tents and wagons, the dancing, the pilgrims and the milling visitors, the artist depicts what appears to be a battle royal taking place in the background within the shadow of the medieval round tower. Describing the pattern at Glendalough, Wilde noted that toward day's end both devotions and dancing ceased, pipers and fiddlers scurried for safety, and vendors secured their goods and gear as best they could. All around them a growing crowd of men gathered, brandishing their sticks and roaring for their respective sides. What Wilde called a "faction fight" was about to begin.[20]

Such battles seem to have been the common coda for many patterns and fairs. T. Croton Croker has a vivid description of how the pattern at Gaugen Barra degenerated into a fight. Donnybrook Fair became famous for its pitched battles "in which much blood is spilled, and many heads broken, but rarely any life lost." In fact, "a donnybrook," became known the world over as a term for Irish recreational fighting—a brawl in other words.[21] Although generally limited to men, faction fights sometimes involved women. Observing a battle at the fair in Cahirciveen, Kerry, Thomas Reid recorded how an "Amazon took off her apron, and enclosed in it a large angular stone, and winding this terrific catapult two or three times around her head, she then left fly at the head of her towering antagonist, still holding the ends of the apron in both of her hands. The blow brought him to the ground streaming with blood; it was not necessary to repeat it; he lay as senseless as a log."[22]

Patrick Logan distinguishes between faction fighting and what he called "stick fighting." He argues that the former involved religious opponents or political factions, often under the control of local landlords, vying for dominance. The less deadly stick fighting, what others have called "recreational fighting," generally involved some skillful fencing with ashplants and blackthorns. Inglis noticed this at the fair in Maum, County Galway, 1834, during a ruction involving the Joyces and a rival clan: "The very flourish of a regular shillelagh

[sic], and the shout that accompanies it, seems to be the immediate precursors of a fractured skull; but the affair, though bad enough, is not so fatal as it appears to be...." Although sticks sometimes did hit heads, mostly they hit each other. Inglis noted that the fight lasted about ten minutes, leaving several men disabled but none killed: "I noticed, after the fight, that some, who had been opposed to each other, shook hands and kissed; and appeared as good friends as before." Needless to say, these fights, whatever their nature, fit all too well into what many tourists would have considered stereotypical Irish behavior carried to the high degree of the exotic. One traveler, observing a donnybrook in Kerry in 1828, described it in Stage-Irish terms: "Cudgels twinkled and Paddies fell in every direction."[23] These mostly ritual combats—"merry wars"— without apparent merit or meaning, simply reinforced the British stereotypes of the Irish as irrational, contrary and pugnacious. And since only Paddies got hurt, visitors seldom took the fights or the participants very seriously.

No humor, however, appears in the reaction of several British and Anglo-Irish writers who recorded their Protestant horror and disgust at the promiscuous mixing of religion and riotous behavior that characterized the patterns. T. Crofton Croker held dim Protestant views regarding the nature of those devotions, but his mind rebelled at the sight of the "drunken men and the most depraved women [who] mingled with those whose ideas of piety brought them to this spot; and a confused uproar of prayers and oaths, of sanctity and blasphemy sounded the same instant on the ear." Observing the pattern at Clonmacnois, Rev. Caesar Otway complained bitterly about "impious blaspheming, the maudlin song, the squeaking bagpipe, and the heavy-footed dance" among those who had spent the earlier part of the day dedicated to devotions. Even Otway, who had a keen appreciation for the folkways of the Irish peasantry, failed to see the ritual nature of these celebrations.[24]

While visitors often regarded these signs of Irishness encountered at fairs and patterns as deeply disturbing, some travel writers found them good copy. James Johnson recognized this as he traveled around Ireland in 1844, a time when Fr. Theobald Mathew's temperance movement was at its height. With tongue in cheek, Johnson complained that Ireland had become a lot quieter than it had been even a decade earlier when Inglis and others "were fortunate enough to travel in times more merry than the present, when furious faction fights, 'ructions,' royal showers of shillelaghs falling on forests of cracked-brain skulls enlivened the scene, and helped to fill up many a page that would otherwise have remained blank and uncut by the reader!... The Star of Ireland's poetry and fun has set forever! We have now no chance of seeing a broken head, a black eye, or a bloody nose.... Prosaic dullness reigns from Kerry to Antrim...." Nonetheless, the power of temperance eventually waned enough for stick fighting to make at least a modest return to fairs and patterns for much of the remainder of the century.[25]

Overall, the seeming contradictory mixture of the sacred and the profane at patterns not only reinforced British stereotypes about the Irish but also feed anti-Catholic attitudes as well. In spite of the attempts on the part of the Roman Catholic clergy to suppress or at least subdue folk, non-liturgical practices, most Protestant observers insisted on seeing in the patterns and pilgrimages examples of Catholicism at its absurd worst. As discussed in Chapter Two, some of the more militantly Evangelical writers even managed to read Popery into the landscape of popular pilgrimage sites such as Lough Derg and Croagh Patrick.

Funerals

As the above examples suggest, the exotic may sometimes go beyond the realm of the expected. Although the milling crowds and hubbub of Ireland's fairs and markets may have been louder and more raucous than similar gatherings in Britain, visitors still had some basis for comparison. Even the recreational fighting that concluded some patterns might have had parallels back home. Few tourists, however, would have been prepared for the sight, much less the sound, of an Irish funeral, even though they had probably read about them prior to their visit. So exotic was the encounter, the Irish funeral procession became one of the set pieces in pre-Famine travel accounts. T. K. Cromwell described one outside of Dundalk. As was usual in Ireland, the hearse was open with a handsome coffin carried under a canopy. Yet, many details of the affair struck the Englishman as "wanting in appropriate solemnity....the mixture of black with every variety of colour—of every degree of respectability from gentility to the threadbare garment, in the dress of the followers—together with that of vehicles of all shapes, sizes, and pretensions, as to soundness and smartness of appearance, in their conveyances—produces ideas rather ludicrous than grave in the unaccustomed spectator." Cromwell reported the amazement of his English driver, who claimed such a sight would never have been encountered back home.[26]

Most travelers greeted the Irish funeral processions as an alien spectacle, although reactions to them varied. The neatness of the mourners' dress in the quarter-mile-long procession she witnessed in Clare impressed Mary Knott. The men had wound white bands about their hats, and they wore blue coats, which set off the whiteness of their shirt collars. The women, mounted behind the men, had dressed in "*warm* blue or scarlet cloaks," their caps displaying a "tasteful variety of form and texture." For some observers, such as a member of the Blake family of Renvyle in Connemara, peasant funerals took on a romantic glow: "I stopped to watch the mournful train wind down the steep declivity, and I can assure you the effect was truly picturesque." Sir Richard Colt Hoare also saw the funeral procession he encountered near

Adair, Limerick within the context of scenic tourism, admiring its "awful and picturesque effect."[27]

Often accompanied by loud lamentations, Irish funeral processions were usually heard before they were seen, assailing the ear before they caught the eye. By the time tourists started arriving in Ireland, keening, the famous "Irish cry" or "howl" had become legendary. Even so, tourist anticipation often fell short of reality, and, whether in processions or at wakes, this loud wailing provided a truly exotic, if not always welcome, experience. An anonymous writer in 1809 complained that, while becoming less common, "the barbarous custom of roaring aloud at funerals is still continued in some places...." On the other hand, James Johnson in 1844 chanced upon a procession that he estimated to have been an "Irish mile" in length. He found that "the ululations of the professed keeners, the cries and sobbings of the female relatives, rendered more distinct and audible by the solemn silence of the long and mournful train, presented a picture unique in its kind, and hardly to be erased by time from memory of the spectator."[28]

The exotic may strike some beholders as grotesque, as well as picturesque, however. Moved indoors into the "wake house," Irish lamentations could be off-putting to any British visitors invited to attend. When he first encountered the "Irish howl," as he called it, the "Sportsman in Ireland" acknowledged that it was "well suited with the liveliness of feeling, which is a strong characteristic of the Irish; the cold formula of an English funeral would ill suit them." However, once inside the wake house, he found "the din was distracting—as, in every variety of tone, men, women, and children, all seemed determined to show their affection for the deceased by the goodness of their own lungs." He then noticed something that caught the eye of other British observers at Irish wakes: "I ventured to look into the faces of the most sonorous of the party—there was almost an instant revulsion to the ridiculous. Not an expression of seriousness even seemed to accompany the howl—the muscles of the face were all perfectly quiescent; On this occasion there were no actual tears being shed." At another wake Anne Plumptre "could not perceive any sign of tears, or the least symptom of real grief upon the continence of any person attending."[29] British Protestant sensibilities were not soothed when visitors noticed that off in the corners whiskey and even jokes were being exchanged.

Only a few travelers recognized something of the ritualistic nature of the Irish wake. Breton Jacques-Louis de Latocayne likened the keening to the "ululatus" of the ancient Romans. Jonathan Binns also recalled the funeral customs of ancient peoples. The Halls described the traditional role of the *bean chnointe* (the female professional mourner) who led the keening. However, they criticized the "merriment" going on at the fringes of the wake. Yet, even this aspect, too, belonged to the ritual of what Gearóid Ó Crualaoich calls the "merry wake," the combination of mourning and celebration that commemorated the death of an older person "whose time had come." The wakes of younger people, on the other hand, were regarded as tragic and treated as such. Most visitors failed to fully recognize and understand the cultural context of Irish funeral customs. This not only trapped such practices in the realms of the exotic, but it placed them in the gallery of half-comic, half-absurd Irish stereotypical behavior.[30] Unfortunately, whether it is viewed positively or negatively, the discovery of the exotic has the effect of increasing the separation between the tourist and the Other.

Hibernian "Orientalism"

Sometimes the search for the exotic inspires a certain exuberance, as the imagination builds an edifice out of a few sticks of reality. Within the context of tourism, travel writers tend to echo each other, and, in doing so, seed expectations among their readers. Galway town is a case in point. There were long-standing historical connections between Galway and Spain. While some Celts may have come to Ireland from the Iberian Peninsula, no doubt more than a bit of Spanish wine—along with other possible influences—flowed through the western port,. This was enough to excite travel writers, who became adept at spotting Moorish, or at least Iberian, influences in Galway and Connemara. For some observers the town, its architecture, even its people carried tantalizing hints of Iberian-Moorish connections. Rev. Robertson went so far as to assert that Ireland had been settled by three races: the Milesians (the "native" Irish), the Scotch and the Spanish.[31]

In the eighteenth century some visitors, such Bishop Pococke and de Latocnaye, claimed to discern Spanish influences in Galway. However, it may have been Henry D. Inglis' widely-read travel account of 1834 that prompted so many subsequent visitors to seek out Iberia on the shores of Galway Bay. Inglis declared that the town's buildings with their wide entries, broad external stairs, arched gateways and courtyards, lacked only the fountains, flowers and little sliding wickets on the doors to make them Spanish. Sir Francis Head, too, found himself intrigued by the "Spanish" architectural influences he perceived "in the wide entries, arched gateways, stone-mullioned windows, and outside stairs of several ancient mansions in town." Not all visitors found Iberian exoticism charming. John Barrow, arriving a year after Inglis, asserted that Galway, "has all the dark and gloomy appearance of which I conceive of a Spanish town, a point upon which all travellers seem to agree—the streets are narrow and dirty—the houses old and dark, with arched gateways that lead into court-yards."[32]

J. Sterling Coyne, for his part, argued that the red petticoats and bright colors of the market women "give a foreign aspect to the population which prepares you somewhat for the completely Italian or Spanish look of most of the streets of the town." The "Sportsman in Ireland" also thought he saw Spanish origins in the dress of Galway women. In 1851 George Preston White claimed that the women of Galway required only "the large combs and graceful mantilla to make the [Spanish] resemblance complete." Some writers even read Moorish features in Galway faces. Sir Francis Head insisted that in the town and throughout Connemara "...I repeatedly met men and women whose countenances, to say nothing of their garb, would anywhere have induced me to address them in Spanish rather than in English." He described one old women "in a mantilla of old blanket, fantastically shrouded over her head, so as to show nothing of an aged face but an *Arab nose*, a pair of piercing eyes, and a very small portion of sallow complexion, there sat at my feet a regular Spanish beggar."[33]

A few travelers extended the Iberian lineage to other parts of Ireland. Lord John Manners found Kilkenny a "Spanish-looking town." William Bennett thought he spied Spanish features in the girls of Valentia Island at the western tip of the coast of Kerry's Iveragh Peninsula. Spencer T. Hall regarded the Clare farmers in their long cloaks and slouched hats as "wanting little to make their costume completely Spanish."[34] Whatever the historical merits of these observations, casting Ireland in an "Oriental" or at least Iberian mode, fulfilled the tourists' impulse to discover the exotic in the host country. Unfortunately, it did little to promote the idea among British visitors that the Irish were their fellow citizens.

Chapter 9

ON THE ROAD—IN SEARCH OF IRELAND

Tourist Space in Ireland

As the preceding chapters have made clear, the Irish Tour involved more than the picturesque. In order to understand the complexity of the tourist experience, it is necessary to investigate "tourist space" in Ireland. The term as used here considers the parts of a country in which tourism occurs, and how deeply into a country tourism may penetrate. Tourist space may be thought of in terms of *traveling to, traveling through* and/or *traveling into* a country. Each involves very different kinds of tourist experiences.

Much tourism today involves the most limited form of tourist space: travel *to* a country. People fly to a location, enjoy a resort, shop around a city, attend a convention or international sporting event, and fly out again. Even on "side trips" to famous ruins or scenic attractions, visitors may move quickly to and from their destinations, encapsulated in buses, planes or helicopters. This sort of point-to-point travel, whatever its joys and rewards, offers a very limited experience of the host country, treating it like a series of unconnected "dots" or sites.

Traveling *through* a country invariably takes more time. In following a well-trod itinerary with little deviation from the guidebook or the route established by the tour guide, this sort of trip may allow the tourist enough time to observe bits of the countryside and the towns along the way; to make brief stops at minor attractions; to visit enough cafes, inns, or food stalls; and talk to enough natives to get some sense of the local as opposed to the international. Instead of seeing just an airport and a resort or a city, the visitor experiencing this broader form of "tourist space" may return home with a very limited tourist's experience.

Alternatively, one may invoke the broadest form of "tourist space" and travel *into* a country. This involves some kind of exploration, by which the visitor may be less interested in "seeing the sights" and more anxious to experience the host country and its people. Travelers, therefore, may pass up the group tour and depart from the beaten path. They may meander along back roads, strolling though small towns and villages not highlighted on the tourist map, observing, chatting and tasting. Whether the trip takes a week or a month, whether it is accomplished in a rented car, on a bicycle or on foot with a backpack, the resulting experience is still limited. Yet, it does offer the opportunity to gain a greater depth of experience, one that can take tourists farther into a country and beyond the clichés of the guidebook and tourist office. It is, of course, quite possible for visitors to mix several modes of travel by, for example, breaking their tours and staying for an extended time in one spot.[1]

Before the development and expansion of the railroads in Ireland, few tourists simply traveled *to* a single destination and then returned directly home without having seen something of the countryside. To have seen anything in pre-Famine Ireland outside of the confines of Dublin or Cork, tourists had to travel at a horse's pace through large portions of the country. In the Ireland of that period tourist space was of necessity broad and deep. In fact, tourist space potentially involved the whole of the island. It included not only picturesque sites but agricultural land, bogs, sparsely settled mountain passes, windswept lake shores and roadside mud cabins. And, as was pointed out in Chapter Two, tourist space could also include social and economic institutions. Almost any aspect of Irish life was open to the tourist, and the tour itself, taking to the road and following the day-to-day itinerary, pulled the disparate parts of the tourists' experience together. In this sense, touring pre-Famine Ireland inevitably meant traveling *into* it. The lovely and the unlovely—all became part of the tourist experience.

And certainly, not everything in Ireland was lovely. For every charming river valley, the traveler would inevitably ride through long stretches of seemingly empty bog land. Some tourists dismissed such areas as dull, if not actually ugly, and endured riding through them as best they could. However, judging from the travel accounts, many visitors were prepared to engage with almost everything they saw. In many cases tourists could take whatever detours they wished and stop their vehicles wherever and whenever they pleased. And when they did, the fields, bogs and cabins became tourist sites in their own right; that is, places or objects that engaged their inquiring gaze and made impressions on their minds. In fact, the mundane sights found along the road were as much a part of the Irish Tour as the famous picturesque attractions. They were the raw materials involved in the search for Ireland itself, its differences, its uniqueness—the real journey *into* Ireland.

Time, Travel and Landscape Perception

As noted earlier, touring in pre-Famine Ireland, either on or behind a horse, was slower than today's faster pace of travel. As a consequence, tourists spent considerable time directly exposed to the elements, to the countryside and to its people. Areas that today's tourist might cover by automobile in twenty minutes might have taken hours to traverse in the in eighteenth and early nineteenth centuries. To some extent, then, the impression made by a landscape depended on the time it took to get through it. As they clopped along the road on horseback or in carriages, the tourists' experiences could be quite different from those they had enjoyed at picturesque sites like Killarney or the Giant's Causeway. There visitors weighed the anticipated with the realized, gauged their reactions, listened to the guides, engaged with vendors, and made their sketches or took their notes. They focused their attention on highly regarded landscape features. Almost every element within such sites had a name and a guidebook description. Along the road, however, only distant mountain ranges, towns and the occasional ruined abbey bore names the visitors might know. And, as Jonathan Culler suggests, "Nothing is more boring than an unnamed landscape."[2] So the tourists had to deal with successions of bogs, hillocks, fields, hamlets and peasants' cabins in a different way. The sublime and the picturesque required no explaining; they did not have to be accounted for—unlike everything else the tourists encountered along the road.

As they traveled through pre-Famine Ireland, the visitors view of the countryside changed slowly, and whatever moods or reactions it induced stayed with the travelers, sometimes for hours. Moreover, they were hostage to bad weather until it decided to change. Owing to a deficiency of funds, Mr. A. Atkinson frequently traveled on foot. In walking through the village of Mohill in Leitrim, he found himself nearly ankle-deep in mud. Slogging along, he had ample time to reflect upon and deplore what he considered the "bleak and undiversified appearance" of the surrounding country. Even the mounted traveler suffered from long exposure to unpleasant or at least unpleasing countryside. In spite of the benefit of horse power, Rev, Caesar Otway was not charmed by the scenery he encountered upon leaving Tuam in Galway as he headed for Mayo. He found the country "exceedingly ugly.... I scarcely could bring myself to believe that a lake could be an ugly thing until I saw some of those in Galway and Mayo, surrounded by dreary rockiness of the uncovered limestone wastes, or by the brown desolation of the bog...." Robert Bell, riding through the drumlin belt in County Cavan in 1809, felt burdened by the equally dismal landscape and weather: "The hills exhibiting nothing but bareness and the hollows between them consisted of a vast morass, whose produce, except a little stunted hay and oats, was turf. Not a tree, not even a tolerable cabin was visible over the face of this country.... The rain set in, in perfect torrents and down the rugged hills, over which we passed the floods poured in tremendous torrents."[3]

Since Ireland's Midlands contained a high percentage of the country's raised or red bogs, anyone traveling through them had to endure stretches of what many considered dull, even depressing landscape. The extensive Bog of Allen, for instance, lay directly in the path of the Dublin-Galway traveler. Originally a network of bogs covering around 770 square miles, it was significantly drained by the cutting of the cross-country canals. Trying to describe this "dreary expanse of brown heath-like herbage," Leitch Ritchie asked his readers to "imagine a plain of this kind, extending as far as the eye can reach, with pools or lakes of black water gleaming in the midst." The scene was not improved by the "miserable" huts of the bog workers, smoke "oozing" from their roofs.[4]

It would be a mistake to assume that such comments were the grumblings of travelers whose aesthetic tastes were so tuned to the sublime and the picturesque that they were unable to appreciate the less spectacular, more mundane landscapes of rural Ireland. On the contrary, visitors also applied the same visual awareness they brought to a place like Killarney to everything else in Ireland. And if visitors did not always enjoy what they saw, they could explain why. For example, they were acutely aware of what they regarded as pleasant rural landscapes, and they could identify the missing elements in the unpleasant ones. So armed, they were quite as prepared to render aesthetic judgments on agricultural land as they were on mountains, lakes and waterfalls. Moving slowly along the road, these visitors had ample time to evaluate what they saw, and when the landscape failed to meet their standards, they also had time to decide who or what was to blame.

The tyranny of horse power began its slow decline during the waning days of the Great Famine. As noted in Chapter One, Ireland's first cross-country rail lines began operating in the 1840s. The contrast between the old and new modes of transportation was obvious. For one thing, the scenery glimpsed from a rail car changed rapidly. In 1852 Sir Francis Bond Head rode the newly completed railroad from Dublin to Mullingar. Settling himself in the "coupe," he declared it "really quite delightful to find oneself in a quiet study with large plate-glass windows, contemplating, not little bits of painted canvas, but Ireland itself, passing in review, with growing crops, living cows, sheep, goats, and horses...." The scenery changed steadily as the train headed into an area of bog land: "Suddenly, from the most beautiful verdure, we passed through a large dark level, looking as if it had been convulsed by an earthquake...." If Head had been riding behind a horse, he would have had plenty of time to contemplate this dreary scene. However, thanks to steam power, "the barren bog...suddenly changed into heather in bloom, in which occasionally appeared heaps of peat; and thus for some time flowers and fuel were to be seen in juxtaposition, in a beautiful variety of different proportions." Spencer T. Hall likened a railway trip to "a photographic process, by which object after object becomes permanently fixed upon it." James Johnson worried, however, that visitors would form "sweeping conclusions...of countries over which they travel at railroad speed...with very little real knowledge..."[5]

Crossing Boundaries

Most tourists had some awareness of the character of the four provinces of Ireland. Leinster contained the capital city, the Glens of Wicklow and rich river valleys and farmlands. Munster combined good farm lands in the east with scenic seacoasts and the beautiful scenery of Kerry. Connacht or "the West" and Ulster or "the North" were of particular interest, because in traveling to them, visitors crossed several sociological, as well as geographical, boundaries.

The West is generally defined as that part of Ireland beyond the Shannon and the Foyle lying along the Atlantic seaboard. It is characterized by bogs, mountains and sea cliffs interspaced by broad bays and many rocky inlets. Although more lush in its scenery, the southwestern portions of Munster, made up of the mountainous parts of Kerry and of West Cork, share many of the characteristics with "The West." In spite of some difficult roads, the Southwest was open to tourists as far as Killarney during the second half of the eighteenth century. For the most part the Iveragh Peninsula and the cliff-walled Clare coast were not readily accessible until the 1820s and 1830s, when new roads were built. Connemara in West Galway could not be easily accessed until the 1840s.

Since the seventeenth century, the British had regarded the West as the most distinctively Irish part of the island.[6] Certainly, much of the region looks starkly different from the rest of Ireland, especially in comparison to the rich agricultural sections of Leinster and the eastern portions of both Munster and Ulster. As the first Northern European landfall for storms coming in from the North Atlantic, the West of Ireland receives the highest rainfall in the country. A relatively treeless region, it contains mountains covered with blanket bogs, with much of the lower-lying areas dotted with raised bogs and small lakes. Its heavy rain and acidic soil make grain cultivation problematic in much of the West. However, the region's peasantry, especially those crowded along the coastal strips, managed to grow potatoes and raise pigs and goats.

Although many found the Western landscape exhilarating, British tourists also found it stark and even alien. The numerous bogs, which failed to meet most tourist's standards of "scenery," were all too easily written off as "wasteland." Moreover, the West contained few settlements that matched British concepts of proper villages, a point to be discussed below. The region was, in fact, Ireland's poorest, something that shocked tourists, even though most would have read something about Irish poverty before leaving Britain. Finally, to add to the region's powerful sense of difference, the West contained the highest proportion of Ireland's Gaelic speakers. For much of the pre-Famine period travelers had to rely on guides or drivers who could also act as translators. Thus, even if Ireland was the "sister island," the West was more like a foreign country. As suggested earlier, tourists leave home precisely to experience difference, but as also noted, such differences can also be disturbing. And so, although the West of Ireland became a tourist Mecca, it nevertheless raised difficult questions in the minds of many visitors about the nature of Ireland and its people.

Traveling northward from Dublin to Ulster, the tourist crossed another, even more complex series of boundaries. In terms of geography, much of the Province of Ulster is divided from the rest of Ireland by the so-called drumlin belt. Drumlins are little hills, the cores of which are made up of glacial till or debris left over from the last Ice Age. Since the thousands of such hills impeded drainage, the land between them became waterlogged, settling into small lakes and bogs. Much of the southern border of Ulster is marked by swarms of drumlin extending from County Down westward along much of the modern political border dividing Northern Ireland from the Republic, until they fan out into Sligo and Mayo further south, forming numerous islands in Sligo Bay and in Clew Bay.[7]

Although few tourists had the geological term for them or realized their extent, most travel writers clearly described drumlins. Robert Bell's impressions of drumlins were noted above. One writer in the 1740s compared those around Downpatrick in County Down to so many "wooden Bowls inverted, or Eggs set in Salt." Theresa Cornwallis West described the land in eastern Monaghan as "tumbled about most strangely; little knolls are quite round while the valleys seem scooped out with a spoon. It is this peculiar conformation which has occasioned County Monaghan to be compared to a *dish of pippins* with its conical rotundities all over the face of it." Years earlier, Gabriel Beranger, passing through Leitrim on his way to Sligo, observed that the hills there appeared endless: "We looked forward from the top we ascended, and were astonished to see others as high before us succeeding one another in chains piled up so that no horizon could be seen."[8]

Starting in County Down, the drumlin belt roughly follows the line that divides Ireland's better-drained soils in the east from the wetter lands as far as County Leitrim in the west.[9] While small farms are successful on some of the drumlins, especially in the dryer eastern portions of Ulster, the agricultural quality of the land tends to deteriorate as one moves westward. As a consequence, travelers were often struck by the poverty they encountered as they traveled through the drumlins heading north into Ulster. Once north of the drumlin belt, however, visitors often encountered stretches of relatively good agricultural land, which they compared favorably to those of rural England. The impression made by these relatively prosperous-looking farms was enhanced by their contrast to what travelers had seen as they spent hours twisting and turning through the poorer and unattractive drumlin regions. The reverse journey, from north to south, with the prosperous farms behind them, tended to underscore for travelers the contrasting destitution of the rest of Ireland.

The drumlins were not the only boundary travelers to Ulster had crossed, however. By the time they were admiring the farms around County Down, the Glens of Antrim or the hinterland of Derry, tourists had passed through a social frontier as well. Ulster contained the largest proportion of Ireland's Protestants, most of them in the eastern half, where they dominated the Province's best agricultural land. The fact that "Protestant Ulster" (essentially four or five out of the nine counties of the Province) appeared so prosperous was not lost on the British tourists, most of whom were Protestant themselves. As a result, Ulster came to be regarded as a unique part of Ireland, *if* it could, in fact, really be considered Irish at all. Henry D. Inglis' statement, noted earlier, that in Belfast "there is, in fact, no trace of an Irish population among any class...," underlined this distinction. An anonymous visitor, having journeyed from Dublin through the drumlin belt into County Armagh, exclaimed: "What a change! The transition from England to Ireland is not more remarkable than that from the south to the north."[10] When they reached County Down, the Halls claimed that, "We began to feel we were in another country; in a district at least where the habits as well as the looks of the people were altogether different from those to which we had been accustomed." Other visitors in the 1830s and 1840s had similar impressions. To them Protestant Ulster became a moral landscape, a superior unIreland by which the rest of the country and its Roman Catholic majority stood judged and condemned.[11]

A Naked, Bleak, Dreary Country

Based on travel accounts, it seems that, in addition to an eye for the sublime and the picturesque, many British tourists brought with them a well-articulated appreciation for rich agricultural landscape, such as they had found in Ulster and eastern Ireland. They based this admiration on a series of cultural "templates" of fields and villages derived from the enclosed rural landscape of England's Home Counties, the heartland of Britain's grain production. Most travelers delighted in neat villages with rose-covered cottages surrounded by well-tilled and maintained fields clearly marked by blooming hedgerows, all set within a verdant countryside dotted with trees. Behind this aesthetic ideal lay a profound sense of economic well-being and social order. In the absence of such scenes, however, a landscape could seem out of kilter. Much of rural Ireland did not look right to British tourists who looked at Ireland but thought of home.

Trees were the first things British tourists found missing in the Irish countryside. Touring Ireland in the 1770s, the English agronomist Arthur Young complained that the greatest part of the country "exhibits a naked, bleak, dreary view for want of wood [trees], which has been destroyed for a century past with the most thoughtless prodigality, and still continues to be cut and wasted as if it was not worth the preservation." Such sentiments echoed throughout virtually every Irish travelogue. As noted earlier, the combination of ancient farming practices, climate change and, during the seventeenth and eighteenth centuries, ruthless colonial exploitation, had destroyed much of Ireland's forests. The resulting treeless landscapes found in many parts of the island were an affront to eye of the British visitors. As a consequence, travelers welcomed any comforting sylvan clump they came upon, especially in the West. Upon seeing the tree-enshrouded Martin house at Ballynahinch in Connemara, a member of the Blake family enthused: "In so wild a country as this, where trees are rarely to be seen, and where the eye generally travels over a dreary waste of bog til it rest on the barren summits of the distant mountains…there is something singularly pleasing in finding yourself embosomed among the trees…."[12]

Perhaps it was a subconscious awareness of the loss of trees back home that accounted for the British tourist's shock at treeless Ireland. Britain, too, had been prodigal with its forests. And although it eventually arrived at better forest management practices than Ireland, by 1800 only one-eighth of England remained under wood. Moreover, because of the losses suffered by the British navy during the Seven Years war, something akin to an oak panic had swept Britain in the later decades of the eighteenth century. Typically, such unpleasant concerns about home do not usually surface in travelogues. They can, however, make the tourist sensitive to similar failings or problems in the host country. Thus, British tourists deplored Ireland's scarcity of trees without explicitly recalling the situation back home.[13]

Besides trees, British tourists also missed the hedgerows of home, or at least the Home Counties. The English hedgerows were and are intricately connected mini-ecologies made up of a variety of plants, trees and animals. With their flowering hawthorn they provided some of the aesthetic pleasure Britons took in the rich agricultural lands around London. Although English-type hedges could be found and were admired in parts of Leinster and Ulster, field boundaries through much of Ireland were more likely to consist of sparse "hedgebanks," a mixture of earth and stone incorporating only a few trees and gorse.[14] In the West fields were divided by dry stone walls. Neither type of boundary division held much aesthetic appeal for the tourists.

To eyes that had learned to appreciate the aesthetics of English agriculture, much of the Irish countryside seemed wrong. Around 1820 T. K. Cromwell wrote: "The face of this country is almost invariably less rich than that of England... the apparent monotony of its surface...is a consequence of the want of trees and hedge-rows rather than of exuberance in the cultivated productions of the soil." Although, as T. K. Cromwell observed, there was much greater cultivation in Ireland than in Scotland or Wales, the Irish countryside just did not look right. Scottish landlord Robert Graham echoed this view when he described the productive farms in Wexford: "If you could substitute quickset [hawthorn] for furze [gorse] fences and could make hedgerows where there are now clay banks, this portion of the country could not easily be surpassed by any agricultural district of the same extent in England."[15]

Cromwell and Graham were sharper observers than most travelers who, shocked by the absence of trees and hedgerows, simply assumed that Irish agricultural productivity was inferior to England's. Theresa Cornwallis West's reaction was typical. Irish fields, she protested, appeared unkempt: "the hedges broken and irregular; the stone walls loose and crumbling that mostly divide the fields, and every third patch of grass-land choked with rag-weed in full growth which ought to have been plucked out by the roots...."[16] Yet, on the eve of the Famine, these unattractive ill-kempt Irish fields allowed Ireland to export enough food to feed two million people in Britain.

More than a well-developed rural aesthetic informed the tourists' horror regarding Ireland's scarcity of trees, "proper" hedgerows and well-maintained fields. The British template for rural beauty rested on the evolution of modern agriculture based upon a complex system of crop rotation, involving alternative plantings of clover, grains, legumes, root crops and pasturage. To manage this system, landlords enclosed previously open or unfenced fields within rectangular sections carefully bordered by hedgerows. This enclosure movement, which continued through the first century of Irish tourism, represented the basis for the Agricultural Revolution that greatly increased England's agrarian output and the incomes of its great estates. In fact, it was the proprietors who drove enclosure bills through Parliament. The resulting checkerboard layout of England's fields not only looked pretty; they also symbolized prosperity and order. And, while the enclosure movement had reached Ireland, it generally took hold only in the best farming lands of Ulster, Leinster and Munster where British travelers recorded their approval, even joy, at the sight of English-looking farms. However, when the visual cues of English-style farming and prosperity were missing, which was often the case, the visitors were disappointed and distressed.[17]

This was particularly true when visitors passed through areas where grazing rather than cultivation dominated the rural economy. At the time of his visit to the Rock of Cashel in southwest Tipperary in 1770s, Reverend Thomas

Campbell complained that the landscape represented nothing more than a "sheep walk": "Agriculture ceases," he declared, "and not a house, not a hedge, not a ditch is to be seen." In England such a tract "would be as beautifully rich as any in the British Empire." Yet, Campbell continued, "with a total neglect of cultivation, there is scarce a tree to be seen.... The squire's country seat, the rich farm house, or even the warm cottage, are here looked for, but looked for in vain...." Compared to cultivated farmland, the look of the grazier economy of the cattle raising lands in Tipperary and East Galway seemed barren, although the land was clearly productive.[18]

Pasturage was not the only reason British visitors often failed to find English-style enclosed fields in Ireland. Small holders in England farmed comparatively less land than their counterparts in Ireland, especially in the West.[19] This was largely the result of the Irish landlords, or their primary renters, who chose to enhance their incomes by permitting subletting among their tenantry, instead of pursuing the more expensive alternative of improving their land. By the nineteenth century Ireland had a fast-growing population of poor peasants working small tracts and living primarily on potatoes. Enclosure proved impractical on this scale of farming. As a result, many small fields were in fact open and unfenced. The aesthetic, social and economic association of enclosed agriculture with prosperity and good order became so in-grained in the British mind that many travelers revealed a distinct prejudice against any sort of unenclosed land, even when given over to crops. Bereft of the sight of their beloved checkerboard fields, Britons suffered from what John Barrell calls "visual discomfort."[20]

Concluding her reminiscences about her stay in Kerry, Lydia Jane Fisher could not help comparing the fields and farms there with those she had seen in England. She described "the soft and verdant wealth of her [England's] landscapes, and the rich glory of her waiting woods,—her fields divided by hedge-rows, and her plains stretching away to the horizon—a sea of verdure—all speaks of peace, industry, and security! Alas, judge if the contrast between those well-remembered scenes and the terrible and sorrowful poverty of these [Kerry's] wastes and wilds does not strike me with a saddening force, akin to envy. How much more melancholy is the difference between the domestic habits and comforts of the two nations!"[21] Like so many visitors, Fisher had indulged herself in a kind of tourist's myopia which compares the best of home to the worst of the host country. In this case she compared Britain's richest agricultural region, the farmland of England's Home Counties, to a part of Ireland where cultivation would always be marginal at best.

In 1809 Joseph Woods tried to sum up what British travelers found missing in so much of the rural landscape of Ireland: "It is not mere wood which gives richness to English landscape but the mixture of wood, cultivation and habitation—the hedge rows, and the trees in them, the sheltered villages & farm houses with their orchards, and the Spire embosomed in Elms or Eughs [sic]. There is nothing of all this in the generality of Irish scenery." Spencer T. Hall complained that in Ireland "few or no villages like our English, Scotch, or Welsh villages, crowned with church spires or towers, could be seen in the distance."[22] It is important to keep in mind that the great proprietors often owned the villages and controlled the livelihoods connected to those spired churches. Clearly then, just as with enclosed fields, the association of aesthetics with apparent productive order biased the eye of the British tourists. As a result, they misread features of Irish agriculture and—looking at Ireland and thinking of England—they imposed their own cultural and socio-economic presumptions on Ireland, making it difficult for them to completely understand the country and its problems.

Irish Poverty and the Tourist Experience

Rundale settlements represented one type of Irish settlement so far removed from the British ideal of a village that it filled visitors with disgust and horror. Sometimes referred to as "clachans," these settlements—mostly clusters of mud cabins—could be found in many parts of Ireland, but were particularly plentiful in the West. Peasants living in such communities would pool their resources to rent and work what was often marginal land. On the infields around their cabins they raised grain and/or potatoes in unfenced, open strips, which were periodically redistributed. In the outfields and rough upland pastures they raised cattle and sheep. Some work was done in common, and the elected village headman, the *airgead rí* ("money king"), collected the rent and paid the landlord. Because arable land was frequently at a premium, cabins were situated on the least productive plots nearest the road, without regard to alignment or order, thus giving the clachan its characteristic jumbled appearance. Although their prototypes might be traced back to the Middle Ages, during the pre-Famine decades, the clachans evolved and spread in the West and in the most densely populated parts of Ulster. They were a natural response to the rapidly growing population of poor peasants who, as Kevin Whelan has pointed out, used the rundale system to pioneer the production of marginal land. The system allowed the poorest peasantry to invest their only resource—their labor. The self-sufficient clachans represented what Whelan characterizes as a "sophisticated response" to the social and ecological problems presented by Ireland's massive population growth.[23]

All of this was usually lost on the visitor who happened upon a clachan. Although most tourists had no term for them, anyone writing about a "jumble" of poor cabins that looked as if they had fallen "in a shower from the sky," was, in most cases, describing one. In 1862, journalist Harry Coulter came upon a clachan that had survived the Famine near Castlebar: "The cottages are built most irregularly, here, there, and everywhere—some parallel with the road, others at right angles with it...the road through the village is ankle deep in mud; and pigs, poultry, and children are to be seen running in every direction. Words fail to convey an adequate idea of the filthy and disorderly appearance which this village presents."[24] In many ways the term "village" was a misnomer. The clachans had none of the infrastructure which the British visitors associated with proper village life—no blacksmith, no shops, no rose-covered cottages, no church, with or without a spire, and no solid houses suggesting a resident middle class. To the visitors the clachans made no sense whatsoever, except as extreme examples of Irish slovenliness, disorder and poverty.

The British had always associated Ireland with poverty, even while happily exploiting its resources. Poverty had thus long been a part of the Irish stereotype, and it is hard to imagine any tourist who had not read something about it before coming to Ireland. And, while the Giant's Causeway or Killarney may have occasionally fallen short of tourist expectations, few travel writers of the pre-Famine period found Irish poverty anything *less* than what they had anticipated. Indeed, most seemed shocked at its reality, even though British tourists should have been well acquainted with poverty back home. Nonetheless, operating once again under tourist amnesia, those who attempted any sort of comparison between Britain and Ireland usually insisted that Irish poverty was worse. In fact, by the eve of the Famine, most travel writers depicted Ireland's dire poverty as uniquely Irish. The anonymous author of *The Irish Tourist*, published in the 1830s, claimed that until he came to Limerick he had no real conception of the depth of poverty and misery.[25] Certainly, poverty in Ireland appeared wide spread and deep. Yet, it is hard to believe that it was worse than what could have been encountered in the slums of England's industrial cities like Manchester.

Spread out along the tourist track, however, Irish poverty was certainly visible. Many Irish peasants dressed in rags. Many went barefoot. Their cabins were often ill-thatched, smoky, mud huts that they shared with their animals. Their main food was the potato, which most British visitors wrongly assumed was less nutritious than the grain diet of English agricultural workers. The potato, in fact, is one of the most nutritious foods in the world, and most travelers had to admit that, except in times of distress, Irish peasants looked relatively healthy in spite of their rags. As Cormac Ó Gráda has pointed out, while Irish life expectancy was a few years lower than that of the English, it was higher than that of several European nationalities. In fact, by the beginning of the nineteenth century, the potato had become the foundation of much of Ireland's rural economy. Its high yields and high nutritional value made it possible to feed Ireland's mushrooming population and underwrite the continued subdivision of holdings. The potato was, moreover, a substitute food. By eating primarily potatoes, farmers could send their more desirable produce to market, thereby sustaining estate incomes and Ireland's agricultural export trade with Great Britain. Of course, when the tuber failed it brought the whole system down with it.[26]

Irish peasants had a few other advantages besides the potato. Although frequently ragged, many peasants did have the benefit of free fuel—peat. And, while their cabins were certainly wretched, some of the dwellings of England's rural and especially urban poor were not much better.[27] Nevertheless, visitors from the other island no doubt found it comforting to assert that the Irish poor were worse off than those back home. To believe otherwise would have raised the kinds of questions about home that tourists rarely entertained abroad.

In assuming the uniqueness of Irish poverty, British visitors sometimes exaggerated its extent. Not all of the "poor" whom tourists encountered were really destitute. Compared to many Irish and British Protestants, Irish Catholic farmers were less likely to invest in appearances. They put less money into their clothes, shoes and houses and more into their cattle, and, even more significantly, education for their children. In fact, Irish Catholic culture did not encourage individuals to appear more prosperous than their neighbors. And this is one reason why Ulster Protestants often looked more prosperous than Catholics. Each group made different choices about what to do with its money. Thus, visitors were sometimes surprised to discover that some ragged farmer in a rough cabin with hardly any furniture was "a man of a hundred cows." In some cases, a poor-looking Catholic tenant might actually have loaned money to his improvident landlord. Furthermore, because the better-off Catholic farmers did not appear superior to their poorer neighbors, visitors were unable to discern a rural middle class in many parts of Ireland. As several travel writers remarked, there seemed to be no one between the landlords and their poverty-stricken tenants. Another reason Protestant tenant farmers, at least in Ulster, appeared more prosperous than their Catholic neighbors had to do with politics. Not only did the Protestants generally occupy and farm the better land, they usually had more advantageous arrangements with their landlords, giving them some protection from evictions and some reimbursement for improvements they made on the land. In most other parts of Ireland, tenants feared that any improvements to dwellings or lands would simply result in higher rents.[28]

Occasionally tourists found themselves sharing the roads with the Irish poor. John Barrow marveled at the deployment of old regimental greatcoats along the Irish roads: "Could you but see the strange-looking characters that have found their way into these coats, carelessly trudging along with a short tobacco-pipe, commonly called a *dudeen*, in the corner of their mouths; the big shilelahs [sic] sloped across their shoulders, and all their worldly possessions tied up in a dirty bundle suspended at the end of it—except, perhaps, some half-dozen brats, one of whom rides *pick-aback*, while the mother brings up the rear with the other five,—you would indeed be astonished how they drag out what must appear to everyone but themselves so miserable an existence." It is very likely that Barrow's pauper family were only seasonal beggars; small conacre farmers who, having planted the year's crop of potatoes, had closed their cabin and taken to road before returning for the harvest and the winter.[29] Sometimes the men went to Britain looking for seasonal work while their wives and children took to the summer roads to beg. Ritchie observed this practice in the 1830s: "If you see…a ragged mother, with a baby on her back, and two or three ragged children at her heels, and more rarely, the ragged father bringing up the rear,—if you see this melancholy cortege glide into the huts by the roadside…you may conclude with absolute certainty, that you have seen a family of pauper peasants…." Ritchie noted that these families rarely bothered the tourists. Instead, they begged from other peasant families only slightly better off than themselves. Stopping for a time in Phillipstown in the 1830s, Jonathan Binns claimed that between two and four hundred such seasonal beggars would pass through the town in any given day.[30]

The Cabin

Ubiquitous as beggars were, British tourists did not regard them as the true representatives of Irish poverty. It was the peasant with his rags, his pig, his mud cabin and numerous family who caught their attention. The poverty that emerges from the travel accounts is not just a generalized picture of deprivation. It can be quite specific and detailed, for any tourist who wished could look Irish poverty in the face and even enter its dwelling. Ironically, the Irish cabins themselves, often poorly thatched one-room mud structures, became a locus for Irish tourism. T. K. Cromwell remarked on the wretchedness of "the rural cabins congregated in petty villages, or scattered still more thickly than in England, over the surface of the country." Surprisingly, at least from the standpoint of modern tourists, visitors to pre-Famine Ireland investigated and described the cabin and its inhabitants, human and otherwise, making it part of the Irish tourist experience. These encounters were as likely to involve encounters with animals as with people. Richard Twiss entered one cottage and entertained a hen on his knee. Mary Knott tolerated the poultry but pointedly requested that the resident pig be kept outside during her visit to a cabin in Clare.[31] Once inside, the visitors took note of the smoke (few of the poorer cabins had chimneys) and the dim interior (few had windows). Very often the visitor might occupy the cabin's only piece of furniture.

The tourists' presence in the cabin resulted from a combination of curiosity, compassion, and a sort of class-based entitlement that allowed gentlemen and ladies to pursue the public interest in the private sphere of the poor. Since the condition of the Irish poor remained an important question not limited to Parliamentary commissions and reports, any visitor to Ireland might make inquiries. The class differences between the well-dressed visitors and their ragged hosts was negotiated through the ritual of Irish hospitality, which ran very deep within Gaelic culture and became an important aspect of Irish tourism. If at all possible, the Irish hosts offered their guests something to eat or to drink. John Melish, caught in a shower between Newry and Belfast, sheltered in a "wretched cabin," where an old woman gave him some *potín*. Dismounting from his car on a steep hill, Henry D. Inglis entered a nearby cabin in which he found an old man who lived by begging potatoes from his neighbors. The host offered his guest a tuber, and in exchange Inglis proffered some tobacco. When available, the visitor might have been given one of the good quality potatoes that the family raised primarily for market. Otherwise, the guest would get what the family ate, a half-cooked "lumper," a prolific if ill-tasting tuber. Such potatoes often had the "bone" in them; that is, they were undercooked so that the center remained almost raw. This meant that it took longer to digest and so, as one peasant told surgeon Thomas Reid, "they stick to our ribs, and we can fast longer that way."[32] Visitors usually left a coin or two behind in return for the treat.

For the one-quarter to one-third of the Irish peasants who occupied the lowest rungs on pre-Famine Ireland's economic ladder, the cabin and its family was the basic unit of survival. Everything around and in it served the tight and merciless logic of that survival. Almost every cabin had at least a "praty garden" or potato patch, the main source for the family's food. Potatoes are not difficult to grow, requiring only spade cultivation. In Ireland they were often grown in raised beds, popularly known as "lazy beds," which tourists took as a kind of metaphor for what they regarded as a lazy man's crop, easy to plant and requiring little tending. The beds, however, represented an ancient and sophisticated method of cultivation in wet soil. They consisted of a ridge made by folding over the sod on the left and right to form a domed ridge. The digging broke the iron pan and provided nutrients to be spread on the ridge, along with the green manure from the turned-over grass. The process also formed drains on either side of the ridges. The potato, planted on the top of the bed, not only grew out of the wet, but it also received maximum sunlight.[33]

Although they would grow almost anywhere, potatoes did require manure, especially in the poor, acidic soils of the West. Therefore, a manure pile (more often a pool) lay before the cabin door, the recipient of what were euphemistically called the "sweepings of the house." To this the family added any animal droppings donated by passing horses and cattle, as well as the invaluable contribution from the resident pig. The manure's proximity to the door shocked and disgusted most tourists, who did not understand that the family's food production depended upon protecting it—no manure, no potatoes.

Although highly nutritious, the potatoes did not last a full year, and, as noted above, those who were largely dependent upon them had to beg during the "hungry months" of summer until the new crop came in. Since any surplus potatoes would not keep, the family fed extra tubers and their stalks to the pig, which acted as a kind of potato bank. Peasant families rarely ate their pig (or any other kind of meat). Instead, the animal was sold at market to help pay the yearly rent. Thus, the frequent reference to the pig as "the gintleman what pays the rent." Pigs are, however, somewhat fragile creatures and cannot be kept outside in the rain and damp. Since few of the poorer families could manage a piggery, much less a barn, the pig, along with whatever other livestock the family had, crowded into the cabin at night to bed down with their owners. This manner of securing livestock against theft and disease horrified the British visitors even more than the door-side manure pile.

Few tourists understood the intricacies of what many took to be a slovenly, catch-as-catch-can approach to agriculture. Few understood how tightly the parts of the system fitted together—or the disaster that awaited a family if any part failed. To the visitors, the cabin, its ragged inhabitants, its resident menagerie and its ill-kept potato patches made no sense, except to bear witness to the careless, chaotic qualities of the Irish character. Indeed, in the Irish cabin the tourist had found the ultimate exotic—the inscrutable Irish Other.

Lord John Manners, visiting Ireland in 1846, learned of some agricultural laborers from Adair who, having gone to England where they earned from twelve to fifteen shillings a week, all soon returned home. They came back, not because of difficulties regarding travel or wages, but because they missed their families: "They would rather lead a life of misery," wrote the astounded baronet, "and struggle among old familiar scenes in Ireland—helping and being helped by relatives and friends, as nearly as miserable…as themselves—than live prosperous among strangers, and enjoy comforts away from the Shannon." His lordship found this incomprehensible, and he then unburdened himself on the hopelessness of the Englishman's attempt to understand the Irish. The Englishman, he wrote, "has one system of government, one key to the human heart, one conception of human virtue, one appreciation of human happiness," But, alas for the Englishman trying to govern the Irishman: "His [the Englishman's] system of government in not government for them; his key to the human heart won't unlock theirs; his conception of human virtues is in their eyes neither Catholic nor Christian; his appreciation of happiness to them is misery; what results?" In Manners' case the results seem to have been anger and frustration.[34]

For other visitors the sense of frustration that Ireland engendered within them went even deeper. It was much more fundamental, and it was directly connected to the very basis of the picturesque tour. Entering Castlebar in Mayo, the anonymous author of *A Sportsman in Ireland* praised the surrounding scenery: "The gorgeous beauty of the sun reflected on the glassy bosom of the Castlebar Lake, and the pure green of the mountains...formed a cheering scene, to which the miserable huts we occasionally passed but ill responded."[35] The more open to the Irish picturesque, the more difficulty a visitor had in reconciling Ireland's natural beauty with its apparent extreme poverty. This is particularly evident in the ten years or so prior to the Famine, when, because of the pressure of the country's population upon an already unstable land system, both the degree and extent of Irish poverty seemed to be growing. As Glenn Hooper shows in *Travel Writing and Ireland*, the optimism that characterized travel accounts just after the Act of Union had begun to wane by the 1830s and on the eve of the Famine had given way to pessimism among some writers. And, if one theme runs through most of the Irish travelogues by the mid-1830s, it is the seeming contradiction between natural splendor and the wretchedness of Irish poverty. In a culture still inclined to associate nature's beauty and bounty with a divinely ordained sense of order, the presence of extreme poverty and its accompanying ugliness seemed a denial of that order.

An anonymous visitor to Killarney in the 1830s could not block out the scenes of the human misery he had so far encountered in Ireland. Referring to the beauty of the Lakes, he wrote: "Time was when my heart would have bounded at the sight, and broke out in raptures of enthusiastic ecstasy; now it sunk within me, and I was silent, if not sullen—a very Trappist, no longer a worthy votary and worshipper of Nature." While on a sketching expedition, Lady Chatterton came across a doorless cottage with holes in its roof: "The contrast of this old smoke-stained and nearly ruined hovel, with the sublime and highly decorated character of the surrounding scenery, was very striking. A picture of distress where all nature seemed to rejoice; a mass of wretchedness amid the perfection of beauty."[36] Similar comments were quite common in the travel literature.

While picturesque tourism is often condemned for allowing tourists to ignore a country's harsh realities (and the literature certainly abounds with examples), the very nature of the Irish tour often forced British visitors to at least acknowledge, and often report on, Ireland's poverty. Sometimes the acknowledgements went very deep. Throughout his two-volume travelogue, *Ireland, Picturesque and Romantic*, Ritchie called almost as much attention to the Irish poverty as to the country's scenery. Toward the end of his work he unburdened himself of his feelings: "To a sincere lover of Nature, the tour I have just finished is one of the most delightful in Europe; but to him who, instead of abandoning himself to the poetry of the world, lives and is living in the joys and sorrows of his own kind, it will be productive of many a bitter thought, and many a melancholy hour."[37]

Lydia Jane Fisher, an Anglo-Irish woman, concluded her book on Kerry with this heart-felt cry for her native land: "I will only insist that it is not the fault of my country that she is so different—so wildly different—so sorrowfully different—so inferior! What has she been but a conquered nation for ages...complete subjugation under the English yoke.... England may be envied for her wealth, for her order, her industry, her peace, and her security—yet, dear, dirty Ireland! we must ever feel for you, pity you, and love you; and dearly do I love you, my beautiful country!" Few of those disturbed by the contradiction between the picturesque and poverty so easily placed the blame on England. The fault more often fell upon Paddy and his landlord. The key to the contradiction could be found, many observers were convinced, in the Irish character.[38]

The troubled conclusions of the books by Ritchie and Fisher were more or less in keeping with many of the accounts written by those who devoted most of their attention to Ireland's social and economic problems. However, both Ritchie and Fisher were primarily interested in the picturesque, and their sentiments would be almost inexplicable had their Romantic tours been taken elsewhere. Yet, as is clear from the preceding chapter, the picturesque tour in Ireland was inevitably an *Irish* tour. Even tourists who had no desire to inquire about wages and rents, traveled through Irish tourist space deep *into* the country. As a result, they moved beyond the realm of the picturesque to confront, as did Ritchie and Fisher, the extent to which the contradiction between the riches of nature and the poverty of man had come to characterize Ireland and the Irish tour on the eve of the Famine.

Chapter 10

THE FAMINE AND AFTER

While Ritchie's and Fisher's conclusions may not be typical of those pursuing the picturesque tour in Ireland, most travel writers did at least take notice of Irish poverty and privation. But if social realities had the power to push their way through the conventions of the picturesque, the reverse is also strangely true. By the time of the Great Famine, the picturesque had so defined Ireland that even some of those who came to observe the crisis and/or to minister to its victims were drawn to Ireland's scenic landscapes. Although the number of "tourists" must have dropped during the Famine, roughly the same number of travel accounts appeared during the most critical years, 1846 and 1849, as had been published between 1840 and 1845, the year the potato blight first appeared.[1]

Relatively few of the travel accounts produced during the Famine described what might be considered conventional picturesque tours. In what may be one of the first examples of "disaster tourism," visitors from Britain came to Ireland during the worst years of the crisis to verify the extent of the problem or to provide relief. Touring during 1847, one of the worst years of the crisis, Rev. John East visited some of the hardest hit areas. An Evangelical who suspected that the Roman Catholic peasantry and their clerical leaders had brought the catastrophe upon themselves, East encountered and described some grim scenes.[2] Yet, he also visited Killarney, Bantry Bay and other scenic locations, which he greatly appreciated. However, given the circumstances of his tour, the already common tourist discomfort at the contrast between suffering and scenery became in East's account a reoccurring theme. He could not admire the beauty of nature without reminding himself and his readers of the disaster taking place around him. Recalling his arrival in Dublin Bay, he wrote: "On that fair scene one could not help dwelling, in almost a transport of pleasure, notwithstanding many sad thoughts—many painful forebodings... before which all the loveliness of the beautiful, and all the grandeur of the sublime in natural scenery, would soon sink into unaffecting insignificance." Under the circumstances East's comments are quite understandable. Yet, acknowledging human suffering while reveling in the beauties of the Irish landscape seems more an effort to assuage the writer's conscience than to voice genuine concern. Interestingly, at the end of his trip, East expressed relief in leaving famine-stricken Ireland by contrasting it to his native England: "It was the climax of earthly happiness, after a rough night at sea," he concluded, "to find myself again on soil of England, to pass through the blooming orchard lands of Worcester...and Summerset, and reach my home...in peace." While one can appreciate such sentiments, they may have served only to further distance readers from the grotesque horrors East had left behind in Ireland.[3]

Scottish political philosopher Thomas Carlyle paid a brief visit to Ireland in 1849, claiming that he felt "driven...as by the point of bayonets at my back" to witness the extent of the debacle. "Ireland really *is* my problem," he claimed, but not out of pity. The country represented "the breaking point of the huge suppuration which all British and all European society now is. Set down in Ireland, one might at least feel, '*Here* is thy problem. In God's name, what wilt thou do with it?'"[4] Published after his death, Carlyle's notes retain their original stark telegraphic quality. Remarkable for their lack of empathy, his observations, nonetheless, provide some arresting glimpses into the crisis. Yet, while, neither the man nor the situation would seem suited to a scenic tour, Carlyle also took in such tourist sites as Glendalough and Killarney, but with a dour solemnity that suggests he derived little joy from his venture into the picturesque.

Some travelers managed to use picturesque techniques to create a comforting distance between themselves and the horrors of the Famine. Along with descriptions of prime tourist sites such as Killarney, Lord John Manners provided some of the relatively few descriptions in the travel literature of fields blackened by the potato blight. Travelling from Dublin to Limerick in 1846, he found that, "though half the country you see is a bog, and the cultivated fields, from the want of timber and hedgerows, and the black destruction of the potato crop, are nearly as black and dreary to look as the redoubtable Bog of Allen itself...*still, as in Italy, the distant view was ever delightful.*"[5] By lifting his eyes to this Claudean horizon, his Lordship provided himself and his readers with some momentary relief from brutal reality.

Even some of those who came to Ireland to provide help could not escape the pull of the picturesque. William Bennett offers an interesting example. A Quaker who traveled around Ireland distributing seeds, Bennett was one of the most effective witnesses to the island's suffering. As Glenn Hooper points out, in writing his *Narrative of a Recent Journey of Six Weeks in Ireland* (1847), Bennett provided testimony of the reality of the crisis.[6] The Society of Friends' commitment to the plain style of communication, characterized by Hooper as "direct, uncomplicated, chastening," proved very effective in this regard. However, Bennett's writing also suggested more than a passing acquaintance with the less restrained style of the picturesque. For example, at one point Bennett stayed with the Rector of Kilconnen in Mayo. In a grim distortion of the picturesque tendency to use windows to frame scenes, Bennett described how, during breakfast, the destitute began to "throng the windows, which presented framed pictures of living groups of want and wretchedness, almost beyond endurance to behold; yet to keep them off the family had long found impossible."[7] What is more striking, however, is Bennett's occasional willingness to depart from his relief duties and momentarily leave behind his Quaker plain style as he directly engaged Irish scenery. Although he did not tour Killarney, he did descend into Michelstown Cave, as noted in Chapter Six. And his description of the mountains of Donegal as seen from around Killybegs is, like most such passages in his book, quite vivid. On Achill Island he was thrilled as "the sun set gloriously across the great Atlantic, and brought out the magnificent features of the coast in bold relief. The scenery wants foliage, but nothing else, to render it most attractive." He enjoyed a boat trip around the harbor of Broadhaven, observing: "On rounding a point eastward, the most beautiful scenery bursts at once upon the astonished beholder. An amphetheatre of cliffs rises stupendous, rugged, black, perpendicular,—their summits sharply pinnacled against the sky, and with some remarkable twists in their structure, that give them a most impending appearance." The cliffs facing his party seemed impenetrable until "...instantly an archway appeared, at the base of those adamantine barriers, of width just sufficient for the oars to play, and within which we caught sight of the sea, writhing and roaring like some prostrate monster enchained."[8] There is probably no better testimony to the power of the picturesque and its association with Ireland than Bennett's breaks from Famine relief for an occasional escape into the country's scenic landscape.

As already noted, the inevitable contrasts voiced by visitors to Ireland between human poverty and natural beauty became even more frequent and disturbing during the Famine. In his *Life and Death in Ireland as Witnessed in 1849*, Rev. Spencer T. Hall recalled enjoying a mild April evening: "The...sky was soft and golden as that of the morning had been clear and bright...[the] beauty was so intense that it filled my bosom with an aching ecstasy; but the knowledge of hunger and hopelessness prevailing through all gave me another ache still more intense and deep." In a similar mood William Bennett, admiring the day breaking over the estuary of Broadhaven, wrote: "The contemplation of the beauty of Nature was, however, soon broken into, by evidences that we were indeed in a land of woe."[9] As the Famine deepened, the tourists' oft expressed sense of a contradiction between natural beauty and human misery had come to define Ireland.

The Contradiction "Resolved"

Writing in the *Edinburgh Review* in 1848, Charles Travelyan, chief administrator for famine relief, announced the end of the Irish crisis.[10] Although the Famine raged on, the British Government wanted to proclaim its end and to move on towards reconstruction. The following year the government promised that the Queen would visit Ireland that summer. Although intended to symbolize the end of the Famine, the Queen's visit to Ireland in 1849 also sought to reassure the traveling public about security in Ireland. The shootings of landlords, as well as the abortive "Rising" of 1848 had reawakened never-quite-dormant fears of Irish violence. While encouraging, the Queen did not venture inland, restricting her visit to ports of Cork, Dublin and Belfast. Nevertheless, the occasion did provide opportunities to remind the British that Ireland was still a Mecca for the picturesque tourist. For example, in the month preceding the Queen's trip, the *Illustrated London News* ran a series of articles on Killarney. Unfortunately, the unidentified correspondent somewhat spoiled the first article with references to roofless cabins in West Cork and a detailed description of the funeral of a child. Subsequent pieces focused exclusively on tourism and scenery.[11] The Queen's visit itself received extensive coverage in the British press. While due emphasis was given to the loyalty and devotion of the Irish people, the visit also sought to promote Irish economic development. *Punch* ran a cartoon titled "Dream of the Future," depicting the Queen gazing into the waters of Lough Neagh, within which she beheld a vision of the prosperous agricultural (but not industrial) Ireland that would allegedly emerge from the ruins of the Famine.[12] In the meantime the actual Famine, as opposed to the fading unpleasantness imagined by bureaucrats and politicians in London, raged on. Later, after the Queen had returned home, the *Illustrated London News* published a series of articles on famine victims and on the evictions proliferating in parts of the West, where potato blight and death continued until 1852.[13]

Around the same time as the Queen's visit, Sir Robert Peel introduced in Parliament a bill that eventually became the "Encumbered Estates Act." He intended the law to facilitate the breakup and sale of the entailed lands of bankrupt Irish landlords to "capable" English and Scottish investors and settlers, who would rejuvenate Irish agriculture, especially in the West of Ireland. The British press referred to Peel's bill as the "new plantation of Ireland."[14] Peel's measure inspired a new type of travel literature, promoting the West of Ireland, especially Connemara, not only for its picturesque qualities but also for its opportunities for settlement and investment. Taking advantage of the Encumbered Estate Act, new landowners would supposedly create verdant fields of grain in place of endless bogs and rushy pastures. The bogs would accordingly be drained and the surviving peasantry, those who had not died or emigrated, would supply a cheap and willing workforce. At the same time, Ireland's expanding rail network would facilitate the movement of the resulting produce. Imagined opportunities to develop fisheries and to exploit mineral resources added glitter to what seemed endless possibilities for a sort of internal colonialism. Happily, some of the most spectacular scenery in the Empire would provide the setting for all of this activity. These dreams of agricultural development and broad economic opportunities were, in fact, built upon the scenic images of the West of Ireland already established by the tourist literature.[15]

The connection between picturesque scenery, tourism and development was not new to Ireland. The Kenmares, Herberts and other landlords had enjoyed some success in attracting visitors as well as businesses to Killarney. Moreover, visions of economic development in the West can be found in almost all of the travel accounts written about the area, starting with the Blakes in their *Letters from the Irish Highlands* (1825). Written by a family intent on establishing a successful estate at Renvyle in Connemara, the book, filled with landscape descriptions, clearly aimed at encouraging broad interest in the region.[16] Henry David Inglis, treking over Connemara's bad roads in 1834, had praised the scenery but also what he imagined to be the region's agricultural potential. Surveying the land around Clifden, he wrote that "it was impossible to cast the eye over the vast inclined plains of bog-lands, skirted by fine water levels, which seemed to invite draining, without feeling a conviction of the immense capabilities of this part of Ireland; and seeing, in perspective, these vast tracts bearing abundant produce...." The next year, John Barrow claimed Connemara "capable of being converted into one of the most fertile and productive districts in the land...." Rev. Caesar Otway was bullish on both expanding tourism and draining the bogs.[17] Just a few years before the Famine, William Makepeace Thackeray, whirling merrily over Alexander Nimmo's new roads through Connemara, rarely saw a bog that could not be drained, or so he believed: "The cultivation of the country is only in its infancy as yet, and it is easy to see how vast its resources are...." He was quite sure that "*a little draining* will convert into thousands of acres of rich productive land." At the same time Thackeray urged his fellow countrymen to visit the West of Ireland and to enjoy its stark beauty. Although Carlyle expressed little interest in tourism, he assumed that bogs could be turned into farmland. Inspecting part of Lord Lucan's estate near Westport, the Scotsman proclaimed: "Abominable bog, thou *shalt* cease to be abominable, and become subject to man!" It is significant that *The Tourist's Illustrated Handbook for Ireland* (1854) mentioned most of these authors as harbingers of tourism in the West. The *Handbook* also touted the railway "Excursion Ticket" system, instituted a few years earlier, which encouraged travelers to prolong their visits so as to enjoy the scenery while exploring the agriculture and business opportunities awaiting them.[18]

Perhaps the most influential promotional book was Rev. John Harvey Ashworth's *A Saxon in Ireland, or the Rambles of an Englishman in Search of a Settlement in the West of Ireland*. It was published in 1851 by Murray, the company that also produced *Murray's Handbook for Travelers in Ireland*. According to the introduction to Ashworth's book, the work was intended "to direct the attention of persons looking out either for investments or for new settlements, to the vast capabilities of the Sister Island, and induce such to visit it, and judge for themselves." Writing anonymously, Ashworth adopted the persona of an individual who had to leave England to seek his fortune. As Glenn Hooper has pointed out, through this device, the fictional narrator voiced all of the supposed disadvantages that Ireland might present. One by one, first by his friends and then by his own experience, these objections were demolished or rendered unimportant. Several of Ashworth's chapters consisted of detailed tours through Connemara and into Erris in County Mayo. Enchanted by the landscape, Ashworth included many descriptions of picturesque scenery. He even took time to enjoy the bugle echoes in the Ballycory Mountains. In fact, at one point he apologized for devoting so much space to the landscape. Yet, he claimed: "I feel that persons of warm imaginations would never think of settling in the flats of Holland or Lincolnshire, though the richness of the land and the pecuniary benefits to be derived therefrom are most manifest. Beautiful scenery will have its influence on the mind of an immigrant…. The more beautiful, sometimes, the more unproductive, is often remarked; but so not here. The mountains often afford the finest pasture, and the valleys the richest soil." Acknowledging the still extensive poverty in the area, Ashworth voiced in its most succinct form the tourist's sense of contradiction in Ireland: "Strange it is that, where nature is so lovely, man should be so degraded and so wretched."[19] At the same time he was keen to emphasize opportunities for reclaiming bog land, and he lauded the examples already provided by new settlers. The book ended with several chapters on issues of interest to would-be settlers, such as the Encumbered Estate Act and religion. He also provided a detailed map of Erris. Ashworth's work was apparently well known. In referring to the rapid changes in land ownership in Connemara, the *Tourist's Illustrated Handbook* claimed that the new owners "and even the tillers of the soil have the stamp of the 'Saxon in Ireland,'" a clear reference to Ashworth's book.

First published in 1849, George Preston White's *A tour in Connemara, with remarks on its great physical capacities,"* was subsequently reissued in 1851. White began his book by stating his preference for the "bold and romantic scenery of Connemara and Joyce's country" over Killarney. Beginning with "Spanish Galway," White devoted several chapters to a tour of Connemara and to fishing expeditions in Killary Harbour and at Maum. The remainder of the book discussed the development potential of the region, including the hope that its harbors would become ports for transatlantic shipping. Quoting extensively from Inglis, White, too, confidently subscribed to the assumption that the "wastelands" of the West could be reclaimed for modern agriculture. He was also convinced that the region possessed "numerous industrial resources," such as minerals, fisheries and harbors. White concluded his book by quoting Sir Humphrey Davy to the effect that, if properly developed, the West of Ireland could become "the richest part of the empire."[20]

The entrepreneurs' first customers are themselves. They must buy into their own visions of the future before they can approach bankers and drum up customers. Therefore, it is not unusual to find fantasy, sometimes tricked out with solemn bits of theory, trumping hard-headed reality. As Henry Nash Smith pointed out years ago in *Virgin Land*, during the decades following the American Civil War, migrants heading west to settle the semi-arid American high plains were spurred on by the quaint theory that rain would follow the plow: that once cultivated, the land would somehow attract the rains. Unfortunately, this was not the case. Pseudo-science did not figure in the dream that Ireland's "Garden of the West" would resolve the contradiction between the Irish picturesque and Irish poverty. However, much irrational exuberance propelled the vision, itself based on the contradiction. To the Romantic mind, poverty amidst the picturesque represented a sort of spiritual affront. The ugly and the squalid were not supposed to be intertwined with the beautiful. Moreover, within the new culture of industrial capitalism, such a contradiction constituted a moral challenge as well. Nature should be useful as well as appealing. In this light, therefore, bogs were not ordained by nature; instead their continued existence spoke of human sloth. Accordingly, only indolence and ignorance kept men from draining them. Inspiring scenery should inspire men to exploit the resources around them. Unfortunately, in the case of the West of Ireland, it encouraged some men to exaggerate, even invent, those resources.

Not everyone assumed that some kind of internal colonialism offered the best solution for Ireland, or that the West of Ireland was as fecund with opportunity as writers like Ashworth and White believed. Traveling through Connemara in 1852, Dr. John Forbes wondered at the many English settlers who seemed so confident that "resolution, when aided by money, can triumph over every disadvantage of the soil and climate."[21] And that was, indeed, the problem. The soil and climate in the West of Ireland did not favor grain production. As far as fisheries were concerned, the region lacked even the most rudimentary infrastructure to support such an industry. Mineral resources, too, had been greatly exaggerated. And while some bogs were successfully drained and the reclaimed land put under cultivation, those who sought to apply the latest techniques of "high farming," with its deep tiled drainage systems, had forgotten one thing. As Prime Minister in 1846, Robert Peel had used the looming crisis caused by the potato blight to repeal the protectionist Corn Laws. Without artificially high prices for domestic grain supported by import duties, the costs of high farming in a region like the West of Ireland could not be sustained over time. During the second half of the nineteenth century, cheap American grain flooded the United Kingdom, with the result that the fortunes of those new Irish landowners who invested in cultivation began to fade. In the West of Ireland cattle and sheep became more numerous, which, given the region's climate and weather patterns, represented a sounder use of the land. Writers such as White, Ashworth and Martineau had so fixated on the idea of the "Saxon" farmer that they failed to notice the speed with which graziers took over much of the newly consolidated holdings in the region. At least in Connemara, the "Garden of the West," intended to resolve the tensions between scenery and poverty, died a failed dream.[22]

If the region had a future, it lay in tourism, a point made by a leader in the *Times* in 1864: "There is nothing in these isles more beautiful and more picturesque than the south and west of Ireland. They who know the fair portions of Europe still find in Ireland that which they have seen nowhere else, and which has charms all its own. One might suppose the island just risen from the sea...and the spirit of light and order beginning its work; such is the infinite confusion of surge and beach, bay, headland, river, lake, grass, of land and sea, sunshine in showers, and rainbow over all." The *Times* predicted the day when an "annual stream of tourists will lead the way" to a future in which "we see in the beauty of Ireland even a surer heritage than in hidden mine or fertile soil." Prosperity would reign, as it did in many other regions, which had "nothing but their beauty and salubrity to recommend them." By this time the Connemara "Loop," also known as the "Circular Tour," had become an established part of the region's tourism.[23]

The internal dynamics of the pre-Famine Irish Tour, characterized by the contradiction between the picturesque and poverty, gradually resolved itself. As Elizabeth Meloy suggests, "...the West of Ireland lost its Otherness in the tourist literature of the immediate post-Famine period. With the sites of death and destruction still visible and the traces of modern life just emerging, the Connemara landscape could be read as an illustration of the central principle of modernity itself: in order for something new to be created, something old must be discarded and destroyed."[24] Poverty, of course, remained a serious problem in Ireland well into the twentieth century. However, its depth and extent were dramatically altered within a decade after the Famine. It is estimated that by the end of the potato blight in 1852, the country may have lost as many as two million people through death and emigration. Many of the squatters and conacre farmers had disappeared into British and American cities or into mass graves. The rural landscape changed dramatically as a result. Through abandonment and eviction, tens of thousands of mud cabins, many unroofed, stood vacant. For a few years their stark remnants troubled tourists, but gradually the gable ends and walls crumbled into the ground, leaving only some stones and fallow lazy beds to mark their location. Many clachans vanished completely. The teeming population hugging Ireland's coasts gradually thinned, as emigration became institutionalized within Irish society. The country's population continued to fall, from an estimated 8.5 million at the start of the Famine, until it reached 4.5 million at the end of the nineteenth century: roughly what its population had been in 1790. Because of the clustering of many peasant settlements off the tourists' beaten track, pre-Famine visitors had often felt that they were travelling through empty sections of the country. After the Famine that emptiness had become real. Only the picturesque scenery remained unchanged.

CONCLUSION

As this book has attempted to demonstrate, in pre-Famine Ireland the average tour could involve two parallel tracks, the combination of which varied for each visitor. One track searched for the picturesque; the other for Ireland, or at least an understanding of Irish society. Curiosity about the people of a host country is, or should be, a proper part of any type of tourism. In the case of British visitors to Ireland, however, their tours contained an implicit imperative, even before the Act of Union. While the picturesque was often a convenient perceptual screen that could blur unpleasant realities, in Ireland reality frequently forced itself upon the traveler. In fact, as suggested several times throughout this study, the picturesque created preconditions whereby Irish problems, especially the country's poverty, were seen as a contradiction to Ireland's natural beauty. As a result, visitors frequently felt that something was "wrong" with Ireland.

Something was, indeed, wrong, and if visitors been willing to look more deeply and honestly into the history and nature of British-Irish relations, the sense of contradiction might have led to useful reforms. However, British blame fell too easily on Irish landlords and peasants. And questions of national character too often pushed aside the recognition of basic economic problems. Once the Famine took hold, both the government and the British public speedily abandoned effective relief and shifted the burden of aiding a starving peasantry onto the shoulders of the already strained Irish property class. This, in effect, represented the ultimate failure of the Irish Tour and the significant literature it had generated to promote real understanding of Ireland. Nevertheless, with so many paupers dead, so many small famers sent on the emigrant's long trail, with the landscape gradually cleared of mud cabins (the icon of Irish poverty), the Famine "resolved" the contradiction, leaving the picturesque landscape and the tourists who continued to pursue it, if not untroubled, then eventually without serious visual challenge.

Touring in and of itself does not constitute tourism. Tourism did not exist in Ireland in 1750 when individuals began taking pleasure tours there. A century later, however, tourism had established itself on the island, as it had in other scenic parts of Europe between 1750 and 1850. One may identify in pre-Famine

Ireland many of the basic elements that contributed to the growth of modern tourism. First of all, Ireland clearly benefited from the shift in cultural attitudes regarding travel—from the Grand Tour to the pleasure tour. Closely tied to this change was the revolution in landscape aesthetics characterized by the concepts of the sublime and the picturesque.

The picturesque pleasure tour greatly increased the size of the touring public. This growth depended upon expanded and improved accommodations, as well as the modernization of the basic transportation infrastructure (both within and between countries). In this regard pre-Famine Ireland offered tourists a relatively good road system and two cross-country canal lines. And, if it lagged a decade or so behind Britain in the application of steam to internal travel, Ireland still benefited from the early appearance of steamships on the Irish Sea, linking the country more closely to the larger island.

While the culture defined tourist sites, each one had to be identified, marked and internally organized, physically and perceptually, to accommodate and engage visitors. Here, the landlords and travel writers played key roles. In both Britain and Ireland landed proprietors opened their parks and country houses to the traveling public. Their great estates themselves were among the first tourist attractions. In Ireland, as noted earlier, many topographical features were either on or visible from estate lands. By opening their grounds, by providing roads, pathways, inns and picnicking facilities, the proprietors were instrumental in inaugurating Irish tourism. Travel writers were equally important in developing modern tourism. Although most who came to Ireland were English, Anglo-Irish authors often brought to their works greater commitment to, as well as knowledge of, Ireland. Taken as a whole, the travelogues and guidebooks proved essential, not only in identifying and publicizing sites, but also in helping to "script" the tourist experiences available at each.

The quality of those experiences resulted from a triangular interaction involving topographical features, the ability of the locals to engage the visitors, and the tourists themselves, each of whom varied according to the extent of his or her preparation, interest, time, resources and attitude. For their part, it was the locals who made tourism function on the everyday level. From hoteliers and shop keepers down to peasant drivers, guides, vendors, porters and even beggars (in business for themselves in the most basic way), all formed a vast entrepreneurial network that mediated between the tourists and the objects they had come to see. The result was a tourist experience that was identifiably Irish. As off-putting as importuning hoards of ragged peasants may have been, close contact with Irish people made a visit to Killarney, for example, memorably different from a trip to the Lake District or to Bodensee.

In a generic sense, most of the above are still among the basic elements of tourism. However, today's student of the industry must consider how businesses, government and nonprofit agencies and organizations cooperate with each other. Such interactions did not exist during the first century of Irish tourism. While the Irish government did involve itself to varying degrees in the creation of most of the country's transportation network, tourism was not its primary motivation. By the same token, tourism was a beneficiary of the desire of individual Irish proprietors to develop their estates and promote their reputations. And the peasants who filled in the details of the tourist experience at popular sites did so, not to serve tourists, but rather from their own desires to earn a few coppers for their families. In fact, tourism as a concept did not exist before 1800. There was no Bord Fáilte in 1750 or 1800 to coordinate public and private efforts. There was no minister or ministry for tourism in College Green, Dublin Castle or in Westminster for that matter. With the possible exception of the publicity surrounding the Queen's visit in 1849, the British government seemed to have had little interest in promoting Irish tourism. There were no plans, no consultants, no grants, no marketing surveys and no advertising campaigns. Until the coming of the railroads, "marketing" was carried out solely through the uncoordinated efforts of a steady stream of travel writers. Thus, the foundations of Irish tourism emerged out of what was essentially a self-organizing system.

It is impossible to say when Irish tourism, having self-organized, became self-aware. However, Samuel Ferguson's three articles, "The Attractions of Ireland," which appeared in *Dublin University Magazine* in 1836, represent a symbolic moment. By that time all of the individual "tours" over the previous half-century or so were beginning to add up to something. "Ireland is at present day unquestionably one of the most interesting portions of Europe," Ferguson asserted. "In the midst of scenery, which alone assures us no inconsiderable share of attention from the ordinary tourist, we exhibit a state of society, in all respects most inviting to the philosophic traveller...." Ferguson's tourist was, no doubt, a mirror image of himself, a middle-class intellectual, confident in his ability to wield the language of the picturesque.[1] Yet, while Ferguson used the word "tourist" frequently in his essays, the new term "tourism" (coined, according to the *Oxford English Dictionary*, in 1815) did not appear.

Nevertheless, by the early 1840s writers such as the Halls and Thackeray were appealing directly to their British readers to pack their bags and cross the Irish Sea. By the 1850s the railroads, with their transportation networks and hotels in scenic areas, had created the rudiments of Ireland's first real tourism system. Thomas Cook, who had begun bringing tourists to Ireland in 1849, established regular excursions in 1852. The Dublin Industrial Exposition in 1853, organized by railway man and entrepreneur William Dargan, attracted visitors who were encouraged to buy excursion tickets to tour the West.[2] Dargan also extended the Dublin-Kingston rail line south to the seaside town of Bray in Wicklow and invested in establishing that town as a prominent resort, eventually dubbed "the Brighton of Ireland." The end of the nineteenth century witnessed purposeful interaction among the various groups interested in tourism—identified by Irene Furlong as "hoteliers, transport companies, peers of the realm whose properties were opened to the public…and some individual entrepreneurs…."[3] As Furlong shows, the final element needed for a modern tourist industry, government involvement, gradually emerged in Ireland during the twentieth century.

Today, there are many varieties of tourism. In Ireland, tourist packages can be built around "heritage" tours, golfing tours, political tours (Bloody Sunday anniversaries, Belfast's sectarian gable-paintings) or bachelor and bachelorette parties. Yet, Ireland's scenery is still the primary drawing card for tourists. Perhaps nothing better symbolizes the extent to which the picturesque imposed itself onto the Irish landscape and Irish tourism than the image used in the first advertising campaign launched by an Irish tourist cross-border initiative around 2001. It depicted a woman in a bridal dress and veil running across the rope bridge at Carrick-a-rede on the North Antrim coast, a tourist fixture since the mid-eighteenth century.

Even if it may be losing its exclusive grip on Irish tourism, the picturesque tour is still very popular, and its major attractions have not changed significantly since it was largely established between 1750 and 1800. Tourists still visit many of the scenic sites that attracted their great-great-grandparents. And while first photographs and now digital images have replaced sketches and watercolors, tourists still tend to use the same picturesque techniques to frame their pictures of landscapes as did their more knowledgeable ancestors in 1800.[4] Certainly, some things have changed or dropped out of fashion. In parts of Ireland McMansions seem more common than the "seats" of Yeats' "hard-riding country gentlemen." The Pigeon Hole near Cong is harder to find in guide books. The visitor to the Gap of Donloe may have to ask his pony-trap driver to shout up an echo, as the old and unique soundscape is no longer an automatic accompaniment to the landscape of Killarney. And, of course, the mobs of guides, vendors, hangers-on and beggars no longer frequent Ireland's tourist sites. Nevertheless, the Irish people, having suffered through a series of stereotypes, still remain an important part of Irish tourism, their friendliness and good humor as permanent a fixture as the scenery.[5]

This is not to suggest that the picturesque will necessarily remain a dominant element in Irish tourism. For a long time it was land that was contested in Ireland, not landscape. Times have changed. Call it the entrepreneurial spirit or a "gombeen man" mentality, but economic opportunities for development over the past half century have not always been gentle to the Irish cityscapes and landscapes long admired by tourists. Continued economic growth may raise new contradictions against Ireland's image as a scenic paradise. Moreover, the aesthetics upon which picturesque tourism were founded have suffered from the gradual erosion of the Romantic view of nature. Endlessly deconstructed by academics and increasingly ignored by an international, urban-oriented popular culture, the picturesque may be on its way to becoming more a touristic habit than an inspiration. Finally, of course, climate change may dim the sheen of the Emerald Isle. On the other hand, new ecological interests and concerns may place picturesque landscapes in a new light. Until that time Irish tourism in the new millennium still retains a remarkable continuity with its origins during its first century, 1750–1850.

NOTES

Introduction

1 These numbers are based on John McVeagh's bibliography, *Irish Travel Writing*. In tabulating the data, I used the date of a tour rather than the date of publication, as some accounts were published well after the journeys they describe. The vast majority of the authors were British or Anglo-Irish. Only around forty of the authors seem to have been from the Continent or the United States.
2 For the Irish Tour see Glenn Hooper, "The Isles / Ireland." For the British Home tour see Ousby, *The Englishman's England* and Moir, *The Discovery of Britain*.
3 Chole Chard, "Introduction," 6. For the Grand Tour see Chard, *op. cit.*, 1–29; Judith Adler, "Origins of Sightseeing," 7–29; John Buzard, "The Grand Tour and After," 37–52. Gina Crandell points out that, while some of those on the Grand Tour described the Italian landscapes they visited, they did so in terms of the landscape paintings they were seeing and buying; *Nature Pictorialized*, 113.
4 Bridges, "Exploration and Travel Outside of Europe," 56.
5 For the cult of Ossian and other aspects of the Celtic Revival see Edward D. Snyder, *The Celtic Revival in English Literature*. See also O'Halloran, *Golden Ages and Barbarous Nations*, 99–103; Leerssen, *Mere Irish and Fíor-Gheal*, 338–49.
6 These numbers are based on John McVeagh's bibliography. For discussions about the Irish travel literature published between 1750 and 1800 see Hooper, *Travel Writing and Ireland*, 36–58; W. Williams, *Tourism, Landscape, and the Irish Character*, 7–13.
7 Hoare, *A Tour in Ireland*, ii, v.
8 Working beyond the genre of travel writing, other scholars have recently contributed to our understanding of British attitudes toward the Irish during these years. For example, see Edward G. Lengel, *The Irish Through British Eyes*; Michael de Nie, *The Eternal Paddy*; Melissa Fegan, *Literature and the Irish Famine*; Leslie A. Williams, *Daniel O'Connell, The British Press and the Irish Famine*.

Chapter 1. Getting There and Getting About

1 Chetwood, *A Tour Through Ireland*, 32–3, 47.
2 Plumptre, *Narrative*, 5; Bush, *Hibernia Curiosa*, 27; Derrick, *Letters*, 1:41–2.
3 Melish, *Travels*, 340; Chetwood, *op. cit.*, 49–50; Bush, *op. cit.*, 10, 11.
4 M. Davies, *That Favored Resort*, 104. See also Clarke, *Tour*, 299; Anon., *Journal of a Tour in Ireland, performed in August 1804*, 6.
5 Plumptre, *op. cit.*, 5, 7; Clarke, *op. cit.*, 298.

6 Hall and Hall, *Hall's Ireland*, 1:xvii, xxix. For ship design and steam see MacDonagh, "Sea Communications," 120–1.
7 Anon., *Walker's Hand-book of Ireland*, 67; Clarke, *op. cit.*, 303; Carr, *The Stranger in Ireland* 27–8; Bowden, *A Tour Through Ireland*, 2; Thackeray, *The Irish Sketch Book*, 6; Head, *A Fortnight in Ireland*, 4.
8 Rynne, *Industrial Ireland*, 393.
9 Plumptre, *ibid.*, 8–9.
10 Pratt, *Imperial Eyes*, 78; Cronin, *Across the Lines*, 68.
11 Reid, *Travels in Ireland*, 149. See also Carr, *op. cit.*, 31–2; Plumptre, *op. cit.*, 11; For the Long Car see C. Maxwell, *Dublin*, 295.
12 See J. L. McCracken, "The Age of the Stage Coach," 52. See also Chetwood, *op cit.*, 142; Bush, *op cit.*, 29; Campbell, *A Philosophical Survey*, 48.
13 For sedan chairs see J. L. McCracken, *op cit.*, 52–3; C. Maxwell, *op cit.*, 77.
14 Hoare, *A Tour in Ireland*, xix. See also Carr, *op cit.*, 36–7; R. Graham, *A Scottish Whig in Ireland*, 152; Bush, *op cit.*, 31–2.
15 For post chaise see Bayne-Powell, *Travellers in Eighteenth-Century England*, 9. For posting costs and turnpike fees see J. L. McCracken, *op cit.*, 50. See also Gough, *An Account of Two Journeys*, 19; Binns, *The Miseries and Beauties of Ireland*, 1:24; Belton, *The Angler in Ireland*, 96.
16 See Ivor Hering, "Traveling Conditions," 6; J. L. McCracken, *op cit.*, 59–60.
17 West, *A Summer Visit to Ireland*, 156; Forbes, *Memorandums Made in Ireland*, 2:186; Plumptre, *op. cit.*, 255–6, emphasis original. It is not clear whether Plumptre was referring to James Beresford's satiric *Miseries of Human Life* published in 1806 or Thomas Rowlandson's collection of prints by the same name, published two years later.
18 J. L. McCracken, *op. cit.*, 53.
19 Otway, *Sketches in Ireland*, 3.
20 J. L. McCracken, *op. cit.*, 58, 61.
21 Barrow, *A Tour Round Ireland*, 48.
22 Ivor Hering, *op. cit.*, 8–9. For coaching schedules and costs see J. L. McCracken, *op. cit.*, 59.
23 Belton, *op. cit.*, 97. For jaunting cars see Hall and Hall, *op. cit.*, 1:29–30; J. L. McCracken, *op. cit.*, 50. Regarding the difference between the "inside" and "outside" car, John Barrow received the following bit of enlightenment from an Irish driver. "The difference, sure, is this:—the inside car has wheels outside, and the outside car the wheels inside"; *op. cit.*, 6–7.
24 Head, *op. cit.*, 114.
25 Hall and Hall, *op. cit.*, 1:28. Colin Rynne states that the Irish mile was equal to 2,240 yards, while the English mile is 1,760 yards; *op. cit.*, 319. As the Halls pointed out, this meant that a destination, which a local claimed to be only eleven miles, would turn out to be 14 miles by British measure; 1:39. See also Anon., *The Sportsman in Ireland*, 1:19; Thackeray, *op. cit.*, 109.
26 See Inglis, *A Journey throughout Ireland*, 1:55. See also O'Neill, "Bianconi and His Cars," 86–7.
27 Johnson, *A Tour of Ireland*, 123.
28 O'Neill, *op. cit.*, 85. For more on prints see 88–9. For Kohl see C. Kelly, *Cork*, 117.
29 Hole, *A Little Tour in Ireland*, 171. See also Binns, *op. cit.*, 2:365; Johnson, *op. cit.*, 123. The Bianconi cars, or "Bians" as they were called, were so popular that they apparently became synonymous with vehicular travel in Ireland. An Irish-American women once told the author that her grandmother, who had emigrated from Ireland early in the twentieth century, used to refer to the family car as the "Bianky," a variation, perhaps, on "Bian" or Bianconi.
30 Rynne, *op. cit.*, 313. Chetwood, *op. cit.*, 99. For Young's quote see Moir, *op. cit.*, 10.

31 Colin Rynne notes that with the establishment of the Irish Post Office and the resulting necessity for regular mail coaches, the Irish Parliament began to address the problem of steep gradients; *op. cit.*, 311. For turnpikes see Rynne, *op. cit.*, 315–16; David Broderick, *An Early Toll-Road*. As an example of the intensity of the competition facing turnpikes, Broderick points out that the Dublin-Dunleer company sued a rival road for having falsified its milestones to make it appear that it offered a shorter route to Dublin; 50.
32 Carr, *op. cit.*, 210; Twiss, *A Tour of Ireland*, 54. For Grand Jury system see Rynne, *op. cit.*, 311–13. See also Freeman, "Land and People, c. 1841," 255–6.
33 See Carr, *op. cit.*, 354. For Beranger see Wilde, "Memoir of Gabriel Beranger," 122. For manhandling carriages over the Cork-Kerry mountains see Otway, *op. cit.*, 393; Inglis, *op. cit.*, 2:205. Even into the nineteenth century there were parts of Ireland where wheeled-vehicles of any sort were a rare sight. As late as 1837, one Donegal parish of some 9000 people contained only one wheeled cart. Wheelless sidecars or drags had long been the common conveyances of the Irish peasantry in the more remote parts of the island; see Ivor Hering, "Bians (II)," 115.
34 For Beranger, see Harbison, *"Our Treasure of Antiquities"*,108–109.
35 Ó Gráda, *Ireland*, 133.
36 In spite of Nimmo's best efforts, Connemara remained almost isolated until after 1840, several years after his death when his road system was completed. See Villiers-Tuthill, *Alexander Nimmo*, xiv, 18, 21, 25, 119–120.
37 See Killen, "Communications," 209–210. For the Board of Works see Rynne, *op. it.*, 320–21. For a critique of the Board see Villiers-Tuthill, *op. it.*, 176.
38 Forbes, *op. it.*, 2:180.
39 See W. Williams, *Landscape, Tourism and the Irish Character*, 81–84. See also James Johnson, *op. it.*, 205, italics original; Rynne, *op. it.*, 311. In his *Exploring the History and Heritage of Irish Landscapes*, Patrick Duffy points out that, in addition to under utilization, the relative lack of trees and hedgerows along Irish roads allowed them to dry out more quickly than England's more muddy roads; 140–41.
40 Duffy, *op. cit.*, 143.
41 George Taylor's brother, Major Alexander Taylor, built the "Military Road" through the mountains south of Dublin. He later became a principal figure in the expansion of the Irish road system. Both Taylors were Scottish-trained engineers. For eighteenth-century Irish road maps see Sir George Herbert Fordham, *Notes on British and Irish Itineraries and Road-Books*.
42 Hoare, *op. cit.*, xv. For the *Companion*, see J. L. McCracken, *op. cit.*, 59.
43 Gough, *op. cit.*, 19.
44 Duffy, *op. cit.*, 143. For Newry Canal see Rynne, *op. cit.*, 338. For background on the Grand and Royal canals see Delany, *A Celebration*, 74–109.
45 See Delany, *op. cit.*, 16; Rynne, *op. cit.*, 339–40.
46 For costs see Cromwell, *Excursions Through Ireland*, 2:159; Delany, op. cit., 89. For the canal's trade barges see Delany 76, 77, 87. For the passenger boats see Delany, 80; Rynne, *op. cit.*, 349.
47 See Freeman, "Land and People," 257. See also Delany, *op. cit.*, 103.
48 See Delany, *op. cit.*, 96, 106; Carr, *op. cit.*, 434–5.
49 For descriptions of flyboats see Hall and Hall, *op. cit.*, 1:186; McCutcheon, "The Transport Revolution," 77; Freeman, *op. cit.*, 256. For the idea of using steamers to tow boats on Grand Canal, see Delany, *The Shannon Navigation*, 155–56. Although this proved infeasible, steamboats were used to pull canal boats on certain stretches of the Shannon Navigation, Delany, 158.

50 Delany, *A Celebration*, 137.
51 Johnson, *op. cit.*, 58; Hall and Hall, *op. cit.*, 1:186.
52 Rynne, *op. cit.*, 350.
53 Delany, *The Shannon Navigation*, 157.
54 See Dickson, "Letters from the Coast of Clare," July–December, 1841, 685; Knott, *Two Months at Kilkee*, 13, 19. See also Murphy, *Before the Famine Struck*, 76.
55 See Forbes, *op. cit.*, 1:207. For Kohl see Delany, *op. cit.*, 157, 160. For origins of the Shannon Navigation and the introduction of steamers on the river see Delany, *op. cit.*, 22, 26, 155–63.
56 Forbes, *op. cit.*, 2:181. See also Hall and Hall, *op. cit.*, 2:239; Head, *op. cit.*, 1.
57 Nowlan, "The Transport Revolution," 96–97. For the Kingston-Dublin railway see K. O'Connor, *Ironing the Land*, 7, 11, 19.
58 O'Connor, *op. cit.*, 45, 54, 56. For the Dublin-Galway line see Nowlan, *op. cit.*, 101–2. See also Hole, *op. cit.*, 33.
59 Fisher, *Letters from the Kingdom of Kerry*, 23; Head, *op. cit.*, 111.
60 Reid, *op. cit.*, 205.
61 Forbes, *op. cit.*, 1:2–3.
62 For M'Gregor see C. Maxwell, *op. cit.*, 92. See also Anon. *Journal of a Tour in Ireland, performed in August 1804*, 32–3; I. Hering, "Traveling Conditions," 2–4, 6; Bush, *op. cit.*, 25–6.
63 Binns, *op. cit.*, 2.328–29. See also Pococke, *Pococke's Tours of Ireland in 1852*, 7–8; Hall and Hall, *op. cit.*, 2:415. For Beranger see Wilde, *op. cit.*, 41.
64 Hoare, *op. cit.*, 188; de Latocnaye, *A Frenchman's Walk through Ireland*. 115; Woods, "A Scientific Tour," 25; Atkinson, *The Irish Tourist*, 342–3.
65 Atkinson, *op. cit.*, 595–6; Derrick, *op. cit.*, 1:52; Clarke, *op. cit.*, 205; Anon., *Sportsman in Ireland*, 1:36.
66 Johnson, *op. cit.*, 130–1; Plumptre. *op. cit.*, 251; Walford, *The Scientific Tourist*, 2:23; Inglis, *op. cit.*, 1:269–70.
67 Hall and Hall, *op. cit.*, 1:3. See also West, *op. cit.*, 171–2, 77, italics original.
68 Robert Graham, *op. cit.*, 258–9; Inglis, *op. cit.*, 2.57; Barrow, *op. cit.*, 220–21.
69 J. L. McCracken, *op. cit.*, 55–6.
70 Hoare, *op. cit.*, 2. For quote see Anon., *Journal of a Tour in Ireland, performed in August 1804*, 8, 23–4.
71 Plumptre, *op. cit.*, 342. Anne Plumptre's confidence was shaken, however, when, upon arriving at Cashel in Tipperary, she discovered that a raid had taken place the previous day and a soldier had been killed. Although in no danger, she left without taking in the ruins of the famous cathedral. For further discussion see Hooper, *Travel Writing and Ireland*, 98–9. See also Inglis, *op. cit.*, 2:92.
72 Ferguson, "The Attractions of Ireland.—III," 310; Ritchie, *Ireland*, 1:52, 2:183; Hall and Hall, *op. cit.*, 1:172.

Chapter 2. Tours Grand and Petite

1 C. Maxwell, *Dublin*, 59. The Irish Parliament building was the first great public Palladian structure in the British Isles; Crookshank, "The Visual Arts, 1740–1850," 499.
2 Bowden, *A Tour Through Ireland*, 78–9. See also Boyd, *Dublin*, 77–9; C. Maxwell, *op. cit.*, 75.
3 See C. Maxwell, *op. cit.* 58. Kildare, the Duke of Leinster, built what was essentially a great country house set down on what was then the very edge of Dublin. He correctly

predicted that much of fashionable Dublin would, as he put it, "follow me wherever I go"; M. Craig, *Dublin, 1660–1860*, 133.
4   M. Craig, *op. cit.*, 164–65.
5   Boyd, *op. cit.*, 47; Clarke, *Tour*, 319. For bringing rural light into the city, see Boyd, 40.
6   C. Maxwell, *op. cit.*, 72–3; Bush, *Hibernia Curiosa*, 13–4; Cromwell, *Excursions Through Ireland*, 1:49.
7   Plumptre, *Narrative*, 52; Campbell, *A Philosophical Survey*, 6.
8   By around the year 2000 as many as 60 of the Georgian houses originally situated around the Green had been demolished. See Pearson, *The Heart of Dublin*, 286.
9   Hoare, *A Tour in Ireland*, 18; Twiss, *A Tour of Ireland*, 11; Campbell, *op. cit.*, 6.
10 Plumptre, *op. cit.*, 51; Hoare, *op. cit.*, 17; Carr, *The Stranger in Ireland*, 130. For the elm trees surrounding the Green, see Pearson, *op. cit.*, 273–4.
11 Clarke, *op. cit.*, 314; Twiss, *op. cit.*, 22–4.
12 See Boyd , *op. cit.*, 49. By the early nineteenth century the handwork of the stuccodore was replaced by plaster casting; see C. Maxwell, *op. cit.*, 82–4. For the plaster work in the Lying-in Hospital's chapel see Curren, *Dublin Decorative Plasterwork*, 51–6; Boyd, *op. cit.*, 67–71.
13 Carr, *op. cit.*, 182–3; Campbell, *op. cit.*, 5. See also C. Maxwell, *op. cit.*, 303.
14 Roughly a half century after the demolition, the city has built a replacement—the 120 meter stainless steel "Monument of Light," better known to the punters as "the Stiletto in the Ghetto."
15 Gough, *A Tour in Ireland*, 140; Campbell, *op. cit.*, 27; Plumptre, *op. cit.*, 41.
16 C. Maxwell, *op. cit.*, 115; Boyd, *op.cit.*, 58.
17 Boyd, *op. cit.*, 79, 95; de Latocnaye, *A Frenchman's Walk through Ireland*, 24.
18 For Berkeley and Chesterfield see C. Maxwell, *op. cit.*, 101. For comparison of Dublin and London society see Maxwell, 114. See also Cromwell, *op. cit.*, 1:50; Bush, *op. cit.*, 19, 21; italics original.
19 Luckombe, *A Tour Through* Ireland, 17; C. Maxwell, *op. cit.*, 320. See also Twiss, *op. cit.*, 8.
20 C. Maxwell, *op. cit.*, 115–16, 185. See also Bowden, *op. cit.*, 25.
21 Ritchie, *Ireland*, 1:4, 7; Bush, *op. cit.*, 11; Twiss, *op. cit.*, 10; Reid, *Travels in Ireland*, 147–8.
22 Cromwell, *op. cit.*, 1:19. See also Campbell, *op. cit.*, 56; Johnson, *A Tour of Ireland*, 26; italics original.
23 Ritchie, *op. cit.*, 1:11, 1:12; Clarke, *op. cit.*, 312; de Latocnaye, *op. cit.*, 17.
24 Anon., *Journal of a Tour in Ireland, performed in August 1804*, 8, 36.
25 For the population of Ireland's cities see McDowell, "Ireland in 1800," 666.
26 Charles de Montbret, "A New View of Cork City in 1790," 2. See also Twiss, *op. cit.*, 146; Campbell, *op. cit.*, 174, 176; Bowen, *op. cit.*, 187.
27 Ritchie, *op. cit.*, 1:183; Anon., "A Tour of the South of Ireland," 595; Plumptre, *op. cit.*, 233.
28 Anon., "A Tour of the South of Ireland," 597.
29 Forbes, *op. cit.*, 1:66; Carr, *op. cit.*, 242; Derrick, *Letters*, 1:72.
30 Ritchie, *op. cit.*, 2:204; Thackeray, *The Irish Sketch Book*, 125, 126; Carr, *op. cit.*, 328; S. T. Hall, *Life and Death in Ireland*, 34.
31 Inglis, *A Journey throughout Ireland*, 2:251–2.
32 Inglis, *op. cit.*, 2:251, italics added.
33 Manners (7th Duke of Rutland), *Notes of an Irish Tour*, 139; Ritchie, *op. cit.*, 2:54–5, 251; Inglis, *op. cit.*, 2:251.
34 Ritchie, *op. cit.*, 2:58, italics original; Inglis, *op. cit.*, 2:252.
35 Johnson, *op. cit.*, 333; Barrow, *A Tour Round Ireland*, 110.
36 For Young see C. Kelly, *Cork*, 45. See also K. Whelan, "Towns and Villages," 187, 188–9.

37 Gough, *An Account of Two Journeys Southward in Ireland in 1817*, 36.
38 See Louis M. Cullen, "Man, Landscape and Roads," 75. See also Bush, *op. cit.*, 56; Cromwell, *op. cit.*, 2:41.
39 For de Tocqueville see C. Kelly, *op. cit.*, 99. See also J. L. McCracken, "The Political Structure, 1714–60," 82–3; John Gough, *An Account of Two Journeys*, 18.
40 Anon., *A Sportsman in Ireland*, 1:278. See also Hoare, *op. cit.*, 60; Plumptre, *op. cit.*, 274–5; Carr, *op. cit.*, 176.
41 S. T. Hall, *op. cit.*, 5.
42 Rojek, "Indexing and Dragging," 52.
43 Cosgrove, *Social Formation and Symbolic Landscape*, 232.
44 Holmes, *Sketches*, 44. The reference is to the Italian painter Salvator Rosa.
45 Hutchinson, *James Arthur O'Connor*, 68–69; Duffy, "The Changing Rural Landscape," 37.
46 See Rynne, *Industrial Ireland*, 75. For various types of Irish iron ores see 107. For charcoal furnaces see Neeson, *A History of Irish Forestry*, 75.
47 Plumptre, *op. cit.*, 181–2; S. Molyneux, "Samuel Monyneux's Tour of Kerry, 1709," 66, 74–5; Anon. *Traveller's New Guide*, 46.
48 Rynne, *op. cit.*, 105.
49 Otway, *Sketches in Ireland*, 347. See also Charles Smith, *County of Kerry*, 94–5, 130; Barton, *Some Remarks*, 8; Holmes, *op. cit.*, 193–4. For the impact of iron smelting on Irish forests, see Rynne, *op. cit.*, 114, 123; Neeson, *op. cit.*, 73–5.
50 Rynne, *op. cit.*, 222; Atkinson, *The Irish Tourist*, 449.
51 Rynne, *op. cit.*, 83. See also Montbret, "A View of Kilkenny City and County, 1790," 30; Bowden, *op. cit.*, 30; Plumptre, *op. cit.*, 224; Cromwell, *op. cit.*, 3:52; Barrow, *op. cit.*, 70.
52 Carr, *op. cit.*, 377; Chetwood, *op. cit.*, 183.
53 Chatterton, *Rambles in the South of Ireland*, 1:79–83. For Ireland's copper mines see Rynne, *op. cit.*, 139, 141–2.
54 See Forbes, *op. cit.*, 1:29. In this passage Forbes was satirically imitating Thomas Moore's language in his well-known song about the Vale of Avoca, "The Meeting of the Waters." See also Pococke, *Pococke's Tours of Ireland in 1852*, 159; Carr, *op. cit.*, 161–173.
55 See Thackeray, *op. cit.*, 264–5. For the mills see Rynne, *op. cit.*, 27. See also Hall and Hall, *op. cit.*, 2:338–9.
56 Barrow, *op. cit.*, 15. See also Rynne, *op. cit.*, 207. For illustration of a bleaching green see Rynne, 214.
57 Barry, *A Walking Tour*, 50; Reid, *op. cit.*, 222; Inglis, *op. cit.*, 2:89.
58 Hall and Hall, *op. cit.*, 1:9; Reid, *op. cit.*, 260.
59 Carlyle, *Reminiscences*, 167, italics original.
60 Manners, *op. cit.*, 29; Inglis, *op. cit.*, 1:65–6.
61 Noel, *Notes on a short tour*, 77.
62 West, *A Summer Visit*, 136; Forbes, *op. cit.*, 1:46; Bennett, *Narrative*, 31.
63 Walford, *The Scientific Tourist*, 6; S. T. Hall, *op. cit.*, Knott, *Two Months at Kilkee*, 61.
64 Thackeray, *op. cit.*, 201; Anon., *Traveller's New Guide*, 316.
65 See Anon., *The Irish Tourist*, 99. For the "confessional landscapes" see W. Williams, *Tourism, Landscape, and the Irish Character*, 48–50.
66 For Otway on the peasantry, *op. cit.*, 112. In *The Bible Wars in Ireland* Irene Whelan has pointed out that while Otway liked to expose the "superstitions" of the peasantry, he could also be good humored about the clash of Protestant and Catholic cultures within his country; 211. He even admitted at one point that individual Catholic clergy were often "kind, generous, hospitable and charitable"; see Otway, *op. cit.*, 108.

67 Anon., *Journal of A Tour in Ireland during the Months of October and November, 1835*, 51.
68 Hall and Hall, *op. cit.*, 2:392–93; Otway, *op. cit.*, 259, 320.
69 See Lengel, *The Irish Through British Eyes*, 142. For the "Second Reformation," see I. Whelan's, *op. cit.*, 153–92.
70 See I. Whelan, *op. cit.*, 135–54.
71 While Dallas came from England, Nangle was born near Athboy in Meath in 1799 or 1800. He was educated at Trinity College and ordained a deacon in the Church of Ireland in 1824; Ní Ghiobúin, *Dugort, Achill Island*, 7.
72 See Irene Whelan, *op. cit.*, 262–65. For visitors to Achill see Ní Ghiobúin, *op. cit.*, 13; for the colony's hotel, see 24. In their guidebook to Connemara, the Halls described the Protestant settlement on Achill but stated they would leave the readers to draw their own conclusions, *Hand-Books for Ireland: The West*, 159–60. After the famine, Nangle's mission purchased most of island under the Encumbered Estates Act. The Roman Catholic archbishop John MacHale of Tuam purchased the rest and established a Franciscan monastery on island. The stage was set for a protracted religious struggle that gradually subsided with the mission's demise in the 1880s. See Branach, "Edward Nangle and the Achill Island Mission," 35–8; Harriet Martineau, *Letters from Ireland*, 95–9. The controversy over Achill even carried over to several readers of John Barrow's *Tour*, one of whom, incensed by the author's support for Nangle, scrawled in his copy that Barrow was "one of the most bigoted and narrow-minded of men"; 1. In a later note the reader complained that Nangle was a "carpetbagger" from England (which was not true). Beneath this statement a second reader wrote "notwithstanding he preached the truth"; 211. This copy of Barrow's book is in the main branch of the Hamilton County Public Library in Cincinnati, Ohio.

Chapter 3. Property, Class and Irish Tourism

1 MacCannell, *The Tourist*, 13.
2 See Tinneswood, *The Polite Tourist*, 63–4; John Brewer, *The Pleasures of the Imagination*, 627.
3 Moir, *The Discovery of Britain*, 20; Ousby, *The Englishman's England*, 61.
4 See Tinneswood, *op. cit.*, 91, 96. See also Moir, *op. cit.*, xv; Ousby, *op. cit.*, 74; Mandler, *The Rise and Fall of the Stately Home*, 9, 10.
5 Carol Fabricant, "The Literature of Domestic Tourism," 57, 256. See also Ousby, *op. cit.*, 62, 65; Tinneswood, *op. cit.*, 99–100.
6 See Toby Barnard, *Making the Grand Figure*, 52; Reeves-Smyth, "Desmesnes," 199. For descriptions of the Irish "big house" in the seventeenth century see Crookshank, "The Visual Arts, 1603–1740," 475–7; MacLysaght, *Irish Life in the Seventeenth Century*, 92–110.
7 See K. Whelan, "Modern Landscape from Plantation to Present," 69. Concerning the building boom, Kevin Whelan notes that, between the seventeenth century and 1740, the number of big houses in County Cork had grown from 25 to 200. Tracking the construction of some 300 big houses constructed between 1700 and 1800, Whelan displays a graph showing that there was a significant surge in building between 1720 and 1740, with a much larger surge coming after 1760; see K. Whelan, *op. cit.*, 68–9; figure 5, page 69. The Penal Laws deprived Roman Catholics of most of their civil rights and threatened their ability to retain ownership of land unless they converted to the Anglican faith. Gary A. Boyd underscores the "urgency" of Ascendancy efforts to build their way into a claim of legitimacy; *Dublin*, 38–9.

8 Barnard, *op. cit.*, 27, 35. See also, Mandler, 7–8, 26. For the Ascendancy's obsession with building see Ray Foster, *Modern Ireland*, 190–93. Although the Anglo-Irish Protestant Ascendancy included all of the recognized Irish peerage, it was also represented by a relatively small number of gentry and urban businessmen who had the franchise. Among these were a few extremely powerful "commoners," such as William Conolly, Speaker of the Irish House of Commons and proprietor of one of Ireland's grandest estates at Castletown, County Kildare; see Toby Bernard, *op. cit.*, 14–5, 24.

9 Guinness, "The Irish House," 15; Bernard, *op. cit.*, 35–52.

10 See Cullen, "Economic Development," 127; O'Kane, *Landscape Design*, 101; MacAodha, "Distribution, Function and Architecture," 21. For Coole Park see Somerville-Large, *The Irish Country House*, 136. Finola O'Kane points out that walled estates often blocked access to land and pathways that had once been treated as commonage; *ibid.*, 34. An anonymous painting, *View of Mount Ivers, Co. Clare*, circa 1737, provides a good example of the Irish walled estate; see Barnard, *op. cit.*, 175.

11 Campbell, *A Philosophical Survey*, 96; Chetwood, *A Tour Through Ireland*, 137, 208.

12 Atkinson, *The Irish Tourist*, 100. See also Anon., "Sketch of a Journey through Part of Ireland," *Walker's Hibernian Magazine*, September, 1807, 617; November, 1807, 675.

13 See Anon., *A Topographical and Chronographical Survey of the County of Down*, 35; Barnard, *op. cit.*, 25. See also O'Kane, *op. cit.*, 1.

14 See Reeves-Smyth, *op. cit.*, 200. See also O'Kane, *op. cit.*, 31, 98. O'Kane reproduces a 1740 painting of the Stradbally Estate on page 96, which provides a good example of the look of Anglo-Dutch estate design.

15 See Charles Smith, *Cork*, 301. For the tree-lined avenues see Reeves-Smyth, *op. cit.*, 200–1. Paintings of Stradbally and Carton, figures 1 and 4 on pages 197 and 199 preceding Reeves-Smyth's essay illustrate the use of these sylvan corridors.

16 Chetwood, *op. cit.*, 208–9, italics original.

17 Chetwood, *op. cit.*, 239. Lord Mornington at Dargan also had a lake with a fort and a man-of-war; J. R. McCracken, 1986, 46. For estate hydraulic systems see O'Kane, *op. cit.*, 21–9, 34.

18. Campbell, *op. cit.*, 169–70; italics original.

19 For an example of the transition from the Anglo-Dutch style to the new natural style of landscape gardening see Finola O'Kane's chapter on Carton House; *op. cit.*, 89–117. O'Kane points out that by the 1730s and 1740s it was considered unfashionable to use canals in landscaping in Ireland; 41. However, the new tastes in landscaping were not universally adopted in eighteenth-century Ireland. O'Kane demonstrates how the Conollys of Castletown, conscious of their middle-class origins, rejected romantic naturalism and clung to the older, more formal, style with its obvious emphasis on power, order and control; 122.

20 T. K. Cromwell quotes Cowper Walker, an earlier visitor to Delville; *Excursions Through Ireland*, 2:18. For Delany see C. Maxwell, *The Stranger in Ireland*, 149.

21 Pococke, *Pococke's Tours of Ireland in 1852*, 98. See also Harden, "Tour in Ireland," July–December, 1955, 83. For a description of the Rock Close see Hall and Hall, *op. cit.*, 1:22. For how it was adapted to tourism see Mark Samuel and Kate Hamlyn, *Blarney Castle*, 65–6.

22 For ha-has in Ireland see Reeves-Smyth, *op. cit.*, 201. For a brief description of the new style of park design see Crookshank, "The Visual Arts, 1740–1850," 509–10. For Leixlip Castle see de Courcy and Maher 1985, *National Gallery of Ireland*, 30; for Ballinrobe House and Westport House see John Hutchinson, *James Arthur O'Connor*, 67, 99; also "Intrusions

and Representations," 93–4. For the sheep at Carton House see Arthur Young, *A Tour in Ireland*, 9. Estate owners did not completely surrender flowers and shrubs to the great expanses of grass. O'Kane points out that at Castletown House small plantings of flowers were carefully tucked into corners of the lawn; *op. cit.*, 61.

23 See Raymond Williams, *The Country and the City*, 133. See also Cormac Ó Gráda, *Ireland*, 125–6. For a map showing the location of estates of more than twenty hectares from 1830–1900, see Reeves-Smyth, *op. cit.*, Figure 8, 202. Finola O'Kane points out that in the eighteenth century, some of the great proprietors went to great efforts to try to make their estate grounds as agriculturally productive as possible, following a "farmlike way of gardening"; *op. cit.*, 35.

24 See John Hutchinson, "Intrusions and Representations," 93–4, 95. Because of the superior quality of the agricultural lands around Dublin, many of the finest houses tended to be in a radius of seventy-mile of the city; see MacAodha, "Distribution, Function and Architecture,"49.

25 See De Latocnaye, *A Frenchman's Walk through Ireland*, 203; C. T. Bowden, *A Tour Through Ireland*, 71. See also Twiss, *A Tour of* Ireland, 22–24; Barrow, *A Tour Round Ireland*, 135, 178; Beaufort, "Rev. Daniel A. Beaufort's Tour of Kerry," 203. For the importance of paintings in the eighteenth-century Irish big house see Barnard, *op. cit.*, 151–187.

26 Chetwood, 137, 142. For a description of Thomastown see Somerville-Large, *The Irish Country House*, 124. For the positioning of the big house in relation to the road, see J. H. Andrews, "Land and People, c1780," 239.

27 Howley, *The Follies and Garden Buildings of Ireland*, 6–7.

28 J. L. McCracken, "Social Structure and Social Life," 46. See also Pococke, *Pococke's Tours of Ireland in* 1852, 4, 137. Lady Tyrone spent 262 days organizing and pasting the shells; Howley, *op. cit.*, 35. For techniques in constructing shell houses see Howley, 34–6.

29 For Mrs. Delaney and her love of shells, see Howley, *op. cit.*, 28. For Poulaphouca see Bowden, *op. cit.*, 71. Concerning grottos, Howley discusses several types. Some, such as the still extant one at Stillorgan in south Dublin, were constructed partially or wholly underground. Others were "natural," being built into hillsides. Others incorporated "plunge pools" for bathing or served as ice houses in winter; 27–30.

30 For follies at Castletown House, see O'Kane, *op. cit.*, 62, 63, 67; Barnard, *op. cit.*, 73; Howley, *op. cit.*, 14.

31 For Beranger see Wilde "Memoir of Gabriel Beranger," 144–5.

32 R. Williams, *op. cit.*, 154; Atkinson, *op. cit.*, 263–4.

33 Forbes, *Memorandums*, 1:14.

34 Barnard, *op. cit.*, 194. For the Civil Survey see Michael Viney, *Ireland*, 89, 247. For lumbering in the seventeenth century see E. McCracken, *The Irish Woods Since Tudor Times*, 30.

35 For estate forestry in Ireland see Neeson, *op. cit*, 91–114. For Robertson's comments see his *The Traveller's Guide*, 128–9. Nineteenth-century estate forestry was successful in stabilizing the acreage of forests in Ireland at roughly 345,000 acres by 1841. However, with land transfers from proprietors to tenants beginning in the 1880s, many landlords quickly sold off their trees. By the end of World War One there were only 130,000 acres of trees left. Since then Ireland's forests, treated as a renewable resource, have expanded; see Eileen McCracken, *op. cit*, 140.

36 See Everett, *The Tory View of Landscape*, 53. Everett notes Tory opposition to the Whig-type of estate improvement, which involved visual separation of the manor house from the

208   CREATING IRISH TOURISM

fields and villages upon which the estate depended. The Tory opposition was not so much to enclosure, a system of farming, but rather to displays of aristocratic ego, such as the destruction of a village to "improve" a park; 64. See also K. Whelan, "Modern Landscape from Plantation to Present," fig. 8, 70; Hutchinson, "Intrusions and Representations," 94.
37 For the picture see de Courcy and Maher, *op. cit*, 27. For a brief description of the estate see Somerville-Large, *op. cit.*, 137.
38 Campbell, *op. cit.*, 167; Young, *A Tour In Ireland*, 8–9, 90; Atkinson, *op.* cit., 264.
39 Thackeray, *op. cit.*, 130. See also Atkinson, *op.* cit., 556; Gough *An Account of Two Journeys Southward in Ireland in 1817*, 4–5.
40 Fabricant, "Binding and Dressing," 117.
41 Atkinson, *op.* cit., 125.
42 *Ibid.*, 214.
43 Somerville-Large, *op.* cit., 139. Tunbridge wares were inlaid wooden boxes, bowels and utensils made by craftsmen from the English spa town of Tunbridge Wells. See also Pococke, *op.* cit., 9. For a description of the Glen of the Downs, see Anon., "A Sketch of an Excursion to the County of Wicklow," 349–50.
44 John Gough, *A Tour in Ireland*, 171–5.
45 O'Kane, *op. cit.*, 170.
46 Young quoted in C. Maxwell, *op. cit.*, 27. For Campbell, *op. cit*, 55. For Thomastown House and for barrack rooms see Somerville-Large, *op. cit.*, 124, 156–7.
47 O'Kane, *op. cit.*, 119.
48 Inglis, *op. cit.*, 1:193; Reid, *op. cit.*, 331; Hutchinson, *op. cit.*, 50, 95.
49 See Guinness, *op. cit.*, 16; Plumptre, *op. cit.*, 215–16.
50 E. Smith, *The Wicklow World*, 122–3. For the decline of tourist interest in the estates, see O'Kane, *op. cit.*, 172, 175; for quote see 170.
51 See Mandler, 71, 72–3; for "Olden Time" see 23–69. For opening of Hampton Court see Tinneswood, *op. cit.*, 139.
52 B. Graham, "Ireland and Irishness," 4.
53 For Powerscourt Garden see Ann Crookshank, *op. cit.*, 488. Edward Hyams suggests that the eighteenth century garden at Powerscourt looked to Italian and French Renaissance examples for inspiration; *Irish Gardens*, 91–97. The great house itself burned in 1975. The walls of the house, along with the gardens survived, and it has been reopened as a tourist center.

Chapter 4. The Sublime and the Picturesque in the Irish Landscape

1 Adler, "Origins of Sightseeing," 9, italics original, 10.
2 Immerwhar, "'Romantic' and its Cognates," 33; Adler, *op. cit.*, 11, 17–8.
3 See M. Andrews, *Landscape and Western Art*, 4; Spirn, *The Language of Landscape*, 16, 17. See also Helsinger, "Land and National Representation in Britain," 15; Crandell, *Nature Pictorialized*, 104.
4 Cosgrove, *Social Formation and Symbolic Landscape*, 15. See also M. Andrews, *op. cit.*, 156; W. J. T. Mitchell, "Imperial Landscape," 2, 5; Spirn, *op. cit.*, 24.
5 This public availability of private paintings was part of the gradual shift of patronage of the arts from aristocratic privacy to the public sphere, representing the general movement of cultural production from the aristocracy toward urban middle-class. See

NOTES

Brewer, *The Pleasures of the Imagination*, xvii; Hemingway, *Landscape Imagery and Urban*, 33, 36–7; Dian Kay Kriz, *The Idea of the English Landscape Painter*, 37.

6   For the print market in Britain see Brewer, *op. cit.*, xvii, 450–3, 458–9.
7   Brewer, *op. cit.*, 457, 449–50, 455. For the relationship of painters to prints see Clayton, *The English Print*, 157, 181. For print rooms see Barrell, *The Idea of Landscape*, 4. For Castletown House see Guinness, "The Irish House," 11.
8   Anon., *The Sportsman in Ireland*, 1:4. See also Standring, "Watercolor Landscape Sketching,"73–84; Kriz, *op. cit.*, 66–7. For the role of periodicals in popularizing landscape painting among amateurs see Ann Pullan, "For Publicity and Profit," 261–84.
9   Axton, "Victorian Landscape Painting," 282.
10 Barrell, *op. cit.*, 13, 7–8; see also Crandell, *op. cit.*, 96–8.
11 Uvedale Price wrote, "When I speak of a painter I do not mean merely a professor, but any man (artist or not) of a liberal mind, with a strong feeling for nature as well as art, who has been in the habit of comparing both together"; quoted in Brewer, *op. cit.*, 620.
12 Dickson, "Letters," July–December, 1841, 678–9; Holmes, *Sketches*, 16.
13 See Derrick, *Letters*, 1:53. Malcolm Andrews suggests that the Poussin most British writers referred to was Gaspard Dughet, Nicholas Poussin's brother-in-law. Gaspard adopted Nicholas' surname. Some 300 paintings attributed to Gaspard were sold in England between 1711 and 1759; *The Search for the Picturesque*, 26.
14 M. Andrews, *Landscape and Western Art*, 131. See also R. Bell, "An Excursion to County Cavan," 496; E. Wakefield, *An Account of Ireland*, 1:51.
15 Chatterton, *Rambles in the South of Ireland*, 1:171 italics added. See also Campbell, *A Philosophical Survey*, 104–5; Ashworth, *A Saxon in Ireland*, 138, italics added.
16 Otway, *Sketches in Ireland*, 8.
17 See Schama, *Landscape and Memory*, 447–8. For "Wens," etc. see Nicolson, *Mountain Gloom, Mountain Glory*, 42.
18 Schama, *op. cit*, 450. For Walpole, Gray and Dennis see Schama, 448–449, italics added. For Nicolson, see *op. cit.*, 272.
19 Burke, *A Philosophical Enquiry*, 58, 60; italics original.
20 Quoted in Gibbons, *Edmund Burke and Ireland*, 2–3.
21 Burke, *op. cit.*, 237–8. For "astonishment" see 95–6.
22 In *Gothic Ireland*, Jarlath Killeen argues that Burke's vision of nature as irrational, uncontrollable and wild represented a direct challenge to the Protestant, Anglo-Irish attempt to impose a sense of control, order and dominance upon Irish landscape; 131–56. See also Gibbons, *op. cit.*, 23.
23 Carr, *The Stranger in Ireland*, 381.
24 Bush, *op. cit.*, 89; italics original. For a discussion of Bush's work see Hooper, *Travel Writing and Ireland*, 17–31.
25 Robertson, *The Traveller's Guide Through*, 146–7. See also Holmes, *Sketches*, 195; italics added.
26 Ritchie, *Ireland*, 1:95; italics added. Ritchie's "torrent" may have been the Poulanass Waterfall, which today is flanked by a set of steep steps equipped with handrails, additions that are convenient but less conducive, perhaps, to sublime imagination.
27 Ousby, *op. cit.*, 140, 146, 148.
28 Burke, *op. cit.*, 339–40. See also 319–20.
29 Atkinson, *The Irish Tourist*, 602.
30 For Rosa's place in landscape appreciation see Barrell, *op. cit.*, 6–7, 50. Some indication of the importance of Rosa to popular landscape aesthetics is suggested by the fact that the Anglo-Irish novelist Lady Morgan (Sidney Owenson) wrote a biography of the artist

in 1822; see Sunderland, "The Legend and Influence of Salvator Rosa," 785. For Rosa's influence on Morgan's landscape descriptions see Susan Egenolf, "Revolutionary landscapes," 48–9, 61–2. Egenolf shows how Owenson worked comparisons of Claude Lorrain and Salvator Rosa into her novel *The Wild Irish Girl* (1806); 55.
31 Monk, *The Sublime*, 211. See also Crandell, *op. cit.*, 99; See also Schama, *op. cit.*, 450–7. Rosa was a much more versatile painter than many of his British admirers realized. They greatly exaggerated his supposed fascination with *banditti*. Sunderland points out that they appear in only a few of his paintings. Although storms were also often associated with Rosa's art, there are no storms in any of his paintings; Sunderland, *op. cit.*, 785–8. For Sunderland's quote see 786.
32 Crandell, *op. cit.*, 101. See also Carr, *op. cit.*, 147–8; Dunn, *op. cit.*, 28–9; White, *A Tour in Connemara*, 26.
33 Burke, *op. cit.*, 150–1.
34 Carr, *op. cit.*, 359–60; italics added. See also Bush, *op. cit.*, 77, italics added. For Beranger see Harbison, *"Our Treasure of Antiquities"*, 140, italics added.
35 Feifer, *Tourism in History*, 189; Batten, Jr., *Pleasurable Instruction*, 11. Boswell's imitation of Addison is a good example of the power of travel writing to set patterns of behavior at tourist sites.
36 See Ousby, *op. cit.*, 136–7, 150–1.
37 Anon., *The Sportsman in Ireland*, 1:102–3. See also de Latocnaye, *A Frenchman's Walk through Ireland*, 72; Bowden, *op. cit.*, 114; Croker, *Researches*, 284.
38 Fisher, *Letters from the Kingdom of Kerry*, 23–4.
39 Burke, *op. cit.*, 96. For "idea of vast power" see 110. For M. Andrews see *op. cit.*, 233.
40 Otway, *A Tour of Connaught*, 389. For "hanging over the Atlantic" see Otway, *Sketches in Ireland*, 91–2. Hy Brazil was a mythical island lying somewhere west of the Aran Islands. It was variously a place of death or an earthly paradise. It appeared on old international charts, and explorers gave its name to the most easterly part of South America; McMahon, O'Donoghue, *Brewer's Dictionary*, 381.
41 Johnson, *A Tour of Ireland*, 331. For "terrible convulsion" see 125.
42 Dunn, *op. cit.*, 61, italics added. See also Herbert, *Retrospections*, 151–2.
43 Fisher, *op. cit.*, 15–6, italics added. See also Gibbons, "Topographies of Terror," 26.
44 Dunn, *op. cit.*, 29, italics added.
45 See Norman Nicholson, *The Lakers*, 38. Gina Crandall suggests that "picturesque" became associated with landscape through the works of the English "Landscape Poets" John Dyer (1699–1757) and James Thompson (1700–1748). The former's *Grongar Hill* and the latter's *Seasons* both appeared in the 1730s; *op. cit.*, 116.
46 Campbell, *op. cit.*, 166–7, italics added. See also Dunn, *op. cit.*, 10; italics added.
47 C. Smith, *Kerry*, 95, 96–7. See also Kriz, *op. cit.*, 63–4.
48 Forbes, *Memorandums*, 1:93. See also Blake Family, *Letters*, 25; Dunn, *op. cit.*, 64–5; Belton, *The Angler in Ireland*, 109, italics original.
49 Lowenthal, Prince, "English Landscape Taste," 196.
50 See M. Andrews, *op. cit.*, 239. See also Standring, *op. cit.*, 78; Ousby, *op. cit.*, 154.
51 Ellul, *The Technological Society*, 63. Technique often leads to a fascination with technology. Even without cameras, the eighteenth and early nineteenth centuries could call upon technology to enhance landscapes. In addition to various tinted glass through which a scene might be viewed, there was the so-called "Claude glass." This was a concave mirror through which the viewer, with his back to the object of interest, inspected the scene. The mirror, which could also be tinted, compressed the scene and emphasized

the sense of perspective, making nature look, indeed, just like a picture. For a time this type of mirror was used to assist artists in sketching their scenes. For the "Claude glass," see Standring, *op. cit.*,75; M. Andrews, *op. cit.*, 63–73; 155–6, 161–3; Moir, *op. cit.*,143; N. Nicholson, *op. cit.*, 53–4. With the exception of A. Atkinson's *The Irish Tourist* (1815), few travel accounts about Ireland refer to the use of "the glass."

52 For Batten see *op. cit.*, 29. Gilpin's approach to landscape had an enormous influence over a generation of British watercolorists, sketchers and travel writers. He recommended sketching (as opposed to oil painting) as an appropriate art form for the middle-class amateur. As Kriz suggests: "Picturesque sketching, then, had the potential of aesthetically empowering a middle-class public"; *op. cit.*, 63, 66.

53 For authenticity in tourism see Jonathan Culler's "The Semiotics of Tourism." For Gilpin's book on the Wye Valley see M. Andrews, *op. cit.*, 86). For "stations" see Moir, *op. cit.*, 141, 144; Kim Ian Michasiw, "Nine Revisionist Theses," 82–4. For Gilpin's approach to scenery see Stephen Copley, "Gilpin on the Wye," 133–56; also M. Andrews, *op. cit.*, 86–94. Gilpin did not invent the principles of the picturesque. Timothy Clayton notes that they had been set forth by William Oran in 1745; *op. cit.*, 158. The Gilpinesque fussiness about finding the right "station" from which to view a scene, the use of various "glasses" and his rather specialized vocabulary inevitably became the target of satire. Gilpin inspired the satire, *The Tour of Dr. Syntax in Search of the Picturesque* (1813) by William Combe and Thomas Rowlandson. Jane Austin had more than a decent amount of fun with Gilpin's picturesque terminology in *Northanger Abbey*. The satire even extended to a comic opera, *The Lakers* by James Plumptre, in which one character, when accused of producing an unrecognizable landscape sketch, retorts, "If it is not like what it *is*, it is what it *ought* to be. I have only made it picturesque"; see Lowenthal, Prince, *op. cit.*, 195.

54 Ousby, *op. cit.*, 158. The guides to the Lake District were written by Gilpin, Thomas Gray and Thomas West (and later by William Wordsworth).

55 The anonymous quote is from "A Tour of the South of Ireland," in *Walker's Hibernian Magazine*, November 1886, 593–8. For Ockenden see *Letters*, 134–5. For more examples see W. Williams, *Tourism, Landscape, and the Irish Character*, 22. For theatrical references to landscape see M. Andrews, *op cit,*, 89. For connection between travel descriptions, landscape painting and theatrical design see John Brewer, *The Pleasures of the Imagination*, 620; Carole Fabricant, "Binding and Dressing," 114. W. F. Axton points out that studio-based landscape painters were frequently called upon to double as theatrical set designers; *op. cit.*, 291.

56 Thomas Gray made his tour of the Lake Districts in 1769, but his descriptions were not published until 1780 as an appendix to Thomas West's *Guide to the Lakes*; see Moir, *op. cit.*, 140. For an account of the influence of the Lake District guidebooks upon picturesque tourism see M. Andrews, *op. cit.*, 153–95. For a detailed account of the writers who popularized the Lake District see N. Nicholson's, *op. cit.* Clayton points out that landscape prints produced in the 1740s and 1750 predated the popular guidebooks of the British Lake District, which were not published until the 1780s; *op. cit.*, 158.

57 Bush, *op. cit.*, 96.

58 Plumptre, *op. cit.*, 75. The bridge is very evident in Francis Wheatly's *Nymphs Bathing at the Salmon Leap* (c. 1782), although the naked nymphs were probably the artist's contribution to the scene. For a detail of the painting see O'Kane, *Landscape Design*, 68. For Strandling see *op. cit.*, 76.

59 Fisher, *op. cit.*, 7–8.

60 Forbes, *op. cit*, 1:143. See also Crandell, *op. cit*, 136.
61 Anon., "An Account and Description of Rostrevor," by M. in *Newry Register*, 1:2 (1815), 106.
62 Barrell, *op. cit.*, 22, 89.
63 Binns, *The Miseries and Beauties of Ireland*, 1:31–2. See also Inglis, *A Journey throughout Ireland*, 2:41; Reid, *Travels in Ireland*, 249. For more on "figures in the landscape" see W. Williams, *op. cit.*, 53–60.
64 Fisher, *op. cit.*, 53.

Chapter 5. Picturesque Tourist Sites in Ireland

1 Moir, *The Discovery of Britain*, 156.
2 Dean MacCannell, *The Tourist*, 41; italics original. Neil Leiper cautions against using words such as "attraction" or "drawing power" in connection with tourist sites. A waterfall or a ruin has no magnetic power to pull in tourists. The impetus for travel and the choice of destinations comes from within tourists themselves and are products of the culture to which they belong. However, once identified, even Leiper has to admit that popular sites do "appear" to attract tourists; "Tourist Attraction Systems," 369.
3 Hutchinson, "Intrusions and Representations," 90, 91.
4 For the Boyne monument see W. Williams, *Tourism, Landscape, and the Irish Character*, 38–40. The monument, erected in 1736, was blown up in an unofficial action of the Free State Army in 1923; see Geraldine Stout, *New Grange*, 145. See also Urry, *The Tourist Gaze*, 9. For the tourist gaze in Ireland see W. Williams, *op. cit.*, 52–60, 107–10.
5 MacCannell, *op. cit.*, 41, 113.
6 Plumptre, *Narrative*, 245.
7 Leiper, *op. cit.*, 370. For the different types of markers see Leiper, 377–80.
8 Young, *A Tour In Ireland*, 31; Pococke, *Pococke's Tours of Ireland in 1852*, 126.
9 See Luckcombe, *A Tour Through Ireland*, 27–8. This book is so thoroughly plagiarized from the works of the author's immediate predecessors that one must wonder if it wasn't concocted in Fleet Street in London.
10 For the painting see O'Kane, *Landscape Design*, 149. See also Carr, *The Stranger in Ireland*, 140–1.
11 Atkinson, *The Irish Tourist*, 617; Clarke, *Tour*, 308–9.
12 Although Moore's lyrics for his *Irish Melodies* could stand alone as poems, he set them to traditional airs, many taken from the last of the Irish harpers by Edward Bunting and his colleagues at the end of the eighteenth century.
13 Tradition provided various reasons as to why the larks did not allegedly sing at Glendalough. Carr reported on one legend, hinted at in Moore's song: "Upon inquiry I was informed, that the lark never gladdens this inhospitable region with its song, owing, no doubt, to the bird being scared away by the horror of its desolation"; *op. cit.*, 185. (For Carr's use of the word "gloomy," see 176.) Hall and Hall related the story of St. Kevin banishing the larks, whose untimely warbles prematurely woke up the workmen building his church; *Hall's Ireland*, 1:254.
14 Ritchie, *Ireland*, 1:89–90.
15 See Wilde, "Memoir of Gabriel Beranger," 450. Sir John Carr, Leitch Ritchie and Sir John Forbes were among the travel writers to also call attention to the industrial pollution at Glendalough.
16 See Carr, *op. cit.*, 117. Many place names in Ireland refer to ancient woodlands. The Gaelic word for "oak" is *doire*, usually rendered in English as "Derry." *Coill*, a common

place name meaning "wood," is often Anglicized as "Kil" or "Kill." Confusion comes from the fact that *cill*, Gaelic for "church" may also rendered in English as "Kill." Without the original Irish name, it is sometimes difficult to know whether a place name refers to a long-gone forest or an ecclesiastical site. See Deirdre and Laurence Flanagan, *Irish Place Names*, 58, 70. For a list of Gaelic tree names with Anglicized forms see E McCracken, *The Irish Woods*, 22–3.

17 Hall and Hall, *op. cit.*, 2:250. For Peacock's painting see Crookshank, Knight of Glin, *Painters of Ireland*, 197. See also Atkinson, *op. cit.*, 589.

18 For Petrie's watercolor see de Courcy and Maher, *National Gallery of Ireland*, 6. See also Coyne, *Scenery and Antiquities*, 287.

19 Cromwell, *Excursions Through Ireland*, 3:128.

20 See Anne Plumptre, *op. cit.*, 297. See also Wakefield, *An Account of Ireland*, 536; italics original. For tree planting procedures in England see Keith Thomas, *Man and the Natural World*, 210, 211. For Ireland see O'Kane, *op. cit.*, 57. For coppice and pollard woods see Oliver Rackham, "Ancient Woodland," 48–67. Eileen McCracken points out that coppicing came late to Ireland. British iron works generally used twenty-five-year-old coppice oak, making it a renewable fuel. In Ireland, where oak had been so plentiful, proprietors often did not bother to coppice their forests until most of them were gone; *op. cit.*, 92.

21 Quoted by Hooper, *Travel Writing and Ireland* 30; see also 33.

22 Bush, *op. cit.*, 76. See also Stafford, *Voyage into Substance*, 242, 272. For the place of waterfalls in modern tourism see Brian J. Hudson's essay, "Waterfalls: Resources for Tourism."

23 See O'Kane, *op. cit.*, 149–50. Barret's painting shows a group of picnickers enjoying the view of the falls from under some trees in the foreground. The painting is in the National Gallery of Ireland; see de Courcy and Maher, *op. cit.*, 24. The Powerscourt waterfall and Barret's painting have remained powerful icons for Ireland's natural scenery. In 2002 artist Margaret Corcoran exhibited *An Enquiry* (a reference to Burke's famous essay on the sublime), a series of paintings set in the National Gallery, several of which incorporate Barret's depiction of the Powerscourt falls. See Corcoran, *Margaret Corcoran: An Enquiry*.

24 Clarke, *op. cit.*, 310. See also Bush, *op. cit.*, 80–1, 83.

25 See Plumptre, 185, italics original. See also Atkinson, *op. cit.*, 615–6. T. Croften Croker claimed that on his visit to Powerscourt he had to pass through six gates and had to pay at each, going and coming. He set this down to a temporary situation, an attempt by the family to recoup the cost of a Royal visit from George IV; *Researches*, 25.

26 Ritchie, *op. cit.*, 1:56. See also Binns, *The Miseries and Beauties*, 12; R. Graham, *A Scottish Whig in Ireland*, 49.

27 Ritchie, *op. cit.*, 1:261. The Blessington Estate lobbied hard for a bridge to be built above the falls, although the main purpose seems to have been to create better road links with Dublin than to accommodate tourists. For an illustrations of the bridge see Trant, *The Blessington Estate*, 133; O'Kane, *op. cit*, 166. For Plumptre quote see *op. cit.*, 216.

28 See the Hall and Hall, *op. cit.*, 2:242–3. Poulaphouca derives from the Gaelic for "Pool of the Pooka." The *Púcaí*, pooka, phooka or phouka was usually depicted as a demonic being, which often took the form of a horse that carried unwary riders over a precipice to their doom. It is this demon who, by spitting on them, ruins the blackberries at Michaelmas time. The Pooka appears in more benign form in several folk tales where it is condemned to toil for others until its work earns it a token gift. See Katharine Briggs, *An Encyclopedia of* Fairies, 325–7. He also turns up in traditional music, in the haunting air *Port Na bPúkaí* and in hard-driving reel "The Black Mare of Fanad,"

a piece associated with the late Donegal fiddler Johnny Doherty. Unfortunately, the falls at Poulaphouca are no longer a part of Ireland's tourist map. A hydroelectric dam built above the gorge in 1930s has left it dry and, as a consequence, virtually unknown.

29 C. T. Bowden in his *A Tour Through Ireland* described Poulaphouca on 71. For his trip to Coolaphooka see 111–14. The moss house at the later site became so well known that it was mentioned in a traditional ballad, "The Streams of Bunclody," which begins, "Oh, were I at the moss house or some other fine place." See also Atkinson, *op. cit.*, 351; E. Smith, *The Wicklow World*, 7.

30 Stafford, *op. cit.*, 112, 116.

31 Hall and Hall, *op. cit.*, 1:155. See also T. Molynuex, "A Journey to Kilkenny," 299; Chetwood, *A Tour Through Ireland*, 193; Plumptre, *op. cit.*, 318; Cromwell, *op. cit.*, 3:52.

32 Inglis, *A Journey throughout Ireland*, 2:234–5. See also Ritchie, *op. cit.*, 2:129.

33 Dickson, "Letters," July–December 1841, 552; see also 550.

34 Corbin, *The Lure of the Sea*, 97, 144.

35 Otway, *Sketches in Ireland*, 211.

36 Plumptre, *op. cit.*, 118.

37 Hardy, *The Northern Tourist*, 291. See also Hamilton, *Letters*, 52; Plumptre, *op. cit*, 128; Barrow, *A Tour Round Ireland*, 74; Hall and Hall, *op. cit*, 2:356–7.

38 The description of the Giant's Causeway and basalt flows is taken from Fedden, *The Giant's Causeway*, 1–4, 18; Holland, *The Irish Landscape*, 134–35; F. Mitchell, *Shell* Guide, 13–15.

39 See Klonk, "From Picturesque Travel," 205–230. See also Stafford, *op. cit.*, 72. In 1788 the controversy inspired a series of very detailed accounts in Dublin newspapers of a "volcanic eruption" near Ballycastle in Antrim. The author of the hoax signed himself "Pliny the Younger"; see Robert Lloyd Preager, *The Way that I Went*, 82–3.

40 See Curwin, *Observations*, 1:192. Rev. William Hamilton was rector of Clondavaddog and Fannet, County Donegal, a remote parish near Lough Swilly. He was a graduate of Trinity College where his studies had included geology and mineralogy. He had been involved in the founding of the Dublin Society. Unfortunately, Hamilton became *persona non grata* to the locals because of his overly vigorous defense of the Anglican Church and the British Government. He was murdered by a mob in 1779.

41 Hamilton, *op. cit.*, 187; Dodd, *The Traveller's Directory*, 213.

42 For Drury's painting see Crookshank and The Knight of Glin, *Painters of* Ireland, 67. Drury, who was interested in science, won a premium from the Dublin society for her painting; Crookshank, "The Visual Arts, 1740–1850," 524. For Drury see also Barnard, *Making the Grand Figure*, 164. For Plumptre see *op. cit.*, 132.

43 Manners, *Notes of an Irish Tour*, 136. See also Twiss, *A Tour of Ireland*, 158; de Latocnaye, *A Frenchman's Walk*, 206; Curwen, *op. cit.*, 1:194; Inglis, *op. cit.*, 2:235–6.

44 Curwen, *op. cit.*, 1:194. See also John Forbes, *op. cit.*, 2:169; James Johnson, *op. cit.*, 337–8. For Richard Pococke and the Giant's Causweay see McVeigh's *Richard Pococke's Irish Tour*. For Plumptre see *op. cit.*, 134. Plumtre's decision to devote a whole chapter to a description of the basaltic rocks illustrates Barbara Marie Stafford's assertion that there was some continuity between eighteenth-century "scientific" accounts of exploration and nineteenth-century travel writing; Stafford, *op. cit.*, xxi.

45 Young, *op. cit.*, 115. See also Duffy, *op. cit.*, 174–7; Holmes, *op. cit.*, 35.

46 Hall and Hall, *op. cit.*, 1:164–5. See also Hoare, *op. cit.*, 49; "Blaymire's Tour of Connaught, 1779," 15, 31. Blaymire's constant poking around old churches caused rumors that he was a Papal legate or, conversely, a representative of the Protestant

Bishop of Meath. Blaymire reported that several Roman Catholic priests caught up with him at Clonmacnois to check him out; 89.
47 Harden, "Tour in Ireland," January–June 1954, 38. See also Hunt, *Gardens and the Picturesque*, 179, 18; Twiss, *op. cit.*, 38; Holmes, *op. cit.*, 183, italics added; Chatterton, *Ramble*, 163, For more discussion about the travelers' emotions surrounding Irish antiquities, see W. Williams, *op. cit.*, 32–8.
48 Weld, *Illustrations*, 25. See also Gibbons, *Gaelic Gothic*, 11. Gibbons argues that "Gaelic Gothic" involved race as well religion.
49 Beranger was a French Huguenot from Rotterdam who settled in Dublin where for a time he ran an artist supply store. He sketched antiquities around Dublin, and in 1779 he was commissioned by the Hiberno Antiquarian Society to record the antiquities in the West; see Harbison, *"Our Treasure of Antiquities"*, 1–14. Early drawings of New Grange, Knoth and Dowth may be seen in G. Stout, *op. cit.*, 40–2, 64. For the Hall's description of New Grange see *op. cit.*, 2:307.
50 O'Hollaran, *Golden Ages and Barbarous Nations*, 6.
51 West, *A Summer Visit to Ireland*, 120–21. See also Hall and Hall, *op. cit.*, 2:452–60. For the round tower controversy see Leersson, *Remembrance and Imagination*, 108–26; O'Halloran, *op. cit.*, 60, 184.
52 See Janowitz, *England's Ruins*, 3–5.

Chapter 6. The Tourist Experience

1 Holmes, *Sketches*, 2. See also Buzard, *The Beaten Path*, 105; Urry, *Consuming Places*, 132.
2 Ritchie: *Ireland*, 1:53; Plumptre, *Narrative*, 269; Belton, *The Angler in Ireland*, 2:7, 8; Weld, *Illustrations*, 17.
3 Barton, *Some Remarks*, 13. See also MacCannell, *The Tourist*. 44.
4 R. Graham, *A Scottish Whig in Ireland*, 108.
5 Hall and Hall, *Hall's Ireland*. 2:364–5. See also Twiss, *A Tour of Ireland*, 43; Plumptre, *op. cit.*, 135.
6 Barrington, *Discovering Kerry*, 203. Kevin Danaher notes that a similar apparition on Lough Gur in County Limerick became associated with another Gaelic political figure, the Great Earl of Desmond; *The Year in Ireland*, 121. Luke Gibbons discusses the political significance of this transfer of magical identities from ancient deities to defeated Gaelic lords; "Topographies of Terror," 31–4.
7 On their visits to Killarney both Ritchie, *op. cit.*, 2:238 and Binns, *The Miseries and Beauties of Ireland*, 120 referred to Moore's song, one of his *Irish Melodies*. "O'Donoghue's Mistress" is a strange but sprightly love song, set to one of Turlough Carolan's harp tunes, "Planxty Irwin."
8 See Hall and Hall, *op. cit.*, 1:74. Donal Horgan points out that much of the rock in and around Lough Leane is limestone. The weathering of these rocks produced the fantastic shapes that sparked the imagination of guides and tourists. Unfortunately, the weathering also collapsed "O'Donoghue's Horse" into the Lough about a century ago; *Echo After Echo*, 22.
9 See Richard M. Dorson's *Folklore and Fakelore*. See also Hall and Hall, *A Week at Killarney*, 136; Gibbons, *op. cit.*, 34. A phenomenon similar to that reported at Killarney has allegedly been seen off the Antrim coast around the Giant's Causeway. Philip Dixon Hardy cited this as an example of the "Fata Morgana," as this type of spectacle is sometimes called. See his *The Northern Tourist*, 322–3.

10 Plumptre, *op. cit.*, 280, italics original.
11 MacCannell, *op. cit.*, 42. The author is quoting Erving Goffman. MacCannell maintains that ritual behavior could even extend to routine tourist complaints about guides.
12 The association of "blarney" with hyperbolic speech supposedly comes from the experience of Lord Carew, whom a later Cormac MacCarthy talked into believing that he, Carew, would be given possession of Blarney Castle. Although often reiterated, the promise was never kept. Some trace the origin of the expression back to earlier chiefs of the clan Carthy who held off the forces of Queen Elizabeth I with frequent promises to surrender the castle. In either case, such promises were "all blarney." See Dolan, *A Dictionary of Hiberno-English*, 29; Share, *Slanguage*, 28. Samuel and Hamley report that the word may be related to the Gaelic *bladhmann*, meaning "boasting" or "bragging"; *Blarney Castle*, 72.
13 Millikin's poem (and song) became a literary marker for Blarney Castle and was often cited in travel accounts. In 1835 Francis Mahony ("Father Prout") added a verse to the Millikin's poem: "There is a stone that whoever kisses,/Oh! He never misses to grow eloquent./'Tis he may clamber to a ladies' chamber,/Or become a member of parliament./A clever spouter he'll soon turn out or/And out-and-outer 'to be left alone.'/Don't hope to hinder him, or to bewilder him/Sure he's a pilgrim from the Blarney Stone"; quoted in Samuel, Hamlyn, *op. cit.*, 67. It may have been Mahony's verse that helped to popularize the term "Blarney Pilgrim" (also the title of a well-known traditional jig) for the visitor in search of "the gift."
14 Plumptre, *op. cit.*, 239. See also Croker, *Researches*, 306.
15 Coyne, *The Scenery and Antiquities*, 238–39. Coyne reports that in order to kiss the "real" stone—the most inaccessible one—the tourist had to be dangled upside down by the heels. In the twentieth century safety bars were eventually installed making access safer but still difficult. For a detailed account of the stones see Samuels and Hamlyn, *op. cit.*, 68–70. See also Plumptre, *op. cit.*, 239; Chatterton, *Rambles*, 2:24; Hall and Hall, *Hall's Ireland*, 1:20–1.
16 Knott, *Two Months at Kilkee*, 164.
17 Edensor, "Staging Tourism," 325–6.
18 Nuñez, "Touristic Studies," 271, italics original; Crang, "Performing the Tourist Product," 141–2, 149.
19 Hall and Hall, *op. cit.*, 1:92–3. See also Wright, *A Guide*, 21.
20 Bennett, *Narrative*, 110. See also Hall and Hall, *op. cit.*, 1:154.
21 Wilde, *Lough Corrib*, 201. Meg Merrilees is the gypsy figure who provides the title for a poem by John Keats. Sir Walter Scott has a character by that name in *Guy Mannering*, one of the Waverly novels. The Firbolgs were one of the mythic peoples of Ireland. See also Hall and Hall, *op. cit.*, 2:392.
22 Ousby, *The Englishman's England*, 167. See also Ritchie, *op. cit.*, 2:125; Thackeray, *Irish Sketch Book*, 278–9; Barry, *A Walking Tour*, 26.
23 West, *A Summer Visit*, 18; Carlyle, *Reminiscences*, 57.
24 Martin Haverty, *The Aran Isles*, 18–9. Tim Robinson, who interviewed one of the last of the "cliffmen" on the largest of the Aran islands, states that the paddling motion enabled the men making the descent to control the oscillations of the rope; *Stones of Aran*, 54.
25 Knott, *op. cit.*, 78, 156–7.
26 Urry, *The Tourist Gaze*, 9.
27 See Anon., *Paddy Land*, 44–5; also Hall and Hall, *A Week at Killarney*, 120.
28 Hall and Hall, *op. cit.*, 2:255, 365.
29 See Dickson, "Letters," July–December 1841, 60, 341, 342, italics original. For reference to concerts see Murphy, *Before the Famine Struck*, 85–86. See also Chatterton, *op. cit.*, 2:215.

30 Anon., *A Sportsman in Ireland*, 1:75–6. See also Dickson, *op. cit.*, July–December, 1841, 60.
31 Ritchie, *op. cit.*, 2:125. See also Edensor, *op. cit.*, 331.
32 Ousby, *op. cit.*, 132–33.
33 For descriptions of the running girls see W. Williams, *op. cit.*, 190–1. See also Binns, *op. cit.*, 2:354–5; Bennett, *op. cit.*, 44; Ritchie, *op. cit.*, 1:132–3; Carlyle, *op. cit.*, 121.
34 Knott, *op. cit.*, 154.
35 Wright, *op. cit.*, 29.
36 Barry, *op. cit.*, 27, 28.
37 Graburn, "Tourism," 33. See also Leiper, *op. cit.*, 380.
38 Hall and Hall, *op. cit.*, 74. See also Hall and Hall, *Hall's Ireland*, 1:121, 2:288–9.
39 Ritchie, *op. cit.*, 2:125. See also Plumptre, *op. cit.*, 142.
40 Thackeray, *op. cit.*, 227, italics original. See also R. Graham, *op. cit.*, 315.
41 Thackeray, *op. cit.*, 311. Alexis de Tocqueville published *Journeys to England and Ireland* in 1834; his friend Gustav Beaumont wrote *Ireland: Social, Political and Religious* in 1839. See also Binns, *op. cit.*, 1:249.
42 Thackeray, *op. cit.*, 275. See also Johnson, *A Tour of Ireland*, 105; Hall and Hall, *op. cit.*, 2:358, emphasis original.
43 Ritchie, *op. cit.*, 2:124. For McMullen guides see Halls and Hall, *op. cit.*, 2:358; Fedden, *op. cit.*, 10.
44 Cronin, *Across the Lines*, 72.
45 Hall and Hall, *op. cit.*, 2:251; for the Halls on the Spillanes see *A Week at Killarney*, 81. See also Plumptre, *op. cit.*, 142; Ritchie, *op. cit.*, 1:82. James Johnson recognized George Wynder from the Halls' description; Johnson, *op. cit.*, 38. Wynder may have been the guide Carlyle encountered in his visit to Glendalough in 1849. Never at a loss at depicting the beggars' rags, Carlyle described a "scarecrow" boatman at Glendalough, "his clothes or rags hung on him like *tapestry*; when the wind blows he expands like a tulip…"; *op. cit.*, 72.
46 Thackeray, *op. cit.*, 213. Thackeray may have intended the reference to Inglis as a joke, since it was Killary Harbour in Connemara, not Glendalough that the Scot had likened to a Norwegian fjord. Samuel Lover (1797–1868) was a popular Anglo-Irish artist, novelist, song writer and entertainer.
47 Otway, *A Tour of Connaught*, 167, italics original. See also Hall and Hall, *A Week at Killarney*, 79.
48 Cronin, "Fellow Travelers," 58.
49 For travel writers' comments on the Irish peasant's character, especially compared to their English counterparts, see W. Williams, *op. cit.*, 105–126. For quotes see West, *op. cit.*, 101, italics original; Crang, *op. cit.*, 151.
50 Inglis, *op. cit.*, 1:76; Barrow, *A Tour Round Ireland*, 301.
51 Reid, *Travels in Ireland*, 236–7, 271. See also Hall and Hall, *Hall's Ireland*, 1:1–2.
52 S. T. Hall, *Life and Death in Ireland*, 36, 77, emphasis original.
53 Pratt, *Imperial Eyes*, 84.

Chapter 7. Killarney—A Case Study of the Irish Tourist Experience

1 Edmund Falconer (Edmund O'Rourke, 1814–1879) was an actor/playwright. Michael William Balfe (1808–1870) was an Irish composer, best known for his *Bohemian Girl*.
2 See Gibbons, "Topographies of Terror," 25. See also Charles Smith, *County Kerry*, 141; John Bush, *Hibernia Curiosa*, 122. For the Lake District see Esther Moir, *The Discovery of*

Britain, 140. Raymond Immerwhar dates the beginning of the fascination with picturesque romantic landscapes from around the mid-1750s and cites Charles Smith's description of Killarney as one of the key texts; see Immerwhar, "'Romantic' and its Cognates," 33–4.

3   Campbell, *A Philosophical Survey*, 26. See also Orrery, "Lord Orrery's Travels," 48–9.
4   Anon., *A Sportsman in Ireland*, 1:126. See also C. Smith, *op. cit.*, 141.
5   Barrington, *Discovering* Kerry, 137; Freeman, *Ireland*, 45.
6   Holmes, *Sketches*, 140–1. See also Barrington, *op. cit.*, 144–5.
7   Peter Somerville-Large, *The Irish Country House*, 115, 116. It helped that, during the period of the Penal Laws, the Brownes had only one male heir in each generation. Thus, the estate was not subdivided among Catholic brothers. After James II's defeat at the Battle of the Boyne, the title of Viscount was granted to a Browne who accompanied the King to France. It was recognized in Ireland as a courtesy title only. However, as a part of the Government's buying of support for the Act of Union, the fifth Viscount became the Earl of Killarney; see Barrington, *op. cit.*, 100, 109.
8   Gibbons, *op. cit.*, 29, 30.
9   For tanneries see Bradshaw, Quirke, "Woodland History," 39–40. For the Muckross iron works see C. Smith, *op. cit.*, 122. Mining at Killarney went back to ancient times; see Freeman, *Pre-Famine Ireland*, 1957, 102–103. Charles Smith claimed that the copper mine at Muckross was once one of the most productive in Europe; *op. cit.*, 125. In 1804 a Col. Hall, who was attached to the local barracks, reopened the Ross copper mine to considerable profit. At that point the miners were working under the lake. However, when they followed a rich vein leading upwards, they cut through the lake bed, and the mine was flooded; Croker, *Researches*, 311–2. Rudolf Erich Raspe, general reprobate and the author of *Travels and Surprising Adventures of Baron Munchausen*, was briefly the manager of the Herbert's cooper mine until his untimely death from typhoid in 1794. He is said to be buried in the grounds of Muckross Friary; Barrington, *op. cit.*, 110, 206, 208.
10 See Hall and Halls, *Hall's Ireland*, 1:67; Otway, *Sketches in Ireland*, 393; Inglis, *A Journey throughout Ireland*, 1:205. For roads to Killarney see Barrington, *op. cit.*, 106, 109.
11 Barrington, *op. cit.*, 110, 198. See also C. Smith, *op. cit.*, 146–7; Anon., *Traveller's New Guide*, 311.
12 Wright, *A Guide*, 6, 10. See also C. Smith, *op. cit.*, 146–7; Young, *A Tour In Ireland*, 119.
13 Anon., *Sportsman*, 1:127. See also Plumptre, *Narrative*, 275; Wright, *op. cit.*, 10.
14 Wright, *op. cit.*, 25. For Pococke see Gibbons, *op. cit.*, 29.
15 Forbes, *op. cit.*, 135. See also D. Herbert, *Retrospections*, 3.
16 Wright, *op. cit.*, 26; italics original. See also R. Graham, 197; Anon., *Sportsman*, 1:107.
17 Harden, "Tour in Ireland," January–June, 1955, 16. See also Dunn, *A Description of Killarney*, 25.
18 Weld, *op. cit.*, 8, 116. After quoting this passage, a reviewer of Weld's book observed that, since much of Killarney's wood had been earlier sacrificed to iron manufacturing, the remaining timber was so valuable on the market that "demand for it will eventually render the whole district a dreary waste"; see Anon., "Review of New Publications," 343. For Weld's statement beginning "it is painful to reflect" see *op. cit.*, 10–1; for "Painful is the task" see 151. For the Earl of Kenmare see Barrington, *op. cit.*, 110. See also Dunn, *op. cit.*, 25; John Harden, *op. cit.*, January–June, 1955, 16.
19 See Hoare, *A Tour in Ireland*, 70, italics original. Bradshaw and Quirke point out that the Herberts were only reintroducing Scots pine, which had been indigenous to the Killarney area until two to three thousand years ago; *op. cit.*, 37, 43. See also E. Wakefield, *An Account of Ireland*, 1:67.

20 Barrow, *A Tour Round Ireland*, 304. See also Dodd, *The Traveller's Directory*, 205–6; Hoare, *op. cit.*, 78.
21 Forbes, *Memorandums*, 141. See also Belton, *The Angler in Ireland*, 3:25–6.
22 Holmes, *op. cit.*, 148–50.
23 For "pseudo-event" see Urry, *The Tourist Gaze*, 7–8. For quote see Anon., *Sportsman*, 1:123–4. The red deer at Killarney represent the only remaining herd of Ireland's indigenous deer. Their survival is due, in part, to the famous hunt, the continuation of which into the nineteenth century necessitated the establishment of a herd management plan; see Horgan, *Echo After Echo*, 4; Barrington, *op. cit.*, 142. In the twentieth century the herd dwindled until it received some state protection. It has been managed by the state for over the past thirty years; see Alan J. Craig, "Killarney National Park," 10. In addition to the red deer, sika deer were introduced from Japan into the Killarney woods during the nineteenth century.
24 Wright also recorded the local legend that one must not injure the tree. He tells of a soldier who stuck his pen knife into bark and died on spot; *op. cit.*, 59. See also Young, *op. cit.*, 115; Harden, *op. cit.*, January–July 1955, 15.
25 W. Williams, *Tourism, Landscape, and the Irish Character*, 46–7.
26 Urry, *op. cit.*, 9–10.
27 The entire poem represents a powerful literary marker for Killarney as a whole. Hallam Tennyson, the poet's son, noted: "It is marvelous that so many of the chief characteristics of Killarney should have found place in a poem so short"; *Alfred Lord Tennyson*, 293. In addition to the echoes the first verse refers to O'Donoghue's castle on Ross Island, as well as the long cataract which falls from the Devil's Punch Bowl from the summit of Mangerton into the lake below. In the twentieth century, British composer Benjamin Britten set the poem to music, famously recorded by tenor Peter Pears.
28 Williams Ockenden, *Letters*, 137–8. As at Killarney, the boats on Derwentwater and Ullswater in the Lake District came equipped with brass cannon and French horn players or buglers; Moir, *op. cit.*, 146. By 1780s there was so much firing that it gave the Lake District the "rustic calm of a battlefield." There were even mock naval engagements. See Norman Nicholson, *The Lakes*, 62–3.
29 Weld, *op. cit.*, 135. See also Holmes, *op. cit.*, 139–40.
30 Bush, *Hibernia Curiosa*, 98–9, 127.
31 Beaufort, "Rev. Daniel A. Beaufort's Tour of Kerry," 7.
32 For quotes see Weld, *op. cit.*, 135; Johnson, *op. cit.*, 115, italics original. See also West, *A Summer Visit*, 106.
33 Weld, *op. cit.*, 151. See also Plumptre, *op. cit.*, 276; Manners, *Notes of an Irish Tour*, 66.
34 Plumptre, *op. cit.*, 276. See also Weld, *op. cit.*, 137; Woods, "A Scientific Tour," 29.
35 Hole, *A Little Tour in* Ireland, 169–70.
36 Hoare, *op. cit.*, 80. See also Woods, *op. cit.*, 28.
37 Plumptre, *op. cit.*, 274. For 1804 quote see Anon., *Journal of a Tour in Ireland, performed in August 1804*, 26.
38 Hall and Hall, *op. cit.*, 1:71. The anonymous author of the *Sportsman*, writing at about the same time as the Halls, claimed that "what with *aiting*, and drinking, and bugling, and humbug," a boat and its crew would cost about two pounds a day; *op. cit.*, 88, italics original. See also Twiss, *A Tour of Ireland*, 117; Wright, *op. cit.*, 9.
39 Belton, *op. cit.*, 2:11–2.
40 Carr quotes from a question-answer echo poem attributed to Swift; 389. Donal Horgan gives a version of the dialogue in his book on Killarney; *op. cit.*, 90.

41 Hall and Hall, *A Week in Killarney*, 142. See also West, *op. cit.*, 106.
42 Hall and Hall, *op. cit.*, 120. See also West, *op. cit.*, 111.
43 Plumptre, *op. cit.*, 273–4.
44 See W. Williams, *op. cit.*, 73. See also Wright, *op. cit.*, 67, italics original; Hall and Hall, *op. cit.*, 110.
45 West, *op. cit.*, 106. See also Hall and Hall, *op. cit.*, 110. For the origins of the cottage see Horgan, *op. cit.*, 84.
46 Allingham, *William Allingham's Diary*, 301. See also Hall and Hall, *Hall's Ireland*, 1:72.
47 Hall and Hall, *A Week in Killarney*, 68, 97. See also Inglis, *op. cit.*, 1:220.
48 Leiper, *op. cit.*, 376.
49 Harden, *op. cit.*, January–June, 1955, 17. See also Urry, *Consuming Places*, 188; Carlyle, *op. cit.*, 124.
50 Urry, *op. cit.*, 174, 192. See also Anon., *A Run Around* Ireland, 20, 22, 24–5; italics original.
51 Thackeray, *Irish Sketch Book*, 125. See also Anon., *Sportsman, op. cit.*, 1:109.
52 Urry, *op. cit.*, 136, 137. There can be elements within a site that may be literally consumed, however. At Killarney two-and-a-half centuries of tourism have taken their toll on the Lakes' flora and fauna. The Killarney fern (*Irichomanes speciorum*) now borders on extinction due to its great popularity with Victorian tourists, who were eager to take samples back with them. The long-extinct golden eagle, which gave its name to the famous Eagle's Nest along the Long Range River, may also have been a victim of tourism. Captive eaglets were once kept by hotels for tourists, some of whom were willing to pay high prices to take one home (Horgan, *op. cit.*, 13, 29–30). Mrs. West's guides suggested that they capture a bird for her in 1846. She declined the offer; *op. cit.*, 106.
53 Cosgrove, *Social Formation and Symbolic Landscape*, 230–1.
54 Michasiw, "Nine Revisionist Theses," 76, 77. Michasiw's revisionism is valid up to a point. It is a good corrective to Terry Eagleton's statement that "aesthetics" has more to do with political ideology than with art. "It denotes instead a whole program of social, psychological and political reconstruction on the part of the early European bourgeoisie…"; see "The Ideology of the Aesthetic," 327. Michasiw may go too far, however, in arguing that the picturesque was *only* a literary convention and that it did not affect the way nineteenth-century writers looked at the world; 77.
55 Inglis, *op. cit.*, 1:228.
56 Monk, *The Sublime*, 203.
57 Wordsworth, *The Preludes* (2:302–22), quoted in Weiskel, *The Romantic Sublime*, 173.
58 Thackeray, *op. cit.*, 128, 129.
59 Buzard, *The Beaten Track*, 11.

Chapter 8. Tourist Semeiotics, Stereotypes and the Search for the Exotic

1 See MacCannell, *The Tourist*; Culler, "The Semiotics of Tourism."
2 Culler, *op. cit.*, 1.
3 De Montbret, "An Eighteenth Century French Traveller in Kildare," 379.
4 Woods, "A Scientific Tour," 31. See also Derrick, *Letters*, 1:76; Thackeray, *Irish Sketch Book*, 193.
5 See Reid, *Travels in Ireland*, 314. The author of the *A Sportsman in Ireland* reported the same custom within the Claddagh outside of Galway town; 1:292. See also Knott, *Two Months at Kilkee*, 42.

6 See Harbison, "*Our Treasure of Antiquities*", For Beranger's dependence on translators see 38. See also Wilde, "Memoir of Gabriel Beranger," 133.
7 Chatterton, *Rambles*, 2:7.
8 I am indebted to Alf MacLochlainn, former director of the National Library of Ireland, for calling Dinnenn's comments to my attention. John Houston reports that the natives of Kilkee referred to the tourists as *ruachach* or "red turd." The term may have come from those whose task it was to empty the visitor's chamber pots. They found the color of the meat-eating tourists' excrement notably different from that of the local potato-eating peasantry; see Houston, "Kilkee,"27n21. *Ruachach*, however, does not appear in Dinneen. See also Head, *A Fortnight in Ireland*, 180–1.
9 Bernard Share, *Slanguage*, 44. See Chetwood, *A Tour Through Ireland*, 125–6, italics original. It is possible that what Chetwood heard was some form of "buggaun" or "buggeen," which Terence Patrick Dolan traces to *bugán*, meaning an egg with no shell, in other words a spineless person, *A Dictionary of Hiberno-English*, 33. See also Atkinson, *The Irish Tourist*, 472.
10 For tourists' tendency to treat accents as exotic see Cronin, *Across the Lines*, 11–16.
11 Ritchie, *Ireland*, 2:184–5. For more discussion of tourism and the Irish dialect see W. Williams, *Tourism, Landscape, and the Irish Character*, 63–7.
12 For more on playing the stereotype see Williams, *op. cit.*, 67–72.
13 S. T. Hall added that "if in addition…she happened to have a child, as was often the case, it occupied the hood, which was thrown behind for the purpose," *Life and Death in Ireland*, 18–9. Artist John Leech's foldout frontispiece for Samuel Reynolds Hole's *Little Tour of Ireland* (1859) depicts an outdoor scene in the Claddagh. Several of the old women in the illustration have a humpy appearance because of the burdens carried under their cloaks. See also the illustrations in Crawford, "Provincial Town Life," 48.
14 Cromwell, *Excursions Through Ireland*, 3:65. See also Logan, *Fair Day*, 57, 171, 172; R. Bell, "An Excursion to County Cavan," 499.
15 Chatterton, *op. cit.*, 1:244–5. See also Ashworth, *A Saxon in Ireland*, 62; Inglis, *A Journey throughout Ireland*, 2:24; Thackeray, *Irish Sketch Book*, 128.
16 Carlyle, *Reminiscences*, 162. See also Ritchie, *op. cit.*, 1:162.
17 Plumptre, *Narrative*, 414. See also Ritchie, *op. cit.*, 1:177–8. For congestion at markets see Logan, *op. cit.*, 66.
18 For cattle and horse fairs see Logan, *op. cit.*, 69–90. "Pattern" is Hiberno-English and derives from the English word "patron," referring to a local saint. The Gaelic word *patrún* can mean both "patron" and "pattern"; see Dolan, *op. cit.*, 195.
19 Cromwell, *op. cit.*, 2:7–8.
20 Wilde, *op. cit.*, 450. For Joseph Peacock's *The Pattern, or, The Festival of St. Kevin at the Seven Churches, Glendalough* see Crookshank, Knight of Glin, *Painters of Ireland*, 197. According to Dr. Wilde, the date of the festival was held around June 23, the date of the old Irish Midsummer's festival.
21 Bernard Share suggests that "Donnybrook," meaning a free-for-all, was actually of Australian and American origin; *op. cit.*, 88. For accounts of Donnybrook Fair see Cromwell, *op. cit.*, 2:7; Logan, *op. cit.*, 152–5. For Gaugen Barra see Croker, *Researches*, 280–1.
22 Reid, *Travels in Ireland*, 281.
23 Anon., "Notes of a Journey in the Kingdom of Kerry," 50. See also Logan, *op. cit.*, 102–8; Inglis, *op. cit.*, 2:52.
24 For Otway, *A Tour of Connaught*, 73. See also Croker, *op. cit.*, 280. Diarmuid Ó Giolláin discusses the cultural basis and ritual nature of the patterns in "The Pattern," 201–21.

For a discussion on the travel writers, patterns and faction fighting see W. Williams, *op. cit.*, 40–5, 76–9.
25   Logan states that stick fighting at markets and fairs continued into the 1920s; *op. cit.*, 1986, 112. For a study of post-Famine recreational fighting see Carolyn Conley, "The Agreeable Recreation of Fighting." For quotation see Johnson, *op. cit.*, 156.
26   Cromwell, *op. cit.*, 2:77.
27   See Hoare, *op. cit.*, 46; Blake, *Letters*, 326–7; Knott, *op. cit.*, 120, italics original.
28   Johnson, *A Tour of Ireland*, 194. See also Anon., "Sketch of a Journey through Part of Ireland," 676.
29   Plumptre, *op. cit.*, 248. See also Anon., *Sportsman*, 1:204, 1:259–60.
30   See Ó Crualaoich, "The 'Merry Wake,'" 192, 196. See also de Latocayne, *A Frenchman's Walk through Ireland*, 90; Binns, *The Miseries and Beauties of Ireland*, 138; Hall and Hall, *Hall's Ireland*, 1:86–7. For more discussion of tourist reactions of Irish funeral customs see W. Williams, *op. cit.*, 72–6.
31   Robertson, *The Traveller's Guide*, 311.
32   Barrow, *A Tour Round Ireland*, 264. See also Pococke, *Pococke's Tours of Ireland*, 104; de Latocnaye, *op. cit.*, 246–7; Inglis, *op. cit.*, 2:22; Head, *op. cit.*, 217.
33   Head, *op. cit.*, 217–18; italics added. See also Coyne, *The Scenery and Antiquities of Ireland*, 133; Anon., *Sportsman*, 1:292; White, *A Tour in Connemara*, 21.
34   S. T. Hall, *Life and Death in* Ireland, 47. See also Manners, *Notes of an Irish* Tour, 112; Bennett, *Narrative*, 122. The Spanish-sounding name of Valentia Island may have helped to fuel tourist fantasies of Iberian Kerry. The name, however, is the Anglicization of the Gaelic *Béal Inse*.

Chapter 9. On the Road—In Search of Ireland

1   In *Across the Lines*, 19, Michael Cronin distinguishes between what he calls "horizontal travel" and "vertical travel." By the former he means "linear progression from place to place"; by the latter, a temporary dwelling or "in-dwelling" at a certain location. The latter represents a special form of what I have called "traveling into" a country.
2   Culler is quoting Prospero Merimée; see "The Semiotics of Tourism," 6.
3   Bell, "An Excursion to County Cavan," 496. See also Atkinson, *The Irish Tourist*, 39; Otway, *A Tour of Connaught*, 186.
4   Ritchie, *Ireland*, 1:195.
5   Johnson, *A Tour of Ireland*, iii. See also Head, *A Fortnight in Ireland*, 110; S. T. Hall, *Life and Death in Ireland*, 7.
6   John Dunton, author of *Dublin Scuffle* (1698) and the manuscript *Teague Land*, was among the first British writers to identify the West and its inhabitants as representing the real Ireland, in all of its "old barbarities." See Leerssen, *Mere Irish and Fíor-Gheal*, 66. See also Andrew Carpenter's introduction to Dunton's *Teague Land*.
7   For drumlins see Freeman, *Ireland*, 28–9; Evans, *The Personality of Ireland*, 27–31; Mitchell, *Shell* Guide, 44–6; Viney, *Ireland*, 23–8.
8   Wilde, "Memoir of Gabriel Beranger," 127. See also Anon., *A Topographical and Chronographical Survey of the County of Down*, 9; West, *A Summer Visit*, 244–5, italics original.
9   In County Leitrim the drainage line moves to the southwest until it reaches Galway Bay. There it drops directly south to Clonakilty Bay on the Cork coast. See Figure 6.6 in Frank Mitchell, *Shell* Guide, 176.

10 Anon., *Journal of A Tour in Ireland during the Months of October and November, 1835*, 208–9.
11 For a detailed discussion of Ulster's "moral landscape" see W. Williams, *Tourism, Landscape, and the Irish Character*, 147–61. For quotes see Inglis, *A Journey throughout Ireland*, 2:328; Hall and Hall, *Hall's Ireland*, 2:335.
12 See Blake, *Letters*, 292. For more on trees see W. Williams, *op. cit.*, 128–30. For Young's quote see his *A Tour in Ireland*, 196.
13 For British navy see Simon Schama, *Landscape and Memory*, 166, 173. For a discussion of the importance of forests in Britain see Stephen Daniels, "Political Iconography of Woodland," 47–8. For British attitudes to Ireland's lack of trees see W. Williams, *op. cit.*, 130–1.
14 For Irish hedgerows and hedgebanks see Aalen and K. Whelan, "Fields," 141. See also Evans, *Irish Folk Ways*, 105–6.
15 R. Graham, *A Scottish Whig in Ireland*, 76. See also Cromwell, *Excursions Through Ireland*, 2:41. For English hedgerows see W. G. Hoskins, *The Making of the English Landscape*, 152.
16 West, *op. cit.*, 50.
17 For enclosure and crop rotations see Mark Overton, *Agricultural Revolution in England*, 21; Brewer, *The Pleasures of the Imagination*, 621, 624. For Irish enclosure see Aalen and K. Whelan, *op. cit.*, 136–9. For a more detailed discussion of British attitudes toward Irish agriculture compared to England's, see W. Williams, *op. cit.*, 127–46.
18 For Campbell see *A Philosophical Survey*, 117, 127. Almost twenty years after Campbell's account, John Gough reported extensive cultivation in the vicinity of the Rock of Cashel; *An Account of Two Journeys Southward in Ireland in 1817*, 39–40. This was probably the result of the temporarily higher grain prices during the Napoleonic wars. For the grazier economy see K. Whelan, "Modern Landscape," 73.
19 Hughes, "The Large Farm," 129.
20 Barrell, *The Idea of Landscape*, 32, 75. In his tour of France Arthur Young recorded his intensely negative reaction to open fields in France; see *Young's Travels in France*, 17.
21 Fisher, *Letters*, 65.
22 S. T. Hall, *op. cit.*, 6. See also Woods, "A Scientific Tour," 21.
23 See K. Whelan, *op. cit.*, 81. For a map of clachans in pre-Famine Ireland see figure 31 on page 79 of Whelan's essay. For more on clahans see K. Whelan, "Settlement Patterns," 62, 64; W. Williams, *op. cit.*, 99–101.
24 Harry Coulter, *The West of Ireland*, 201–2. For a description of the clachans and for the quote, "in a shower from the sky," see Evans, *op. cit.*, 29–30.
25 Anon., *The Irish Tourist* (1837), 148.
26 For summaries on the socio-economic role of the potato in pre-Famine Ireland, see J. Donnelly, Jr., *The Great Irish Potato Famine*, 4–11; W. Williams, *op.cit.*, 95–9.
27 For Irish life expectancy and trade-offs see Ó Gráda, *Ireland*, 32; "Industry and Communications," 111. For conditions in English country cottages see W. Williams, *op. cit.*, 111–3.
28 For more on British attitudes towards Irish rural poverty see W. Williams, *op. cit.*, 107–10.
29 Barrow, *op. cit.*, 246, italics original. The conacre system was a form of sharecropping. A family would rent some land for eleven months. The rent was usually due in advance. The landlord plowed and manured the land and perhaps supplied seeds. The family then planted the crop, gambling that the harvest and its price would pay for next year's rent. See Oliver MacDonagh, "The Economy and Society," 219.
30 Binns, *op. cit.*, 2:52. See also Ritchie, *op. cit.*, 2:24–5.

31 Knott, *Two Months at Kilkee*, 133. See also Cromwell, *op. cit.*, 1:47; Twiss, *A Tour of Ireland*, 75.
32 See Reid, *Travels in Ireland*, 204. For "bone" in the spud see also Johnson, *op. cit.*, 313–4. The underdone potato might not have been limited to peasant households. Visiting Ireland in 1846 Theresa Cornwallis West dined at a hotel in Naas where she was served a potato with its uncooked center, *op. cit.*, 43. See also Melish, *Travels*, 349; Inglis, *op. cit.*, 1:59–60. For more on the tourists and the potato see W. Williams, *op. cit.*, 96–9, 159–60.
33 For lazy-bed cultivation see Evans, *The Personality of Ireland*, 40–41; K. Whelan, "Modern Landscape," 88; P J. O'Connor, *Living in a Coded Land*, 20–21; A. Bourke, *"The Visitation of God"?*, 66.
34 Manners, *op. cit.*, 25–6.
35 Anon., *Sportsman*, 1:117.
36 Chatterton, *Rambles*, 102. See also Anon., *Journal of A Tour in Ireland during the Months of October and November, 1835*, 62.
37 Ritchie, *op. cit.*, 2:262–3.
38 This argument is developed in W. Williams 2008, 105–26. For quote see Fisher, *op. cit.*

Chapter 10. The Famine and After

1 Working with John McVeagh's bibliography of Irish travel writing, the author has counted around 102 books published during the decade 1840–1849. A total of 51were published from 1840 to 1845, the year that the potato blight first appeared, and an additional 51appeared between 1846 to 1849.
2 East's book includes a chapter on the "Dingle Reformation," and the book ends with a call for more proselytizing in Ireland. For more on East see Hooper, *Travel Writing and Ireland*, 136–9.
3 East, *Notes and Glimpses of Ireland*, 2, 120.
4 Carlyle, *Reminiscences*, iii; italics original.
5 Manners, *Notes of an Irish Tour*, 10–11, italics added.
6 Hooper, *op. cit.*, 131. As Melissa Fegan points out, Ireland suffered from a "question of reliability." Since the British public would not rely on Irish testimony, those who traveled to Ireland, "felt obliged to witness at first hand"; *Literature and the Irish Famine*, 78.
7 William Bennett, *Narrative*, 19. For the Quaker's plain style see Hooper, *op. cit.*, 127, 136–7. Using the window to frame a scene was one of Lady Chatterton's favorite devices. See W. Williams, *Tourism, Landscape, and the Irish Character*, 60–1. Gina Crandell states that when they looked out of their windows, the proprietors wanted to see scenes that looked like pictures; *Nature Pictorialized*, 112.
8 Bennett, *op. cit.*, 38, 41, 42.
9 Bennett, *op. cit.*, 19. See also S. T. Hall, *Life and Death in Ireland*, 24.
10 See L. A. Williams, *Daniel O'Connell*, 257–279. See also Robin Haines, *Charles Travelyan*, 400–13. Travelyan did not state that the Famine was necessarily over but only that governmental responsibility for the crisis was at an end.
11 See L. A. Williams, *op. cit.*, 316–8.
12 The cartoon refers to one of Thomas Moore's songs, "Let Erin Remember the Days of Old," itself based on the legend of a drowned city under the waters of Lough Neagh in Country Antrim. For the cartoon see *Punch*, xvii, 1849, 87. For a discussion of this and other material on the Queen's visit see L. A. Williams, *op. cit.*, 318–325.
13 For the *ILN* coverage see L. A. Williams, *op. cit.*, 326–40.

14 For Encumbered Estates Act see Peter Gray, *Famine, Land and Politics*, 217–24, 325–7.
15 Elizabeth Meloy points out that Irish pamphlets and articles on post-Famine Connemara did discuss the expansion of tourism; see "Touring Connemara." For internal colonialism see W. Williams, *op. cit.*, 178–9.
16 See K. Whalen's "Introduction" to his edition of the Blakes' *Letters*. The Blakes' attempts to establish productive agriculture on their estate and to exploit Connemara marble never quite paid off, and the family went bankrupt during the Famine.
17 See Otway, *Tour*, 238, 272, 341. See also Inglis, *A Journey throughout Ireland*, 2:64; Barrow, *A Tour Round Ireland*, 244–5. For more about tourists' enthusiasm for development in the West of Ireland see W. Williams, *op. cit.*, 168–9.
18 See *The Tourist's Illustrated Handbook for Ireland*, 173, 174. For more on the *Handbook* see Meloy, *op. cit.*, 22–4. For a more detailed discussion of the role of travel writers optimism regarding the economic potential of Connemara see W. Williams, *op. cit.*, 164–72. For quotes see Thackeray, *The Irish Sketch Book*, 210–11; Carlyle, *op. cit.*, 174, italics original.
19 For Ashworth's quotes see *A Saxon in Ireland*, A3, 206, 97, 40. For a detailed discussion of Ashworth's book see Hooper, *op. cit.*, 157–62.
20 For White's quotes see *A Tour in Connemara*, viii, 30, 145. See also Anon., *Tourists Illustrated Handbook*, 173. White's publisher, W. H. Smith and Sons, initially presented this work in the context of tourism. In the beginning of the first edition the company advertised its guidebooks to County Wickow, Killarney and the Giant's Causeway. More to the point, the 1849 edition had two titles. The first was tourist oriented: *Handbook to Connemara and Joyce's Country*. The second title, *A Tour of Connemara, with remarks on its great physical capabilities*, suggested development as well as tourism. Later editions used only the second title.
21 Forbes, *Memorandums*, 1:259.
22 See D. Jones, "The Transfer of Land"; M. Turner, *After the Famine*, 10, 15–6, 18, 35.
23 For the "Loop" see Meloy, *op. cit.*, 26–7. For *The Times* see Anon., *Handbook for Travelers in Ireland*, v-vi.
24 Meloy, *op, cit.*, 45.

Conclusion

1 Ferguson, "The Attractions of Ireland.—I, Scenery," 112. In her study of Ferguson Eve Patten argues that his essays represent an attempt to bring both the picturesque and the Irish countryside, especially Wicklow, into the cultural hegemony of the Dublin middle-class intellectual; *Samuel* Ferguson, 77–87.
2 For the impact of railways on Irish tourism in the 1850s see Furlong, *Irish Tourism*, 15–8; for Thomas Cook, *Ibid.*, 17. For Dublin Industrial Exposition and railways, see Dube, "'Enabling Institutions' and Disabling Illustrations," 77.
3 Furlong, *op. cit.*, 210. For Dargan and Bray see M. Davies, *That Favored Resort*, 145–7, 154–7.
4 Writing near the end of the twentieth century, Gina Crandell points to the continuing power of the picturesque. "The eighteenth century remains the primary source for landscape design that echoes a pictorialized nature," 112.
5 Nothing is really permanent, of course. If the Celtic Tiger revives and reverts to its recent tendency to use cheap immigrant labor to interface with tourists, Ireland's geniality may start to go the way of its Georgian buildings.

BIBLIOGRAPHY

Anon. "An Account and Description of Rostrevor, and of the Gentlemen's Seats, Castles, & c. in its Vicinity by M." *Newry Register.* 1, no. 2 (May-June, 1815), 103–13
Anon. "The Irish Tourist." *Fraser's* Magazine. 15 (June, 1837), 765
Anon. *The Irish Tourist or, the People and the Provinces of Ireland.* London: Barton, Haravey 1837
Anon. *The Itinerant: A Select Collection of Interesting and Picturesque Views of Great Britain and Ireland, Engraved from Original Paintings and Drawings by Eminent Artists.* London: John Walker 1799
Anon. *Journal of A Tour in Ireland during the Months of October and November, 1835.* London 1836
Anon. *Journal of a Tour in Ireland, performed in August 1804, with Remarks on the Character, Manners and Customs of the Inhabitants.* London: Richard Phillips 1806
Anon. "A Journey through part of Province of Munster by 'J. W.'" *Walker's Hibernian Magazine: Or Compendium for Entertaining Knowledge.* (October 17, 1794) 355–8; (November, 1794) 433–47; (December, 1794) 483–5; (January, 1795) 20–4; (February, 1795) 112–4
Anon. *Murray's Handbook for Travelers in Ireland,* 4th rev. ed. London: John Murray 1878
Anon. "Notes of a Journey in the Kingdom of Kerry." *Gentleman's Magazine.* 144 (January, 1828) 49–54
Anon. "Observations made in a Tour from Dublin to Lucan." *Irish Magazine* [*Cox's Magazine*]. 7, no. 5 (1814) 196–203
Anon. *The Pleasure Tour in Ireland with a Map, an Itinerary on a new plan and elegant engravings.* 2nd ed. Edinburgh: John Thompson 1827
Anon. "Review of New Publications." *Gentleman's Magazine* 103 (April, 1809) 343
Anon. *A Rollicking Irish Tour, by Rag, Tag and Bobtail, with Free and Easy Sketches by A. R-A.* Paisley, Scotland 1877
Anon. *A Run Around Ireland in August 1850, by "A" and "B."* [reprinted from the *Scotsman*] [1850]
Anon. "A Sketch of an Excursion to the County of Wicklow, in September, 1825," by "Delta." *Bolster's Quarterly Magazine.* 1, no. 4 (November 26, 1826) 349–55
Anon. "Sketch of a Journey through Part of Ireland." *Walker's Hibernian Magazine.* (September, 1807) 545–7; (October, 1807) 616–9; (November, 1807) 675–80; (August, 1808) 497–8
Anon. "Sketches from a Tourist's Notebook," by "E. G. A." *Belfast Monthly Magazine.* 12 (March, 1814) 191–7
Anon. *Sketches of Society in France and Ireland in the Years 1805–6–7. By a Citizen of the United States in Two Volumes.* Dublin 1811
Anon. *The Sportsman in Ireland, with his Summer route through the Highlands of Scotland by a Cosmopolite,* 2 vols. London: Henry Colburn 1840
Anon. *A Three Day's Tour in the County of Wicklow.* London 1849
Anon. *A Topographical and Chronographical Survey of the County of Down.* Dublin 1740

Anon. "Tour of Sligo and Longford in 1837," MS. Royal Irish Academy
Anon. "A Tour of the South of Ireland," *Walker's Hibernian Magazine*. (July, 1783) 362–4; November, 1786) 593–8; (December, 1786) 642–6
Anon. *The Tourist's Illustrated Handbook for Ireland*. London, Crownynill: Jones, Lover 1854
Anon. *Traveller's New Guide through Ireland....* Dublin: John Commings 1815
Anon. *Walker's Hand-book of Ireland, an Illustrated Guide for Tourists and Travellers*, 2nd ed. Dublin, London: n. d. [1872]
Aalen, F. H. A. "The Irish Rural Landscape: Synthesis of Habitat and History." *Atlas of the Irish Rural Landscape*. Edited by F. H. A. Aalen, *et al*. Cork: Cork University Press, 31–63, 1997
———. *Man and the Landscape in Ireland*. London: Academic Press 1978
———. "Synthesis of Habitat and History." *Atlas of Rural Landscape*. Edited by F. H. A. Aalen, *et al*. Cork: Cork University Press, 4–30, 1997
———. and Kevin Whelan. "Fields." *Atlas of Rural Landscape*. Edited by F. H. A. Aalen, *et al*. Cork: Cork University Press, 134–44, 1997
Adler, Judith. "Origins of Sightseeing." *Annals of Tourism Research*. 16 (1989) 7–29
Allingham, William. *William Allingham's Diary*. Fontwell, Sussex: Centar Press 1967
Andrews, J. H. "Land and People, c1780." *A New History of Ireland, IV: Eighteenth-Century Ireland, 1691–1800*, ed. T. W. Moody, W. E. Vaughn. Oxford: Clarendon, 236–264, 1986
Andrews, Malcolm. *Landscape and Western Art*. Oxford; New York: Oxford University Press 1999
———. *The Search for the Picturesque: Landscape Aesthetics and Tourism in Britain, 1760–1800*. Stanford, California: Stanford University Press 1989
Ashworth, John Harvey. *A Saxon in Ireland: or the Rambles of an Englishman in Search of a Settlement in the West of Ireland*. London: Murray 1851
Atkinson, A. *The Irish Tourist: in a Series of Picturesque Views, Travelling Incidents and Observations Statistical, Political, and Moral on the Character and Aspect of the Irish Nation*. Dublin: Courtney 1815
Axton, W. F. "Victorian Landscape Painting: A Change in Outlook." *Nature and the Victorian Imagination*. Edited by U. C. Knoepflmacher and G. B. Tennyson. Berkeley, California: University California Press, 281–96, 1977
Barnard, Toby. *Making the Grand Figure: Lives and Possessions in Ireland, 1641–1770*. New Haven, Connecticut: Yale University Press. 2004
———. *A New Anatomy of Ireland: The Irish Protestants 1649–1770*. New Haven, Connecticut: Yale University, [1980] 2003
Barrell, John. *The Dark Side of Landscape: The Rural Poor in English Painting 1730–1840*. Cambridge, UK: Cambridge University Press 1980
———. *The Idea of Landscape and the Sense of Place, 1730–1840: An Approach to the Poetry of John Clare*. Cambridge, UK: Cambridge University Press 1972
Barrington, T. J. *Discovering Kerry: Its History, Heritage & Topography*. Cork: Collins [1976] 1999
Barrow, John. *A Tour Round Ireland, Through the Sea-Cast Counties, in the Autumn of 1835, with plates drawn and etched by Daniel Maclise and app. containing a letter from a lady giving an account of the Achill mission*. London: John Murray 1836
Barry, William Whittaker. *A Walking Tour Around Ireland in 1865, by An Englishmen*. London: Richard Bentley 1867
Barton, Richard. *Some Remarks, towards a full description of Upper and Lower Lake Lene* [sic], *near Killarney, in the County of Kerry*. Dublin: S. Powell 1751
Batten, Jr., Charles L. *Pleasurable Instruction: Form and Convention in Eighteenth-Century Travel Literature*. Berkeley, California: University California Press 1978

Bayne-Powell, Rosamond. *Travellers in Eighteenth-Century England*. London: J. Murray 1952
[Beaufort, Daniel Augustus]. "Rev. Daniel A. Beaufort's Tour of Kerry, 1788." Edited by Gerard J. Lyne. *Journal of the Kerry Archeological and Historical Society*. 18 (1985) 183–214
Bell, J. "The Improvement of Irish Farming Techniques Since 1750: Theory and Practice." *Rural Ireland 1600–1900: Modernization and Change*. Edited by Patrick O'Flanagan, *et al* Cork: Cork University Press, 24–41, 1987
[Bell, Robert]. "An Excursion to County Cavan 1809." Edited by Séamus O Loinsigh. *Breifne*. 2 no. 8 (1965) 495–504
Belton, William. *The Angler in Ireland, or an Englishman's ramble Through Connaught and Munster during the summer of 1833*. 2 vols. London: Richard Bentley 1834
Bennett, William. *Narrative of a recent journey of six weeks in Ireland....* London: C. Gilpin, Hatchard 1847
[Beranger, Gabriel]. See Harbison, Peter; Wilde, Sir W. R
Berghoff, Hartmut, and Barbara Korte. "Britain and the Making of Modern Tourism." *The Making of Modern Tourism: The Cultural History of the British Experience, 1600–2000*. Edited by Hartmut Berghoff, *et al*. New York: Palgrave, 1–20, 2002
Bermingham, Ann. *Landscape and Ideology: The English Rustic Tradition, 1740–1860*. Berkeley, California: University California Press 1986
———. "The Picturesque and Ready-to-Wear Femininity." *The Politics of the Picturesque: Literature, Landscape and Aesthetics Since 1770*. Edited by Stephen Copley and Peter Garside. Cambridge: University California Press, 81–119, 1994
Binns, Jonathan. *The Miseries and Beauties of Ireland*. 2 vols. London: Longman, Orme, Brown 1837
Blake Family of Renvyle House [Henry Blake, Martha Louise Blake, Anne Attersol]. *Letters from the Irish Highlands*. London: John Murray 1825
Blaymire. [?]. "Blaymire's Tour of Connaught, 1779," MS. Royal Irish Academy
Bohls, Elizabeth A. *Women Travel Writers and the Language of Aesthetics, 1716–1818*. New York: University California Press 1995
Bourke, Austin. *"The Visitation of God"? The Potato and the Great Irish Famine*. Edited by Jacqueline Hill and Cormac Ó Gráda. Dublin: Lilliput 1993
Bourke, Marie. "Rural Life in Pre-Famine Connacht: A Visual Document." *Ireland: Art into History*. Edited by Raymond Gillespie and Brian P. Kennedy. Dublin: Town House, 61–74, 1994
Bowden, C[harles] T[opham]. *A Tour Through Ireland*. Dublin: Corbet 1792
Boyd, Gary A. *Dublin 1745–1922: Hospitals, Spectacle and Vice*. The Making of Dublin City, series. Edited by Joseph Brady and Anngret Simms. Dublin: Four Courts 2006
Bradshaw, Richard, and Bill Quirke. "Woodland History." *Killarney National Park: A Place to Treasure*. Edited by Bill Quirke. Cork: Collins, 31–50, 2001
Branach, Niall R. "Edward Nangle and the Achill Island Mission," *History Ireland*. 8 no. 3 (Autumn, 2000) 35–8
Brewer, John. *The Pleasures of the Imagination: English Culture in the Eighteenth Century*. New York: Farrar, Straus,Giroux 1997
Bridges, Roy. "Exploration and Travel Outside of Europe (1720–1914)," *The Cambridge Companion to Travel Writing*. Edited by Peter Holme and Tim Youngs. New York: University California Press, 53–69, 2002
Briggs, Katharine. *An Encyclopedia of Fairies: Hobgoblins, Brownies, Bogies and Other Supernatural Creatures*. New York: Pantheon 1976
Broderick, David. *An Early Toll-Road: The Dublin-Dunleer Turnpike, 1731–1855*. Maynooth Studies in Local History. Edited by Raymond Gillespie. Dublin: Irish Academic Press 1996

Burke, Edmund. *A Philosophical Enquiry into the Origin of our Ideas of the Sublime and Beautiful*, eighth edition. London: J. Dodsley [1757] 1776

Bush, John. *Hibernia Curiosa: A Letter from a Gentleman in Dublin to his Friend at Dover in Kent Giving a general View of the Manners, Customs, Dispositions, &c. of the Inhabitants of Ireland*. Dublin: J. Potts, J. Williams 1769

Buzard, James. *The Beaten Track: European Tourism, Literature, and the Ways to Culture, 1800–1918*. Oxford, UK: Clarendon 1993

———. "The Grand Tour and After (1660–1840)," *The Cambridge Companion to Travel Writing*. Edited by Peter Hulme and Tim Young. New York: University California Press, 37–52, 2002

Campbell, Thomas. *A Philosophical Survey of the South of Ireland in a Series of Letters to John Watkinson, M.D.* Dublin: Whitestone 1778

Carlyle, Thomas. *Reminiscences of My Irish Journey in 1849*. Preface by J. A. Froude. New York: Harper 1882

Carr, Sir John. *The Stranger in Ireland, or A Tour in the Southern and Western Parts of that Country in the year 1805*. London: Richard Phillips 1806

Chard Chloe. "From the Sublime to the Ridiculous: The Anxieties of Sightseeing." *The Making of Modern Tourism: The Cultural History of the British Experience, 1600–2000*. Edited by Hartmut Berghoff, et al. New York: Palgrave, 47–68, 2002

———. "Introduction." *Transports: Travel, Pleasure, and Imaginative Geography, 1600–1830. Studies in British Art 3*. Edited by Chloe Chard, Helen Langdon. New Haven: Yale California Press, 1–29, 1996

Charlesworth, Michael. "The Ruined Abbey: Picturesque and Gothic Values." *The Politics of the Picturesque: Literature, Landscape and Aesthetics Since 1770*. Edited by Stephen Copley and Peter Garside. Cambridge: Cambridge University Press, 62–80, 1994

Chatterton, Lady Henrietta. *Rambles in the South of Ireland during the year 1838*, 2 vols. London: Saunders, Otley 1839

Chetwood, William Rufus. *A Tour Through Ireland, In Several Entertaining Letters… To Which is prefix'd a description of the road from London to Holy-Head. By Two English Gentlemen*, 2nd ed. Dublin 1748

Clarke, Edward Daniel. *Tour Through the South of England, Wales and Part of Ireland, made during the Summer of 1791*. London: Minerva Press 1793

Clayton, Timothy. *The English Print, 1688–1802*. New Haven, Connecticut: Yale University Press 1997

Colbert, Benjamin. "Aesthetics of Enclosure: Agricultural Tourism and the Place of the Picturesque." *European Romantic Review*. 13, no. 1 (March, 2002) 23–34

Colley, Linda. *Britons: Forging the Nation 1707–1837*. New Haven, Connecticut: Yale University Press 1992

Conley, Carolyn. "The Agreeable Recreation of Fighting." *Journal of Social History*. 33, no. 1 (Fall, 1999) 57–72

Connolly, S. J. *Priests and People in Pre-Famine Ireland, 1780–1845*. Dublin: Four Courts 2001

Copley, Stephen. "Gilpin on the Wye: Tourists, Tintern Abbey, and the Picturesque." *Prospects for the Nation: Recent Essays in British Landscape, 1750–1880, Studies in British Art., No. 4*. Edited by Michael Rosenthal, et al. New Haven, Connecticut: Yale University Press, 133–156, 1997

———. "William Gilpin and the black-lead mines." *The Politics of the Picturesque: Literature, Landscape and Aesthetics Since 1770*. Edited by Stephen Copley and Peter Garside. Cambridge: Cambridge University Press, 42–61 1994

Corbin, Alain. *The Lure of the Sea: The Discovery of the Seaside in the Western World, 1750–1840.* Translated by Jocelyn Phelps. Berkeley, Los Angeles, California: University California Press 1994
[Corcoran, Margaret.] *Margaret Corcoran: An Enquiry.* Notre Dame, Indiana: Snite Museum of Art 2005
Cosgrove, Denis E., *Social Formation and Symbolic Landscape.* Totowa, New Jersey, Barnes, Noble 1984
Coulter, Harry. *The West of Ireland: its existing condition, and prospects.* Dublin: Hodges, Smith 1862
Coyne, J. Sterling. *The Scenery and Antiquities of Ireland Illustrated.* Drawings by W. H. Bartlett. London: Mercury [1842] 2003
Craig, Alan J. "Killarney National Park — An Introduction." *Killarney National Park: A Place to Treasure.* Edited by Bill Quirke. Cork: Collins, 7–14, 2001
Craig, Maurice. *Dublin, 1660–1860: A Social and Architectural History.* Dublin: Allen Figgis 1969
Craik, Jennifer. "The Culture of Tourism." *Touring Cultures: Transformations of Travel and Theory [1997].* Edited by Chris Rojek and John Urry. London, New York: Routledge, 113–36, 2000
Crandell, Gina. *Nature Pictorialized: "The View" in Landscape History.* Baltimore: Johns Hopkins University Press 1993
Crang, Philip. "Performing the Tourist Product." *Touring Cultures: Transformation of Travel and Theory.* Edited by Chris Rojek and John Urry. London: Routledge, 137–54, [1997] 2000
Crawford, W. H. "Provincial Town Life in the Early Nineteenth Century: An Artist's Impressions." *Ireland: Art into History.* Edited by Raymond Gillespie and Brian P. Kennedy. Dublin: Town House, 43–59, 1994
Croker, T[homas] Croften. *Researches in the South of Ireland: Illustrative of the Scenery, Architectural Remains and the Manners and Superstitions of the Peasantry with an Appendix Containing a Private Narrative of the Rebellion of 1798.* New York: Barnes, Noble [1824] 1969
Cromwell, Thomas K. *Excursions Through Ireland, Comprising Topographical and Historical Delineations of Leinster,* 3 vols. London: Longman, Hurst, Rees, Brown 1820
Cronin, Michael. *Across the Lines: Travel, Language, Translation.* Cork: Cork University Press 2000
_____. "Fellow Travelers: Contemporary Travel Writing and Ireland." *Tourism in Ireland: A Critical Analysis.* Edited by Barbara O'Connor and Michael Cronin. Cork: Cork University Press, 51–67, 1993
Crookshank, Ann. "The Visual Arts, 1603–1740." *A New History of Ireland, IV: Eighteenth-Century Ireland, 1691–1800.* Edited T. W. Moody, W. E. Vaughn. Oxford: Clarendon, 471–98, 1986
_____. "The Visual Arts, 1740–1850." *A New History of Ireland, IV: Eighteenth-Century Ireland, 1691–1800.* Edited T. W. Moody, W. E. Vaughn. Oxford: Calrendon, 499–541, 1986
_____. and The Knight of Glin. *Painters of Ireland c. 1660–1920.* London: Barrie, Jenkins 1978
Cullen, Louis M. "Economic Development, 1750–1800." *A New History of Ireland, IV: Eighteenth-Century Ireland, 1691–1800.* Edited T. W. Moody, W. E. Vaughn. Oxford: Clarendon, 159–95, 1986
_____. *The Emergence of Modern Ireland, 1600–1900.* New York: Holmes, Meier 1987
_____. "Man, Landscape and Roads: The Changing Eighteenth Century." *The Shaping of Ireland: The Geographical Perspective.* Edited by William Nolan. Cork: Mercier, 123–37, 1986
Culler, Jonathan. "The Semiotics of Tourism," http://homepage.mac.com/allanmcnyc/textpdfs/culler1.pdf 1990

Curran, C. P. *Dublin Decorative Plasterwork of the Seventeenth and Eighteenth Centuries*. London: Alec Tiranti 1967

Curwen, J. C. *Observations on the State of Ireland, Principally directed to its Agricultural and Rural Population; in a Series of Letters written on a Tour of that Country*. 2 vol. London: Baldwin, Cradock, Joy 1818

Danaher, Kevin. *The Year in Ireland*. Cork: Mercier, 1972

Daniels, Stephen. "Political Iconography of Woodland in Late Georgian England." *The Iconography of Landscape: Essays on the Symbolic Representation, Design and Use of Past Environments*. Edited by Daniel E. Cosgrove and Stephen Daniels. Cambridge, UK: Cambridge University Press, 43–82, 1988

———. "Re-visioning Britain: Mapping and Landscape Painting, 1750–1820." *Glorious Nature: British Landscape Painting, 1750–1850*. Edited by Katharine Baetjer. New York: Hudson Hills, 61–72, 1993

———. and Charles Watkins. "Picturesque Landscaping and Estate Management: Uvedale Price and Nathaniel Kent at Foxley." *The Politics of the Picturesque: Literature, Landscape and Aesthetics Since 1770*. Edited by Stephen Copley and Peter Garside. Cambridge: Cambridge University Press, 13–41, 1994

Davies, Gordon L. Herries. "The Concept of Ireland." *The Shaping of Ireland: The Geographical Perspective*. Edited by William Nolan. Cork: Mercier, 13–27, 1986

Davies, Mary. *That Favored Resort: The Story of Bray, Co. Wicklow*. Bray, County Wicklow: Woodwell 2007

De Courcy, Cathreine, and Ann Maher. *National Gallery of Ireland: Fifty Views of Ireland*. Dublin: National Gallery of Ireland 1985

De Latocnaye, Jacques-Louis. *A Frenchman's Walk through Ireland: 1796–7 (Promenade d'un Francais dans l'Irlande)*. Translated by John Stevenson. Dublin: Hodges, Figgis 1917

De Montbret, Charles Etienne Coquebert. "A Frenchman's Impressions of County Cork in 1790." Edited by Sile Ní Chinnéide. *Journal of the Cork and Archaeological Society*. 78 (1973–74) 117–23; 79 (1973–74) 14–25

———. "A Frenchmen's Impressions of Limerick, Town and People in 1791." Edited by Sighle Kennedy [Sile Ní Chinnéide]. *North Monster Antiquarian Society Journal*. 5, no. 4 (1948) 96–116

———. "A Frenchman's Tour of Connacht in 1791." Edited by Sile Ní Chinnéide. *Journal of the Galway Archaeological and Historical Society*. 35 (1976) 52–66

———. "A Journey from Cork to Limerick in 1790." Edited by Sile Ní Chinnéide. *North Munster Antiquarian Journal*. 54 (1971) 65–74

———. "A New View of Cork City in 1790." Edited by Sile Ní Chinnéide. *Journal of the Cork Historical and Archaeological Society*. 78 (1973) 1–13

———. "A New View of the Eighteenth Century Life in Kerry." Edited by Sile Ní Chinnéide. *Journal of the Kerry Archaeological and Historical Society*. 6 (1973) 83–100

———. 1974. "A View of Kilkenny City and County, 1790." Edited by Sili Ní Chinnéide. *Journal of the Royal Society of Antiquaries*. 104 (1974) 29–38

———. "An Eighteenth Century French Traveller in Kildare," ed, Sile Ní Chinnéide. *Journal of the Kildare Archaeological Society*. 15, no. 4 (1974) 376–86

———. "Coquebert de Montbret's Impressions of Galway City and County in the Year 1791." Edited by Sile Ní Chennéide. *Journal of the Galway Archaeological and Historical Society*. 25, no. 1–2 (1952) 1–14

De Nie, Michael. *The Eternal Paddy: Irish Identity and the British Press, 1798–1882*. Madison, Wisconsin: University Wisconsin Press 2004

De Tocqueville, Alexis. *Alexis de Tocqueville's Journey in Ireland, July-August, 1835.* Translated and edited by Emmet Larkin. Washington, D. C.: Catholic University of America Press 1990
Delany, Ruth. *A Celebration of 250 Years of Ireland's Inland Waterways.* Belfast: Apple Tree [1986] 1992
―――――. *The Shannon Navigation.* Dublin: Lilliput, 2008
Derrick, Samuel. *Letters Written from Liverpool, Chester, Corke, the Lake of Killarney, Dublin, Tumbridge-Wells, Bath,* 2 vols. London: L. Davis, C. Reymers 1767
[Dickson, M. F.]. "Letters from the Coast of Clare." by M. F. D. *Dublin University Magazine.* 27 (January-June, 1841) 355–68, 517–23, 770–76; 28 (July-December, 1841) 59–67, 161–79, 336–49, 429–38, 544–54, 678–87, 770–76. Later published as *Scenes on the Shores of the Atlantic.* 2 vols. London, T. C. Newby, 1845
Dodd, James Solas. *The Traveller's Directory through Ireland, being a topographical description....* Dublin: J. Stockdale 1801
Dolan, Patrick Terence. *A Dictionary of Hiberno-English: The Irish Use of English.* Dublin: Gill, Macmillan 1999
Donnelly, Jr., James S. *The Great Irish Potato Famine.* Thrupp Strand, Glouchestershire: Sutton 2001
Dorson, Richard M. *Folklore and Fakelore: Essays Toward a Discipline of Folk Studies.* Cambridge, Massachusetts: Harvard University Press, 1976
Dube, Colleen Margaret. " 'Enabling Institutions' and Disabling Illustrations: Images of Connemara in Tourist Handbooks, 1850–1880." M.Phil. Dissertation, University College, Galway 1994
Dufferin, Lord Frederick Temple. *Narrative of a Journey from Oxford to Skibbereen, During the Year of the Irish Famine.* Oxford: J. H. Parker 1847
Duffy, P[atrick] J. "The Changing Rural Landscape 1750–1850: Pictorial Evidence." *Ireland: Art into History.* Edited by Raymond Gillespie and Brian P. Kennedy. Dublin: Town House, 26–42 1994
―――――. *Exploring the History and Heritage of Irish Landscapes.* Maynooth Research Guides to Irish Local History, Number 12. Dublin: Four Court 2007
―――――. "Writing Ireland: Literature and art in representation of Irish place." In *Search of Ireland: A Cultural Geography.* Edited by Brian Graham. London: Routledge, 64–86 1997
Dunn, [?]. *A Description of Killarney.* London: J. Dodlsey 1776
Dunton, John. *Teague Land: Or A Merry Ramble to the Wild Irish (1698).* Transcribed from the manuscript, edited and introduced by Andrew Carpenter. Dublin: Four Courts 2003
Eagleton, Terry. "The Ideology of the Aesthetic." *Poetics Today.* 9, no. 2 (1988) 327–338
East, Rev. John. *Notes and Glimpses of Ireland in 1847.* London: Hamilton, Adams 1847
Edensor, Tim. "Staging Tourism: Tourists as Performers." *Annals of Tourism Research.* 27, no. 2 (2000) 322–44
Egenolf, Susan. "Revolutionary landscapes: the picturesque, Salvator Rosa and the *Wild Irish Girl. Land and Landscape in Nineteenth-Century Ireland.* Edited by Una Ní Bhroiméil and Glenn Hooper. Dublin: Four Courts, 48–62, 2008
Ellison, C. C. *The Hopeful Traveller: The Life and Times of Daniel Augustus Beaufort. LL.D, 1739–1829.* Kilkenny, County Kilkenny: Boethius 1987
Ellul, Jacques. *The Technological Society.* Translated by John Wilkinson. New York: Vintage 1984
Evans, E. Estyn. *Irish Folk Ways.* London: Routledge, Kegan, Paul 1957
―――――. *The Personality of Ireland: Habitat, Heritage and History* Dublin: Lilliput [1973, 1981] 1992

Everett, Nigel. *The Tory View of Landscape*. The Paul Mellon Centre for Studies in British Art. New Haven, Connecticut: Yale University Press 1994

Fabricant, Carole. "The Aesthetics and Politics of Landscape in the Eighteenth Century." *Studies in Eighteenth-Century British Art and Aesthetics*. Edited by Ralph Cohen. Berkeley, California: University of California Press, 49–81, 1985

――――. "Binding and Dressing Nature's Loose Tresses: The Ideology of Augustan Landscape Design." In *Studies in Eighteenth-Century Culture*, vol. 8. Edited by Roseann Runte. Madison, Wisconsin: University Wisconsin Press, 109–35, 1979

――――. "The Literature of Domestic Tourism and the Public Consumption of Private Property." *The New Eighteenth Century: Theory, Politics, English Literature*. Edited by Felicity Nussbaum and Laura Brown. New York: Methuen, 254–75, 1987

Fedden, Robin. *The Giant's Causeway: An Illustrated Account*. London 1971

Fegan, Melissa. *Literature and the Irish Famine*. New York. Clarendon/Oxford University Press 2002

Feifer, Maxine. *Tourism in History: From Imperial Rome to the Present*. New York: Stein, Day 1986

[Ferguson, Samuel]. "The Attractions of Ireland.—I, Scenery." *Dublin University Magazine* 8 (July, 1836) 112–131

――――. "The Attractions of Ireland.—II, Scenery and Society." 8 (September, 1836) 315–33

――――. "The Attractions of Ireland.—III, Society." 8 (December, 1836) 658–75

[Fisher, Lydia Jane]. *Letters from the Kingdom of Kerry in the Year 1845*. Dublin: Webb, Chapman 1847

Flanagan, Deirdre, and Laurence Flanagan. *Irish Place Names*. Dublin: Gill, Macmillan 1994

Forbes, Dr. John. *Memorandums Made in Ireland in the Autumn of 1852*, 2 vols. London: Smith, Elder 1853

Fordham, Sir Herbert George. *Notes on British and Irish Itineraries and Road-Books*. Hertford, UK: Stephen Austin 1912

Foster, R. F. *Modern Ireland, 1600–1973*. London: Allen Lane/Penguin 1988

Freeman, T. W. *Ireland: Its Physical, Historical Social and Economic Geography*. London: Metheum [1950] 1960

――――. "Land and People, c. 1841." In *New History of Ireland: Ireland Under the Union, I, 1801–70*, vol. 5. Edited by W. E. Vaughan. Oxford, UK: Clarendon, 242–71, 1989

――――. *Pre-Famine Ireland: A Study in Historical Geography*. Manchester, UK: Manchester University Press 1957

Furlong, Irene. *Irish Tourism: 1880–1980*. Dublin, Portland, Oregon: Irish Academic Press, 2009

Gailey, Alan. "Changes in Irish Rural Housing, 1600–1900." In *Rural Ireland 1600–1900: Modernisation and Change*. Edited by Patrick O'Flanagan, *et al*. Cork: Cork University Press, 86–103, 1987

Gibbons, Luke. *Edmund Burke and Ireland*. Cambridge, UK: Cambridge University Press 2003

――――. *Gaelic Gothic: Race, Colonization, and Irish Culture*. Galway: Arlen House 2004

――――. "Topographies of Terror: Killarney and the Politics of the Sublime." *South Atlantic Quarterly*. 95, no. 1 (Winter, 1996) 23–45

[Gough, John.] *An Account of Two Journeys Southward in Ireland in 1817*. Dublin n. d. The title page states "by John Gough, intended as a supplement to 'A Tour of Ireland.'" See next entry

[Gough, John.] *A Tour in Ireland, in 1813 & 1814; with an appendix, written in 1816, on another capital visit to that Island. By an Englishman*. Dublin: R. Meyer 1817. The catalog entry in the library of the Royal Irish Academy attributes this work to John Gough as does John McVeagh

Graburn, Nelson H. H. "Tourism: The Sacred Journey." In *Hosts and Guests: The Anthropology of Tourism*. 2nd ed. Edited by Valene L. Smith. Philadelphia: University Pennsylvania Press, 21–36, [1977] 1989

Graham, Brian. "Ireland and Irishness: Place, Culture and Identity." In *Search of Ireland: A Cultural Geography*. Edited by Brian Graham. London: Routledge, 1–16, 1997

Graham, Robert. *A Scottish Whig in Ireland, 1835–1838: The Irish Journals of Robert Graham of Redgorton*. Edited by Henry Heaney. Dublin: Four Courts 1999

Gray, Peter. *Famine, Land and Politics: British Government and Irish Society, 1843–1850*. Dublin: Irish Academic Press 1999

Guinness, Desmond. "The Irish House." *Ascendancy Ireland: Papers read at Clark Library Seminar, 28 September 1985*. Edited by Desmond Guinness and Denis Donohue. Los Angeles, California: University California Press, 3–25, 1986

Haines, Robin. *Charles Travelyan and the Great Irish Famine*. Dublin: Four Courts, 2004

[Hall, Anne Maria and Samuel Carter]. 1984. *Hall's Ireland: Mr. and Mrs. Hall's Tour of 1840*. Edited by Michael Scott, 2 vol. London: Sphere Books [1841–1843] 1984

———. *Hand-Books for Ireland: The West and Connemara*. Dublin: J. McGlashan 1853

———. *A Week at Killarney, Descriptions of the Routes Thither from Dublin, Cork & etc.* London: Virtue Brothers [1843] 1865

Hall, Spencer T. *Life and Death in Ireland as Witnessed in 1849*. Manchester: J. T. Sparkes 1850

Hamilton, Rev. William. *Letters Concerning the Northern Coast of the County of Antrim....* Dublin: George Bonham 1786

Hansbrow, Rev. G. *An improved topographical and historical Hibernian Gazetteer; describing the various boroughs, baronys, buildings, cities, counties, etc.* Dublin: Richard Moore Tims, *et al.* 1835

Harbison, Peter. *"Our Treasure of Antiquities": Beranger and Bigari's Antiquarian Sketching Tour of Connaught in 1779*. Bray, Co. Wicklow: Wordwell 2002

[Harden, John]. "Tour in Ireland by John Harden in 1797." Communicated by Michael Quane. *Journal of the Cork Historical and Archeological Society*. Series 2. 58, no. 187 (January-June, 1953) 26–32; 58: no. 188 (July-December, 1953) 81–90; 59, no. 189 (January-June, 1954) 34–41; 59, no. 190 (July-December, 1954) 69–77; 60, no. 191 (January-June, 1955) 15–21; 60, no. 197 (July-December,1955) 80–87

Hardy, Philip Dixon. *The Northern Tourist, or Stranger's guide to the north and north west of Ireland, including a particular description of Belfast, the Giant's Causeway and every object of picturesque interest in the district referred to*. Dublin: William Curry, Jun. 1830

Haverty, Martin. *The Aran Isles: Or, a Report of the excursion of the ethnological Section of the British Association from Dublin to the Western Isles of Aran in September, 1857*. Dublin: Dublin University 1859

Head, Sir Francis Bond. *A Fortnight in Ireland*. London: John Murray 1852

Helsinger, Elizabeth K. "Land and National Representation in Britain." *Prospects for the Nation: Recent Essays in British Landscape, 1750–1880, Studies in British Art, No. 4*. Edited by Michael Rosenthal, *et al.* New Haven, Connecticut: Yale University Press, 13–36, 1997

———. *Rural Scenes and National Representation: Britain, 1815–1850*. Princeton, New Jersey: Princeton University Press 1997

Hemingway, Andrew. *Landscape Imagery and Urban Culture in Early Nineteenth-Century Britain*. Cambridge, UK: Cambridge University Press 1992

Herbert, Dorothea. *Retrospections of Dorothea Herbert, 1770–1789*. London: Gerald Howe 1929

Hering, Ivor. "Bians (II): Their place among Irish Vehicles." *Ulster Journal of Archeology*. Series 3 (July, 1940) 115–122

———. "Traveling Conditions in the Early Nineteenth Century." *Ulster Journal of Archeology.* Series 3, 4 (1941) 2–11

[Hering, Johann Friedrich]. "Select Documents XLI: Johann Friedrich Hering's Description of Connaught, 1806–7." Edited by Christopher Wood. *Irish Historical Studies.* 25, no. 99 (May, 1987) 311–21

Heuston, John. "Kilkee—the Origins and Development of a West Coast Resort." *Tourism in Ireland: A Critical Analysis.* Edited by Barbara O'Connor and Michael Cronin. Cork: Cork University Press, 13–28, 1993

Hill, H. "Diary of an Itinerary in Ireland in 1831." *Cork Historical and Archaeological Society.* 2nd series. 37: no. 147: (January-June, 1933) 30–7

Hoare, Sir Richard Colt, Bart. *A Tour in Ireland, A.D. 1806.* Dublin: Miller, J. Archer, Mahon 1807

[Hole, Samuel Reynolds]. *A Little Tour in Ireland. Being a Visit to Dublin, Galway, Connemara, Athlone, Limerick, Killarney, Glengarriff, Cork, etc., By an Oxonian. With Illustrations by John Leech.* London: Bradbury, Evans 1859

Holland, Charles Hepworth. *The Irish Landscape: A Scenery to Celebrate.* Edinburgh: Dunedin Academic Press 2003

Holmes, G[eorge]. *Sketches of Some of the Southern Counties of Ireland, Collected During a Tour in the Autumn, 1797, in a Series of Letters.* London: Longman, Rees 1801

Hooper, Glenn. "Anne Plumptre: An Independent Traveller." *Gender Perspectives in Nineteenth-Century Ireland: Public and Private Spaces.* Edited by Margaret Kelleher and James H. Murphy. Dublin: Irish Academic Press, 129–139, 1997

———. "The Isles / Ireland: the Wilder Shore." *The Cambridge Companion to Travel Writing.* Edited by Peter Hulme and Tim Young. New York: Cambridge University Press, 174–190 2002

———. *Travel Writing and Ireland, 1760–1860: Culture, History, Politics.* New York: Palgrave, Macmillan 2005

Horgan, Donal. *Echo After Echo: Killarney and Its History.* Cork: Blackface Publications 1988

Hoskins, W. G. *The Making of the English Landscape.* London: Hodder, Stroughton [1955] 1988

Howkins, Alun. "Land, Locality, People, Landscape: The Nineteenth-Century Countryside." *Prospects for the Nation: Recent Essays in British Landscape, 1750–1880, Studies in British Art., No. 4.* Edited by Michael Rosenthal, *et al.* New Haven, Connecticut: Yale University Press, 97–114, 1997

Howley, James. *The Follies and Garden Buildings of Ireland.* New Haven, Connecticut, Yale University Press 1993

Hudson, Brian J. "Waterfalls: Resources for Tourism." *Annals of Tourism Research.* 25, no. 4 (1998) 958–973

Hughes, T. Jones. "The Large Farm in Nineteenth Century Ireland." *Gold Under the Furze: Studies in Folk Tradition Presented to Caoimhín O Danachair.* Edited by Alan Gailey and Dáithí Ó hOgáin. Dublin: Glendale, 104–41 1982

Hunt, John Dixon. *Gardens and the Picturesque: Studies in the History of Landscape Architecture.* Cambridge, Massachusetts: MIT, 1992

Hussey, Christopher. *The Picturesque: Studies in a Point of View.* Hamden, Connecticut: Archon 1967

Hutchinson, John. "Intrusions and Representations: The Landscape of Wicklow." *The GPA Irish Arts Review Yearbook.* 91–9, 1989–90

———. *James Arthur O'Connor.* Dublin: National Gallery Ireland, 1985

Hyams, Edward. *Irish Gardens.* London: Macdonald, 1967

Immerwhar, Raymond. " 'Romantic' and its Cognates in England, Germany and France before 1790." *"Romanticism" and its Cognates: The European History of a Word*. Edited by Hans Eichner. Toronto, University of Toronto, 17–97, 1972

Inglis, Henry D. *A Journey throughout Ireland, during the spring, summer, and autumn of 1834*. 3rd ed., 2 vols. London: Whittaker 1835

Janowitz, Anne. *England's Ruins: Poetic Purpose and the National Landscape*. Cambridge, Massachusetts: Basil Blackwell 1990

Johnson, James. *A Tour of Ireland with Meditations and Reflections*. London: S Highley 1844

Jones, David S. "The Transfer of Land and the Emergence of the Graziers during the Famine Period." *The Great Famine and the Irish Diaspora in America*, Edited by Arthur Gribben. Amherst: University of Massachusetts, 65–103, 1999

Kelly, Cornelius. *The Grand Tour of Cork*. Cork: Cailleach, 2003

Kennedy, Líam, Paul S. Ell, E. M. Crawford and I. A. Clarkson. *Mapping the Great Irish Famine: A Survey of the Famine Decades*. Dublin: Four Courts 1999

Killeen, Jarlath. *Gothic Ireland: Horror and the Irish Anglican Imagination in the Long Eighteenth Century*. Dublin: Four Courts 2005

Killen, James. "Communications," *Atlas of the Irish Landscape*. F. H. A, Allen, *et al*. Cork: Cork University Press, 206–219 1997

Kilroy, Patricia. *The Story of Connemara*. Dublin: Gill, Macmillan 1989

Klonk, Charlotte. "From Picturesque Travel to Scientific Observation: Artists' and Geologists' Voyages to Staffa." *Prospects for the Nation: Recent Essays in British Landscape, 1750–1880, Studies in British Art., No. 4*. Edited by Michael Rosenthal, *et al*. New Haven, Connecticut: Yale University Press, 205–30 1997

Knott, Mary John. *Two Months at Kilkee*. Ennis, County Clare: Claps [1836]1997

Knox, Alexander. *The Irish Watering Places, their Climate, Scenery, and Accommodations....* Dublin: William Curry, Jun. 1845

Korte, Barbara. *English Travel Writing from Pilgrimages to Postcolonial Explorations*. Translated by Catherine Matthais. New York: Macmillan/St. Martin's 2000

Kriz, Dian Kay. *The Idea of the English Landscape Painter: Genius as Alibi in the Early Nineteenth Century*. New Haven, Connecticut: Yale University Press 1997

Leerssen, Joep. *Mere Irish and Fíor-Gheal: Studies in the Idea of Irish Nationality, its Development and Literary Expression Prior to the Nineteenth Century*. Critical Conditions: Field Day Essays and Monographs, 3. Edited by Seamus Deane. Notre Dame, Indiana: University Notre Dame Press [1986] 1997

———. *Remembrance and Imagination: Patterns in the Historical and Literary Representation of Ireland in the Nineteenth Century*. Critical Conditions: Field Day Essays and Monographs, 4. Edited by Seamus Deane. Notre Dame, Indiana: University Notre Dame Press 1997

Leiper, Neil. "Tourist Attraction Systems." *Annals of Tourism Research*. 17 (1990) 367–384

Lengel, Edward G. *The Irish Through British Eyes: Perceptions of Ireland in the Famine Era*. Westport, Connecticut: Praeger 2002

Lewis, Samuel. *Lewis's Dublin: A Topographical Dictionary of the Parishes, Towns and Villages of Dublin City and County*. Compiled by Christopher Ryan. Cork: Collins 2001

Logan, Patrick. *Fair Day: The Story of Irish Fairs and Markets*. Belfast: Appletree 1986

———. *Making the Cure: A Look at Irish Folk Medicine*. Dublin: Talbot 1972

Lovett, Richard. *Ireland 100 Years Ago: The Beauty of Ireland Illustrated*. London: Bracken 1985. Originally published as *Irish Pictures drawn with Pen and Pencil*. London: 1888

Lowenthal, David, Hugh Prince. "English Landscape Taste." *Geographical Review*. 55 (1965) 186–222

Luckombe, Philip. *A Tour Through Ireland in 1779*. London: Lowndens 1780

MacAodha, Breandán. "Distribution, Function and Architecture." *The Big House in Ireland: Reality and Representation*. Edited by Jacqueline Genet. Savage, Maryland: Barnes, Noble, 43–57, 1991

McAuliffe, John. "Taking the Sting out of the Traveller's Tale: Thackeray's *Irish Sketchbook*." *Irish Studies Review*. 9, no. 1 (2001) 25–40

———. "Women's Travel Writing in Mid-Nineteenth Century Ireland." *Gender Perspectives in Nineteenth-Century Ireland: Public and Private Spaces*. Edited by Margaret Kelleher and James H. Murphy. Dublin: Irish Academic Press, 140–7 1997

MacCannell, Dean. *The Tourist: A New Theory of the Leisure Class*. New York: Schocken Books 1976

McCracken, Eileen. *The Irish Woods Since Tudor Times: Their Distribution and Exploitation*. Institute of Irish Studies, Queens University Belfast. Newton Abbot, Devonshire: David, Charles 1971

McCracken, J. L. "The Age of the Stage Coach." *Travel and Transport in Ireland*. Edited by Kevin B. Nowlan. Dublin: Gill, Macmillan, 47–64, [1973] 1993

———. "The Political Structure, 1714–60," *A New History of Ireland, IV: Eighteenth-Century Ireland, 1691–1800*. Edited by T. W. Moody, W. E. Vaughn. Oxford: Clarendon, 57–83, 1986

———. "Social Structure and Social Life, 1714–1760." *A New History of Ireland, IV: Eighteenth-Century Ireland, 1691–1800*. Edited by T. W. Moody, W. E. Vaughn. Oxford: Clarendon, 31–56, 1986

McCutcheon, W. A. "The Transport Revolution: Canals and River Navigations." *Travel and Transport in Ireland*. Edited by Kevin B. Nowlan. Dublin: Gill, Macmillan, 64–81, [1973] 1993

MacDonagh, Oliver. "The Economy and Society, 1830–1845." *New History of Ireland: Ireland Under the Union, I, 1801–70*. Vol. 5. Edited by W. E. Vaughan. Oxford, UK: Clarendon, 218–41, 1989

———. "Sea Communications in the Nineteenth Century." *Travel and Transport in* Ireland. Edited by Kevin B. Nowlan. Dublin: Gill, Macmillan, 120–21, [1973] 1993

McDowell, R. B. "Ireland in 1800." *A New History of Ireland, IV: Eighteenth-Century Ireland, 1691–1800*. Edited by. T. W. Moody, W. E. Vaughn. Oxford: Clarendon, 657–711, 1986

Mac Lochlainn, Alf. "Social Life in County Clare, 1800–1850," *Irish University Review*. 2, no. 1 (1972) 55–78

MacLysaght, Edward. *Irish Life in the Seventeenth Century*. Dublin: Irish Academic Press 1979

McMahon, Sean, Jo O'Donoghue. *Brewer's Dictionary of Irish Phrase and Fable*. London: Weidenfeld, Nicolson 2004

McManus, Rev. Henry. *Sketches of the Irish Highlands: Descriptive, Social and Religious with Special Reference to Irish Missions in West Connaught since 1840*. London: Hamilton, Adams 1863

McVeagh, John. *Irish Travel Writing: A Bibliography*. Dublin: Wolfhound Press 1996

Mandler, Peter. *The Rise and Fall of the Stately Home*. New Haven, Connecticut: Yale University Press 1997

Manners, John James Robert, 7th Duke of Rutland. *Notes of an Irish Tour in 1846*. Edinburgh: Blackwell [1849]

Martineau, Harriet. *Letters from Ireland*. Edited by Glenn Hooper. Dublin: Irish Academic Press [1852] 2001

Mason, Williams Shaw. *A Statistical Account or Parochial Survey of Ireland Drawn from the Communications with the Clergy*. 2 vols. Dublin: Graisberry, Campbell 1814

Maxwell, Constantia. *Dublin Under the Georges* [1936]. Dublin: Lambay 1997

―――. *The Stranger in Ireland: From the Reign of Elizabeth to the Great Famine*. London: Jonathan Cape 1954

Maxwell, William Hamilton. *Wild Sports of the West of Ireland, Also Legendary Tales, Folk-lore, Local Customs and Natural History* [1832]. Southhampton, UK: Ashford Press 1886

Melish, John. *Travels in the United States of America, in the years 1806–1807, and 1809, 1810, & 1811...*. 2 vols. Philadelphia [Published by the author] 1813

Meloy, Elizabeth. "Touring Connemara: Learning to Read a Landscape of Ruins, 1850–1860." *New Hibernia Review*. 13, no. 3 (Autumn, 2009), 21–46

Michasiw, Kim Ian. "Nine Revisionist Theses on the Picturesque." *Representation* 38 (1992) 76–100

Mitchell, Frank. *Shell Guide to Reading the Irish Landscape (Incorporating the Irish Landscape)*. Rev. ed. Dublin: Michael Joseph/Country House 1990

Mitchell, W. J. T. "Imperial Landscape." *Landscape and Power*. Edited by W. J. T. Mitchell. Chicago: University Chicago Press, 5–34 1994

Moir, Esther. *The Discovery of Britain: The English Tourists*. London: Routledge, Kegan, Paul 1964

[Molyneux, Samuel]. "Samuel Monyneux's Tour of Kerry, 1709." Edited by K. Theodore Hoppen. *Journal of the Kerry Archeological and Historical Society*, 3 (1970) 59–80

[Molyneux, Thomas]. "A Journey to Kilkenny in the Year 1709, From the Manuscript Notes of Dr. Thomas Molyneux." Edited by Rev. James Graves. *Journal of the Royal Society of Antiquaries of Ireland*. 5 (1860–61) 296–303

Monk, Samuel H. *The Sublime: A Study of Critical Theories in XVIII-Century England*. Ann Arbor, Michigan: Ann Arbor Paperback/University of Michigan [1935] 1960

Murphy, Ignatius. *Before the Famine Struck: Life in West Clare 1834–1845*. Dublin: Irish Academic Press 1996

Murray, K. A., D. B. McNeill. *The Great Southern & Western Railway*. Dublin: Irish Railway Record Society 1976

Nash, Catherine. " 'Embodying the Nation'—The West of Ireland Landscape and Irish Identity." *Tourism in Ireland: A Critical Analysis*. Edited by Barbara O'Connor and Michael Cronin. Cork: Cork University Press, 86–111, 1993

Nash, Dennison. "Tourism as a Form of Imperialism." *Hosts and Guests: The Anthropology of Tourism*. 2nd ed. Edited by Valene L. Smith. Philadelphia: Pennsylvania University Press, 37–52 [1977] 1989

Neave, Sir Digby, Bart. *Four Days in Connemara*. London: Richard Bentley 1852

Neeson, Eoin. *A History of Irish Forestry*. Dublin: Lilliput 1991

Nicholson, Norman. *The Lakers: The Adventures of the First Tourists*. London: Robert Hale 1995

Nicolson, Marjorie Hope. *Mountain Gloom, Mountain Glory: The Development of the Aesthetics of the Infinite*. Ithaca, New York: Cornell University Press 1959

Ní Ghiobúin, Mealla. *Dugort, Achill Island 1831–1861: The Rise and Fall of a Missionary Community*. Maynooth Studies in Irish Local History. Edited by Raymond Gillespie. Dublin: Irish Academic Press 2001

Noel, Baptist Wriothesley. *Notes on a short tour through the midland counties of Ireland in the summer of 1836, with observations on the condition of the peasantry*. London: J. Nisbet 1837

Nowlan, Kevin B. "The Transport Revolution: The Coming of the Railways." *Travel and Transport in Ireland*. Edited by Kevin B. Nowlan. Dublin: Gill, Macmillan, 96–109 [1973] 1993

Nuñez, Theron. "Touristic Studies in Anthropological Perspective." *Hosts and Guests: The Anthropology of Tourism*. 2nd ed. Edited by Valene L. Smith. Philadelphia: Pennsylvania University Press, 265–79, [1977] 1989

O'Connor, Barbara. "Myths and Mirrors: Tourist Images and National Identity." *Tourism in Ireland: A Critical Analysis*. Edited by Barbara O'Connor and Michael Cronin. Cork: Cork University Press, 68–85, 1993

O'Connor, Kevin. *Ironing the Land: The Coming of the Railways to Ireland*. Dublin: Gill, Macmillan 1999

O'Connor, Patrick J. *Living in a Coded Land*. Irish Landscape Series No. 1. Limerick, County Limerick 1992

Ó Crualaoich, Gearóid. "The 'Merry Wake.' " *Irish Popular Culture: 1650–1850*. Edited by James S. Donnelly, Jr. and Kerby A. Miller. Dublin: Irish Academic Press, 173–200 1998

Ó Giolláin, Diarmuid. "The Pattern." In *Irish Popular Culture: 1650–1850*. Edited by James S. Donnelly, Jr. and Kerby A. Miller. Dublin: Irish Academic Press, 201–21,1998

Ó Gráda, Cormac. "Industry and Communications, 1801–45." *New History of Ireland: Ireland Under the Union, I, 1801–70*. Vol. 5. Edited by W. E. Vaughan. Oxford, UK: Calrendon, 137–57, 1989

———. *Ireland: A New Economic History 1780–1939*. Oxford, UK.: Clarendon 1995

———. "Poverty, Population, and Agriculture, 1801–45." *New History of Ireland: Ireland Under the Union, I, 1801–70*. Vol. 5. Edited by W. E. Vaughan. Oxford, UK: Clarendon,108–133 1989

O'Halloran, Clare. *Golden Ages and Barbarous Nations: Antiquarian Debate and Cultural Politics in Ireland, c. 1750–1800*. Cork: University Cork Press 2004

O'Kane, Finola. *Landscape Design in Eighteenth-Century Ireland: Mixing Foreign Trees with the Natives*. Cork: University Cork Press 2004

O'Neill, Timothy P. "Bianconi and His Cars." *Travel and Transport in Ireland*. Edited by Kevin B. Nowlan. Dublin: Gill, Macmillan, 83–96 [1973] 1993

Ockenden, William. *Letters Describing the Lakes of Killarney, and Muckruss* [sic] *Gardens*. Appended without attribution to volume two of Samuel Derreck's *Letters Written from Liverpool*, etc. London 1767

[Orrery, Sixth Earl of; John Boyle.] "Lord Orrery's Travels in Kerry, 1735." Edited by Desmond Fitzgerald, Knight of Glin. *Journal of the Kerry Archeological and Historical Society* 5 (1972) 46–59

Otway, Rev. Caesar. *Sketches in Erris and Tyrawly, By the Author of Sketches in Ireland, A Tour of Connaught, &c. With A Map and other illustrations*. Dublin, William Curry, Jun. 1841

———. *Sketches in Ireland, Descriptive of Interesting, and Hitherto Unnoticed Districts in the North and South*. Dublin: William Curry, Jun. 1827

———. *A Tour of Connaught, Comprising Sketches of Clonmacnoise* [sic], *Joyce Country and Achill. By the Author of Sketches in Ireland. With Illustrations engraved on wood*. Dublin: William Curry, Jun. 1839

Ousby, Ian. *The Englishman's England: Taste, Travel and the Rise of Tourism*. Cambridge, UK: Cambridge University Press 1990

Overton, Mark. *Agricultural Revolution in England: The Transformation of the Agrarian Economy, 1500–1850*. Cambridge Studies in Historical Geography, 23. Edited by Alan R. H. Baker, et al. Cambridge, UK: Cambridge University Press 1996

Patten, Eve. *Samuel Ferguson and the Culture of Nineteenth-Century Ireland*. Dublin: Four Courts 2004

Payne, Christiana. *Toil and Plenty: Images of the Agricultural Landscape in England, 1780–1890*. New Haven, Connecticut: Yale University Press 1993

Pearson, Peter. *The Heart of Dublin: Resurgence of a Historic City*. Dublin: O'Brien 2000

Plumptre, Anne. *Narrative of a Residence in Ireland during the Summer of 1814, and that of 1815. By Anne Plumptre, author of a Narrative of Three Years Residence in France*. London: H. Colburn 1817

[Pococke, Richard]. *Pococke's Tours of Ireland in 1852.* Edited George. T. Stokes. Dublin: Hodges, Figgis 1891

———. "Pococke's Tour of South and South West Ireland in 1758." Edited by Pádraig Ó Maidín. *Journal of the Cork Historical and Archaeological Society.* (July-December, 1956) 73–94

———. *Richard Pococke's Irish Tours.* Edited by John McVeagh. Blackrock, County Dublin: Irish Academic 1995

Praeger, Robert Lloyd. *The Way that I Went.* Dublin: Allen Figgis, 1969

Pratt, Mary Louise. *Imperial Eyes: Travel Writing and Transculturation.* London: Routledge 1992

Pullan, Ann. "For Publicity and Profit." *Prospects for the Nation: Recent Essays in British Landscape, 1750–1880, Studies in British Art., No. 4.* Edited by Michael Rosenthal, et al. New Haven, Connecticut: Yale University Press, 261–284, 1997

Quirke, Bill. "The People of the Glens." *Killarney National Park: A Place to Treasure.* Edited by Bill Quirke. Cork: Collins, 83–105, 2001

Rache, Hermann. "German Travelers in the West, 1828–1858." *Journal of Galway Archeological and Historical Society.* 47 (1995) 87–107

Rackham, Oliver. "Ancient Woodland and Hedges in England." *The English Landscape: Past, Present, and Future.* Edited by S. R. J. Woodell. Oxford: Oxford University Press, 48–67, 1985

Reeves-Smyth, Terence. "Desmesnes." *Atlas of the Rural Irish Landscape.* Edited by F. H. A. Aalan et al. Cork: Cork University Press, 197–205, 1997

Reid, Thomas. *Travels in Ireland in the Year 1822, exhibiting brief sketches of the moral, physical, and political state of the country. With reflections on the best means of improving its condition.* London: Longman, Hurst, Rees, Orme, Brown 1823

Ritchie, Leitch. *Ireland, picturesque and romantic, With engravings from drawings by D. M'Clise, Esq., A. R. A., and T. Creswick,* 2 vols. London: Rees, Orme, Brown, Green, Longman 1837

Robertson, Rev. Joseph. *The Traveller's Guide Through Ireland, or a Topographical Description of that Kingdom....* Edinburgh: Denham, Dick 1806

Robinson, Tim. "Connemara, County Galway." In *Atlas of the Irish Rural Landscape.* Edited by F. H. A. Aalen et al. Cork: University Cork Press. 329–45, 1997

———. *Stones of Aran: Pilgrimage.* New York 1990

Rojek Chris, "Indexing and Dragging and the Social Construction of Tourist Sights." *Touring Cultures: Transformations of Travel and Theory.* Edited by Chris Rojek and John Urry. London, New York: Routledge, 52–74, [1997] 2000

———. John Urry. "Transformations of Travel and Theory." *Touring Cultures: Transformations of Travel and Theory.* Edited by Chris Rojek and John Urry. London, New York: Routledge, 1–19, [1997] 2000

Rosenthal, Michael. "Introduction." *Prospects for the Nation: Recent Essays in British Landscape, 1750–1880, Studies in British Art., No. 4.* Edited by Michael Rosenthal, et al. New Haven, Connecticut: Yale University Press, 1–12, 1993

———. "Landscape as High Art." *Glorious Nature: British Landscape Painting, 1750–1850.* Edited by Katharine Baetjer. New York: Hudson Hills, 14–30, 1993

Rutland, 7th Duke of. See Manners, John James Robert

Rynne, Colm. *Industrial Ireland, 1750–1930: An Archaeology.* Cork: Collins 2006

———. "Mining Power and Water: Mining and Quarrying." *Atlas of the Irish Landscape.* Edited by. F. H. A. Aalan, et al. Cork: University Cork Press, 221–25 1997

Samuel, Mark, Kate Hamlyn. *Blarney Castle: Its History, Development and Purpose,* Cork: Cork University Press, 2007

Schama, Simon. *Landscape and Memory.* New York: Alfred A. Knopf 1995

Share, Bernard. *Slanguage: A Dictionary of Irish Slang and Colloquial English in Ireland.* New and Expanded Edition. Dublin: Gill, Macmillan [1997] 2003

Simms, Anngret. "The Origin of Irish Towns." *Irish Country Towns*. Edited by Anngret Simms and J. H. Andrews. Cork/Dublin: Mercier, 11–20 1994

[Slade, Robert]. "Robert Slade's Narrative of a Journey to the North of Ireland, 1802." Edited by Diarmuid O'Doibhlin. *Journal of the South Derry Historical Society*. 2 (1981–2) 130–95

Smith, Charles. *The ancient and present state of the County and City of Cork...*, Published with the Approbation of the Physico-Historical Society. Dublin: W. Wilson [1750] 1774

———. *The antient and present state of the County of and City of Waterford, Being a Natural, Civil, Ecclesiastical, Historical, and topographical Description thereof.... Published with the Approbation of the Physico-Historical Society*. Dublin: W. Wilson [1746] 1774

———. *The Antient and Present State of the County of Kerry, Being a Natural, Civil, Ecclesiastical, Historical, and Topographical Description thereof...,Undertaken with the Approbation of the Physico-Historical Society*. Dublin: W. Wilson [1756] 1774

[Smith, Elizabeth]. *The Wicklow World of Elizabeth Smith,1840–1850*. Ed. Dermot James and Séamas Ó Maitiú. Dublin: Woodfield 1996

Smith, Joseph Denham. *Connemara, Past and Present*. Dublin: John Robertson 1853

Smyth, William J. "A Plurality of Irelands: Regions, Societies and Mentalities." *Search of Ireland: A Cultural Geography*. Edited by Brian Graham. London: Routledge, 19–42 1997

Snyder, Edward D. *The Celtic Revival in English Literature, 1760–1800*. Gloucester, Massachusetts: Peter Smith, 1965

Somerville-Large, Peter. *The Irish Country House: A Social History*. London: Sinclair Stevenson 1995

Spirn, Anne Whiston. *The Language of Landscape*. New Haven, Connecticut: Yale University Press 1998

Stafford, Barbara Maria. *Voyage into Substance: Art, Science, Nature, and the Illustrated Travel Account, 1760–1840*. Cambridge, Massachusetts: Massachusetts Institute of Technology 1984

Standring, Timothy J. "Watercolor Landscape Sketching During the Popular Picturesque Era in Britain." *Glorious Nature: British Landscape Painting, 1750–1850*. Edited by Katharine Baetjer. New York: Hudson Hills, 73–84 1993

Stout, Geraldine. *New Grange and the Bend of the Boyne: Irish Rural Landscapes*, Vol. 1. Edited by F. H. A. Aalen, ed al. Cork: University Cork Press 2002

Sunderland, John. "The Legend and Influence of Salvator Rosa in England in the Eighteenth Century." *Burlington Magazine*. 115 (December, 1973) 785–789

Taylor, George, and Andrew Skinner. *Taylor and Skinner's Maps of the Roads of Ireland, Surveyed 1777*. Dublin: W. Wilson 1778

Tennyson, Hallam. *Alfred Lord Tennyson: A Memoir, by his Son*. Edited by Cary Nelson Grossberg and Paula A. Teichler. New York: Macmillan 1897

Thackeray, William Makepeace. *The Irish Sketch Book: 1842*. New York: P. F. Collins [1843] 1902

Thomas, Keith. *Man and the Natural World: A History of the Modern Sensibility*. New York, Pantheon 1983

Tinniswood, Adrian. *The Polite Tourist: Four Centuries of Country House Visiting*. London: National Trust [1989] 1998

Trant, Kathy. *The Blessington Estate, 1667–1908*. Dublin: Anvil Books 2004

Turner, Katherine. *British Travel Writers in Europe 1750–1800: Authorship, Gender and National Identity*. Studies in European Cultural Transition, vol. 10. Aldershot, UK: Ashgate 2001

Turner, Michael. *After the Famine: Irish Agriculture, 1850–1914*. Cambridge, UK: Cambridge University Press 1996

Twiss, Richard. *A Tour of Ireland in 1775 with a Map, and a View of the Salmon-Leap at Ballyshannon*. London: Robson, Walker, Robinson, Kearsly 1776

Urry, John. *Consuming Places.* London: Routledge 1995
———. *The Tourist Gaze: Leisure and Travel in Contemporary Societies.* London: Sage 1990
———. "The Tourist Gaze 'Revisited.' " *American Behavioral Scientist.* 36, no. 2 (November-December, 1992) 172–86
Villiers-Tuthill, Kathleen. *Alexander Nimmo and the Western District.* Clifden, Galway: Connemara Girl 2006
———. *Beyond the Twelve Bens: A History of Clifden and District 1860–1923.* Clifden, Galway: Connemara Girl 1986
Viney, Michael. *Ireland: A Smithsonian Natural History.* Washington, D.C: Smithsonian Books 2003
Wakefield, Edward. *An Account of Ireland, Statistical and Political.* 2 vols. London: Longman, Rees 1812
[Walford, Thomas]. *The Scientific Tourist Through Ireland…. A sequel to Scientific Tourist through England, Wales and Scotland,* 2 vols. London: Booth 1818
Walton, John K. *The English Seaside Resort: A Social History, 1750–1914.* New York: Leicester University Press 1983
Weiskel, Thomas. *The Romantic Sublime: Studies in the Structure and Psychology of Transcendence.* Baltimore: Johns Hopkins University Press 1976
Weld, Isaac. *Illustrations of the Scenery of Killarney and the Surrounding Country.* London: Longmans, Hurst, Rees, Orme, Brown [1807] 1812
West, Theresa Cornwallis. *A Summer Visit to Ireland in 1846.* London: Richard Bentley 1847
Whelan, Irene. *The Bible War in Ireland: The "Second Reformation" and the Polarization of Protestant-Catholic Relations, 1800–1840.* Dublin: Lilliput 2005
———. "The Stigma of Souperism." *The Great Irish Famine.* Edited by Cathal Póirtiér. Cork: Mercier, 135–54 1995
Whelan, Kevin. "The Famine and Post-Famine Adjustment." *The Shaping of Ireland: The Geographical Perspective.* Edited by William, Nolan. Thomas Davis Lecture Series. Edited by Michael Littleton. Cork: Mercier, 151–64 1986
———. "Introduction." *Letters from the Irish Highlands* [1825]. Edited Kevin Whelan. Clifden, County Galway: Gibbons Publications 1995
———. "Modern Landscape from Plantation to Present." *Atlas of the Irish Rural Landscape.* Edited by F. H. A. Aalen, et al. Cork, Cork: University Press, 67–103 1997
———. "Settlement Patterns in the West of Ireland in the Pre-Famine Period." *Decoding the Landscape: Papers Read at the Inaugural Conference of The Centre for Landscape Studies.* Edited by Timothy Collins. Galway, County Galway: Centre for Landscape Studies, 60–78, 1994
———. "Towns and Villages." *Atlas of the Irish Rural Landscape.* Edited by F. H. A. Aalen, et al. Cork: Cork University Press, 180–96, 1997
———, F. H. A. Aalen. "Fields." *Atlas of the Irish Rural Landscape.* Edited by F. H. A. Aalen, et al. Cork: Cork University Press, 134–44, 1997
White, George Preston. *A Tour in Connemara, with remarks on its great physical capabilities.* London: W. H. Smith 1849
Wilde, William. R. *The Boyne and the Blackwater.* Headford, County Galway: Kevin Duffy [1849] 2002
———. *Lough Corrib, Its Shores and Islands: with Notices of Lough Mask.* Headford, County Galway: Kevin Duffy [1867] 2002
———. "Memoir of Gabriel Beranger, and His Labours in the Cause of Irish Art, Literature, and Antiquities from 1760–1780, with Illustrations." By Sir W. R. Wilde, *Journal of the Royal Society of Antiquaries of Ireland.* 1:4th series (1870–71), 33–64, 121–52, 236–60; 2:4th series (1872–7), 445–85; 4:4th series (1876–78) 111–56

Williams, Leslie A. *Daniel O'Connell, The British Press and the Irish Famine: Killing Remarks*. Aldershot, UK: Ashgate 2003

Williams, Raymond. *The Country and the City*. Frogmore, St. Albans, Hertshire: Paladin 1975

Williams, William H. A. "Blow, Bugle, Blow: Romantic Tourism and the Echoes of Killarney." *Travel Essentials: Collected Essays on Travel Writing*. Edited by Santiago Henríquez. Las Palmas de Gran Canaria, Spain: Chandlon Inn, 133–47 1998

———. *Tourism, Landscape, and the Irish Character: British Travel Writers in Pre-Famine Ireland*. Madison, Wisconsin: University of Wisconsin 2008

[Woods, Joseph]. 1985. "A Scientific Tour Through Munster, the Travels of Joseph Woods, Architect and Botanist, in 1809." Edited by G. J. Lyne and M. Mitchel. *North Munster Archeological Journal*. 27 (1985), 15–61

Wright, Rev., G. N. *A Guide to the Lakes of Killarney, Illustrated by engravings after the designs of G. Petrie, Esq.* London: Baldwin, Cradock, Joy 1822

Wykehamist, A. [pseudonym]. *Paddy Land and the Lake of Killarney*, London: John Chapman 1853. John McVeagh identifies the author as John Ashley. The catalog in the National Library of Scotland lists Fred Gale of Edinburgh as the author

Young, Arthur. *A Tour In Ireland With General Observations on the Present State of That Kingdom Made in the Years, 1776, 1777 and 1778*. Edited by Constantia Maxwell. London: Cambridge University [1780] 1925

———. *Young's Travels in France During the Years 1787, 1788, 1789*, Edited by M. Bentham-Edwards. London: G. Bell 1913

INDEX

accommodations in Ireland: 20–23; in "big house" 62; quality of inns 20–22; quality of service 22
Achill Island (Mayo): 48, 185, 205n72
Act of Union: xiv, 16, 43, 62–3,181
Addison, Joseph: 81
Adler, Judith: 69
agriculture: *see* tourism and agriculture
Alps: xi–xii
Andrews, Malcolm: 70, 73–4, 80, 84
Anti-Catholic attitudes: *see* religion and tourism
Antiquities: 103–6, 137–38; aesthetic appreciation of 104; anti-Catholic gothic 104–5, 215n46; antiquarian landscape 102–6; and graveyards 103–4; and melancholy 104; origins of 105–6; and national identity 106; round towers 105–6; *see also* patterns
Aran Islands: 117
arbutus unedo: 130
arrival in Ireland: *see* travel to Ireland
Ashworth, Rev. John Harvey: 74, 157, 187–8
Atkinson, A.: on accommodations 22; on coal mines 42; on estates 52, 57, 59, 60–61; on Glen of the Dargle 91–2; on Glen of the Downs 78; on Glendalough 93; on Hiberno-English 155; on landscape 167; on Poulaphouca Falls 97; on Powerscourt Falls 96
Auden, W. H.: 150
Austin, Jane: 211n53
authenticity and tourism: 211n53
Avoca, Vale of (Wicklow): 41–2, 43, 82
Axton, W. F.: 72

Balfe, William: 129
Barnard, Toby: Irish estates 51–2
barracks, military: *see* "petite tour"
Barrell, John: 73, 87–8, 174
Barret, George, the Elder: 41–2, 55, 91, 95, 213n23
Barrington, T. J.: 130
Barrow, John: and Achill Island 48, 205n72; and beggars 126, 177; on bleaching greens 44; on Carrick-a-rede 100; on coaches 9; on Connemara 187; on Derry 38; and estate tourism 63; on Flynn's Half-Way House 24; on Killarney 136; on Kilkenny coal 43; on paintings 55–6; on "Spanish" Galway 163;
Barry, William Whittaker: 45, 116, 121
Barton, Richard: 42, 109
basalt columns: *see* Giant's Causeway
Battle of the Boyne Monument: 89
Beaufort, Rev. Daniel A.: 56, 140
beggars: 33, 126–7, 146–7, 177; reciprocity 127
Belfast: 35, 37–8, 44, 171
Bell, Robert: 73, 157, 167
Belton, William: on anticipation 108; on Killarney 108, 136, 143; on jaunting cars 10; on post–chaise 8; on variety of landscape 83–4
Bennett, William: on Catholic priests 46; on Michelstown Caves 115; peasants 120; on picturesque scenery 184–5; and Quaker "plain style" 184–5; on "Spanish" Irish 164
Beranger, Gabriel: 13, 215n49; on country inns 21; on drumlins 170; and Gaelic 154; and Newgrange

Beranger, Gabriel (*Continued*) 105; on "wilderness" garden 56–7; on waterfalls 79
Beresford, James: 200n17
Bianconi, Carlo: 11
"big house": *see* estate tourism
Bigari, Angelo Maria: 105
Binns, Jonathan: on beggars 178; on "Bians" 11–12; and estate tourism 63; on guides 123; on inns 21; on laments 162; on peasantry 88, 120; post-chaise 8; on Powerscourt 76; sketching 72
Blackrock (Dublin): 8
Blakes of Renvyle: 83, 160, 172, 187, 225n16
Blarney Castle: 39, 54, 112, 216n12; and Rock Close 54
Blarney Stone: 113, 216n15
Blaymire [?]: 103, 214n46
Blessington estate: 213n27
Bligh, Captain William: 6
Board of Public Works: *see* roads, Irish
boats and boatmen: *see* Giant's Causeway; Killarney
Bog of Allen: 168
bogs, bog land, tourist attitude towards: 166, 167, 169, 186–7
Boorstin, Daniel: 137
Boswell, James: 80
boundaries in Ireland (geographical, linguistic, social): 169–71
Bowden, C. T.: 6; on Coolaphouka 97; on dueling 32; on echoes 80; on Marino estate 27; on paintings 56
Boyne Monument: *see* Battle of the Boyne Monument
Bratten, Jr., Charles: 85
Bray (Wicklow): 196
Brennan, Edward: 24
Bridges, Roy: xii
Bristol (England): 4, 5
British Institution: 71
Brownes of Killarney: see Kenmare estate
Bulkeley, Sir Richard: 100–1
Burke, Edmund: 75–7, 79–81, 209n22; *see also* sublime
Bush, John: xii, on cabins 39; on chaise-marine 8; on Dublin 28, 32; on Dublin society 32; on echoes 139–40; on Glen of the Downs 76–7; on hotels 21; on Killarney 86, 139–40; on "noddies" 7; and tourism as scenes 86; traveling to Ireland 4, 5; vocabulary of the sublime 129; on waterfalls 79, 95–6
Buzard, James: 108, 150

cabins: 178–82; as suburbs of towns 39; *see also* tourism and poverty
Campbell, Rev. Thomas: on agriculture 173–4; on big house accommodations 62; on cabins 39; on Cork 35; on Dublin 29, 30, 31, 33; on estates design 51, 53–4, 59; on Kilkenny Castle 74; on Killarney 129; on nature as artist 74; on "noddies" 7; on picturesque 83;
canals: 15–17; fly (or Scotch) boats 17; Grand Canal 15–16; Newry Canal 15; Royal Canal 16; *see also* Shannon River
Carlyle, Thomas: on bogs 187; and the Famine 184; at Glendalough 116–7; on guides 217n45; at Killarney 145; on peasantry 116–7, 120, 158; on workhouses 45, 116
Carr, John: 40; on canals 16; on Devil's Glen 78; on Dublin 29, 30; on Dublin Bay 6; on Gap of Dunloe 76; on Glen of the Dargle 91; on Glendalough 92, 93, 212n13; on "jingles" 7–8; on Irish roads 13; on Kilkenny coal 43; on industrial pollution 43; on Ringsend 7; on waterfalls 79
Carrick-a-rede rope bridge (Antrim): 100, 196
Carton House (Kildare): 52, 54, 59
Castle (Cassel), Richard: 30–1
Castletown House (Kildare): 52, 62, 71
caves and tourism: 97–9, 114–6; Dunmore Caves 98; Mitchelstown 109–10, 115; Pigeon Hole 115–6; Portcoon 98; sea caves 98–9
Chard, Chloe: xi

Charlemont, Lord (William Chambers): 27,
Chatterton, Lady Henrietta: xii; and
    "amphitheatre" at Kilkee 119; on
    antiquities 104; on Blarney Stone
    113; on contradiction of scenery
    and poverty 181; on Gaelic 154,
    157; on markets 157; and mines 43;
    on nature as artist 74; sketching 72
Chester (England): 3
Chesterfield, Lord: 32
Chetwood, William Rufus: on Dunmore
    Caves 98; on estates 51, 53, 56; and
    Hiberno-English 155; on Irish roads
    12; on Kilkenny coal 43; on
    "noddies" 7; traveling to Ireland 3, 4
clachans: *see* rundale settlements
Clarke, Dr. Edward Daniel: on Dublin
    28, 30, 33; on Glen of the Dargle
    92; on quality of service 22;
    traveling to Ireland 4, 5, 6; on
    waterfalls 96
Claude: (Lorrain): 71, 72–4, 78, 85
"Claude Glass": 210n51
Combe, Williams: 211n53
conacre farmers: 178, 190, 223n29
Conley, Carolyn: 222n25
Connemara: developmental proposals
    186–91; roads 13
Cook, James: xii
Coolaphouka Falls: *see* waterfalls and
    tourism
coppice wood: 94, 135, 213n20
Corbin, Alain: 99
Corcoran, Margaret, *An Enquiry*: 213n23
Cork, city of: 35–36
Corn Laws, Repeal of: 189–90
Cosgrove, Denis: 70, 148
Coulter, Harry: 176
Coyne, J. Stirling: 84, 113, 163–4; 216n15
Crandell, Gina: 78, 87, 225n4
Crang, Philip: 114, 125
Croagh Patrick: 47, 79
Croker, Thomas Crofton: on Blarney
    Stone 113; on echoes 80; and
    Killarney 110; on pattern at
    Gaugen Barra 160; on Powerscourt
    Falls 213n25
Cromwell, T. K.: on agriculture 173; on
    cabins 178; on canals 16; on
    Donnybrook Fair 158; on Dublin
    28–9, 33; on Dublin society 31; on
    Dunmore Caves 98; on funerals
    160; on Glendalough 94; on
    Kilkenny coal 43; on markets 157
Cronin, Michael: 6, 124, 125, 155, 222n1
Cullen, Louis: 51
Culler, Jonathan: 153, 167
Curraghmore House (Waterford): 59
Curwin, J. C.: xii, 101, 102–3

Dalles, Rev. Alexander: 48
Danaher, Kevin: 215n6
Dargan, William: 195–6
De Latocnaye, Jacques-Louis: on
    accommodations 22; on Dublin
    poverty 33–4; on Dublin society
    31;on echoes 80; on Giant's
    Causeway 102; on laments 162; on
    paintings 56
De Montbret, Charles: 35, 42, 43, 153–4
De Tocqueville, Alexis: 40
Delany, Mary: 54, 56
Delany, Dean Patrick: 54
Delville estate: 54
Dennis, John: 75
Derrick, Samuel: 4, 22, 36, 73, 154
Derry (Londonderry), city of: 35, 38
Devil's Glen (Wicklow): 78
Dickson, Mary Frances: on Kilkee 118–9;
    on landscape 73; on naming 118;
    on sea caves 99; on steam boats 18;
Dingle, town of (Kerry): 88, 118
Dinish Island (Killarney): 133–4
Dinneen, Fr. Patrick: 155
Dodd, James Solas: 92, 101, 135
Donaghadee: 3, 4
Donnybrook Fair: 158, 221n13
Dorson, Richard: 111
drumlins: 167, 170–1
Drury, Susannah: 102, 214n42
Dublin, city of: 27–34; bridges 27: dueling
    32; Georgian architecture 28, 30–1,
    203n8; and Grand Tour 27, 30; "the
    Liberties" 33; Nelson's Pillar 30;
    plaster work 30; pleasure grounds
    31; poverty 32–4; Ringsend 6–7, 33;
    Sackville Street 28–9; St. Stephen's
    Green 28–9; squares 27, 28–9

Dublin Bay: 5–6
Dublin Castle: 28
Dublin Lying-in Hospital 27: pleasure grounds 31; Rotunda 31; plaster work 30
Dublin society: 31–2
The Dublin Society: 58
Duffy, Patrick J.: 103, 201n39
Dunloe, Gap of: see Gap of Dunloe
Dunmore Caves (Kilkenny): see caves
Dunn [?]: on Eagle's Nest 78–9, 82, on estate forestry 134; on mountains of Killarney 81; and the picturesque 82; on waterfalls 82–3; on variety of landscape 83
Dunton, John: 222n6

Eagle's Nest (Killarney): 78–9, 82, 139, 140–1
Eagleton, Terry: 220n54
East, Rev. John: 183–4,
echoes and tourism:79–80, 138–41, 43–4
Edensor, Tim: 119
Edgeworth, Maria: 13
education and tourism: 45–6
Egenolf, Susan: 209n30
Ellul, Jacque: 85
enclosure movement: see tourism and agriculture
Encumbered Estates Act: 186
engravings: see prints (engravings)
estate design: and agriculture 207n23, n24; Anglo-Dutch design 52–3, 206n19; and the big house 54–7, 62, 205n7, 206n8; and Claudean order 76; economics of 54–5; lawns 54–5, 206n22; Palladian style 52; and Protestant ideology 51–2; Romantic design 54–7, 61–2; use of trees 58–61; waterways 52–3; "wilderness" gardens 56–7; see also estate forestry; estate tourism
estate forestry: 57–60, 134–5, 207n35; and Irish tourism 93–5, 134–5; see also woodlands in Ireland
estate tourism, Britain: 49–50, 64
estate tourism, Ireland: 50–7, 131–4; and the "big house" 50–2, 54–7, 62;

critiquing estates 60–61; decline of 62–65; follies 56; grottos 56, 207n29; landlords organize for tourism 61–2; paintings 55–6; prints of estates 73, 89; and picturesque sites 55; shell houses 56; walls 51–2, 57, 133; see also estate design; estate forestry; waterfalls and tourism
Evangelicalism: see religion and tourism
Everett, Nigel: 59, 207n36
Excursion Ticket system: 187

Fabricant, Carol: 50, 60
faction fighting (stick fighting): 159–60, 222n25
Fair Head (Antrim): 99–100
fairs and markets: 156–61
fakelore: see tourism and folklore
Falconer, Edmund: 129
The Famine: 183–91, 193; contradiction of scenery and suffering 183,185; contradiction "resolved" 185–91, 193
Fata Morgana: 215n6, n9; see also O'Donoghue Mór
Fegan, Melissa: 224n6
Ferguson, Samuel: 25, 195, 225n1
Fisher, Jonathan: 62
Fisher, Lydia Jane: on agriculture 174; contradiction of scenery and poverty 88, 182; on echoes 80; on Kerry landscape 82; and picturesque description 87, 88; on rail travel 20;
Flynns Half-Way House (Connemara): 23–24
folklore: see tourism and folklore
Forbes, Dr. John: on accommodations 20, 45; on Connemara 189; on Cork 36; on estates 57; on Giant's Causeway 102; on industrial pollution 43; on Killarney 87, 134, 136; on post-chaise 8–9; on religion 46, 48; on roads 14; on steam boats 18; on travel to Ireland 19; on variety of landscape 84
Foster, John, Baron of Oriel: 57, 59
France: xiii
Franchini brothers: 30

INDEX

Freeman, T. W.: 12–13, 16
funerals: 151–3
Furlong, Irene: 196

Gaelic language: 153–5, 169; *see also* Hiberno-English
Galway, town of: 163–4
Gap of Donloe (Killarney): 76, 82, 132, 145
Gardiner, Luke: 28
geology and tourism: 100–3, 214n39, 214n44; see also Giant's Causeway; Hamilton, William; Klonk, Charlotte; Stafford, Barbara
Georgian architecture: *see* Dublin, city of
Giant's Causeway (Antrim): boatmen at 122–3; description of 100–3; guides at 116, 119–20, 124; naming at 110; souvenirs at 122; tourist theater 116; vendors at 121, 122
Gibbons, Luke: 81, 104, 111, 129, 131, 215n6
Gilpin, Rev. William: 85–6, 87, 211n52, n53
Glen of the Dargle (Wicklow): 65, 91–2, 97
Glen of the Downs (Wicklow): 61, 76–7, 78
Glendalough, (Wicklow): 92–3, 94; fair at 159; graffiti 118; pollution at; *see also* St. Kevin, legends of
Gougane Barra (Cork): 80, 90, 94, 160
Gough, John: 40; on agriculture 223n18; on Caher 39; on Dublin 31; on estates 60, 62; on post-chaise 8; on travel within Ireland 15;
Graburn, Nelson H. H.: 122
Graham, Brian: 65
Graham, Robert: on agriculture 173; and estate tourism 63; Flynn's Half-Way House 24; on Giant's Causeway 122; on Killarney 134; on Michelstown caves 109–10; on Powerscourt 96–7
Grand Canal: *see* canals
Grand Tour: xi–xii, 27, 30, 34–5; 41, 69, 71, 75, 199n3,
Grattan, Henry: 91

Graveyard, bones: 103–4
Gray, Thomas: 75, 211n56
grazier economy: 173–4, 190, 223n18
Great Southern and Western Railway: *see* railroads, Ireland
Gregory, Robert: 51
Guinness, Desmond: 51, 63

"ha-ha": 54, 206n22
Hall, Anna Maria and Samuel Carter: on antiquities 103–4, 105; on beggars 126; on Blarney Stone 113; on canal boats 17; on Carrick-a-rede 100; on caves 98; on expenses 143; on Giant's Causeway 110, 124; on Glendalough 93–4, 212n13; on guides 124–5, 145–6; on inns 21; on jails 45; on jaunting cars 10; on Killarney 111, 115, 142, 143–4, 145; on laments 162; on Mitchelstown Cave 115; and Newgrange 105; on O'Donoghue Mór 111, 143–4; on peasant performance 118; on Pigeon Hole 115; on Poulaphouca 97; portrait of 23; on religion 48, 205n72; security in Ireland 25; on Sion Mills 44; on souvenirs 122; travel to Ireland 5, 19; travel within Ireland 10–11; on Ulster 171
Hall, Rev. Spencer T: 46; on beggars 126–7; on Famine 185; on peasant dress 221n13; on poverty 36; on rail travel 168; on "Spanish" Irish 164; on towns 40; on villages 175;
Hamilton, Rev. William: 100, 101, 214n40
Harden, John: on antiquities 104; on Blarney Castle 54; on Killarney 134, 138, 143, 147
Hardy, Philip Dixon: 100,
Haverty, Martin: 117
Head, Francis Bond: on Dublin Bay 6; on Gaelic 155; on jaunting cars 10; on rail travel 168; on "Spanish" Galway 163, 164; travel to Ireland 19
Herbert, Dorothea: 81, 133–4

Herbert estate (Killarney): 61, 65, 133–4; iron works 42, 132
hedgerows (hedgebanks); 172, 173
Hering, Ivor: 21
Hiberno-English 155–6
Hoare, Richard Colt: xiv, 25, 40; on accommodations 22; on antiquities 103; on Dublin 29; on estate forestry 135; on funerals 160–1; on Killarney 135, 135, 142; on traveling in Ireland 8
Hole, Samuel Reynolds: 12, 141
Holmes, George: 42; on anticipation 108; on antiquities 103, 104; on echoes of Killarney 139; on landscape 73; on Rock of Cashel 73; on Killarney 131, 136–7; in Knockmealdown Mountains 76; on Silvermines, Tipperary 41
Holy Cross Abbey (Tipperary): 103
Holyhead (Wales): 3, 4, 5
Home tour, Britain: ix, 49
Hooper, Glenn: xiv, 181, 184, 188
Horgan, Donal: 215n8, 219n40
hotels: *see* accommodations in Ireland
Houston, John: 221n8
Howley, James: 56
Howth, Hill of: 6
Hudson, Brian J.: 213n22
Hunt, John Dixon: 104
Hutchinson, John: 55, 63, 89,
Hy Brazil: 81, 210n40

Illustrated London News: 186
Immerwhar, Raymond: 217n2
industrial sites and tourism: *see* "petite tour"
Inglis, Henry D.: xii,; on accommodations 23; on beggars 126; on Belfast 37; on "Bians" 11; in cabins 179; on Connemara 13, 187; on estates 63; on Flynn's Half-Way House 23–24; on Giant's Causeway 102; Killarney 132, 146, 149; on peasantry 88, 157; on religion 45, 46, 67; on sea caves 98; security in Ireland 25; on "Spanish" Galway 163; on sublime 149; on Ulster 171

Innishfallen (Killarney): 65, 131, 133, 134, 137
Irish character: xiv, 20, 37, 156, 180, 182, 192
Irish economy: 14,
Irish mile: 200n25
Irish Tour: xi, xiii, xv,
iron works: 41, 42, 132

jaunting cars: *see* traveling within Ireland
Johnson, James : 48; on accommodations 23; on "Bians" 11; on canal boats 17; on Derry 38; on echoes of Killarney 140; on guides 123–4; on Irish roads 14; on laments 162; on poverty 33; on rail travel 168–9; on sublime seascapes 81; on temperance in Ireland 160
Johnson, Samuel: 102

Kate Kearney's Cottage (Killarney): 145
Kenmare estate (Killarney): 61, 65, 131–6 *passim*, 140, 142, 218n7
Kilcolman Castle (Cork): 89
Kilkee (Clare): the "amphitheater" 118–9; travel to 18;
Kilkenny, coals of: 43
Kilkenny, town of: 35
Kilkenny Castle: 74
Killarney, Lakes of: 129–50; accommodations 132–3; anticipated 108–9; antiquities at 137–8; beggars at; boating at 142–3; climate of 130–1; costs; description of 129–31; echoes of 138–41, 143–4, 148–9, 219n40; and estate forestry 134–5, 218n18; and estate tourism 131–4; expenses 141–3, 219n38; flora 130; folklore (legends) 110–11; guides at 125, 145–6; industry at 132, 218n9; mountains of 81; naming at 109, 112; O'Sullivan's Cascade 82–3; overcrowding 147–8; peasantry at 121; performance (tourist "theater") at 86, 143–4; red deer hunt 136–7, 219n23; rituals at 112, 114–5; rock formations 215n8; as series of

scenes 86; souvenirs at 122; tours of 135–6; variety of landscape 83; waterfalls and tourism; *see also* Gap of Donloe; Eagle's Nest; Herbert estate; Innishfallen; Kate Kearny's Cottage; Kenmare estate; O'Donoghue Mór

Killarney, town of: 35, 132–3, 146

Killary Harbour: 79,

Kingstown: 33

Kingstown-Dublin railroad: *see* railroads, Ireland

Klonk, Charlotte: 101

Knight, Payne: 85,

Knockmealdown Mountains: 76, 86

Knott, Mary: in cabins 178; on cliff rappelling 117–8; on funerals 160; on peasants 117–8, 121, 154; on the Sabbath 46; on steam boats 18; on "thread" ritual 113–4;

Kohl, Johann Georg: 11, 18

Kriz, Kay Dian: 71, 83, 211n52

Lake District (Britain): 85–6, 134, 142, 211n56, 219n28

lakes and tourism: 95; *see also* specific lakes, loughs

laments: *see* funerals

landscape, meaning of word: 70; *see also* antiquities; landscape aesthetics

landscape aesthetics: 69–72, 80–1: contradiction of scenery and poverty 88, 181–2; *see also* Claude (Lorrain); mountains; picturesque; sublime; tourism and agriculture

language: *see*; Gaelic; Hiberno-English; tourism and language

Leinster, Duke of: 202n3

Leinster House: 28, 202n3

Leiper, Neil: 90, 212n2

Leixlip Castle: 54

Lengel, Edward: 48

Leslie, John 131

Lhywd, Edward: 105

"Liberties": *see* Dublin, city of:

Limerick: 35, 36–7

linen industry and tourism: 21, 44–5,

Lismore Castle (Waterford): 104

Listowel (Kerry): 87

Liverpool (England): 4, 5

Logan, Patrick: 159–60, 222n25

Londonderry: *see* Derry

Lough Derg (Donegal): 47

Lowenthal, David: 84

Luckcombe. Philip: 91,

MacCannell, Dean: 49, 89, 90, 109, 112, 153

McCarthy, Cormac: 112, 126n12

Mac Coul, Finn: 110,

MacHale, John, Archbishop: 205n72

Maclochlainn, Alf: 221n8

MacPherson, James: xiii

McVeagh, John: 199n1, 224n1

Mahony, Francis: 113, 216n13

Mandler, Peter: British estates 50–1; estate tourism 50;

Manners, Lord John (7th Earl of Rutland): on Belfast 37, 46, 102, 141; on Famine landscape 184; on governing the Irish 180; on "Spanish" Irish 164

maps, Ireland: 14–15

Mardyke (Cork): 36

markers for tourist sites: 89–90: literary 91–2l, 216n13; meta-markers 102; *see also* Moore, Thomas

markets: *see* fairs and markets

Martineau, Harriet: 48,

Meg Merrilies: 115–6, 216n21

melancholy: 84, 93, 104, 174

Melish, John: 4, 179

Meloy, Elizabeth: 190, 225n15, 225n18

Merrion Square (Dublin): 29

Michasiw, Ian: 148–9, 220n54

Millikin, Richard: 113

mining and tourism 42–3

Miseries of Human Life: 9, 200n17

Mitchell, W. J. T.: 70

Mitchelstown Caves (Tipperary): *see* caves and tourism

Moir, Esther: 49, 89

Molyneux, Samuel: 42

Molyneux, Thomas: 100

Monk, Samuel H.: 78, 149

Monument of Light (Dublin): 203n14

Moore, Thomas: 92, 111,116, 137, 204n54, 215n7; 224n12
Morgan, Lady (Sidney Owenson): 92, 145, 209n30
moss houses: 214n29
Mosse, Bartholomew: 31
mountains and tourism: xii, 74–5, 81
Muckross Abbey (Killarney): 103, 104–5, 136, 219n24
Muckross estate (Killarney): *see* Herbert estate

naming sites: *see* tourist sites
Nangle, Edward: 48, 205n71, 205n72
Naples (Italy): 6, 33
Nash, Dennison: 123
Neave, Sir Digby: 48
Neeson, Eoin: 58,
Nelson's Pillar: *see* Dublin, city of
Newgrange (Meath): 105
Ní Ghiobúin, Mealla: 205n72
Nicholson, Norman: 210n45
Nicolson, Marjorie: 75
Nimmo, Alexander: 13–14, 97
Noel, Baptist Wriothesley: 46
North of Ireland: *see* Ulster, Province of
Nuñez, Theron: 114

O'Connor, Arthur: 42, 54
Ó Crualaoich, Gearóid: 162–3
O'Donoghue Mór: 111–2, 143–4, 215n7
O'Donovan, John: 9
Ó Giolláin, Diarmuid: 221n24
Ó Gráda, Cormac: 55, 176
O'Halloran, Clare: 105
O'Kane, Finola: 52–3, 62, 63–4
O'Sullivan's Cascade (Killarney): see waterfalls
Ockenden, William: 86, 111, 139
Ogilby, John: 14
Oran, William: 211n53
Oriel estate: *see* Forster, John
"orientalism," Irish: 163–4; and origin of antiquities 105–6;
Orrery, Sixth Earl of: 129, 130
Ossian, Cult of: xiii
Otway, Rev. Caesar: on coach travel 9; on Connemara 187; on guides 125; on landscape 167; on patterns 160; on religion 42, 47–48, 74, 204n66; on Killarney 132; and sublime seascapes 81, 99;
Ousby, Ian: on estate tourism 49–50; on Lake District 85–6; on picturesque 84; on guides and the sublime 116; on vocabulary of the sublime 77, 84;

paintings: 208n5; landscape 71–4, 78–9; of Giant's Causeway 101–2; *see also* estate tourism, Ireland; prints (engravings)
Parkgate (England): 3
Patten, Eva: 225n1
patterns and pilgrimages: *see* religion and tourism
Peacock, Joseph: 93
Peak District (England): 120
peasantry: *see* tourism and peasantry
Peel, Sir Robert: 186, 189
Penal Laws: 205n7
"petite tour": 34–48; barracks 39–40; cities 34–8; towns 38–40; industrial sites 40–5, 132; institutions 45–8; workhouses 45; *see also* religion and tourism
Petrie, George: 94, 105–6
picturesque: 81–8, 225n4; as common language 86–7; and comparing scenes 87–8; contradiction to poverty 88, 93; future of 196–7; and industrial sites 41–2; and landscape poets 210n45; and melancholy 84; and painting 87; and peasantry 88; and sublime 81–4; as technique 84–8; and word pictures 86–7; and variety 83–4; *see also* Gilpin, William
pigs: 180
Pigeon Hole (Mayo): *see* caves and tourism
Pigeon House (Dublin): 6
plaster (stucco) work: *see* Dublin, city of; Dublin Lying-In Hospital
pleasure gardens: *see* Dublin, city of; Dublin Lying-In Hospital

Plumptre, Anne: 40, 42; on accommodations 23; and anticipation 108; arriving in Ireland 6, 7; on Blarney Stone 113; on Carrick-a-rede 100; on Cork 35–6; on Dublin 28, 29–30, 31; on Dunmore Caves 98; on echoes 140–1; on estate tourism 63; on expenses 142, 144–5; on Fair Head 100; on Giant's Causeway 102, 110, 122; on guides 124, 144–5; on illustrators 72; on Kilkenny coal 43; on Killarney 94–5, 112, 133, 140–1, 142, 144–5; on laments 162; and picturesque description 87; on Poulaphouca Falls 97; on post-chaise 9; on Powerscourt 96; and ritual 112; on security in Ireland 25, 202n71; and tourism marker 90; travel to Ireland 4, 5;

Plumptre, James: 211n53

Pococke, Bishop Richard: 43; on country inns 21; on estate design 54, 56, 61; and Giant's Causeway 102; on glens of Wicklow 91; on Killarney 133

Poulaphouca Falls (Wickolw): *see* waterfalls and tourism

pollard wood: 94

pollution and tourist sites: 43, 93, 212n15

Port Patrick (Scotland): 3, 4

Portcoon: *see* caves and tourism

The Post Chaise Companion: 15

Post-Famine plans for Ireland: 186–91

potato: 176–7, 179–80, 224n32

Poulanass Waterfall (Wicklow): *see* waterfalls and tourism

Poussin, Gaspard (Dughet): 209n13

Poussin, Nicholas: 71, 73, 209n13

poverty: *see* tourism and poverty

Powerscourt estate (Wicklow): 55, 64, 65, 91, 208n53; *see also* waterfalls and tourism

Poyning's Law: 28

Pratt, Mary Louise: 6, 127

Price, Uvedall: 82, 209n11

Prince, Hugh: 84

prints (engravings): 11, 62, 71–3, 83, 88–9

Protestant Ascendancy: 28; and Claudean order 76; and estate design 51–53; and estate tourism 50–1; and estate towns 38–9; and Irish nation 65; and sublime landscapes 209n22

Punch: 186

Quakers: *see* Society of Friends

railroads, Ireland: 18–20, 225n2; Great Southern and Western Railway 19–20; Kingstown-Dublin railroad 6, 19; *see also* travel, modes of

Reeves-Smyth, Terence: 52–3

Reid, Thomas: accommodations 20, 45; arrival 7; on beggars 126; Dublin poverty 33; on estates 63; on faction fighting 159; on peasantry 88, 154; on prisons 45; on potato 179

religion and tourism: 46–8; anti-Catholic attitudes 47–8, 104–5, 160–1, 215n46 ; "confessional landscape 47–8; Evangelicalism 48; patterns and pilgrimages 47–8, 104, 158–60, 221n13, 221n24

Ringsend: *see* Dublin, city of

Rising of 1798: *see* United Irishmen's Rising of 1798

Ritchie, Leitch: on beggars 33, 178; on Belfast 37; on Bog of Allen 168; on contradiction of scenery and poverty 181–2; on Cork 36; on exaggeration 109; on Giant's Causeway 116, 119–20, 122; on Glen of the Dargle 97; on Glendalough 77, 93; on guides 124; and Hiberno-English 155–6; on markets 158; on peasantry 122; on Poulaphouca Falls 97; on Portcoon sea cave 98; on Poulanass Falls 209n26; on poverty 36–7; on security in Ireland 25

roads, Irish: 12–14, 201n39; Board of Public Works 14; Grand Jury roads 12; turnpikes 12, 201n31; *see also* maps

Roberts, James: 71

Roberts, Thomas Sautelle: 59

Robertson, Rev. Joseph: 77, 163
Robinson, Tim: 216n24
Rock Close: *see* Blarney Castle
Rock of Cashel (Tipperary): 73, 103–4, 173–4, 202n71, 223n18
Rojek, Chris: 40–1,
Rosa, Salvator: 71, 78–9, 209n30, 210n31
Ross Castle (Killarney): 138–9, 143, 219n27
Rotunda: *see* Dublin Lying-In Hospital
round towers: *see* antiquities
Rowlandson, Thomas: 200n17, 211n53
Royal Academy of Art (England): 71
Royal Canal: *see* canals
Ruins: *see* antiquities:
rundale settlements: 175–6; 223n23
Russell, John Scott: 17
Rutland Square (Dublin):
Rynne, Colin: on roads 14, 200n25, 201n31

Sackville Street: *see* Dublin, city of
St. Kevin, legends of: 116–7
St. Stephen's Green (Dublin): *see* Dublin, city of
Schama, Simon: 75
schools: *see* education and tourism
Scott, Sir Walter: 92
sea caves: *see* caves and tourism
seascapes: 81, 98–100
security: *see* tourism and security
Shannon Harbour: 16
Shannon, River 16: steam boats on 17–18
shell houses: 56
semeiotics and tourism: 153, 155
Silvermines (Tipperary): 41
Simms, Anngret: 38
sketching: 71–2; *see also* watercolor painting
Skinner, Andrew: 14–15
Slieve Gullion (Armagh): 77
Smith, Charles: 42, 217n2; estate design 53; on Killarney 130, 132; on Muckross estate 132; on variety in landscape 83
Smith, Elizabeth : 64, 97
Smith, Henry Nash: 189
Society of Friends: 185

soundscapes and tourism; 79–80: *see also* echoes and tourism
souvenirs: *see* tourist experience
Spirn, Anne Whiston: 79
The Sportsman in Ireland: 40; on contradiction of scenery and poverty 181; on echoes 80; on exploitation of peasantry 119; on Gap of Donloe 130; on Killarney 133, 134, 137, 147–8, 219n38; on jaunting cars 10; on laments 162; on quality of service 22; on sketching 72; on "Spanish" Galway 164;
Stafford, Barbara: 95, 97–8, 101, 214n44
Stage Irish: *see* tourist guides
Standring, Timothy J: 84, 86
steam boats in Ireland: *see* travel in Ireland
Stradbally estate (Cork): 52
sublime 74–91: aesthetics of the irrational 80–1; in paintings 78–9; paradox of 81; and picturesque 81–4; and power 148; and seascapes 99–103; in sounds 79–80; terror of 75–81; vocabulary of 77–8; *see also* picturesque; Rosa, Salvator

Taylor, Alexander: 201n41
Taylor, George: 14–15, 201n41
Tennyson, Alfred Lord: 138–9, 219n27
Thackeray, William Makepeace: on Belfast linen mills 44–5; on Connemara 187; on Cork 36; on Croagh Patrick 47; on Dublin Bay 5–6; on Giant's Causeway 116, 122–3, 124; on guides 123; on jaunting cars 10; on Killarney 148, 150; on peasant speech 154, 157; sketching 72; on trees 60
theatrical set design and tourism: 86, 95
Thomastown House: 62
tourism and agriculture: 168, 170–5; British-Irish agrarian landscape compared 171–3; enclosed landscape 173–174, 207n36; *see also* grazier economy; pigs; potato,

Trinity College: 27–8
Tunbridge ware: 61, 208n43
Twiss, Richard: on antiquities 104; in cabins 178; on Dublin 29, 32–3; on Dublin society 32; on Irish roads 13; on Killarney 142; on paintings 55; tourism markers 90;

United Irishmen's Rising of 1798: xiii–xiv, 25
Ulster, province of: 170–71; as "moral landscape 223n11; as "unIrish"
urban Ireland (towns, cities): *see* "petite tour"; *see also* Dublin, city of; *see also* specific cities and towns
Urry, John: on markers 89, 118, 137, 138, 146, 147

Valentia Island (Kerry): 80, 222n34
Victoria, Queen: 64, 90, 186, 195
villages: 175; see also rundale settlements
visual education and imagination: *see* tourism and visual imagination

Wakefield, Edward: 73, 94, 135
Walford, Thomas: 23, 46–7
Walker's Hand-Book of Ireland 6
walls: *see* estate tourism, Ireland
Walpole, Horace: 50, 75
watercolor painting: 71–2, 211n52; : *see also* sketching
waterfalls and tourism: 79, 95–8, 213n22; Coolaphouka 97; Poulaphouca 56, 80, 97, 213n28; Poulanass 209n26; Powerscourt falls 95–7, 213n23, n25; O'Sullivan's Cascade 82–3; and the sublime 95
Weld, Rev. Isaac: 104, 109, 135, 139, 141

West, Therese Cornwallis: 46, 220n52; on accommodations 23; on agriculture 173; on drumlins 170; on Glendalough 117; on guides 125; on Killarney 143, 144, 145; on post-chaise 9; and potato 224n32; on round towers 106
West of Ireland: description 169; post-Famine development 187–91; roads 13–14:
Wheatly, Francis: 211n58
Whelan, Irene: 204n66
Whelan, Kevin: 38, 50, 59–60, 205n7
White, George Preston: 79, 164, 188–9, 225n20
Wicklow, County: estates of 55, 61–2; Glens of 90–3; *see also* the Devil's Glen; glens the Dargle, the Downs; Glendalough; Vale of Avoca,
Wicklow Mountains: 6, 109
Wilde, Sir William: 93, 115–6, 159–60
Williams, Raymond: 55, 57
woodland in Ireland: destruction of forests 57–8, 93–4; and Gaelic place names 212n16; reforestation; scarcity of 172; *see also* coppice wood; estate forestry; pollard wood
Woods, Joseph: 22, 141, 142, 154, 174–5
Wordsworth, William: 149–50
Wright, Rev. George: on expenses 142; *Guide to Wicklow* 63; on Killarney 114–5, 121, 133, 134, 135–6, 138

Young, Arthur: on Blarney Castle 39; Carton House 54, 59; Glen of the Dargle 91; on Killarney 132–3; on Muckross Abbey 103, 138; on open fields 223n20; on scarcity of trees 172

INDEX

tourism and folklore: 110–12, 115; fakelore 111; *see* also tourism and literature

tourism and language: 124–5, 155–6; *see also* Gaelic; Hiberno-English

tourism and literature (legends): 89, 116–7; *see also* Thomas Moore; tourism and folklore

tourism and peasantry 88: clachans; cliff rappelling 117–8, 216n24; as drivers (jarvies) 123–6; exploitation of 117–9; at Killarney 143–6; rendering sales/services 120–23; venders; *see also* beggars; faction fighting; funerals; tourist experience; tourist guides

tourism and poverty: 34, 175–82; British-Irish poverty compared 34, 36, 176–7, 183,185; contradiction of scenery and poverty 88, 181–2; in Dublin 32–4; Irish poverty exaggerated 177; in Limerick 36; *see also* beggars, cabins; pig; potato; rundale settlements

tourism and security: 24–5

tourism and social space: 119–21, 123–4; heterogeneous space 119; mixed purpose site 119; social "contamination" of 146–50; *see also* tourist guides—as nuisance

tourism and theater: *see* tourist experience— performance

tourism as self-organizing system: 61, 120–21, 193–5

tourist attractions: *see* tourist sites

tourist experience: 107–27, 194; anticipation 107, 108–9; arrival 5–7; and the exotic 155, 156, 163–4; expenses 141–3, 219n38; graffiti 118; and landscape 166–9, 171–5; and nature 148–50; peasant speech 125–6, 153–6; performance (theater) 86, 114–9, 126–7, 143–4; as ritual 112–4; and semeiotics 153, 155–6; souvenirs 121–2; and stereotypes 156, 162; and tour duration 135–6; and travel time 166–9; *see also* accommodations in Ireland; beggars; cabins; faction fighting; fairs and markets; funerals; "orientalism," Irish; tourism and peasantry; tourism and poverty; tourism and social space; tourist guides; tourist space;

tourist gaze: 86, 89, 118, 148, 155

tourist guides: 123–6, 145–6: as nuisance 116, 119–20, 123–4; 144–6; and performance (theater) 114–5, 123–6, 143–4; and Stage Irishman 125–6, 156; as translators 123–4, 169–70

tourist ritual: *see* tourist experience

tourist sites: 89–93, 95, 106: accessibility 107–8; attractions 89–90, 212n2; complex sites 109, 127, 135; "consumption" of 148, 220n52; definition of 89; discovery of 107; meta-sites 90, 102; naming 109–10, 118–9; *see also* markers for tourist sites; social space

tourist space: 165–6, 222n1

tourists and visual awareness, visual imagination: 69–72; *see also* Claude (Lorrain); sublime; tourism and agriculture 71–2; see also paintings; prints (engravings); sketching; sublime; tourism and agriculture; watercolor painting

travel accounts: xi, xii, xiii, 108, 199n1, 199n1, 224n1

travel to Ireland: 3–5; arrival 5–7; sailing ships 3–5; steam 18–20

travel within Ireland: "Bians" 11–12, 200n29; chaise-marine 8; coaches 910; Long Coach 7; jaunting car (also outside car) 10–11, 200n23; "jingles" 7–8; modes of 78, 168; noddies 7; post-chaise 8–9; sedan chairs 8; sidecars 201n32; steam boats 17–18; *see also* canals; roads, Ireland; railroads, Ireland;

travel writers: xiv, xv

traveling public: xi, 50

Traveller's New Guide through Ireland:

Travelyan, Charles: 185–6, 224n10

trees, scarcity of: *see* woodland in Ireland;

www.ingramcontent.com/pod-product-compliance
Lightning Source LLC
Chambersburg PA
CBHW021822300426
44114CB00009BA/283